The Soviet Air and Strategic Rocket Forces, 1939–1980

*The Soviet Air and Strategic Rocket Forces,
1939–1980:*

A Guide to Sources in English

Myron J. Smith, Jr.

With a Foreword by
Kenneth R. Whiting

INSTITUTE FOR DEFENSE ANALYSES
TECHNICAL INFORMATION SERVICES OFFICE

ABC-Clio

Santa Barbara, California   Oxford, England

Copyright © 1981 by Myron J. Smith, Jr.
All rights reserved.
This book or any part thereof may not be
reproduced in any form without written permission
of the publishers.

Library of Congress Cataloging in Publication Data

Smith, Myron J.
  The Soviet air and strategic rocket forces, 1939-1980.

  (The War/peace bibliography series; no. 10)
  Includes index.
  1. Aeronautics, Military—Russia—Bibliography.
2. Strategic forces—Russia—Bibliography. I. Title.
Z6724.A38S63 [UG635.R9] 016.3584'00947 80-22514
ISBN 0-87436-306-3

ABC-Clio, Inc.
Riviera Campus
2040 Alameda Padre Serra, Box 4397
Santa Barbara, California 93103

Clio Press Ltd.
Woodside House, Hinksey Hill
Oxford, OX1 5BE, England

Manufactured in the United States of America

The War/Peace Bibliography Series

RICHARD DEAN BURNS, EDITOR

This Series has been developed in cooperation with the Center for the Study of Armament and Disarmament, California State University, Los Angeles.

1 *Songs of Protest, War & Peace*
A Bibliography & Discography
R. SERGE DENISOFF

2 *Warfare in Primitive Societies*
A Bibliography
WILLIAM TULIO DIVALE

3 *The Vietnam Conflict*
Its Geographical Dimensions, Political Traumas & Military Developments
MILTON LEITENBERG & RICHARD DEAN BURNS

4 *The Arab–Israeli Conflict*
A Historical, Political, Social & Military Bibliography
RONALD M. DEVORE

5 *Modern Revolutions and Revolutionists*
A Bibliography
ROBERT BLACKEY

6 *Arms Control & Disarmament*
A Bibliography
RICHARD DEAN BURNS

7 *The United States in World War I*
A Selected Bibliography
RONALD SCHAFFER

8 *Uncertain Judgment*
A Bibliography of War Crimes Trials
JOHN R. LEWIS

9 *The Soviet Navy, 1941–1978*
A Guide to Sources in English
MYRON J. SMITH, JR.

#10 *The Soviet Air and Strategic Rocket Forces, 1939–1980*
A Guide to Sources in English
MYRON J. SMITH, JR.

#11 *The Soviet Army* (tentative title)
A Guide to Sources in English
MYRON J. SMITH, JR.

#12 *The Secret Wars*
A Guide to Sources in English
Volume I: Intelligence, Propaganda and Psychological Warfare, Resistance Movements, and Secret Operations, 1939–1945
MYRON J. SMITH, JR.

#13 *The Secret Wars*
A Guide to Sources in English
Volume II: Intelligence, Propaganda and Psychological Warfare, Covert Operations, 1945–1980
MYRON J. SMITH, JR.

#14 *The Secret Wars*
A Guide to Sources in English
Volume III: International Terrorism, 1968–1980
MYRON J. SMITH, JR.

About the War/Peace Bibliography Series

With this bibliographical series, the Center for the Study of Armament and Disarmament, California State University, Los Angeles, seeks to promote a wider understanding of martial violence and the alternatives to its employment. The Center, which was formed by concerned faculty and students in 1962–63, has as its primary objective the stimulation of intelligent discussion of war/peace issues. More precisely, the Center has undertaken two essential functions: (1) to collect and catalogue materials bearing on war/peace issues; and (2) to aid faculty, students, and the public in their individual and collective probing of the historical, political, economic, philosophical, technical, and psychological facts.

This bibliographical series is, obviously, one tool with which we may more effectively approach our task. Each issue in this series is intended to provide a comprehensive "working," rather than definitive, bibliography on a relatively narrow theme within the spectrum of war/peace studies. While we hope this series will prove to be a useful tool, we also solicit your comments regarding its format, contents, and topics.

RICHARD DEAN BURNS
SERIES EDITOR

Other Bibliographies by Myron J. Smith, Jr.

Navies in the American Revolution. Vol. I of the American Naval Bibliography Series.
The American Navy, 1789–1860. Vol. II of the American Naval Bibliography Series.
American Civil War Navies. Vol. III of the American Naval Bibliography Series.
The American Navy, 1865–1918. Vol. IV of the American Naval Bibliography Series.
The American Navy, 1918–1941. Vol. V of the American Naval Bibliography Series.
The European Theater. Vol. I of *World War II at Sea: A Bibliography of Sources in English.*
The Pacific Theater. Vol. II of *World War II at Sea: A Bibliography of Sources in English.*
General Works, Naval Hardware, Home Fronts, Special Studies, and the "All Hands" Chronology (1941–1945). Vol. III of *World War II at Sea: A Bibliography of Sources in English.*
General Works, European and Mediterranean Theaters of Operations. Vol. I of *Air War Bibliography, 1939–1945: English-language Sources.*
The Pacific Theater; Airpower, Strategy and Tactics; Escape, Evasion, Partisans, and POW Experiences. Vol. II of *Air War Bibliography, 1939–1945: English-language Sources.*
Multi-theater Studies and the Air Forces. Vol. III of *Air War Bibliography, 1939–1945: English-language Sources.*
The Aircraft. Vol. IV of *Air War Bibliography, 1939–1945: English-language Sources.*
World War I in the Air: A Bibliography and Chronology.
Cloak-and-Dagger Bibliography: An Annotated Guide to Spy Fiction, 1937–1975.
Air War Southeast Asia, 1961–1973: An Annotated Bibliography and 16mm Film Guide.
Men-at-Arms: A Fiction Guide.
The War Stories Guide: An Annotated Bibliography of Military Fiction.
Sea Fiction Guide. With Robert C. Weller.

for Gary McAllister, colleague and friend

One who has few must prepare against the enemy; one who has many makes the enemy prepare against him.

Sun Tsu, 400–320 B.C. *The Art of War*

Contents

Foreword/ xvii
Introduction/ xxi
Selected Chronology/ xxix

1/ Reference Works/ 1
    A. Bibliographies/ 3
    B. Abstracts/ 7
    C. Indexes/ 7
        1. Newspapers/ 7
        2. Periodicals/ 8
        3. Documents/ 9
    D. Encyclopedias and Handbooks/ 9
    E. Annuals and Yearbooks/ 12
    F. Dictionaries/ 15
    G. Biography: General/ 17

2/ The Era of World War II, 1939–1945/ 19
    A. The Russo-Finnish Wars, 1939–1944/ 21
    B. The Great Patriotic War, 1941–1945/ 22
        1. General Studies/ 22
        2. War on the Eastern Front/ 24
          a. General Studies/ 24
          b. Air Force Opponents/ 27
            (1) The German Luftwaffe/ 27
            (2) The Soviet Air Force/ 30
          c. Specific Campaigns/ 35
            (1) "Operation Barbarossa," The German Invasion, 1941/ 35
            (2) The Battle of Moscow, 1941–1942/ 36
            (3) Stalingrad, 1942–1943/ 37
            (4) Leningrad and the Northern War/ 38

             (5) The Southern Region, 1941–1943/ 38
             (6) Kursk, 1943/ 39
             (7) Counterattack, 1943–1945/ 40
                (a) Forcing the Dneiper, 1943/ 40
                (b) Combat in Byelorussia, 1944/ 41
                (c) Poland and Czechoslovakia,
                    1939–1944/ 41
                (d) Into Germany, 1945/ 42
             (8) War in Manchuria, 1945/ 43
          3. Lend-Lease and Foreign Air Cooperation/ 44
             a. Lend-Lease/ 44
             b. British Assistance/ 46
             c. American Bombers and "Operation
                Frantic"/ 46
          4. Biographies/ 47
             a. General Studies/ 47
             b. Specific Personalities/ 48
          5. Aircraft: Soviet and Lend-Lease/ 49
             a. General Studies/ 49
             b. Fighters/ 51
                (1) General Studies/ 51
                (2) Specific Aircraft/ 52
             c. Bombers/ 54
                (1) General Studies/ 54
                (2) Specific Aircraft/ 54
             d. Transports/ 56

3/ *The Soviet Economy and Defense Establishment*/ 57
       A. The Soviet Defense Establishment/ 63
          1. Organization/ 63
             a. General Studies/ 63
             b. The Soviet High Command/ 66
          2. The Communist Party and the Military/ 68
          3. Military Policy and Doctrine, Theory and
             Strategy/ 72
       B. The Soviet Economy and the Military/ 82
          1. Defense Expenditures/ 82
          2. Weapons Procurement/ 86
             a. General Studies/ 86
             b. The Aircraft and Missile Industry/ 89
             c. Air/Missile Shows and Displays/ 92
             d. Famous Designers/ 94
                (1) General Studies/ 94
                (2) Specific Individuals/ 94

Contents

4/ *Soviet Aerospace Forces, 1946 to the Present/ 97*
    A. General Studies/ 99
    B. The Soviet Air Force (Voyenno-Vozdushnyye Sily—VVS)/ 102
        1. General Studies/ 102
        2. Mission and Doctrine, Strategy and Tactics—VVS/ 107
        3. Specific VVS Air Arms/ 110
            a. Frontal Aviation (Frontovaya Aviatsiya—FA)/ 110
                (1) General Studies/ 110
                (2) Airmobile/ 112
            b. Long-Range Aviation (Dal'nyaya Aviatsiya—DA)/ 113
            c. Military Transport Aviation (Voyenno-Transportnaya Aviatsiya—VTA)/ 114
    C. The Soviet National Air Defense Forces (Voyska Protivovozdushnoy Oborony Strany—PVO-Strany)/ 115
        1. General Studies/ 115
        2. Mission and Doctrine, Strategy and Tactics—PVO-Strany/ 118
        3. Incidents of Home Defense/ 120
            a. The U-2 Incident, 1960/ 120
            b. Other Incidents/ 122
    D. The Strategic Rocket Forces (Raketnyye Voyska Strategicheskogo Naznacheniya—SRF)/ 122
        1. General Studies/ 122
        2. Mission, Doctrine, and Nuclear Strategy/ 124
    E. Personnel, Training, and Exercises/ 131
        1. Personnel/ 131
            a. General Studies/ 131
            b. Defectors/ 133
        2. Training/ 134
            a. Aviation/ 134
            b. Missiles/ 141
        3. Exercises/ 143
    F. Logistics, Bases, and Technical Support/ 144
    G. Soviet Satellite Reconnaissance/ 146

5/ *Soviet Aerospace Weapons Systems/ 151*
    A. Aircraft/ 155
        1. General Studies/ 155
        2. Specific Systems/ 160

xiv *Contents*

        a. Fighters/ 160
          (1) General Studies/ 160
          (2) Specific Types/ 162
        b. Bombers/ 168
          (1) General Studies/ 168
          (2) Specific Types/ 169
        c. Reconnaissance/Liaison/ECM/ 172
          (1) General Studies/ 172
          (2) Specific Types/ 172
        d. Transport/ 173
          (1) General Studies/ 173
          (2) Specific Types/ 173
        e. Training/ 174
          (1) General Studies/ 174
          (2) Specific Types/ 174
        f. Helicopters/ 175
          (1) General Studies/ 175
          (2) Specific Types/ 177
        g. V/STOL and Experimental/ 178
     3. Aircraft Armament and Munitions/ 179
  B. Missiles/ 180
    1. AA Missile Systems/ 180
      a. General Studies/ 180
      b. Specific Types/ 181
    2. Strategic and Battlefield Missile Systems/ 182
      a. General Studies/ 182
      b. Specific Types/ 187

6/ *Arms Competition, Arms Control, and the Balance of Power/ 189*

  A. Arms Competition/ 191
  B. Arms Control/ 199
  C. The Balance of Power/ 204

7/ *Soviet Aerospace Arms and Assistance around the Globe, 1945–1980/ 213*

  A. General Studies/ 215
  B. Soviet Aerospace Arms and Assistance Deployment by Region/ 219
    1. Europe: The Warsaw Pact vs. the West/ 219
      a. General Studies/ 219
      b. Northern Europe and the Atlantic/ 225
      c. Central Europe/ 227

                    d. Southern Europe and the Mediterranean/ 229
                 2. Cuba/ 230
                    a. General Studies/ 230
                    b. The Cuban Missile Crisis, 1962/ 230
                 3. The Middle East and the Persian Gulf/ 232
                    a. Helping the Arabs/ 232
                       (1) General Studies/ 232
                       (2) Egypt/ 239
                       (3) Syria/Jordan/ 242
                    b. The Arab-Israeli Wars/ 243
                       (1) The Six-Day War, 1967/ 243
                       (2) The Yom Kippur War, 1973/ 244
                    c. The Persian Gulf Region/ 248
                 4. Africa/ 249
                    a. General Studies/ 249
                    b. Specific Nations/ 250
                       (1) Angola/ 250
                       (2) Congo/Zaire/ 251
                       (3) Ethiopia/ 252
                       (4) Libya/ 253
                       (5) Somalia/ 253
                 5. Asia/ 253
                    a. China/ 253
                    b. North Korea and the Korean War/ 254
                    c. Afghanistan/ 256
                    d. The Indo-Pakistani Conflicts/ 257
                    e. Indochina/ 261
                 6. The Pacific Area/ 264
                    a. Indonesia/ 264
                    b. Japan and the Kuriles/ 264

Appendix I: Late Entries, to May 1980/ 265
Appendix II: List of Journals Consulted/ 271
Appendix III: Selected Soviet Aerospace Biographies/ 275
Appendix IV: Charts/ 297
Author Index/ 305

Foreword

THERE HAS LONG been a need for a comprehensive bibliography dealing with Soviet aviation. Professor Myron J. Smith, Jr. has filled that vacuum admirably. The Soviet Air Force (VVS) has for some time been more than just another esoteric collection of planes and pilots for the cognoscenti to study and write about. The VVS is an important part of the greatest martial array ever put together by one nation. Information about the VVS has been increasing at an exponential rate, so much so that bibliographies such as this are a sine qua non for the student, the analyst, and the serious reader.

The Communist regime had hardly come to power when Lenin, in December 1918, helped Nikolay Ye. Zhukovsky establish the Central Institute for Aerodynamics and Hydrodynamics (TsAGI). In view of the pitiful collection of aircraft available to the new regime and the marginal value of aviation during the Civil War (1918–21), Lenin showed great foresight in his support of Zhukovsky. His support set the tone for the Soviet attitude toward airpower right down to the present. With the backing of Lenin and his government, Zhukovsky was able to assemble a cadre of such outstanding people as Tupolev, Polikarpov, and Mikulin, to name a few.

Although the will was there and the talent available, the infrastructure necessary for a flourishing aviation industry was lacking. It was not until the 1930s when Stalin whipped the Soviet Union into industrializing at an accelerated tempo that the wherewithal for a respectable aircraft industry came into being. Simultaneously, the paramilitary organization *Osoaviakhim* provided technical training for millions of young citizens, many of them fresh off the farm. The Soviet pilots tested their training and aircraft against the Germans and Italians in the Spanish Civil War and against the Japanese in China and Outer Mongolia at the end of the 1930s.

The real test, however, came in the Great Patriotic War, i.e., the Soviet segment of World War II. After an almost unbelievably disastrous beginning in 1941, the Soviet Air Force gradually improved until by

1944 it dominated the air over the Soviet Union. This accomplishment was due partly to German commitments on other fronts and partly to the fact that the Soviets outproduced the Germans in aircraft. A reasonably definitive account of the German–Soviet air war, however, is still to be written. The official Soviet histories of the air war are stingy indeed about the adversities suffered by the VVS in the Great Patriotic War and extremely boastful about successes, while the German accounts by Schwabedissen, Plocher, Suchenwirth, Galland, Rudel, Berenbrok, et al tend to be apologies rather than accurate history. Putting the Soviet and German accounts side by side does not bring the picture entirely into focus. The Soviet archives are a terra incognita for Western scholars and the citations appearing in Soviet histories and articles in historical journals serve more to tantalize than to satisfy. Fortunately, the production of memoirs, historical articles, and books dealing with the Soviet experience in World War II has become a "national industry" over the last two decades. With such a quantity of materials available, a more balanced picture of the German–Soviet air war may emerge.

The immediate postwar period, the late 1940s and early 1950s, is rather lean in materials about Soviet aviation and weapon systems. The student has to make do with memoirs such as Aleksandr S. Yakovlev's *The Aim of a Lifetime,* secondary works describing the Soviet acquisition of technology and technicians in conquered Germany, and evaluations of Soviet aircraft, radar, and air-defense weapons gained the hard way in the Korean conflict. As long as Stalin was alive, just about everything related to the military, however remotely, was subsumed under the rubric of "state secrets." It was not until Khrushchev came to power in the mid-1950s that the outside world received anything other than the glorification of Stalin's "permanently operating factors" for victory from Soviet military writers.

From the late 1950s to the present, the Western scholar has been inundated by a flood of Soviet military writings—memoirs, descriptions of just about every battle from 1918 to the present, and an inordinate amount of repetitious material on military doctrine and strategy. The quantity is there, but the quality leaves much to be desired. For example, the descriptions of political work in the armed forces and exhortations to improve it long ago reached the ad nauseam level, but the flow continues unabated. Material on civil defense or the role of DOSAAF is abundant, while the literature on such interesting areas as air defense or the missile forces is sparse, and that which is available reveals little in the way of hard information. All of which suggests that the advantage of reading Russian is somewhat dubious. As the present bibliography illustrates in listing numerous translations from the Russian, the student who does not read Russian has access to an enormous amount of translated Soviet material. These translations, on the whole, represent the best works, although it is necessary to read the mediocre and worst to appreciate that fact. The voluminous output of the Joint Publications Research Service (JPRS), the U.S. Air Force project of translating and publishing the best in Soviet military thought, and the numerous other translations available make research and reading in the field of Soviet aviation easy for the English-speaking public. The volume of the literature makes the present bibliography an essential reference work.

If materials on the PVO and the SRF are less than voluminous, writings on the Soviet projection of power around the globe are plentiful—over seven hundred items listed in this bibliography, and only a few of the items deal with the war in Vietnam. The proliferation of the literature on Soviet global ploys is easy to understand—it reflects the change from the Soviet continental-defensive stance of the Stalin period to projection of power on a global scale during the Khrushchev and Brezhnev regimes. It is also noteworthy that earlier writings about the Soviet military, especially those dealing with aviation, tended to be just that—writings about the military. Now many of the books and articles treat the projection of Soviet power as an amalgam of military and political power—two sides of the same coin. Until the 1960s, Western observers tended to regard the military in the Soviet Union as the province of the military specialist, an arcane subject of only peripheral interest to the political analyst. But Soviet forays into the Middle East, Africa, and Asia, the arming and utilization of proxies, and the recent invasion of Afghanistan literally force the political analyst to look more closely at the Soviet capabilities for projecting power far beyond the borders of the Soviet Union. Thus it is no accident that Section 7 of this bibliography is an excellent guide for those interested in Soviet foreign policy in recent decades.

At a time when so-called experts disagree over what constitutes "parity" and "superiority" in strategic weaponry and about which of the superpowers has the advantage, and in a period when the ratification of SALT II, not to mention the negotiation of SALT III, is controversial, the section on arms control and the balance of military power is vital. The literature is extensive—another reminder that Soviet military power is no longer exclusively the concern of experts. Everyone will be affected, if through the failure of negotiations the military balance gets too far out of whack. The books and articles listed should provide a varied menu for even the most avid buff and a good reading list for the interested citizen.

It is a pleasure to write the foreword for Professor Smith's excellent book. I am confident that it will be used widely by students of Soviet studies and especially by those whose area of special interest is the Soviet military. I never cease to marvel at those good people whose persistence and toil make bibliographies possible, but they have my fervent gratitude.

Kenneth R. Whiting
Documentary Research Division
Air University Library

Introduction

Background

THE GROWTH OF Soviet aerospace activity, as reflected in the Air Force (VVS), the National Air Defense Force (PVO-Strany), and the Strategic Rocket Force (SRF), has been one of the most dramatic war/peace developments in the post-World War II period. Today the Soviet Union is an aerospace power at least equal in strength to the United States and one which, despite various disarmament talks, shows every evidence of seeking superiority.

Russian military aviation dates back to before World War I when the Czar's air force ranked among the top three in the world, with the air forces of Germany and France. Plagued by inadequately trained pilots and technicians, poor quality aircraft (mostly imported), and maintenance and logistical problems, the Russian air service proved to be inferior to that of the Germans during the Great War.

Immediately following the Communist Revolution, the Soviets accomplished little toward the creation of an air arm for the Red Army. They did, however, lay plans for the long-term development of aviation research, production, education, and military power. With the inauguration of the five-year production plans in 1928, aircraft production accelerated and the aviation industry began to grow. By 1932, the Soviet Army Air Force (GU-VVS) had 2,000 warplanes and 50,000 personnel, ranking first in the world in number of heavy bombers and airborne capability. By 1939–1940, the GU-VVS ranked, quantitatively at least, among the great military air powers, but substance was lacking. Suffering from weaknesses in organization, training, and equipment, overall Soviet air capability lagged behind the major Western nations throughout the 1930s. Morale was seriously affected by Stalin's purges with over one-half of the highest ranking and many middle and lower ranking GU-VVS officers eliminated for various reasons.

The German attack on the USSR in late June 1941 dealt a severe blow to the GU-VVS. The Soviets lost thirty-eight hundred aircraft in the first six days of fighting as German panzers, supported by the Luftwaffe, overran a large number of airfields, disrupting the entire air organization in the western part of the country.

Early in the war, with the relocation of aircraft plants to the east, the Russians took steps to increase their aircraft production to provide numerical air superiority over the Luftwaffe on the Eastern Front. By mid-1943, the GU-VVS was usually able to gain local air supremacy in supporting a major ground offensive. Moreover, large numbers of tactical aircraft were able to participate with armor and artillery in the support of ground attacks against deeply echeloned German defenses. The greatest weaknesses exhibited by Russian air units during the Great Patriotic War were in pilot proficiency, long-range bombing, night and instrument flying, and aircraft service ability and maintenance.

After World War II, Moscow reorganized the army's air arm, forming the Soviet Air Force and elevating it in 1946 to a status equal to that of the Ground Forces and the Navy. The VVS became one of the three basic branches of the armed forces. The Russians spent the next five years consolidating the reorganization of aircraft on hand as well as some transitional types. Soviet emphasis was placed on building an embryonic air defense force (PVO) in the wake of the Korean War, parallel in time with the U.S. strengthening of SAC. Between 1950 and 1956, the first generation of jet aircraft was introduced into the VVS and by 1960 the air force inventory consisted largely of jet planes, many with long-range strategic capability. In 1962, the VVS was judged the world's largest air force.

Since the early 1960s the Soviets have continued to develop improved aircraft with high performance capabilities. Strategic aviation developments were cut back in line with the decision to concentrate on intercontinental ballistic missiles (ICBMs). During the past decade, the air leaders of the USSR have given high priority to the development of an airmobile capability, the creation of a transport force, and revitalization of front or tactical air support. Similar developments occurred in what would become two additional forces, PVO-Strany and the SRF; similar duties in America are usually handled by the U.S. Air Force.

The Soviets established their first antiaircraft artillery regiment in Leningrad in 1924, and by 1939, most major Russian cities were defended by AAA organized in corps, divisions, and brigades. Many organizational changes during World War II led to centralized control of AAA under the Red Army Chief of Artillery and cooperation at the army level between fighter aviation and antiaircraft artillery.

The Soviet air defense organization entered its main period of growth in the 1950s. Antiaircraft artillery was replaced by AA missile forces, and air defense fighter aviation (IA-PVO) was reequipped with missile-armed jet interceptors. In the mid-1950s, the Soviets deployed their first surface-to-air missiles (SA-1) around Moscow and between 1957 and 1960 employed an improved SAM system of SA-2s throughout the USSR and Warsaw Pact countries. PVO-Strany was elevated to a major separate service in 1955, equal to the Navy, VVS, and Ground Forces. Thereafter, all elements of a first-rate strategic air defense system were evident in the USSR. Features included a comprehensive early warning network deployed in depth, thousands of specially trained fighter pilots and good interceptor aircraft, and an elaborate, three-tier defense system around most Soviet boundaries.

The status and prestige of PVO-Strany has continued to increase since the 1950s. One clear indication of this came in 1960–1962 when it received fifteen hundred to two thousand fighter aircraft from the Soviet Navy. By 1965, PVO-Strany accounted for approximately one-half of the USSR's operational fighters. "National Air Defense Forces Day" was proclaimed on 13 April 1975, initiating an annual holiday to honor the achievements and deeds of this service.

Although Russian interest in missiles and rockets preceded the war, organized research into their technology began in 1945 when the Soviets gained control of a number of German rocket research and test facilities as well as access to many German techniques. The use of native Soviet efforts and skills, and the exploitation of the efforts of many captured rocket engineers and technicians, culminated in the launching of the first Soviet ballistic missiles in the early 1950s. Soviet capabilities were dramatically demonstrated to the world in 1957 when Sputnik I, the first artificial earth satellite, was launched. In August of that year, Russian technicians conducted the first successful test launching of a Soviet ICBM, the SS-6 Sapwood, and during the Fortieth Anniversary of the October Revolution ceremonies, three of these missiles were displayed in Moscow. Over the next few years research continued, involving deployment of missiles and development of an organization and role for missile troops.

Following debate within Russian military circles spurred by Khruschev's desire for a strategic missile force, the Soviets established their Strategic Rocket Force (SRF) in December 1959. Commanded by a deputy minister of defense and controlling all land-based missiles with a range over six hundred fifty miles, the SRF thus became the fifth major service of the USSR, equal in status to the Ground Forces, Navy, VVS, and PVO-Strany, although the SRF is usually considered first in importance. Since 1959, the SRF has been concerned with the training of personnel, development of command and control and the logistics support systems, construction of launch facilities, deployment of new missile systems, and the integration and training of personnel to attain and maintain continual combat readiness.[1]

Recent Department of Defense data reported in the American media demonstrate just how successful the Soviets have been in building up the VVS, SRF, and PVO-Strany. Less than twenty years ago, the United States held a commanding military edge over Russia in military power. In 1964, for example, America held a 7–1 advantage over Russia in long-range bombers, a 4–1 lead in ICBMs, and a 17–1 superiority in nuclear warheads. This overwhelming power gave the United States national security, foreign policy flexibility, and the ability to provide the Free World with a shield against Soviet aggression.

In 1980, the Soviet Union holds a position of rough parity in aerospace power with the United States. For over a decade, according to intelligence estimates, Russia has poured between eleven and fourteen percent of its gross national product (GNP) into the military. America, in contrast, has averaged between five and eight percent. This huge expenditure, which has proved a crushing burden on the civilian Soviet economy, has allowed the Kremlin leadership to build formidable land-sea-air power.

In the area of strategic aerospace power, the Soviets have increased their ICBM inventory in quality as well as number. From four hundred missiles in 1964, the troops of the SRF now man silos and portable launchers capable of hurling 1,398 space machines. In the same period, the Russian stockpile of nuclear warheads has grown from four hundred to six thousand. Added to this missile capability of the SRF are some nine hundred fifty submarine-launched ballistic missiles (SLBMs) of the Soviet Navy and 156 intercontinental bombers of the VVS's Long-Range Aviation (DA) fleet.[2]

Keeping pace with strategic developments, the conventional power of the Soviet armed forces has grown continuously since the mid-1960s. In addition to a growth of some four hundred thousand personnel, hundreds of new and improved weapons have been added to inventory.

Significant gains have been registered in the conventional aerospace area. The addition of several thousand late-model jet aircraft has greatly enhanced the interceptor capability of PVO-Strany and the air superiority/air support capability of VVS. In keeping with decisions to upgrade tactical air support, reconnaissance, airlift, and airmobile capacity, Russian factories produced five hundred new warplanes and three hundred fifty helicopters between 1977 and 1979, or about twice as many in each category as were made in the United States.

The impressive growth of a first-rate nuclear umbrella and the development of formidable conventional forces, particularly those of

Introduction xxv

an aerospace nature, has given the Soviet Union a sense of security and foreign policy flexibility once enjoyed by the United States alone. To a great extent, Russian activity in the Third World may be directly attributed to the Kremlin's expanded military protection capability. The airlifts to the Middle East, Angola, and Ethiopia, from 1973 to 1978, and the role of helicopter gunships and fighter bombers in Afghanistan, from 1979 to 1980, are indications of a new Soviet ability and willingness to influence situations outside the traditional satellite region. These events, coupled with continuing large-scale arms expenditures and an apparent breakdown in detente, have given rise to new Western concerns for the future.

Objectives

THIS BIBLIOGRAPHY, THE first on its subject, is intended to serve as a working guide to English language sources written during the years 1939 to 1980 concerning the Soviet Air Force, the National Air Defense Force, and the Strategic Rocket Force. While aimed primarily at scholars and graduate and undergraduate students, it will also prove useful to librarians, general readers, journalists, policymakers, and aviation rocket enthusiasts.

This guide is not definitive, but it attempts comprehensiveness in that virtually all factors concerning Russian aerospace forces are covered, with the exception of those administered by the Soviet Navy. As a reference tool, it permits its user to quickly determine what material is available as an aid in establishing a basis for further research. In general, the items cited are those the user might reasonably expect to find in large university, public, or government libraries. Should the user be unable to find a given reference in his area, almost every citation is available through interlibrary loan.

Although this is my first bibliography exclusively devoted to a foreign aerospace force, it is not the first aviation-missile guide with which I have been associated. The criteria for selection in this compilation are the same as those employed in my *World War I in the Air: A Bibliography and Chronology* (Metuchen, N.J.: The Scarecrow Press, 1977), *Air War Southeast Asia, 1961–1973: An Annotated Bibliography and 16mm Film Guide* (Metuchen, N.J.: The Scarecrow Press, 1979), and *Air War Bibliography Series, 1939–1945* (Manhattan, Kans.: Military Affairs/Aerospace Historian for the USAF Historical Foundation, 1977–). The following types of published material are represented: books and monographs; scholarly papers, including appropriate numbers from the RAND corporation and International Institute for

Strategic Studies; periodical and journal articles; U.S. government documents; doctoral dissertations, master's theses, and research projects, including several from the U.S. Air University, Army and Navy War Colleges, and Navy Postgraduate School. A list of journals consulted will be found in Appendix II.

Although much has been included, it was necessary to omit certain kinds of information. Excluded materials include fiction, children's works, newspaper articles (unless reprinted), poetry, and book reviews.

The context, content, and emphasis of English language literature on Soviet aerospace forces has changed greatly over the past four decades. Much of what was published in 1944 or 1954 or even 1974 or 1976 is now outdated or "historical." In that respect, much of this guide can be considered "historical" in that its citations will be dated by the time the book is published. To keep abreast of new works and current events as they concern our topic, the user will find it necessary to continuously consult the reference works provided in Section I.

Arrangement

THE SEVEN MAIN sections in the Contents, with their subsections, form a classified subject index to this guide and the key to how the book is laid out. Within the text, each section receives an introduction and after the first section, is arranged alphabetically under the headings "books," "articles," and "documents, papers, and reports." Each section also contains a note on further references within the book designed to guide the reader to related information.

Each reference receives an entry number. These entry numbers run consecutively throughout the guide. An author index keyed to entry numbers is provided.

Acknowledgments

FOR THEIR ADVICE, assistance, or encouragement in the formulation, research, and completion of this endeavor, the following are gratefully acknowledged:
- Mr. Robert B. Lane, Director, Air University Library
- Mr. Stanley Kalkus, Director, Navy Department Library
- LTC Benjamin C. Glidden, Director, Air Force Academy Library
- Mr. Louis E. Foster, Defense Intelligence Agency
- Ms. Joyce Eakin, Assistant Director for Libraries, Army Military History Institute

Introduction

LTC Howard Wright, USAF (Ret.)
West Virginia University Library

Special appreciation is reserved for my colleagues at Salem College, without whose backing and aid this project would still be a dream. President James C. Stam, Deans Ronald O. Champagne, and Gary McAllister provided continuous support and the encouragement to proceed. Sue Webreck, Margaret Allen, Jacqueline Isaacs, Sara Casey, and Stu Godfrey of the Benedum Learning Resources Center provided support, bibliographic help, and interlibrary loan assistance.

Finally, hearty thanks are due to Dr. Kenneth R. Whiting, Chief of the Documentary Research Division at Air University, for his splendid foreword, and to series editor Dick Burns for his support, guidance, and kind words.

Myron J. Smith, Jr.
Salem, West Virginia

Notes

1. Much of the data noted above is drawn from the U.S. Department of Defense, Defense Intelligence Agency, *Handbook on the Soviet Armed Forces* (Washington, D.C.: U.S. Government Printing Office, 1979), pp. 10/1–10, 11/1, and 12/1.

2. Harold Brown, *Report of the Secretary of Defense to the Congress on the FY 1981 Budget, FY 1982 Authorization Request, and FY 1981–1985 Defense Programs, January 29, 1980* (Washington, D.C.: U.S. Government Printing Office, 1980), pp. 31–38. The SLBM force and Naval Air Force are covered in my *The Soviet Navy, 1941–1978: A Guide to Sources in English* (Santa Barbara, Calif.: ABC-Clio, 1980).

Selected Chronology

Introduction

THE CHRONOLOGY WHICH follows is designed to demonstrate certain "high points" in Soviet aerospace developments since 1939 but should not be regarded as definitive. Many events have occurred during the past forty-one years which we have been unable to include here.

1939 Soviet air force general Ya. Smushkevich is named head of the GU-VVS.
Soviet air and ground units attack Finland on November 30.

1940 M. M. Kaganovich is replaced as head of the Aviation Industry Commissariat by A. I. Shakhurin.
On January 6 Finnish ace Jorma "Zamba" Sarvanto, flying a Fokker D-21 of HLeLv-24, intercepts seven VVS DB-3s and downs six.
Soviet pilot V. P. Fedorov test-flies a rocket plane in April.
Soviet air and ground forces, under Gen. S. K. Timoshenko, crush the Finnish armed forces bringing the "Winter War" to a close.
Gen. Ya. Smushkevich, VVS commander during the "Winter War," is removed from his command; he will be executed in October 1941.
Gen. Pavel Rychagov succeeds Smushkevich as GU-VVS commander.

1941 The expansion and reequipment of the GU-VVS is approved in a February decree, "On the Reorganization of the Red Air Force."

On June 22 Luftwaffe units, as part of the opening of Operation Barbarossa, the German invasion of Russia, destroy one thousand two hundred Soviet aircraft, including eight hundred caught on the ground.

On June 23 near Jassy, Lt. Aleksandr I. Pokryshkin, flying a MIG-3 of the 55th Fighter Air Regiment as part of the escort of a DB-3 mission, downs an intercepting Luftwaffe Me-109 of JG-77 for the first of his fifty-nine victories.

The Russian high command or "Stavka" reorganizes the GU-VVS command structure at the end of June and names Gen. Pavel F. Zhigarev to the new post of Commander/Deputy Commissar of Defense.

On June 30 the German Oberkommando der Wehrmacht (OKW) claims that 4,017 Soviet aircraft have been destroyed since June 22 for the loss of one hundred fifty Luftwaffe warbirds.

The first Soviet rocket battery, under Capt. I. A. Flerov, fires on German troops in the Orsha region in July.

In August Soviet bombers, under Col. Preobrazhensky, bomb Berlin in a propaganda effort.

The GU-VVS Rear Services Command is established in August.

British-manned RAF Hurricanes of No. 151 Wing fly their first combat sorties in defense of the Russian port of Murmansk in September.

Beginning in October, in an effort to improve the defense of Moscow, all Soviet air units in the region are placed under the single command of Gen. S. A. Khudiakov.

During October Soviet warplanes fly twenty-six thousand sorties over the Western Front—eighty percent close air support—claiming 228 Nazi planes destroyed for the loss of 120.

During October and November in a series of day/night raids on Luftwaffe airfields supporting the German drive on Moscow, Russian flyers claim one thousand one hundred Nazi aircraft destroyed.

In November four Red Air Force air divisions and over one thousand aircraft are transferred to the defense of Moscow from the Far East Military District; for the first time, the Russians gain a numerical superiority over the Germans, but poor weather keeps the number of sorties flown low.

On December 6 Stalin names six air regiments as "Guards" units for their work in Moscow's defense; these are the first air force units to win the coveted honor.

Selected Chronology   xxxi

Soviet forces around Moscow counterattack forcing a German retreat.

Marina Raskova forms three women's air regiments (588th [46th Guards] Night Bomber, 586th Fighter Air Regiment, and 587th [125th Guards] Bomber Regiment); thirty women in these units will be made Heroines of the Soviet Union during the course of the war.

1942 In March the Long-Range Air Force (ADD) is established under the command of Gen. A. E. Golovanov.

In April Gen. A. A. Novikov succeeds Gen. Zhigarev as GU-VVS Commander; the new chief immediately combines front and army air units into air armies, assigning one to each front, and creates the air corps of the Stavka Reserve.

In August the Stalingrad Front is divided into the Stalingrad and Southeastern Fronts; support for the former is provided by the new 16th Air Army under Gen. P. S. Stepanov while the 8th Air Army assists the latter.

Col. P. S. Danilin's 287th Fighter Air Division—the first unit equipped with the new Lavochkin La-5—arrives in the Stalingrad area on August 20 to reinforce the 8th Air Army.

In late September, north of Stalingrad, the new 17th Air Army under Gen. S. A. Krasovsky is created to aid Gen. N. F. Vatutin's newly-organized Southwestern Front.

After heavy late summer combat in the Stalingrad area, Gen. T. T. Khriukin's 8th Air Army has only 188 operational warplanes by October 3.

Soviet forces counterattack at Stalingrad on November 19; within four days, units will link up west of the city trapping the German 6th Army inside.

At the end of November, Luftwaffe transport units unsuccessfully begin an airlift into Stalingrad, meeting prohibitive resistance from the CU-VVS and encountering fierce winter weather.

Enroute to Stalingrad on December 11, sixteen Luftwaffe Ju-52s, covered by four Me-109s, are attacked by seventeen 235th FAD La-5s and YAK-1s which down nine German transports.

1943 Free French manned fighter squadrons of the 303rd FAD are expanded in January to form the Normandie-Nieman FAR.

German forces in Stalingrad surrender in February.

According to Soviet figures, aircraft of the 2nd, 17th, 16th, and 8th Air Army and the long-range bomber force flew 35,929 sorties between November 19, 1942 and February 2, 1943 in the Stalingrad campaign; Soviet units claimed the destruction of three thousand Luftwaffe planes.

Air units support the Army in early April in a campaign which will become known as the Battle for the Kuban Bridgehead.

Col. Gen. S. A. Khudiakov is named GU-VVS Chief of Staff in May.

In early May, AAD IL-4s and Lend-Lease B-25s begin a week of attacks on German rail yards at Minsk, Orsha, Gomel, and Bryansk; other bomber units mount four concentrated strikes on twenty Luftwaffe airfields west of Kursk.

The Kuban air battles end on June 7; since April 17, GU-VVS aircraft have mounted thirty-five thousand sorties with flyers claiming the destruction of one thousand one hundred German aircraft, including eight hundred in aerial combat.

In an effort to check German bombing raids on Russian industrial targets, GU-VVS aircraft attack twenty-eight Luftwaffe air bases west of Kursk between June 8 and 10.

In an effort to check a Luftwaffe 8th Air Corps raid in support of the opening of "Operation Citadel" (the Battle of Kursk) on July 5, the GU-VVS sends four hundred bombers against sixteen air bases near Kharkov; alerted by radar, German interceptors from JG-3 and -52 break up the attacks and down one hundred twenty Soviet warplanes.

GU-VVS units, which had shown poor operation on the opening day of "Citadel," correct their deficiencies with new tactics; following huge fighter sweeps on July 6, 16th Air Army Il-2s and Pe-2s decimate German 9th Army units in the Okhlovatka sector in two massive strikes.

On July 7 in a concentrated twenty-minute attack, GU-VVS Il-2s, equipped with new anti-tank cannon, destroy seventy German 9th Panzer Division armored vehicles. Before Hitler cancels "Citadel" later in the day, Luftwaffe and GU-VVS air units engage over Prokorovka while, on the ground, one thousand five hundred Nazi and Soviet armored vehicles fight history's largest tank battle.

Soviet ground and air forces begin to mount a two-pronged counter offensive at Kursk; in a little over a month, Belgorod, Orel, and Kharkov will be liberated.

To hamper the German withdrawal from the Kursk area,

Selected Chronology

In February the first Luftwaffe Me-262 jet encountered in the east is downed by Soviet ace Ivan N. Kuzhedub. GU-VVS warplanes support the Soviet ground drive on Berlin; in late April, Soviet 16th and 18th Air Army bombers, in "Operation Salute," pound the defenses around the German capital.

Pilots I. A. Malinovsky of the 1st Guards FAR and K. V. Trovoselov of the 115th Guards FAR drop red banners over the Reichstag.

Germany surrenders unconditionally on May 8.

Since June 1941, GU-VVS units have mounted 3,808,136 combat sorties, dropping 696,268 tons of bombs, expending 1,628,059 tons of fuels and lubricants, and claiming forty-four thousand German aircraft destroyed in the air and thirteen thousand on the ground; loss estimates, never revealed in total, are placed at seventy to eighty thousand Russian warplanes.

From 1939 to 1945, Soviet aircraft factories have produced 158,218 aircraft for the VVS; in the same period, they received 14,018 Lend-Lease aircraft (P-39s, P-40s, P-63s, B-25s, C-47s, A-20s, AT-6s, and PBYs) from the U.S. and 2,950 Hurricane and Spitfire fighters from Britain.

Beginning on August 9, Soviet 9th, 10th, and 12th Air Army units attack industrial and communications targets in Manchuria and North Korea in support of Marshal A. M. Vasilevsky's drive against the Japanese Kwantung Army; Stalin declares the Manchurian campaign successfully completed on August 23.

In December Stalin dismisses A. I. Shakhurin as Minister of Aircraft Production and names M. V. Khrunichev in his place.

1946 Throughout 1945 and 1946, the Soviets capture and examine German scientists and advanced air and missile technology as well as interned U.S. aircraft, especially four B-29s.

Marshal Novikov, GU-VVS commander, is dismissed in March by Stalin and replaced by Gen. K. A. Vershinin; the GU-VVS is reorganized into the Soviet Air Force (VVS), coequal in status with the Army and Navy.

The Soviet Long-Range Air Force (DA) is reconstituted under Marshal A. Ye. Golovanov, becoming a separate service of Soviet arms.

The MIG-9 Fargo becomes the first Soviet-designed

Selected Chronology

ADD Il-4s and B-25s bomb the rail yar⟨ 194
July.
The Trans-Siberian Ferry Route is set u₁
I. S. Semyonov to receive U.S. Lend-L
Alaska.
Soviet ground and air units battle for th
Don Basin through the fall.
In October, Lt. K. A. Yevstigneyev of the
twelve German warplanes in nine air battles
war with fifty-six victories.
Kiev is liberated on November 6.
VVS units play an important role in haltin₁
terattack on the right bank of the D
November–December.

1944 In late January Luftwaffe transports mount an₁
port seven German 8th Army divisions trapped
on the Dnieper; thirty-two Ju-52s will be lost
fighters within a two week period.
A fighter command (LA-PVO) is established
national air defense force.
17th Air Army warplanes support the liberatio
in April.
GU-VVS units support the summer liberatior
Russia, Lithuania, Latvia, and the eastern part of
From July 13 through July 27, units of the 2nd Ai
thirty thousand five hundred sorties in support of th
offensive on Lvov, and claim three hundred fifty
aircraft destroyed.
Soviet ground and air units force Rumania out of
on August 24.
GU-VVS units support the Russian offensive in Belo
American B-17s mount "shuttle bombing" raids on
theater targets.
Finland surrenders to Russia in September; durii
course of their "Continuation War," FAF pilots have cl
the destruction of 1,567 GU-VVS warplanes for the l
536.
Also during September, La-5s of the Soviet-sponsore
Independent Czech FAR fly from Tri Duby airdrome in
port of the Slovak uprising.

turbojet fighter to fly and enter service.

In August the jet-powered Yak-15 and MIG-9 are first exhibited over Tushino.

1947 The Tu-4 Bull, Russian copy of the U.S. B-29, makes its first public appearance during the May Day flypast over Moscow.

The first ballistic missile successfully launched in Russia makes its flight in mid-October.

The Red Army deploys a small number of SS-1 "Scunner" missiles, which are essentially improved German V-2s.

The Soviets purchase fifty-five Rolls Royce jet engines which greatly aid their jet aircraft development.

The first officially verified flight of the MIG-15 occurs in December.

1948 Stalin orders start of an ICBM research program.

National Air Defense Force personnel are detached from the Red Army Artillery to form an independent service under Marshall Leonid Govorov.

In July the Antonov bureau begins the delivery of the first of some eighteen thousand An-2 "Colt" general purpose biplanes.

The VVS receives its first MIG-15 jet fighters in August; the same month, the Il-28 "Beagle" jet bomber is first test-flown.

The first production helicopter in the Soviet Union, the Mi-1, is flown by a test pilot from Mikhail L. Mil's design bureau.

The Lavochkin La-11, the last piston-engined fighter produced in Russia, enters VVS inventory.

1949 Marshall P. F. Zhigarev is named VVS commander, a post he will hold until 1957.

The first Russian A-bomb is tested in August.

1950 In February a MIG-15 reaches the speed of sound in level flight.

The Il-28 "Beagle" tactical jet bomber is first publicly displayed during the May Day flypast over Moscow.

In late May over Korea thirty-six U.S. F-86s engage fifty North Korean MIGs, some flown by Russian "advisors," and down three without loss.

By June a rudimentary radar system extends across the Soviet Union from the Baltic to the Far East.

In Korean War action in June, five USAF F-82s meet five YAK-9s south of Seoul and down three; USAF F-80Cs attack eight NKAF Il-10s over Kimpo and destroy four.

On October 23, some one hundred MIGs attack eight US B-29s, escorted by fifty-five F-84s and F-86s, and down three Superfortresses and a Thunderjet for the loss of three interceptors.

In the first all-jet combat, Lt. Russell J. Brown, flying a USAF 51st Fighter Interceptor Wing F-80, engages and downs a NKAF MIG-15 on November 8.

1951 On November 30, twelve NKAF Tu-2s, escorted by sixteen La-9s and sixteen MIG-15s, bomb an offshore South Korean garrison; intercepted by U.S. 4th FIW F-86s, the Communists lose eight bombers and four fighters for no American loss.

1952 On February 10, a NKAF MIG-15 flown by Chiang Chi-Wei downs Mjr. George A. Davis, U.S. 14-victory F-86 ace, over Korea.

1953 Following a three year period of organizational independence, a unified Soviet Ministry of Defense is established for the second time since 1946.

In June combat over Korea, USAF F-86s engage 501 Chinese and NKAF MIG-15s, downing 77 without loss.

Mjr. Grigori Sedov test-flies the first MIG-19 Farmer in September.

1954 In May Marshall Leonid Govorov is officially named PVO commander and Deputy Minister of Defense.

The Myashishchev M-4 Bison bomber is flown over Moscow during May Day celebrations.

The SA-1 Guild SAM enters Soviet air defense service.

Selected Chronology xxxvii

1955 Marshall Georgi Malenkov is forced out of office as Khrushchev and his loyal generals reorganize the Soviet high command.

Gen. S. S. Biryuzov is appointed PVO commander.

The Warsaw Defense Pact is concluded between Russia and her eastern European satellites in May.

The Yak-25 strategic interceptor is publicly displayed at Tushino in July during the Aviation Day flypast.

The Tupolev Tu-16 Badger and Tu-20 Bear bombers are first publicly displayed at Tushino on Aviation Day; these aircraft create fears in the west of a "bomber gap."

Acting through Czechoslovakia, the Soviets sign an agreement with Egypt to exchange aircraft, advisors, and other technical assistance for cotton.

1956 During the summer certain VVS units are "officially" withdrawn from East Germany.

The first SAM missile defense system is deployed around Moscow.

The Su-7, -9, and -11 fighters are publicly revealed at July's Tushino air show.

The Soviet sponsored East German Air Force (Luftstreitkraefte or LSK) is formed.

1957 The SS-1B Scud A medium range battlefield missile enters Red Army service.

The first full range test of a Soviet ICBM, the SS-6 Sapwood, takes place in August in secret.

On October 4, Sputnik I, the first artificial earth satellite, is launched into orbit by an SS-6 Sapwood.

The SS-3 Shyster MRBM is first publicly displayed during a November Red Square parade.

1958 In February the VVS begins taking delivery of its first MIG-21 "Fishbed" interceptors.

In combat over the Formosa Strait in September, six Nationalist Chinese F-86s engage twenty PRC MIGs and down ten without loss.

1959 The SS-4 Sandal MRBM is deployed.

Flying a MIG-21F on October 31, test pilot G. K. Mosolov establishes an absolute world speed record of 2,388 km/hr.

Soviet MIG-21Fs are supplied to China (PRC).

The Mil bureau begins delivery of the Mi-6 "Hook" helicopter.

On December 17, the Strategic Rocket Force is established by a decree of the USSR Council of Ministers; Marshall Mitrofan I. Nedelin is named commander with Gen. Vladimir F. Tulubko as his first deputy.

1960 In a January 14 speech to the Supreme Soviet, Nikita Khrushchev suggests cutting back the armed forces and placing Russian security under a blanket of strategic nuclear missiles.

On May 1 the U-2 reconnaissance plane flown by Francis G. Powers is downed by a SAM over Sverdlovsk.

In July, VVS MIGs down a U.S. RB-47 reconnaissance plane over the Barents Sea.

More than three hundred people, including SRF commander Nedelin, are killed when a missile explodes during a test launch in October.

In December Marshall Kirill S. Moskalenko is named the new commander of the SRF.

Throughout the year, VVS transports have attempted an unsuccessful airlift into the Congo.

1961 The SS-7 Saddler ICBM enters SRF service.

In April an SS-6 Sapwood ICBM fitted with an upper stage launches Yuri Gagarin into earth orbit aboard Vostok I.

The Indonesian Air Force takes delivery of an initial group of Soviet Tu-16 bombers in July.

The Tu-22 Blinder and M-50 Bounder bombers are first publicly displayed at the Tushino air show in July.

Pakistan begins to take delivery of Soviet MIG-19 fighters.

1962 In April Gen. V. A. Sudets succeeds Marshall Biryuzov as commander of PVO; in the same month, SRF chief Moskalenko is promoted and succeeded by Marshall Biryuzov.

Spanish Civil War and Great Patriot War veteran Marshall

Selected Chronology   xxxix

F. A. Agal'tsov is named commander of the Long-Range Air Force.

In late summer Soviet engineers and SRF personnel begin construction of SS-4 Sandal MRBM sites in Cuba.

In mid-October U.S. reconnaissance planes discover the Soviet missiles in Cuba, leading to a crisis which forces the Russians to remove them.

Russia signs an agreement with India in December to deliver MIG-21s and the plants in which to build them.

1963   The SS-8 Sasin ICBM enters SRF inventory.

In February the Indian Air Force takes delivery of an initial group of MIG-21s.

SRF chief Biryuzov is named chief of the General Staff in March; the new SRF commander is Marshall Nikolai I. Krylov.

VVS tactical reconnaissance aircraft fly electronic ferret missions over West Germany in the spring.

The Finnish Air Force receives a dozen Soviet MIG-21Fs.

1964   Soviet SS-4s and SS-5 Skean MRBM are deployed in Western parts of the Soviet Union targeted on Western Europe.

In March VVS MIGs down a U.S. RB-66 reconnaissance plane over East Germany.

The SS-8 Sassin ICBM is first publicly displayed during a November military parade in Moscow.

1965   In April, North Vietnamese (NVAF) MIGs down three USAF F-105s making American raids on targets in support of the increased U.S. role in the Vietnam war.

SS-13 "Savage" ICBMs, Russia's first solid-propellant missiles, are displayed publicly for the first time in May.

The SS-9 Scarp ICBM is deployed, targeted against U.S. Titan and Minuteman ICBM bases.

The Red Army displays the AT-3 Sagger anti-tank missile during a Moscow military parade.

The SS-1C Scud B battlefield missile is deployed with Red Army units.

Soviet advisors, SAMs, and MIGs, begin to augment the air defense of North Vietnam.

Selected Chronology

1966   Flying a Soviet-supplied MIG-21, Capt. Nguyen Van Bay becomes the first ace of the Vietnam War, claiming for the NVAF the destruction of four U.S. F-105s, two F-4s, and an F-100.

        In July Gen. Pavel Batitski succeeds Marshall Sudets as PVO commander.

        The 23rd CPSU Party Congress elects to upgrade the SRF, VVS, and Soviet Navy.

1967   Israeli Mirages down six Soviet-supplied Syrian MIG-21s during April dogfights.

        In the first hours of the June War, Israeli Air Force fighter bombers destroy the Jordanian Air Force and claim 300 out of 340 Egyptian warplanes attacked on nineteen airfields in the Canal Zone and Sinai; during the second day, the IAF destroys the Syrian Air Force and completes the decimation of the Egyptian Air Force for the reported loss of twenty-six warplanes.

        Gen. Pavel S. Kutakhov is named VVS 1st Deputy Commander in July.

        Three VTA An-22 Cocks display assault capability during Aviation Day festivities; during the same flypast, the swing-wing MIG-23 Flogger is first publicly displayed.

        VVS units participate in field exercises in Belorussia and the Ukraine.

        In November the Red Army first displays the SS-12 Scaleboard battlefield rocket in a Moscow military parade.

1968   The SS-13 Savage and SS-14 Scapegoat are deployed.

        The Moscow Air Defense District is awarded the Order of Lenin in February by order of the Presidium of the Supreme Soviet.

        Pioneer cosmonaut Yuri Gagarin is killed in March when his MIG-15 trainer crashes.

        SRF engineers begin construction near Plesetsk of some sixty SS-13 Savage ICBM silos.

        A four-year debate begins within the Soviet military establishment regarding service priorities.

        The Sukhoi Su-7 Fitter is replaced as a standard PVO-Strany interceptor by the Su-11 Fishpot.

Selected Chronology

1969 Col. Gen. V. V. Reshetnikov succeeds Marshall Agal'tsov as DA commander.
  The Sukhoi Su-15 Flagon interceptor enters PVO service.
  The Mi-12 Homer helicopter is introduced and establishes a world-lift record of 88,636 pounds.
  U.S. spy satellites first observe the Tu-26 Backfire bomber.

1970 On January 31 famed helicopter designer Mikhail L. Mil dies after a long illness.
  In February the USSR passes the U.S. in the numbers of operational ICBMs deployed.
  Soviet air and ground forces participate in the large-scale "Dvina" maneuvers.
  Soviet crews simulate SS-1C Scud B firings in April.
  The first Indian-built MIG-21 is delivered to the Indian Air Force.
  On December 9 Hero of the Soviet Union and famed aircraft designer Artem Mikoyan dies at age 65.

1971 VVS MIG-23s enter operational service in East Germany.
  MIG-25 "Foxbat Bs" gather reconnaissance over Israel with impunity.
  During the Indo-Pakistani war of December, Indian MIG pilots claim ninety-four enemy warplanes downed for the loss of fifty-four; a VVS Tu-126 AWACS "Moss" and its crew assist the Indian Air Force during the conflict.

1972 MIG-25 Foxbat Bs fly tactical reconnaissance over Central Europe during January.
  The Sukhoi Su-17 Fitter C begins service with PVO-Strany.
  Soviet Su-15 Flagons are given to Egypt.
  North Vietnamese soldiers employ shoulder-fired SA-7 SAMs against U.S. warplanes.
  SRF chief Krylov dies in office and is succeeded by Marshall Tulubko.
  During the summer VVS units participate in the Warsaw Pact "Shield" exercises.
  In November SRF personnel test-fire two SS-17 ICBMs into the Pacific.

U.S. B-52s bomb Hanoi in December losing fifteen Stratofortresses to North Vietnamese SAMs; tailgunners claim two intercepting NVAF MIGs shot down.

1973 The VTA begins to take delivery of the Ilyushin Il-76 Candid jet transport.

U.S. spy satellites first detect the SS-16 ICBM.

MIG-25 Foxbat Bs overfly Iran with impunity.

PVO-Strany deploys the Tu-126 AWACS "Moss" in small numbers.

In August the Soviets test the "cold-launching" of ICBMs.

In combat during the Yom Kippur War of October, the Israeli Air Force destroys 450 Soviet-supplied Arab aircraft while losing 115, most to Soviet-supplied SAMs.

During the Arab-Israeli conflict, Egyptian Tu-16 Badgers fire air-to-surface missiles at Israeli targets while the Egyptian Army launches three Soviet-supplied SS-1C Scud B battlefield rockets, all of which miss their targets.

During and after the Yom Kippur War, VTA transports airlift supplies and equipment to the front line Arab states.

1974 The SRF begins to deploy the SS-18 ICBM.

By April the SS-17 ICBM has successfully completed seventeen test flights.

The SALT I pact is signed in December.

The Tu-26 Backfire bomber begins to enter VVS inventory; similarly, the first modern fighter designed for the ground attack role, the Su-19 Fencer, enters service.

The Mi-24 Hind helicopter gunship enters Soviet service and is first witnessed during maneuvers in East Germany.

1975 The SS-20 missile is extensively tested.

The SRF begins to deploy the SS-16, -17, and -19 as well as the SS-18 equipped with MIRV warheads.

Soviet SS-11 silos are modified to take SS-17 and -19 ICBMs.

In April Western interceptors encounter the Backfire bomber during long overseas missions.

In July Soviet ICBM strength peaks at 1,599 missiles, before the SRF begins to phase out its SS-7s and SS-8s.

The Soviets establish a large presence in Somalia.

VVS An-12s and An-22s airlift supplies and equipment to Luanda and Henrique de Carvalho fields, Angola, for use by the MPLA.

In November the Syrian Army test fires a Soviet-supplied SS-1C Scud B battlefield rocket over a range of 155 miles.

The SA-8 Gechko and SA-9 Gaskin SAMs are first publicly displayed in a November parade in Moscow.

1976 The VVS airlift to Angola is continued, bringing Cubans in Il-62s.

SRF SS-20s are reported deployed on the Kamchatka Peninsula in May.

Western experts receive their first close up look at the MIG-25 when a defecting Soviet pilot lands one in Japan in September; the plane is eventually returned to Russia by the Japanese.

The Egyptian Air Force shows off its new Soviet-supplied Su-20 Fitter Cs in a flyby commemorating the Yom Kippur War.

Sukhoi Su-19 Fencers are deployed by Frontal Aviation units.

The last MIG-17s are withdrawn from VVS units stationed in East Germany.

1977 The Soviet Union delivers thirty-six Su-20s to Peru.

VVS units participate in the "Berezina" exercises.

VVS and PVO-Strany interceptors participate in long-range overwater exercises.

1978 The SRF begins to deploy the SS-16 ICBM in substantial numbers.

By March some 120 Backfire bombers are in VVS inventory.

MIG-25s and Su-15s of PVO-Strany are deployed to the Far East to guard against a growing Chinese bomber threat.

In July, Marshall of Aviation Aleksandr I. Koldunov, a top VVS ace of World War II, becomes Commander-in-Chief of PVO-Strany and Deputy Minister of Defense.

VVS transports mount a massive airlift to Ethiopia.

VVS MIG-23s begin to fly combat air patrol over Cuba in November.

1979 The SALT II Treaty is signed in Vienna, but ratification is held up by the U.S. Senate.

In December, Soviet air and ground units move into Afghanistan in force as aircraft, helicopters, and other advisor-assisted machinery have not proved sufficient to put down guerrilla attacks on the Marxist government.

1980 Soviet involvement in Afghanistan grows.

1/ *Reference Works*

Introduction

THE PURPOSE OF this section is twofold: first, to present tools that should prove useful in updating this guide and for additional research into the complexities of the Soviet Air Force, National Air Defense Force, and Strategic Rocket Force; second, to point out those titles that have, in different ways, a general impact either on the topic or on the formation of background knowledge for those who wish to deal with it.

Current and retrospective English language sources on Russian aerospace forces may be located in the bibliographies, abstracts, and indexes cited in sections A, B, and C. Data on the operational and political impact of Soviet aerospace power are often reviewed in citations provided in sections D and E. Terminology useful in interpreting language or concepts in some of the works cited in this book can be found in the dictionaries numbered in section F. General biographies of people of importance involved in some way with Soviet aerospace power during our period are included among the citations of section G. Users should also check the footnotes and bibliographies presented in all of the books and scholarly articles noted in this guide.

A. Bibliographies

1. *ABC POL SCI: A Bibliography of Contents: Political Science and Government.* Santa Barbara, Calif.: ABC-Clio, 1969–. vol. 1–.

2. *A.B.S. Guide to Recent Publications in the Social and Behavioral Sciences.* New York: American Behavioral Scientist, 1965.

   ———. *Supplements.* Beverly Hills, Calif.: Sage, 1966–.

3. *American Book Publishing Record.* New York: R. R. Bowker, 1960–. vol. 1–.

4. American Historical Association. *Writings on American History.* Washington, D.C.: U.S. Government Printing Office, 1947–1961.

5. ———. ———. *1962–1973.* 4 vols. New York: Kraus Reprint, 1975.

6. ———. ———. *1974–.* New York: Kraus Reprint, 1976–.

7. ———. Committee for the Study of War Documents. *Guides to German Records Microfilmed at Alexandria.* Washington, D.C.: U.S. National Archives, 1958–. no. 1–.

8. Attar, Chand. *Bibliography of Indo-Soviet Relations, 1947–1977.* New York: Sterling Publications, 1978. 152p.

9. Bayliss, Gwyn M. *Bibliographic Guide to the Two World Wars: An Annotated Survey of English-Language Reference Materials.* New York: R. R. Bowker, 1977. 578p.

10. *Bibliography of Asian Studies.* Ann Arbor, Mich.: Association for Asian Studies, 1957–. vol. 1–.

11. Bloomberg, Marty and Hans H. Weber. *World War II and Its Origins: A Select Annotated Bibliography of Books in English.* Littleton, Colo.: Libraries Unlimited, 1975. 311p.

12. "Books and Ideas." In: *Air University Review.* Maxwell AFB, Ala.: Air University, 1959–. vol. 10–.

13. *British Books in Print: The Reference Catalogue of Current Literature—Author, Title, and Subject Index.* London and New York: R. R. Bowker, 1967–. vol. 1–.

14. Burns, Richard D. and Susan Hoffman, comps. *The SALT Era: A Selected Bibliography.* Political Issues Series, vol. 6, no. 1. Rev. ed. Los Angeles: Center for the Study of Armament and Disarmament, California State University, 1979. 59p.

15. Burt, Richard. *Congressional Hearings on American Defense Policy, 1947–1971: A Bibliography.* Lawrence: University Press of Kansas, 1974.

16. Cooling, B. Franklin, 3rd and Alan Millett. *Doctoral Dissertations in Military Affairs: A Bibliography.* Bibliography Series, no. 10. Manhattan: Kansas State University Library, 1972. 153p. Updated in the annual April issue of *Military Affairs,* 1973–.

17. *Cumulative Bibliography of Asian Studies.* 2 vols. Boston: G. K. Hall, 1969–1972.

18. *The Cumulative Book Index.* New York: H. W. Wilson, 1939–.

19. Council on Foreign Relations. *The Foreign Affairs 50-Year Bibliography: New Evaluations of Significant Books on International Relations, 1920–1970.* New York: R. R. Bowker, 1970.

20. DeVore, Ronald M. *The Arab-Israeli Conflict: A Historical, Political, Social, and Military Bibliography.* War/Peace Bibliography Series, no. 4. Santa Barbara, Calif.: ABC-Clio, 1976. 273p.

21. Enser, A. G. S. *A Subject Bibliography of the Second World War: Books in English, 1939–1974.* Boulder, Colo.: Westview, 1977. 592p.

22. Estep, Raymond. *An Aerospace Bibliography.* 3 vols. Maxwell AFB, Ala.: Air University, 1962, 1965, 1967.

23. *Forthcoming Books.* New York: R. R. Bowker, 1966–. vol. 1–.

24. Freidel, Frank, ed. *Harvard Guide to American History.* 2 vols. Rev. ed. Cambridge, Mass.: Harvard University Press, 1974.

25. Funk, Arthur L. *The Second World War, A Bibliography: A Select List of Publications Appearing Since 1968.* Gainesville, Fla.: American Committee on the History of the Second World War, 1972. 32p.

26. Great Britain. British Museum. Department of Printed Books. *Catalogue of Printed Books: Additions.* London: Clowes, 1963–. vol. 1–.

27. _____. Public Records Office. *The Second World War: A Guide to Documents in the Public Records Office.* Handbook, no. 15. London: H. M. Stationery Office, 1972. 303p.

28. Hammond, Thomas T., ed. and comp. *Soviet Foreign Relations and World Communism: A Selected, Annotated Bibliography of 7,000 Books in Thirty Languages.* Princeton: Princeton University Press, 1965. 1,240p.

29. Higham, Robin, ed. *Official Histories: Essays and Bibliographies from Around the World.* Manhattan: Kansas State University Library, 1970. 644p.

Reference Works

30. Holler, Frederick L., comp. *Information Sources of Political Science.* 3rd ed. Santa Barbara, Calif.: ABC-Clio, 1981.

31. *International Bibliography of Political Science.* Chicago: Aldine, 1952–. vol. 1–.

32. *International Information Service: A Quarterly Annotated Index of Selected Materials on Current International Affairs.* Chicago: Library of International Affairs, 1963–. vol. 1–.

33. Kucherov, Bertha, comp. *Aeronautical Sciences and Aviation in the Soviet Union: A Bibliography.* Washington, D.C.: Library of Congress, 1955. 274p.

34. Michel, Henri and Jean Marie D'Hoop. *The Two World Wars: Selective Bibliography.* New York: Pergamon, 1964. 246p.

35. "The Military Library." In: *Military Affairs.* Washington, D.C.: American Military Institute, 1939–. vol. 3–.

36. Morton, Louis. "World War II: A Survey of Recent Writings." *American Historical Review,* LXXV (December 1970), 1987–2009.

37. New York Public Library. Research Libraries. *Subject Catalog of the World War II Collection.* 3 vols. Boston: G. K. Hall, 1977.

38. *Paperbound Books in Print.* New York: R. R. Bowker, 1955–. vol. 1–.

39. Parrish, Michael. *The Soviet Armed Forces: Books in English, 1950–1967.* Hoover Institution Bibliographical Series, no. 48. Stanford, Calif.: Hoover Institution Press, 1970. 128p.

40. Remington, Robin A. *International Relations of Eastern Europe: A Guide to Information Sources.* International Relations Information Guide Series, no. 8. Detroit, Mich.: Gale Research Co., 1978. 273p.

41. Rubner, Michael, comp. *Middle East Conflict from October 1973 to July 1976: A Selected Bibliography.* Political Issues Series, vol. 4, no. 4. Los Angeles: Center for the Study of Armament and Disarmament, California State University, 1977. 82p.

42. Scott, William F. *Soviet Sources of Military Doctrine and Strategy.* New York: Published for the National Strategy Information Center by Crane, Russak, 1975. 72p.

43. Simon, Reeva S. *The Modern Middle East: A Guide to Research Tools in the Social Sciences.* Modern Middle East Series, no. 10. Boulder, Colo.: Westview, 1978. 283p.

44. Smith, Myron J., Jr. *Air War Bibliography, 1939–1945: A Guide to Sources in English.* Manhattan, Kans.: Military Affairs Aerospace Historian Publications for the USAF Historical Foundation, 1976–. vol. 1–.

45. *Soviet Analyst.* London: Castle Press, 1971–. vol. 1–.

46. *Subject Guide to Books in Print.* New York: R. R. Bowker, 1957–. vol. 1–.

46a. United States. Air Force. Academy. Library. *Airpower and Warfare.* Special Bibliography Series, no. 59. Colorado Springs, Colo., 1978. 101p.

47. _____. Army. *U.S.S.R.: Analytical Survey of Literature.* Bibliographic Surveys of Strategic Areas of the World. DA 550–6–1. Washington, D.C.: U.S. Government Printing Office, 1976. 232p.

48. _____. _____. *U.S.S.R.: Missiles, Rockets, and Space Effort—a Bibliographic Record, 1956–1960.* DA 70–5–8. Washington, D.C.: U.S. Government Printing Office, 1960. 49p.

49. _____. _____. Military Academy. Library. *Subject Catalog of the Military Art and Science Collection.* 6 vols. Westport, Conn.: Greenwood Press, 1969.

50. _____. _____. Military History Institute. *The Era of World War II.* Special Bibliography Series, no. 16. Washington, D.C.: U.S. Government Printing Office, 1977–. vol. 1–.

51. _____. Library of Congress. General Reference and Bibliography Division. Arms Control and Disarmament Bibliography Section. *Arms Control and Disarmament: A Quarterly Bibliography with Abstracts and Annotations.* 10 vols. Washington, D.C.: U.S. Government Printing Office, 1964–1973.

52. _____. _____. _____. *Library of Congress Catalog, Books–Subjects: A Cumulative List of Works Represented by Library of Congress Printed Cards.* Washington, D.C.: U.S. Government Printing Office, 1950–. vol. 1–.

53. *Verticle File Index.* New York: H. W. Wilson, 1939–. vol. 8–.

54. Ziegler, Janet. *World War II: Books in English, 1945–1965.* Hoover Institution Bibliographical Series, no. 45. Stanford, Calif.: Hoover Institution Press, 1971. 224p.

B. Abstracts

55. *Abstracts of Military Bibliography.* Buenos Aires, Argentina: Navy Publications Institute, 1968–. vol. 1–.

56. *America: History and Life.* Santa Barbara, Calif.: ABC-Clio, 1964–. vol. 1–.

57. Congressional Information Service. *C.I.S. Annual: Abstracts of Congressional Publications and Legislative Histories.* Washington, D.C., 1969–. vol. 1–.

58. *Dissertation Abstracts, v. 2–30.* Ann Arbor, Mich.: University Microfilms, 1939–1968.

59. *Dissertation Abstracts International: "A" Schedule.* Ann Arbor, Mich.: University Microfilms, 1969–. vol. 1–.

61. *Historical Abstracts: Part B: Twentieth Century Abstracts (1914–Present).* Santa Barbara, Calif.: ABC-Clio, 1955–. vol. 1–.

62. *International Political Science Abstracts.* Oxford, England: Basil Blackwell, 1952–. vol. 1–.

63. *Masters Abstracts.* Ann Arbor, Mich.: University Microfilms, 1962–. vol. 1–.

64. RAND Corporation. *Selected RAND Abstracts.* Santa Monica, Calif., 1962–. vol. 1–.

65. United States. Air Force. Air University. Library. *Abstracts of Student Research Reports.* Maxwell AFB, Ala., 1949–. vol. 1–.

C. Indexes

1. Newspapers

66. American Association for the Advancement of Slavic Studies. *Index to Pravda.* Columbus, Ohio, 1950–1977.

67. *California News Index.* Claremont, Calif.: Center for California Public Affairs, 1970–. vol. 1–.

68. *The Christian Science Monitor Index.* Corvallis, Oreg.: Helen M. Cropsey, 1960–. vol. 1–.

69. *Editorials on File.* New York: Facts on File, 1970–. vol. 1–.

70. *The German Tribune.* Hamburg: Friedrich Verlag, 1956–. vol. 1–.

71. Joint Committee on Slavic Studies. *Current Digest of the Soviet Press.* Ann Arbor, Mich., 1949–. vol. 1–.

72. *The National Observer Index.* Flint, Mich.: Newspaper Indexing Center, 1970–. vol. 1–.

73. *Newspaper Index.* Wooster, Ohio: Bell & Howell, 1972–. vol. 1–.

Covers *Chicago Tribune, Washington Post, Los Angeles Times,* and *New Orleans Times-Picayune.*

74. *New York Times. New York Times Index.* New York, 1939–.

75. *Reprints from the Soviet Press.* New York: Compass Publications, 1965–. vol. 1–.

76. *Times of London. Index to the Times.* London, 1939–.

77. *The Wall Street Journal Index.* New York: Dow Jones, 1958–. vol. 1–.

2. Periodicals

78. *Access: The Supplementary Index to Periodicals.* Syracuse, N.Y.: Gaylord, 1975–. vol. 1–.

79. Botlorff, Robert M., ed. *Popular Periodical Index.* New York, 1973–. vol. 1–.

80. Burke, John G., ed. *The Access Index to Little Magazines.* Syracuse, N.Y.: Gaylord, 1977–. vol. 1–.

81. *Humanities Index.* New York: H. W. Wilson, 1975–. vol. 1–.

82. *Index to the Contemporary Scene.* Detroit, Mich.: Gale Research, 1973–. vol. 1–.

83. *Index to U.S. Government Periodicals.* Chicago: Infordata International, 1975–. vol. 1–.

84. *International Relations Digest of Periodical Literature.* Berkeley: Bureau of International Relations, University of California, 1950–. vol. 1–.

85. *The New Periodicals Index.* Boulder, Colo.: Mediaworks, 1977–. vol. 1–.

86. Public Affairs Information Serivce. *P.A.I.S. Bulletin.* New York, 1939–. vol. 24–.

87.   *Reader's Guide to Periodical Literature.* New York: H. W. Wilson, 1939–.

88.   *Social Sciences and Humanities Index.* New York: H. W. Wilson, 1939–1974.

89.   *Social Sciences Index.* New York: H. W. Wilson, 1975–. vol. 1–.

90.   United States. Air Force. Air University. Library. *Air University Library Index to Military Periodicals.* Maxwell AFB, Ala., 1949–. vol. 1–.

3. Documents

91.   Bernan Associates. *Checklist of Congressional Hearings and Reports.* Washington, D.C., 1958–. vol. 1–.

92.   Congressional Quarterly, Inc. *C.Q. Weekly Report.* Washington, D.C., 1945–. vol. 1–.

93.   ———. *Congressional Quarterly Almanac.* Washington, D.C., 1945–. vol. 1–.

94.   Great Britain. *Catalogue of Government Publications.* London: H. M. Stationery Office, 1939–. vol. 1–.

95.   United Nations. Dag Hammerskjold Library. *United Nations Documents Index.* New York, 1950–. vol. 1–.

96.   United States. National Technical Information Service. *Government Reports Announcements.* Springfield, Va., 1946–. vol. 1–.

97.   ———. Superintendent of Documents. *Monthly Catalog of U.S. Government Publications.* Washington, D.C.: U.S. Government Printing Office, 1939–.

98.   *United States Political Science Documents.* Pittsburgh, Pa.: Publications Center, University Center for International Studies, University of Pittsburgh, 1975–. vol. 1–.

D. Encyclopedias and Handbooks

99.   Banks, Arthur S., ed. *Political Handbook of the World, 19–: Governments, Regional Issues, and Intergovernmental Organizations as of January 1, 19–.* New York: McGraw-Hill, 1939–. vol. 11–.

100. Bowman, Norman J. *The Handbook of Rockets and Guided Missiles.* 2nd ed. Newtown Square, Pa.: Perastadion Press, 1963. 1,008p.

Encyclopedias and Handbooks

101.   Brown, Joseph M. *Helicopter Directory.* New York: Hippocrene Books, 1976. 128p.

102.   Chant, Christopher et al. *The Encyclopedia of Air Warfare.* New York: T. Y. Crowell, 1976. 256p.

103.   Dean, Donald W., ed. *World Aviation Directory.* Washington, D.C.: Ziff-Davis, 1976. 1,486p.

104.   Dupuy, R. Ernest and Trevor N. *The Encyclopedia of Military History.* Rev. ed. New York: Harper & Row, 1976. 1,488p.

105.   Dupuy, Trevor N., Grace P. Hayes, and John A.C. Andrews. *The Almanac of World Military Power.* Rev. ed. San Rafael, Calif.: Presidio Press, 1980. 416p.

106.   *The Epic of Flight.* 10 vols. New York: Time-Life Books, 1979.

107.   Green, William, comp. *The Macdonald Aircraft Handbook.* Garden City, N.Y.: Doubleday, 1966. 596p.

108.   Gunston, William T. *The Encyclopedia of the World's Combat Aircraft: A Technical Directory of Major Warplanes from World War I to the Present Day.* New York: Chartwell Books, 1976. 229p.

109.   _____. *The Illustrated Encyclopedia of the World's Modern Military Aircraft.* London: Salamander Books, 1977. 256p.

110.   _____, Bill Sweetman, and Michael Hewish. *Soviet Air Power: An Illustrated Encyclopedia of the Warsaw Pact Air Forces and Their Equipment.* New York: Chartwell Books, 1978. 192p.

111.   Gurney, Gene. *A Chronology of World Aviation.* New York: Franklin Watts, 1965. 252p.

112.   Jones, David R., ed. *Military-Naval Encyclopedia of Russia and the Soviet Union.* Gulf Breeze, Fla.: Academic International Press, 1978–. vol. 1–.

113.   Keegan, John. *World Armies.* New York: Facts on File, 1979. 1,016p.

114.   _____, ed. *The Rand McNally Encyclopedia of World War II.* Chicago: Rand McNally, 1977. 256p.

115.   Krivinyi, Nikolaus et al. *World Military Aviation: Aircraft, Air Forces, and Weaponry.* New York: Arco, 1973. 224p.

116.   Kurian, George T. *Encyclopedia of the Third World.* 2 vols. New York: Facts on File, 1979.

117.   Labrie, Roger P., ed. *SALT Handbook: Key Documents and Issues, 1972–1979*. AEI Studies, no. 214. Washington, D.C.: American Enterprise Institute for Public Policy Research, 1979. 736p.

118.   Mallory, Walter H. *Political Handbook and Atlas of the World*. New York: Council on Foreign Relations, 1939–. vol. 12–.

119.   *The Marshall Cavendish Illustrated Encyclopedia of Aviation*. 20 vols. London: Marshall Cavendish, 1978.

120.   *The Marshall Cavendish Illustrated Encyclopedia of World War II*. 25 vols. Hicksville, N.Y.: Marshall Cavendish, 1972–1974.

121.   Mondey, David, ed. *Complete Illustrated Encyclopedia of the World's Aircraft*. New York: A. & W. Publishers, 1978. 320p.

122.   Norby, M. O., ed. *Soviet Aerospace Handbook*. AF Pam. 200–21. Washington, D.C.: Headquarters, Department of the Air Force, 1978. 222p.

123.   Paneth, Donald. *Current Affairs Atlas, 1979–80*. New York: Facts on File, 1979. 224p.

124.   Parkinson, Roger. *The Encyclopedia of Modern War*. New York: Stein and Day, 1976.

125.   Parrish, Thomas, ed. *The Simon and Schuster Encyclopedia of World War II*. New York: Simon and Schuster, 1978. 765p.

126.   Parsons, Iain, ed. *The Encyclopedia of Air Warfare*. New York: T. Y. Crowell, 1975. 256p.

127.   *Plane and Pilot Magazine,* Editors of. *Aircraft International Directory.* New York: Werner and Werner, 1977. 178p.

128.   Reid, Alan. *A Concise Encyclopedia of the Second World War*. Reading, England: Osprey, 1974. 234p.

129.   Sellers, Robert C., ed. *Armed Forces of the World: A Reference Handbook*. 4th ed. New York: Praeger, 1977. 288p.

130.   Stockholm International Peace Research Institute (SIPRI). *Armaments and Disarmament in the Nuclear Age: A Handbook*. New York: Humanities Press, 1976. 308p.

131.   Taylor, John W. R. *Encyclopedia of World Aircraft*. London: Odhams, 1966. 159p.

132.   _____ et al. *Air Facts and Feats*. Rev. ed. New York: Sterling Publishers, 1978. 240p.

133. Taylor, Michael J. H. and John W. R., eds. *Encyclopedia of Aircraft*. London: Weidenfeld and Nicolson, 1978. 253p.

134. United States. War Department. *Handbook of U.S.S.R. Military Forces, 1945*. TM 30–430. Washington, D.C., 1945. 765p.

135. ———. ———. ———. Springfield, Va.: John Sloan, 1977. 765p.

136. Wieczynski, Joseph L. *The Modern Encyclopedia of Russian and Soviet History*. Gulf Breeze, Fla.: Academic International Press, 1976–. vol. 1–.

137. Wise, Terence. *Military Flags of the World in Color*. New York: Arco, 1978. 184p.

138. "World Missile/Space Encyclopedia." *Missiles and Rockets*, XV (July 27, 1964), 39–140; XVII (July 26, 1965), 37–149.

E. Annuals and Yearbooks

139. Aerospace Industries Association of America. Economic Data Service. Aerospace Research Center. *Aerospace Facts and Figures*. New York: Aviation Week and Space Technology, 1952–. vol. 1–.

140. *The Aerospace Yearbook*. Washington, D.C.: American Aviation Publications, Inc., 1939–. vol. 16–.

141. *Africa South of the Sahara*. London: Europa Publications, 1970–. vol. 1–.

142. *The Aircraft Yearbook*. New York: Aeronautical Chamber of Commerce of America, 1939–. vol. 19–.

143. *American Reference Books Annual*. Littleton, Colo.: Libraries Unlimited, 1970–. vol. 1–.

144. *The Annual Register of World Events: A Review of the Year* ———. London: Longmans, Green, 1939–. vol. 179–.

145. *Arab Report and Record*. London, 1965–. vol. 1–.

146. Berner, Wolfgang, ed. *The Soviet Union, 1973–*. New York: Holmes and Meier, 1975–. vol. 1–.

147. Crozier, Brian. *Annual of Power and Conflict*. London: Institute for the Study of Conflict, 1973–. vol. 1–.

Reference Works 13

148. *The Europa Yearbook: A World Survey and Directory of Countries and International Organizations.* London: Europa Publications, 1950–. vol. 1–.

149. Facts on File, Editors of. *News Dictionary.* New York: Facts on File, 1965–. vol. 1–.

150. ———. *Facts on File Yearbook: The Indexed Record of World Events.* New York: Facts on File, 1941–. vol. 1–.

151. Green, William, comp. *The Observer's Book of Aircraft.* New York: Warne, 1961–. vol. 1–.

152. Hoeber, Francis P., David B. Kassing, and William Schneider, Jr. *Arms, Men, and Military Budgets: Issues for Fiscal Year 19–.* New York: Crane, Russak, 1975–. vol. 1–.

153. *Information Please Almanac.* New York: Viking, 1946–. vol. 1–.

154. Institute of World Affairs. *The Yearbook of World Affairs.* London: Stevens, 1947–. vol. 1–.

155. Intelligence International, Ltd. *Intelligence Digest: A Review of World Affairs.* Cheltenham, England: 1939–. vol. 2–.

156. *Interavia ABC, 19–: World Directory of Aviation and Astronautics.* New York: Interavia, USA, 1952–. vol. 1–.

157. International Institute for Strategic Studies. *The Military Balance.* London, 1958–. vol. 1–.

158. *The International Yearbook and Statesman's Who's Who.* London: Burke's Peerage, 1953–. vol. 1–.

159. *Jane's All the World's Aircraft.* New York: McGraw-Hill, 1939–. vol. 6–.

160. *Jane's Weapons Systems.* New York: Franklin Watts, 1969–. vol. 1–.

161. Jones, David R., ed. *Soviet Armed Forces Review Annual.* Gulf Breeze, Fla.: Academic International Press, 1977–. vol. 1–.

162. *Kessing's Contemporary Archives.* London: Kessing's Publications, 1939–. vol. 8–.

163. Legum, Colin, ed. *Africa Contemporary Record.* New York: Holmes and Meier, 1969–. vol. 1–.

Annuals and Yearbooks

164. _____. *Middle East Contemporary Survey.* New York: Holmes and Meier, 1978–. vol. 1–.

165. Marriott, John, ed. *R.U.S.I. and Brassey's Weapons Technology: A Survey of Current Developments in Weapons Systems.* London: Brassey's International, 1975–. vol. 1–.

166. *The Middle East and North Africa.* London: Europa Publications, 1953–. vol. 1–.

167. Rake, Alan, ed. *New African Yearbook.* New York: Franklin Watts, 1978–. vol. 1–.

168. *Reader's Digest 19– Almanac and Yearbook.* New York: Norton, 1967–. vol. 1–.

169. Royal Institute of International Affairs. *Survey of International Affairs: Post-War Series, Since 1947.* London: Oxford University Press, 1952–. vol. 1–.

170. Scherer, John L., ed. *U.S.S.R. Facts and Figures Annual.* Gulf Breeze, Fla.: Academic International Press, 1977–. vol. 1–.

171. *Soviet Aerospace.* Washington, D.C.: Space Publications, Inc., 1971–. vol. 1–.

172. Staar, Richard F., ed. *Yearbook of International Communist Affairs.* Stanford, Calif.: Hoover Institution Press, 1970–. vol. 1–.

173. *The Statesman's Year-Book: Statistical and Historical Information of the States of the World for the Year* _____ . New York: St. Martin's Press, 1939–.

174. Stebbins, Richard P. and Alba Amoia. *The World This Year.* New York: Simon and Schuster, 1971–. vol. 1–.

175. Stockholm International Peace Research Institute (SIPRI). *World Armaments and Disarmament: The SIPRI Yearbook.* New York: Humanities Press, 1969–. vol. 1–.

176. Taylor, John W. R., ed. *Aircraft, 19–.* London: Ian Allan, 1971–. vol. 1–.

177. United States. Congress. House. Committee on Armed Services. Subcommittee on Department of Defense Appropriations. *Department of Defense Appropriations for Fiscal Year* _____ *: Hearings.* Washington, D.C.: U.S. Government Printing Office, 1948–.

178. _____. _____. _____. _____. *Hearings on Military Posture, etc.* Washington, D.C.: U.S. Government Printing Office, 1961–.

Reference Works 15

179. _____. _____. Senate. Committee on Armed Services. *Military Procurement Authorization, Fiscal Year* _____ *: Hearings.* Washington, D.C.: U.S. Government Printing Office, 1948–.

180. _____. _____. _____. _____. Subcommittee on Department of Defense Appropriations. *Department of Defense Appropriations for Fiscal Year* _____ *: Hearings.* Washington, D.C.: U.S. Government Printing Office, 1948–.

181. _____. Department of Defense. *Report of the Secretary of Defense.* Washington, D.C.: U.S. Government Printing Office, 1948–.

182. Whitaker, Joseph. *Almanack.* London: Whitaker, 1939–. vol. 71–.

183. *World Almanac and Book of Facts.* Garden City, N.Y.: Doubleday, 1939–. vol. 70–.

F. Dictionaries

184. "Atomic Warfare Glossary." *Annals of the American Academy of Political and Social Sciences,* CDXXX (March 1977), 175–177.

185. Crowe, Barry. *Concise Dictionary of Soviet Terminology, Institutions, and Abbreviations.* London and New York: Pergamon Press, 1969. 182p.

186. Foye, James. *Aircraft Technical Dictionary.* Fallbrook, Calif.: Aviation Book Company, 1978. 193p.

187. Gale Research Company. *Acronyms and Initialisms Dictionary.* 3rd ed. Detroit, 1970. 484p.

188. Garber, Max and P. S. Bond. *A Modern Military Dictionary.* 2nd ed. Washington, D.C.: Bond, 1942. 272p.

189. Garman, W. Y. *A Dictionary of Military Uniforms.* New York: Scribner's, 1977.

190. Hanrieder, Wolfram F. and Larry V. Buel. *Words and Arms: A Dictionary of Security and Defense Terms, with Supplemental Data.* Boulder, Colo.: Westview, 1979. 250p.

191. Hayward, P. H. C., comp. *Jane's Dictionary of Military Terms.* London: Macdonald and Jane's, 1975. 201p.

192. Heflin, W. A. *Aerospace Glossary.* Maxwell AFB, Ala.: Research Studies Institute, Air University, 1959. 159p.

Dictionaries

193.   Lanz, J. E. *The Lanz Aviation Dictionary in Nine Languages.* New York: Perkins, 1944. 430p.

194.   Luttwak, Edward. *A Dictionary of Modern War.* New York: Harper & Row, 1971. 224p.

195.   Partridge, Eric, ed. *A Dictionary of Forces' Slang, 1939–1945.* Freeport, N.Y.: Books for Libraries, 1970. 212p.

196.   Plano, Jack C. and Milton Greenberg. *The American Political Dictionary.* 5th ed. New York: Holt, 1979. 488p.

197.   _____ and Roy Olton. *The International Relations Dictionary.* New York: Holt, 1969. 337p.

198.   Quick, John. *Dictionary of Weapons and Military Terms.* New York: McGraw-Hill, 1973. 527p.

199.   Raymond, Walter J. *Dictionary of Politics: Selected American and Foreign Political and Legal Terms.* 6th ed., rev. Lawrenceville, Va.: Brunswick Publishing Co., 1978. 956p.

200.   Ruffner, Frederick G., Jr. and Robert C. Thomas, eds. *Code Names Dictionary.* Detroit, Mich.: Gale Research Company, 1963. 555p.

201.   Schwarz, Urs and Laszlo Hadik. *Strategic Terminology: A Trilingual Glossary.* New York: Praeger, 1966. 156p.

202.   Taylor, A. Marjorie. *The Language of World War II.* Rev. ed. New York: H. W. Wilson, 1948. 265p.

203.   Union of Soviet Socialist Republics. Ministry of Defense. *Dictionary of Military Terms: A Soviet View.* Translated from the Russian. Soviet Military Thought Series, no. 9. Washington, D.C.: Published under the auspices of the U.S. Air Force by the U.S. Government Printing Office, 1976. 256p.

204.   United States. Arms Control and Disarmament Agency. *SALT Lexicon.* ACDA Publication, no. 71. Washington, D.C.: U.S. Government Printing Office, 1974.

205.   _____. Army. *Dictionary of U.S. Army Terms.* Army Reg. 310-25. Washington, D.C., 1972.

206.   _____. Department of Defense. *Glossary of Soviet Military and Related Abbreviations.* TM 30-546. Washington, D.C., 1957. 178p.

207.   _____. _____. Joint Chiefs of Staff. *Department of Defense Dictionary of Military and Associated Terms.* JCS-1. Rev. ed. Washington, D.C.: U.S. Government Printing Office, 1979. 377p.

208. _____. War Department. *Russian Military Dictionary.* TM 30-544. Washington, D.C.: U.S. Government Printing Office, 1945. 478p.

209. Wragg, David W. *A Dictionary of Aviation.* New York: Frederick Fell, 1974. 86p.

G. Biography: General

210. *Biography Index.* New York: H. W. Wilson, 1947–. vol. 1–.

211. *Current Biography.* New York: H. W. Wilson, 1940–. vol. 1–.

212. *Current World Leaders.* Pasadena, Calif., 1957–. vol. 1–.

213. Facts on File, Editors of. *Obituaries on File* [1940–1978]. 2 vols. New York, 1979.

214. *The International Who's Who.* London: Europa Publications, 1939–. vol. 4–.

215. Keegan, John and Andrew Wheatcroft. *Who's Who in Military History* [1450–1974]. London: Weidenfeld and Nicholson, 1976. 367p.

216. Martell, Paul and Grace P. Hayes. *World Military Leaders.* New York: R. R. Bowker, 1974. 268p.

217. *New York Times,* Editors of. *New York Times Obituary Index, 1858–1968.* New York: *New York Times,* 1970. 1,136p.

218. *Times of London,* Editors of. *Obituaries from the Times, 1961–1970.* Reading, England: Newspaper Archive Developments, 1976. 952p.

219. Windrow, Martin and Francis K. Mason. *A Concise Dictionary of Military Biography.* London: Osprey, 1975. 337p.

2/ The Era of World War II, 1939–1945

Introduction

STARTING BARELY THREE months after the German invasion of Poland, the Russo-Finnish "Winter War" is often regarded as a kind of "warm-up" for Soviet involvement in the Second World War. In December 1939 the Red Army moved on Finland in what would become a short, costly, and embarrassing contest. Before regrouping in the spring of 1940 and applying maximum power, the Soviets witnessed the loss of nine hundred aircraft to the gallant and numerically inferior Finnish air force. The leaders of the Luftwaffe as well as other Western air forces observed this aerial engagement with wonder and great applause. Later, when Hitler turned on the USSR, the Finns rejoined the effort against Moscow in a "Continuation War" on the side of the Third Reich.

On June 22, 1941, German armies and Luftwaffe air units attacked Russia in "Operation Barbarossa." Within nine hours of the invasion's commencement, the Soviets had lost twelve hundred aircraft, including four hundred downed in aerial combat. The Red Air Force which began the month as the largest in the world finished it with the loss of five thousand warplanes.

As the Germans pushed deeper into western Russia, surviving Soviet air elements were dispersed under the control of various army (ground) commanders. With fewer aircraft and smaller front lines, the Russians were able to centralize control over their air units. As Hitler's men approached Moscow in late 1941, aircraft from all Soviet armies, later supplemented by fifteen hundred planes from Siberia, were concentrated at the Russian capital.

It was not until the spring of 1943 that the Soviets were able to rebuild their air inventory to the point where it had an effect on the war effort. Between August 1941 and August 1942, aircraft production was slowed down as the Soviet defense industry was relocated east of the Ural mountains. Starting in 1943, production reached thirty-five thousand machines per year. That same year the bulk of fourteen thousand aircraft began to arrive in the USSR from the Anglo-American Lend-Lease program. Until that point, limited Soviet air assets remained under centralized control and were deployed in concentrations for major battles, such as those fought at Stalingrad in the winter of 1942–1943. It was not until the destruction of the German "Operation Citadel" in the July 1943 Battle of Kursk—a major tank battle which saw the destruction of fourteen hundred Luftwaffe warplanes—that the Russian air force captured air superiority.

Following the decisive Kursk engagement, Soviet air superiority had a three-to-one numerical advantage. Throughout the war, pilots of the Russian air force flew approximately four million operational sorties, of which almost half were ground support missions, a third were air superiority missions, and only two percent were strategic bombing. As the Soviets emerged from the war it became clear that they had placed the major emphasis of their air power on support of the ground forces.

In addition to Lend-Lease aid, both the British and Americans made overtures to Stalin to provide direct air support. Always suspicious of his Western allies, the Soviet dictator granted only limited eastern theater air privileges to the RAF and USAAF.

In the fall of 1941, Hurricane fighters of RAF No. 151 Wing arrived in crates at Murmansk. When the planes were reassembled, their pilots flew them for a few weeks from nearby airfields before turning them over to Soviet airmen.

The Americans, meanwhile, were able to convince Russian leaders of possible value in a certain number of "shuttle bombing" raids on German targets in the eastern theater. A few raid by B-17s and long-range fighters from both Britain and Italy were mounted. This precision bombardment had no significant effect on the combined war effort and with the disaster at Poltava raising additional suspicions, may actually have contributed to the growing discord between the Big Three.[1]

The references in this section cover the air war on the Finnish and Eastern Fronts from 1939 to 1945. Data is provided not only on campaigns and battles, but on the opposing air forces, noteworthy people, attempted British and American assistance, and Soviet/Lend-Lease aircraft. A few additional references of a general nature which have bearing here will be found in Section 1:D above and 4:B and 5 below.

---

1. The material in this introduction is based on the references cited below and M. O. Norby, ed. *Soviet Aerospace Handbook*. (Washington, D.C.: U.S. Government Printing Office, 1978), pp. 32–33.

A. The Russo-Finnish Wars, 1939–1944

Books

220. Anttonen, Ossi. *The Luftwaffe in Finland, 1941–1944*. Helsinki: Kirja–Lento, 1976. 144p.

221. Condon, Richard. *The Winter War: Russia Against Finland*. Ballantine's Illustrated History of the Violent Century. New York: Ballantine Books, 1972. 160p.

222. Engle, Eloise and Lauri Paananen. *The Winter War: The Russo–Finnish Conflict, 1939–40*. New York: Scribner's, 1973. 176p.

223. Luukkanen, Eino A. *Fighter Over Finland: The Memoirs of a Fighter Pilot*. Translated from the Finnish. London: Macdonald, 1963. 254p.

224. Lundin, Charles L. *Finland in the Second World War*. Bloomington: Indiana University Press, 1957. 303p.

225. Ward, Richard and Christopher F. Shores. *The Finnish Air Force, 1918–1968*. Aircam Aviation Series. New York: Arco, 1969. 96p.

Articles

226. Barclay, Glen St. J. "Diversion in the East: The Western Allies, Scandinavia, and Russia, November 1939–April 1940." *Historian*, XLIII (May 1979), 483–498.

227. "Bombers Over Finland." *Newsweek*, XV (February 12, 1940), 26–27.

228. "Cities and Towns of Finland Crumple and Burn Under the Hail of Russian Bombs." *Life*, VIII (March 11, 1940), 24–25.

229. "Flying Finns Roll Back Invading Reds in a Rout of Historic Stature." *Newsweek*, XV (January 15, 1940), 19–20.

230. Jokinen, Pertti. "The Finnish Air Force." *Aerospace Historian*, XXVI (December 1979), 221–232.

231. Kozlov, L. "Liberation of the Baltic Region." *Soviet Military Review*, no. 11 (November 1974), 49–51.

232. Salminen, S. "The Raid on Runeberg's Town." *American-Scandinavian Review*, XXVIII (September 1940), 223–230.

233. Salo, Mauno A. "Arctic Air War." *RAF Flying Review*, XVII (April 1962), 22–24.

234. Sarvanto, James. "Fighter Over Finland." *RAF Flying Review*, XI (July–August 1956), 28–29, 29–30, 37.

235. Shores, Christopher F. "Finland's Air War." *Air Pictorial*, XXX (June–July 1968), 192–196, 231–234.

236. Whiting, Kenneth R. "Soviet Aviation and Air Power Under Stalin." In: Robin Highan and Jacob W. Kipp, eds. *Soviet Aviation and Air Power: A Historical View*. Boulder, Colo.: Westview, 1977. pp. 47–68.

Documents, Papers, and Reports

237. Anzulovic, J. V. "The Russian Record of the Winter War, 1939–1940." Unpublished Ph.D. Dissertation, University of Maryland, 1968.

B. The Great Patriotic War, 1941–1945

1. General Studies

238. Adams, Henry H. *1942: The Year That Doomed the Axis*. New York: McKay, 1967. 544p.

239. _____. *Years of Deadly Peril: The Coming of the War, 1939–1941*. New York: McKay, 1969. 559p.

240. _____. *Years of Expectation: Guadalcanal to Normandy*. New York: McKay, 1973. 430p.

241. _____. *Years to Victory*. New York: McKay, 1973. 507p.

242. *Air Power: A Modern Illustrated Military History*. London: Phoebus Books, 1979. 391p.

243. Arnold-Foster, Mark. *The World at War*. New York: Stein and Day, 1973. 340p.

244. Baldwin, Hanson W. *Great Mistakes of the War*. New York: Harper, 1950. 114p.

245. _____. *The World at War: Volume I, The Crucial Years, 1939–1941*. New York: Harper & Row, 1976. 516p.

246. Brown, David, Christopher F. Shores, and Kenneth Macksey. *The Guinness History of Air Warfare*. London: Guinness Superlatives, 1977. 247p.

247. Calvocoressi, Peter and Guy Wint. *Total War: The Story of World War II*. New York: Pantheon, 1972. 959p.

248.   Carmichael, Thomas N. *The Ninety Days* [October 4, 1942–January 1, 1943]. New York: Bernard Geiss, 1971. 302p.

249.   Carter, Kit and Robert Mueller, comps. *The Army Air Forces in World War II: Combat Chronology, 1941–1945*. Washington, D.C.: U.S. Government Printing Office, 1973. 991p.

250.   Churchill, Winston S. *The Second World War.* 6 vols. Boston: Houghton Mifflin, 1948–1953.

251.   Collier, Basil. *A History of Air Power.* New York: Macmillan, 1974. 358p.

252.   ———. *The Second World War.* New York: Morrow, 1967. 640p.

253.   Craven, Wesley F. and James L. Cate, eds. *The Army Air Forces in World War II*. 7 vols. Chicago: University of Chicago Press, 1948–1958.

254.   Dupuy, R. Ernest. *World War II: A Compact History.* New York: Hawthorn, 1969. 334p.

255.   Encyclopedia Americana, Editors of. *A Concise History of World War II*. New York: Praeger, 1964. 434p.

256.   Fitzsimons, Bernard, ed. *Warplanes and Air Battles of World War II*. New York: Beekman House, 1974. 160p.

257.   Gurney, Gene. *The War in the Air: A Pictorial History of World War II Air Forces in Combat.* New York: Crown, 1962. 352p.

258.   Higham, Robin. *Air Power: A Concise History.* New York: St. Martin's Press, 1972. 282p.

259.   *History of the Second World War.* 96 pts. London: Purnell Publishers. 1966–1967.

260.   Hoyle, Martha B. *A World in Flames: A History of World War II.* New York: Atheneum, 1970. 356p.

261.   Jablonski, Edward. *Air War.* 4 vols. Garden City, N.Y.: Doubleday, 1971–1972.

262.   Liddell-Hart, Basil. *History of the Second World War.* New York: Putnam, 1970. 768p.

263.   Lukas, John. *The Last European War.* Garden City, N.Y.: Doubleday, 1976. 562p.

264.   Maule, Henry. *The Great Battles of World War II.* London and New York: Hamlyn, 1972. 448p.

265. Michel, Henri. *The Second World War.* Translated from the French. London: Deutsch, 1975. 947p.

266. Mollow, Andrew. *Naval, Marine, and Air Force Uniforms of World War II.* London: Blandford Press, 1975. 231p.

267. Pimlot, John. *The Strategy and Tactics of Air Warfare.* London: Marshal Cavendish, 1979. 80p.

268. Shirer, William L. *The Rise and Fall of the Third Reich: A History of Nazi Germany.* New York: Simon and Schuster, 1960. 1,245p.

269. Snyder, Louis L. *The War: A Concise History, 1939–1945.* New York: Messner, 1960. 579p.

270. Stamps, T. Dodson and Vincent J. Esposito, eds. *A Military History of World War II.* 2 vols. Westpoint, N.Y.: Department of Military Art and Engineering, U.S. Military Academy, 1953.

271. Taylor, Alan J. P., ed. *The Second World War: An Illustrated History.* New York: Putnam, 1975. 285p.

272. *Time Magazine,* Editors of. *Time Capsule: History of the War Years.* 7 vols. in 1. New York: Bonanza Books, 1967.

273. Williams, Mary H. *Chronology, 1941–1945.* United States Army in World War II: Special Studies. Washington, D.C.: Office of the Chief of Military History, Department of the Army, 1960. 660 p.

274. Wright, Gordon. *The Ordeal of Total War, 1939–45.* New York: Harper & Row, 1969, 315p.

275. Young, Peter. *Atlas of the Second World War.* New York: Putnam, 1974. 288p.

276. _____ , ed. *Decisive Battles of the Second World War: An Anthology.* London: Barker, 1967. 439p.

2. War on the Eastern Front

a. GENERAL STUDIES

Books

277. Allen, William E. D. and Paul Maratoff. *The Russian Campaigns of 1941–1943.* Harmondsworth, England: Penguin Books, 1944. 192p.

278. _____ . *The Russian Campaigns of 1944–1945.* Harmondsworth, England: Penguin Books, 1946. 332p.

The Era of World War II, 1939–1945

279. Anders, Wladyslaw. *Hitler's Defeat in Russia*. Chicago: Regnery, 1953. 267p.

280. Armstrong, John A., ed. *Soviet Partisans in World War II*. Madison: University of Wisconsin Press, 1964. 792p.

281. Clark, Alan. *Barbarossa: The Russian–German Conflict, 1941–1945*. New York: Morrow, 1965. 522p.

282. Gallagher, Matthew P. *The Soviet History of World War II: Myths, Memories, and Realities*. New York: Praeger, 1963. 205p.

283. Germany. Wehrmacht. Oberkommando. *Blitzkrieg to Defeat: Hitler's War Directives, 1939–1945*. New York: Holt, 1965. 231p.

284. Grechko, Andrei A. *Liberation Mission of the Soviet Armed Forces in the Second World War*. Moscow: Progress Publishers, 1972.

285. Guderian, Heinz. *Panzer Leader*. Translated from the German. New York: E. P. Dutton, 1952. 528p.

286. Higgins, Trumbull. *Hitler and Russia: The Third Reich in a Two-Front War*. New York: Macmillan, 1966. 310p.

287. Jacobsen, Hans A. and Jurgen Rohwer, eds. *Decisive Battles of World War II: The German View*. New York: Putnam, 1965. 509p.

288. Kallistov, D. P. *History of the U.S.S.R., Part 3: From the Beginning of the Great Patriotic War to the Present Day*. Moscow: Progress Publishers, 1977. 326p.

289. Kesselring, Albert. *Kesselring: A Soldier's Record*. Translated from the German. New York: Morrow, 1954. 381p.

290. Levinthal, David and Garry Trudeau. *Hitler Moves East: A Graphic Chronicle, 1941–1943*. Kansas City, Mo.: Sheed Andrews and McMeel, 1977. 95p.

291. Lyons, Graham. *The Russian Version of the Second World War: The History of the War as Taught to Soviet School Children*. Hamden, Conn.: Shoestring Press, 1977. 142p.

292. McCagg, William O. *Stalin Embattled, 1943–1946*. Detroit, Mich.: Wayne State University Press, 1978. 423p.

293. Minasyan, M. M., ed. *Great Patriotic War of the Soviet Union*. Moscow: Progress Publishers, 1974. 469p.

The official Russian history of the war was published by the USSR Ministry of Defense in the 6 volume 1960 title *History of the Great Patriotic*

War of the Soviet Union. The United States firm of United Translation translated the title into English and a few copies have been distributed to military libraries by the Office of the Chief of Military History, Department of the Army.

294.   Mrazkova, Damela and Vladimir Remes. *The Russian War, 1941–1945.* New York: E. P. Dutton, 1977. 152p.

295.   Preston, Anthony, ed. *Decisive Battles of Hitler's War.* London and New York: Hamlyn, 1977. 256p.

296.   Salisbury, Harrison, E. *The Unknown War.* New York: Bantam Books, 1978. 219p.

297.   Schmidt, Paul K. *Hitler Moves East* [1941–1942]. By Paul Carrell, pseud. Translated from the German. Boston: Little, Brown, 1965. 640p.

298.   _____ . *Scorched Earth: The Russian-German War, 1943–1944.* By Paul Carrell, pseud. Translated from the German. Boston: Little, Brown, 1970. 556p.

299.   Seaton, Albert. *The Russo-German War, 1941–1945.* New York: Praeger, 1971. 628p.

300.   Shtemenko, Sergei M. *The Last Six Months: Russia's Final Battles With Hitler's Armies in World War II.* Translated from the Russian. Garden City, N.Y.: Doubleday, 1977. 436p.

301.   Strategy and Tactics, Editors of. *War in the East: The Russo-German Conflict, 1941–1945.* Strategy and Tactics Staff Study, no. 1. New York: Simulations Publications, dist. by Hippocrene, 1977. 186p.

302.   Strawson, John. *Hitler's Battles for Europe.* New York: Scribner's, 1972. 256p.

303.   United States. Military Academy. Department of Military Arts and Engineering. *Operations of the Russian Front.* 3 vols. in 1. West Point, N.Y., 1945–1946.

304.   Von Manstein, Erich. *Lost Victories.* Translated from the German. Chicago: Regnery, 1958. 574p.

305.   Werth, Alexander. *Russia at War, 1941–45.* New York: E. P. Dutton, 1964. 1,100p.

306.   Zhukov, Georgii K. *Marshal Zhukov's Greatest Battles* [Moscow, Stalingrad, Kursk, Berlin]. Translated from the Russian. New York: Harper & Row, 1969. 304p.

307.   Ziemke, Earl F. *Stalingrad to Berlin: The German Defeat in the East.* Army Historical Series. Washington, D.C.: Office of the Chief of Military History, Department of the Army, 1968. 599p.

308.   Zubkov, I., ed. *The Second World War.* Moscow: Progress Publishers, n.d. 560p.

Articles

309.   Gentili, Roberto. "The Italian Air Force in Russia." *Air Classics,* VIII (October 1972), 20–27.

310.   Goodspeed, D. J. "War on the Eastern Front." *Canadian Army Journal,* III (December 1949–March 1950), 1–6, 10–14, 4–10, 7–12.

311.   Guderian, Heinz. "The Experiences of War in Russia." *Military Review,* XXXVII (July 1957), 90–97.

312.   Martell, Paul. "The Soviet Concept of Waging Major Operations in World War II." *History, Numbers, and War,* I (Spring 1977), 24–33.

313.   Shores, Christopher F. "Air Combat the World Over, 1932–1945." In: *Fighter Aces.* London and New York: Hamlyn, 1975. pp. 48–136.

314.   Tulubko, Vladimir F. "The Great Exploit of the Soviet People: Translated from *Ekonomicheskaya Gazeta,* May 3, 1978." *Translations on U.S.S.R. Military Affairs,* no. 1355 (May 30, 1978), 48–52.

315.   "World War II in the Air: April 1941–September 1942." *Aero Album,* III (1970), 30–41; IV (1971), 2–23; V (1972), 26–37; VI (1973), 20–33.

316.   Zakharov, M. "The Triumph of Soviet Military Strategy During the War." *Soviet Military Review,* no. 4 (April 1970), 10–13.

b. Air Force Opponents

(1) The German Luftwaffe

Books

317.   Bartz, Karl. *Swastika in the Air: The Struggle and Defeat of the German Air Force, 1939–1945.* Translated from the German. 2nd ed. London: Kimber, 1956. 203p.

318.   Baumbach, Werner. *The Life and Death of the Luftwaffe.* Translated from the German. New York: Coward-McCann, 1960. 224p.

319.   Bender, Roger J. *Air Organizations of the Third Reich*. Palo Alto, Calif: Aurora, 1967. 192p.

320.   Berenbrok, Hans D. *The Luftwaffe War Diaries*. By Cajus D. Bekker, pseud. New York: Ballantine Books, 1966. 580p.

321.   Bloemertz, Günther. *Heaven Next Stop: Impressions of a German Fighter Pilot*. Translated from the German. London: Kimber, 1953. 189p.

322.   Chant, Christopher. *The Mechanics of War: Ground Attack*. Warren, Mich.: Squadron/Signal Publications, 1976. 72p.

323.   Faber, Harold, ed. *Luftwaffe: A History*. New York: Times Books, dist. by Harper & Row, 1977. 267p.

324.   Feist, Uwe and René J. Francillon. *Luftwaffe in World War II*. Fallbrook, Calif.: Aero Publishers, 1973. 96p.

325.   Galland, Adolf. *The First and the Last: The Rise and Fall of the German Fighter Forces, 1938–1945*. Translated from the German. New York: Ballantine Books, 1957. 368p.

326.   _____ et al. *The Luftwaffe at War, 1939–1945*. Chicago: Regnery, 1973. 247p.

327.   Great Britain. Air Ministry. *The Rise and Fall of the German Air Force*. London: H. M. Stationery Office, 1948. 422p. Reprinted 1970.

328.   Irving, David. *The Rise and Fall of the Luftwaffe: The Life of Field Marshal Erhard Milch*. Boston: Little, Brown, 1974. 443p.

329.   Killen, John. *The Luftwaffe, a History*. Garden City, N.Y.: Doubleday, 1968. 324p.

330.   Knoke, Heinz. *I Flew for the Führer: The Story of a German Airman*. New York: Holt, 1954. 187p.

331.   Lee, Asher. *The German Air Force*. New York: Harper, 1946. 310p.

332.   Mizrahi, Joseph V. *Knights of the Black Cross*. Granada Hills, Calif.: Sentry Books, 1972. 102p.

333.   Morzik, Friedrich. *German Air Force Airlift Operations*. USAF Historical Studies, no. 167. Washington, D.C.: Office of Air Force History, Department of the Air Force, 1961. 417p.

334. Nielsen, Andreas. *The German Air Force General Staff.* USAF Historical Studies, no. 173. Washington, D.C.: Office of Air Force History, Department of the Air Force, 1959. 256p.

335. Philpott, Bryan. *German Bombers Over Russia.* WWII Photo Album Series, no. 8. New York: Aztec Corp.; dist. by E. P. Dutton, 1979. 96p.

336. Plocher, Hermann. *The German Air Force Versus Russia, 1941.* USAF Historical Studies, no. 153. Washington, D.C.: Office of Air Force History, Department of the Air Force, 1965. 335p.

337. _____. *The German Air Force Versus Russia, 1942.* USAF Historical Studies, no. 154. Washington, D.C.: Office of Air Force History, Department of the Air Force, 1966.

338. _____. *The German Air Force Versus Russia, 1943.* USAF Historical Studies, no. 155. Washington, D.C.: Office of Air Force History, Department of the Air Force, 1967.

339. Price, Alfred. *Luftwaffe: Birth, Life, and Death of an Air Force.* Ballantine's Illustrated History of the Violent Century. New York: Ballantine Books, 1970. 160p.

340. _____. *Luftwaffe Handbook, 1939–1945.* New York: Scribner's, 1977. 111p.

341. _____. *Pictorial History of the Luftwaffe, 1933–1945.* New York: Arco, 1970. 64p.

342. Rudel, Hans-Ulrich. *Stuka Pilot.* Translated from the German. New York: Ballantine Books, 1958. 259p.

343. Schertl, Alfons. *The Last Battle.* By Peter Henn, pseud. Translated from the German. London: Kimber, 1954. 214p.

344. Shores, Christopher F. *Luftwaffe Fighter Units, Russia: June 1941–1945.* Aircam Aviation Series. London: Osprey, 1978. 48p.

345. Smith, Peter C. *The Stuka at War.* New York: Arco, 1971. 192p.

346. Suchenwirth, Richard. *Command and Leadership in the German Air Force.* USAF Historical Studies, no. 174. Washington, D.C.: Office of Air Force History, Department of the Air Force, 1969. 351p.

347. _____. *Historical Turning Points in the German Air Force War Effort.* USAF Historical Studies, no. 189. Washington, D.C.: Office of Air Force History, Department of the Air Force, 1969. 143p.

348. Windrow, Martin and Richard Ward. *Luftwaffe Colour Schemes and Markings, 1935–1945.* Aircam Aviation Series. London: Osprey, 1971. 40p.

Articles

349. Baumbach, Werner. "Why We Lost: An Ex–Luftwaffe Pilot." *RAF Flying Review,* VII (September 1952), 30–31.

350. Galland, Adolf. "Defeat of the Luftwaffe: Fundamental Reasons." *Air University Quarterly Review,* VI (Spring 1953), 18–36.

351. Green, William, comp. "Luftwaffe Operational Directory, 1939–1945." *RAF Flying Review,* XIV (March 1959), 25–32.

352. Paquier, Col. "The Germans and Air Superiority." *Military Review,* XXIX (September 1949), 103–108.

353. Toliver, Raymond F. and Trevor J. Constable. "Air War in the East." In: *Fighter Aces of the Luftwaffe.* Fallbrook, Calif.: Aero Publishers, 1977. pp. 240–301.

354. Van Ishoven, Armand. "Above Tundra, Ice, and Steppe." In: *Messerschmitt Bf-109 at War.* New York: Scribner's, 1977. pp. 60–70.

355. Wood, Tony and William T. Gunston. "Russia, 1941–1944." In: *Hitler's Luftwaffe.* New York: Crescent Books, 1978. pp. 78–84.

Documents, Papers, and Reports

356. Kreipe, Werner. "The Kreipe Diary (22 July–2 November 1944)." Unpublished paper, Foreign Military Studies Program, Historical Division, U.S. Army, Europe, 1950. 69p.

357. United States. Air Forces in Europe. *Fighter Operations of the German Air Force: Tactical Employment.* 2 vols. Wiesbaden, 1945.

(2) The Soviet Air Force

Books

358. Coates, William P. *Why Russia Will Win: The Soviet Military, Naval, and Air Power.* London: Eldon, 1942. 104p.

359. Drum, Karl. *Airpower and Russian Partisan Warfare.* USAF Historical Studies, no. 177. Maxwell AFB, Ala.: Research Studies Institute, Air University, 1962. 63p.

360. Erickson, John. *The Soviet High Command: A Political-Military History, 1918–1941.* New York: St. Martin's Press, 1962. 889p.

361.   Guillaume, Augustin. *Soviet Arms and Soviet Might: The Secrets of Russia's Might.* Washington, D.C.: Infantry Journal Press, 1949. 212p.

362.   Howard, John. *The Other R.A.F.: The Story of the Red Air Force.* London: Russia Today Society, 1944. 20p.

363.   Jackson, Robert. *Red Falcons: The Soviet Air Force in Action, 1919–1969.* New York: International Publications Service, 1970. 236p.

364.   Kerr, Walter B. *The Russian Army: Its Men, Its Leaders, and Its Battles.* New York: Alfred A. Knopf, 1944. 250p.

365.   Kilmarx, Robert A. *A History of Soviet Air Power.* New York: Praeger, 1962. 359p.

366.   Kournahoff, Sergei N. *Russia's Fighting Forces.* New York: Duell, 1942. 258p.

367.   Schwabedissen, Walter. *The Russian Air Force in the Eyes of German Commanders.* USAF Historical Studies, no. 175. Washington, D.C.: Office of Air Force History, Department of the Air Force, 1960. 434p.

368.   Shtemenko, Sergei M. *The Soviet General Staff at War, 1941–1945.* Moscow: Progress Publishers, 1975. 389p.

369.   Stroud, John. *The Red Air Force.* London: Pilot, 1943. 48p.

370.   Uebe, Klaus. *Russian Reactions to German Airpower in World War II.* USAF Historical Studies, no. 176. Washington, D.C.: Office of Air Force History, Department of the Air Force, 1964. 146p.

371.   Union of Soviet Socialist Republics. Ministry of Defense. *The Soviet Air Force in World War II: The Official History.* Translated from the Russian. Garden City, N.Y.: Doubleday, 1973. 440p.

372.   White, D. Fedotoff. *The Growth of the Red Army.* Princeton, N.J.: Princeton University Press, 1944. 486p.

Articles

373.   Chedleyev, N. "Defending Communications." *Soviet Military Review*, no. 1 (January 1977), 55–57.

374.   "Close to the Earth." *Time*, XLIV (July 31, 1944), 18–20.

375.   Denisov, Nikolai. "The Soviet Air Force After a Year of War." *Aviation*, XLI (August 1942), 90–92.

376. Erickson, John. "Radio-Location and the Air Defense Problem: The Design and Development of Soviet Radar, 1934–1940." *Science Studies*, II (1972), 241–263.

377. Fuller, Curtis. "How the Red Air Force Fights." *Flying*, XXXVI (May 1945), 21–23.

378. Garthoff, Raymond L. "Soviet Employment of Airpower." In: *Soviet Military Doctrine*. Glencoe, Ill.: Free Press, 1953. pp. 321–360.

379. Greenwood, John T. "The Great Patriotic War, 1941–1945." In: Robin Higham and Jacob W. Kipp, eds. *Soviet Aviation and Air Power: A Historical View*. Boulder, Colo.: Westview, 1977. pp. 69–136.

380. Gromov, Mikhail M. "Russia's Fighter Command." *Flying*, XXXII (January 1943), 27–28.

381. Hotz, Robert. "Ramming Russians." *Flying*, XXXI (October 1942), 32.

382. "How the Reds Won Air Power." *Aviation Age*, XIX (January 1953), 27–29.

383. Hurley, James A. "Soviet Air Support to Insurgents." *Marine Corps Gazette*, XLVII (January 1963), 13–14.

384. Karikh, A. "Air Support." *Soviet Military Review*, no. 9 (September 1972), 19–22.

385. Kochnovskii, N. A. "The Russian Use of Air OP in World War II." *U.S. Army Aviation Digest*, IX (March 1963), 42–43.

386. Komarov, N. "Wartime Tactics of Air Defense Aviation Reviewed: Translated from *Voyenno-Istoricheskiy Zhurnal*, December 1978." *Translations on USSR Military Affairs*, no. 1414 (March 1, 1979), 47–55.

387. Kozhevnikov, M. "Air Force and Infantry Operations in World War II: Translated from *Voyenno-Istoricheskiy Zhurnal*, February 1979." *Translations on USSR Military Affairs*, no. 1441 (May 24, 1979), 21–29.

388. _____. "Birth of the Air Armies" *Aerospace Historian*, XXII (June 1975), 73–76.

389. Kutakhov, Pavel S. "The Conduct of Air Operations." In: William F. Scott, ed. *Selected Soviet Military Writings, 1970–1975: A Soviet View*. Soviet Military Thought Series, no. 11. Washington, D.C.: Published under the auspices of the U.S. Air Force by the U.S. Government Printing Office, 1977. pp. 240–251.

390. Laird, Lael. "The Royal Air Force on the Red Air Force." *Life,* XII (May 4, 1942), 12.

391. Mets, David R. "The Origins of Soviet Air Theory and Doctrine." *Military Review,* LV (August 1975), 36–48.

392. Miryukov, L. "Wartime Experiences in Employing Attack Aviation Reviewed: Translated from *Voyenno-Istoricheskiy Zhurnal,* January 1979." *Translations on USSR Military Affairs,* no. 1414 (March 1, 1979), 98–108.

393. "The Normandie Regiment." *Air Progress,* XXII (January 1966), 26–27.

394. Parrish, Michael. "Command and Leadership in the Soviet Air Force During the Great Patriotic War." *Aerospace Historian,* XXVI (Fall 1979), 194–197.

395. Potts, Ramsay D., Jr. "The Foundations of Soviet Air Power: A Historical and Managerial Interpretation." *Annals of the American Academy of Political and Social Sciences,* CXCIX (May 1955), 38–48.

396. Pshenyanik, G. "Wartime Control of Air Armies at Front Level Discussed: Translated from *Voyenno-Istoricheskiy Zhurnal,* June 1978." *Translations on USSR Military Affairs,* no. 1375 (September 7, 1978), 17–27.

397. Ray, G. D. "I Saw Russia's Air Power." *Aviation,* XLII (May 1944), 122–123.

398. "Red Falcons: Russia's Mighty Air Force." *Scholastic,* XLIV (March 13, 1944), 28.

399. Reshetnikov, Vasilii V. "Reshetnikov on the Employment of Strategic [ADD] Aviation: Translated from *Voyenno-Istoricheskiy Zhurnal,* February 1978." *Translations on USSR Military Affairs,* no. 1344 (April 7, 1978), 57–63.

400. Rieckhoff, Herbert J. "A German View of the Soviet Air Force." *Military Review,* XXIX (April 1949), 73–78.

401. Rougeron, Camille. "Russian Air Strategy." *Military Review,* XXX (November 1950), 94–99.

402. Savitskii, E. "Co-Operation Between Fighter Planes and Tanks." *Military Review,* XXVI (August 1946), 89–91.

403. Shtemenko, Sergei M. "The General Staff During the War." *Soviet Military Review,* nos. 1–5 (January–May 1969), 47–49, 46–51, 2–5, 45–48, 50–53.

404. _____. _____. *Soviet Military Review,* nos. 3–11 (March–November 1974), 58–61, 58–62, 54–56, 52–55, 53–56, 59–61, 55–57.

405. _____. "Strategic Leadership During the War." *Soviet Military Review,* nos. 1 and 2 (January–February 1971), 46–48, 37–39.

406. Simakov, Ye. "Air Force Wartime Camouflage and Deception Measures: Translated from *Voyenno-Istoricheskiy Zhurnal,* December 1977." *Translations on USSR Military Affairs,* no. 1329 (February 10, 1978), 3–13.

407. "The Soviet World War II Air Force." *Air Classics,* VII (March 1971), 6–18.

408. Spaight, James M. "Russia's Air Strength." *19th Century,* CXXVI (August 1939), 165–171.

409. Tokaev, G. A. "Background of the Soviet Air Force." *Flight,* LV (May 12, 1949), 561–564.

410. Veraksa, Ye. "Air Offensive." *Soviet Military Review,* no. 4 (April 1973), 38–41.

411. _____. "Co-Operation of Aviation with Land Forces in World War II." *Soviet Military Review,* no. 10 (October 1976), 54–56.

412. _____. "Fighter Sweep Missions." *Soviet Military Review,* no. 12 (December 1972), 54–55.

413. _____. "Fighter Tactics." *Soviet Military Review,* no. 3 (March 1978), 35–37.

414. _____. "Fighters Attack an Airfield." *Soviet Military Review,* no. 7 (July 1971), 39–41.

415. _____. "The Struggle for Air Supremacy." *Soviet Military Review,* no. 10 (October 1975), 48–50.

416. Whiting, Kenneth R. "Soviet Air Power in World War II." In: Alfred F. Hurley and Robert C. Ehrhart, eds. *Air Power and Warfare: The Proceedings of the Eighth Military History Symposium, United States Air Force Academy, 18–20 October 1978.* Washington, D.C.: U.S. Government Printing Office, 1979. pp. 98–127.

417. "Women's Guards (Air) Regiment." *Soviet Military Review,* no. 3 (March 1972), 46–48.

418. Zacharoff, Lucien. "Civil Aviation Cooperates in the Russian War Effort." *Aviation,* XL (November 1941), 50–51.

The Era of World War II, 1939–1945

Documents, Papers, and Reports

419. Hoeffding, O. *Soviet Interdiction Operations, 1941–1945.* RAND Report R-556-PR. Santa Monica, Calif.: RAND Corporation, 1970. 38p.

420. Kilmarx, Robert A. "History of the Soviet Air Force Through World War II." Unpublished Ph.D. Dissertation, Georgetown University, 1958.

421. Peresypkin, I. T. *Communications During the Great Patriotic War.* Translated from the Russian. Arlington, Va.: Joint Publications Research Service, 1974. 65p.

422. Whiting, Kenneth R. *Soviet Air Power, 1917–1976.* Maxwell AFB, Ala.: Aerospace Studies Institute, Air University, 1976.

c. Specific Campaigns

(1) "Operation Barbarossa," The German Invasion, 1941

Books

423. Bethell, Nicholas W. B. *Russia Besieged.* World War II Series. New York: Time Life Books, 1977. 208p.

424. Blau, George E. *The German Campaign in Russia: Planning and Operations, 1940–1942.* DA Pamphlet. Washington, D.C.: Department of the Army, 1955. 197p.

425. Caldwell, Erskine. *All-Out on the Road to Smolensk.* New York: Duell, 1942. 230p.

426. Cecil, Robert. *Hitler's Decision to Invade Russia, 1941.* London: Davis Poynter, 1975. 192p.

427. Critchley, Julian. *Warning and Decision.* New York: Crane, Russak, 1978. 123p.

428. Erickson, John. *The Road to Stalingrad: Stalin's War with Germany.* New York: Harper & Row, 1975. 595p.

429. Germany. Auswartiges Amt. *Nazi-Soviet Relations, 1939–1941.* Department of State Publication, no. 3023. Washington, D.C.: U.S. Government Printing Office, 1948. 362p.

430. Keegan, John. *Barbarossa: Invasion of Russia, 1941.* Ballantine's Illustrated History of the Violent Century. New York: Ballantine Books, 1971. 160p.

431.   Kirkpatrick, Lyman B., Jr. "Barbarossa." In: *Captains Without Eyes: Intelligence Failures in World War II.* New York: Macmillan, 1969. Chpt. 1.

432.   Leach, Barry R. *German Strategy Against Russia, 1939–1941.* Oxford, England: At the Clarenden Press, 1973. 388p.

433.   Petrov, Vladimir. *"June 22, 1941": Soviet Historians and the German Invasion, Including a Complete Translation of Aleksandr M. Nekrich's "1941, 22 Iyunia."* Columbia: University of South Carolina Press, 1968. 322p.

434.   Whaley, Barton. *Codeword Barbarossa*. Cambridge, Mass.: MIT Press, 1973. 376p.

Articles

435.   Dreisziger, N. F. "New Twist to an Old Riddle: The [Soviet] Bombing of Kassa, June 26, 1941." *Journal of Modern History,* XLIV (June 1972), 232–242.

436.   Liddell-Hart, Basil H. "Was Russia Close to Defeat?" *Military Review,* XXX (July 1950), 10–15.

437.   Sas, Anthony. "The Invasion of Russia." *Military Review,* LI (June 1971), 38–46.

438.   Sella, Amnon. "Barbarossa: Surprise Attack and Communications." *Journal of Contemporary History,* XII (July 1978), 555–583.

Documents, Papers, and Reports

439.   Whaley, Barton. "Operation Barbarossa: A Case Study of Soviet Strategic Information Processing Before the German Invasion." Unpublished Ph.D. Dissertation, Massachusetts Institute of Technology, 1969.

(2) The Battle of Moscow, 1941–1942

Books

440.   Jukes, Geoffrey. *The Defense of Moscow.* Ballantine's Illustrated History of the Violent Century. New York: Ballantine Books, 1970. 160p.

441.   Seaton, Albert. *The Battle for Moscow, 1941–1942.* New York: Stein and Day, 1971. 320p.

442.   Seth, Ronald S. *Operation Barbarossa: The Battle for Moscow.* London: Blond, 1964. 191p.

443. Turney, Alfred W. *Disaster at Moscow:* [Fedor] *von Bock's Campaigns, 1941–1942.* Albuquerque: University of New Mexico Press, 1970. 228p.

444. Werth, Alexander. *Moscow War Diary.* New York: Knopf, 1942. 297p.

Articles

445. Liddell-Hart, Basil H. "How Hitler Failed at Moscow." *Marine Corps Gazette,* XLI (March 1957), 28–30.

446. Mikhaylenko, I. "Wartime Air Defense of Moscow: Translated from *Veyenno-Istoricheskiy Zhurnal,* December 1977." *Translations on USSR Military Affairs,* no. 1329 (February 10, 1978), 14–17.

447. Panov, B. "Sharp Turn." *Soviet Military Review,* no. 12 (December 1971), 34–37.

448. Vasilevsky, A. "The Battle of Moscow." *Soviet Military Review,* no. 11 (November 1976), 10–13.

(3) Stalingrad, 1942–1943

Books

449. Chuikov, Vasilii I. *The Battle for Stalingrad.* Translated from the Russian. New York: Holt, 1964. 364p.

450. Craig, William. *Enemy at the Gates: The Battle for Stalingrad.* New York: Reader's Digest Press, dist. by E. P. Dutton, 1973. 462p.

451. Goerlitz, Walter. *Paulus and Stalingrad.* Translated from the German. New York: The Citadel Press, 1963. 301p.

452. Jukes, Geoffrey. *Stalingrad: The Turning Point.* Ballantine's Illustrated History of the Violent Century. New York: Ballantine Books, 1968. 160p.

453. Kerr, Walter B. *The Secret of Stalingrad.* Garden City, N.Y.: Doubleday, 1978. 274p.

454. Kluge, Alexander. *The Battle.* Translated from the German. New York: Morrow, 1962. 127p.

455. Schroter, Heinz. *Stalingrad.* Translated from the German. New York: E. P. Dutton, 1958. 263p.

456. Seth, Ronald. *Stalingrad—Point of Return: The Story of the Battle, August 1942 to February 1943.* New York: Coward-McCann, 1959. 254p.

457. Shaw, John. *Red Army Resurgent.* World War II Series. New York: Time-Life, 1980. 206p.

458. Werth, Alexander. *The Year of Stalingrad.* New York: Knopf, 1947. 480p.

459. Zieser, Benno. *The Road to Stalingrad.* Translated from the German. New York: Ballantine Books, 1956. 152p.

Articles

460. Henzel, H. W. "The Stalingrad Offensive." *Marine Corps Gazette,* XXXV (August–September 1951), 56–63, 46–57.

461. Pickert, Wolfgang. "The Stalingrad Airlift: An Eyewitness Commentary." *Aerospace Historian,* XVII (December 1971), 183–185.

462. Selle, Herbert. "The German Debacle at Stalingrad." *Military Review,* XXXVII (September–October 1957), 3–13, 37–47.

463. Zvenzlovsky, A. "Victory on the Upper Don." *Soviet Military Review,* no. 3 (March 1973), 57–59.

(4) Leningrad and the Northern War

Books

464. Fadeyev, Aleksandr A. *Leningrad in the Days of the Blockade.* Translated from the Russian. Westport, Conn.: Greenwood Press, 1971. 104p.

465. Malaparte, Curzio. *The Volga Rises in Europe.* Translated from the Italian. London: Alvin Redman, 1957. 281p.

466. Pavlov, Dmitri. *Leningrad, 1941: The Blockade.* Translated from the Russian. Chicago: University of Chicago Press, 1965. 186p.

467. Salisbury, Harrison E. *The 900 Days: The Siege of Leningrad.* New York: Harper & Row, 1969. 635p.

Article

468. Grushevoy, K. "The Liberation of Northern Norway." *Soviet Military Review,* no. 10 (October 1969), 47–49.

(5) The Southern Region, 1941–1943

Book

469. Grechko, Andrei A. *Battle for the Caucasus.* Moscow: Progress Publishers, 1971. 366p.

Articles

470. Kotov, Mikhail. "Immortal Exploit [Novorosiisk]" *Soviet Literature,* no. 7 (July 1978), 136–143.

471. Kurov, N. "Liberation of the Crimea." *Soviet Military Review,* no. 4 (April 1974), 47–49.

472. Lederrey, E. "Operations of Marshal von Manstein in Southern Russia, December 1942–March 1943." *Military Review,* XXXVII (January 1958), 98–101.

473. Schultz-Naumann, Joachim. "The Demyansk Pocket." *Military Review,* XXXVII (December 1957), 77–84.

474. Vershinin, Konstantin A. "Air Battle in the Kuban, Spring 1943." *Soviet Military Review,* no. 6 (June 1968), 42–44.

475. Von Manstein, Erich. "The Campaign in the Crimea, 1941–1942." *Marine Corps Gazette,* XL (May 1956), 32–47.

476. _____. "Defensive Operations in Southern Russia, 1943–1944." *Marine Corps Gazette,* XLI (April 1957), 40–53.

477. Yakubovsky, I. "In Battles in the Right-Bank Ukraine." *Soviet Military Review,* nos. 8–9 (August–September 1969), 38–42, 39–41.

(6) Kursk, 1943

Books

478. Caidin, Martin. *The Tigers are Burning.* New York: Hawthorn Books, 1974. 243p.

479. Chant, Christopher. *Kursk.* London: Almark, 1975. 48p.

480. Jukes, Geoffrey. *Kursk, the Clash of Armor.* Ballantine's Illustrated History of the Violent Century. New York: Ballantine Books, 1969. 160p.

481. Solovyov, Boris. *The Battle of Kursk.* Moscow: Novosti Press Agency Publishing House, 1973. 40p.

Articles

482. Christyakov, I. "The Victory at Kursk: An Interview." *Soviet Military Review,* no. 7 (July 1978), 42–45.

483. Erickson, John. "Kursk." In: Noble Frankland and Christopher Dowling, eds. *Decisive Battles of the Twentieth Century.* New York: McKay, 1976. pp. 222–238.

484. Holder. L. D. "Kursk: The Breaking of the Panzer Corps." *Armor,* LXXXIV (January–February 1975), 12–17.

485. Koltunov, G. A. "Kursk: The Clash of Armor." In: Bernard Fitzsimons, ed. *Tanks and Weapons of World War II.* New York: Beekman House, 1973. pp. 81–97.

486. "The Kursk Battle—30 Years." *Soviet Military Review,* no. 6 (June 1973), 2–39.

487. Parrish, Michael. "The Battle of Kursk." *Army Quarterly,* XCIX (October 1969), 39–51.

488. Ratley, Lonnie O., 3rd. "Air Power at Kursk: The Confrontation of Aircraft and Tanks—a Lesson for Today." *Journal of the Royal United Service Institution for Defence Studies,* CXXII (June 1977), 25–29.

489. Rokossovsky, K. "The Kursk Battle, July 5–August 23, 1943." *Soviet Military Review,* nos. 7–8 (July–August 1968), 2–7, 30–36.

490. Shutov, Z. "In the Enemy Rear." *Soviet Military Review,* no. 12 (December 1973), 45–47.

491. Von Manstein, Erich. "Operation Citadel." *Marine Corps Gazette,* XL (August 1956), 44–47.

492. Zhukov, Georgii K. "The Battle of Kursk, 1943." *Military Review,* XLIX (August 1969), 82–96.

Documents, Papers, and Reports

493. Thach, Joseph E. "The Battle of Kursk, July 1943: Decisive Turning Point on the Eastern Front." Unpublished Ph.D. Dissertation, Georgetown University, 1971.

(7) Counterattack, 1943–1945

(a) FORCING THE DNEIPER, 1943

494. Frolov, B. "Battle for the Dneiper." *Soviet Military Review,* no. 10 (October 1978), 46–49.

495. Konev, I. "The Rush to the Dneiper." *Soviet Military Review,* no. 8 (August 1973), 50–52.

496. Lashchenko, P. "Battle by Battle." *Soviet Military Review,* nos. 9–12 (September–December 1973), 53–55, 56–59, 60–62, 56–58.

497. Moskalenko, Kirill S. "The Battle for the Dneiper." *Soviet Military Review,* no. 9 (September 1968), 34–40.

498. Shutov, Z. "Battle for the Dneiper." *Soviet Military Review*, no. 9. (September 1973), 48–51.

499. Turbiville, Graham H., Jr. "Paradrop at the Bukrin Bridgehead: An Account of the Soviet Dneiper Operation." *Military Review*, LVI (December 1976), 26–40.

500. Vorontsov, G. "The Army Forces the Dneiper." *Soviet Military Review*, no. 7 (July 1970), 12–15.

(b) COMBAT IN BYELORUSSIA, 1944

Book

501. Grossman, Vasilii S. *With the Red Army in Poland and Byelorussia.* Translated from the Russian. London: Hutchinson, 1945. 52p.

Articles

502. Batov, P. I. "The Blow in Byelorussia: An Interview." *Soviet Military Review*, no. 6 (June 1979), 16–18.

503. Fitzgerald, Charles G. "Operation Bagration." *Military Review*, XLIV (May 1964), 59–72.

504. Novikov, A. "Attack Aircraft Versus Tanks." *Soviet Military Review*, no. 2 (February 1968), 40–43.

505. Rudenko, Sergii I. "The Belorussian Air Offensive." *Aerospace Historian*, XX (March 1973), 17–26.

506. Shutov, Z. "The Jassy-Kishinev Operation." *Soviet Military Review*, no. 9 (September 1974), 56–58.

507. Vasilevsky, A. "Operation Bagration." *Soviet Military Review*, no. 6 (June 1974), 2–55.

(c) POLAND AND CZECHOSLOVAKIA, 1939–1944

Books

508. Bethell, Nicholas W. B. *The War Hitler Won: The Fall of Poland, September 1939.* New York: Holt, 1973. 472p.

509. Cynk, Jerzy B. *History of the Polish Air Force, 1918–1968.* Berkshire, England: Osprey, 1972. 307p.

510. London. Instytut Historyczny imienia Generala Sikorskiego. *Documents on Polish-Soviet Relations, 1939–1945.* 2 vols. London: Heinemann, 1961–1967.

511. Maks, Leon. *Russia by the Back Door.* Translated from the Polish. London and New York: Sheed and Ward, 1954. 264p.

512.   Titz, Zdenek. *Czechoslovakian Air Force, 1918–1970.* Aircam Aviation Series. New York: Arco, 1971. 96p.

Articles

513.   Konev, I. "From the Vistula to the Oder." *Soviet Military Review,* no. 2 (February 1970), 44–48.

514.   Lelyushenko, D. "The Prague Operation." *Soviet Military Review,* no. 5 (May 1970), 46–49.

515.   Lukas, Richard C. "The Big Three and the Warsaw Uprising." *Military Affairs,* XXXIV (October 1975), 129–136.

516.   McFarland, Marvin W. "Air Power and the Warsaw Uprising." *Air Power Historian,* III (October 1956), 186–194.

517.   Shtemenko, Sergei M. "Across the Carpathians into Slovakia." *Soviet Military Review,* no. 10 (October 1974), 8–11.

518.   Szkoda, W. E. "Soviet Tactics Against the Polish Resistance in World War II." *Military Review,* XLIV (September 1964), 88–93.

519.   Titz, Zdenek. "Lavochkins Over Slovakia: The Story of the First Czechoslovak Fighter Regiment on the Eastern Front During World War II." *Air Pictorial,* XXVIII (March 1966), 92–96.

(d) INTO GERMANY, 1945

Books

520.   Chuikov, Vasilii I. *The Fall of Berlin.* Translated from the Russian. New York: Holt, 1968. 261p.

521.   Kuby, Erich. *The Russians and Berlin, 1945.* Translated from the German. New York: Hill and Wang, 1968. 372p.

522.   Ryan, Cornelius. *The Last Battle.* New York: Simon and Schuster, 1966. 571p.

523.   Strawson, John. *The Battle for Berlin.* New York: Scribner's, 1974. 182p.

524.   Tully, Andrew. *Berlin: Story of a Battle, April–May 1945.* New York: Simon and Schuster, 1963. 304p.

525.   Ziemke, Earl F. *The Battle for Berlin: End of the Third Reich.* Ballantine's Illustrated History of the Violent Century. New York: Ballantine Books, 1968. 160p.

Articles

526. Denisov, Nikolai. "The Aerial Battle of Berlin." *Military Review*, XXV (December 1945), 94–97.

527. Prokofyev, N. "The Storming of Königsberg." *Soviet Military Review*, no. 4 (April 1969), 42–44.

528. Zhukov, Georgii K. "The Berlin Operation." *Soviet Military Review*, no. 4 (April 1970), 14–19.

(8) War in Manchuria, 1945

Articles

529. Betit, Eugene D. "The Soviet Manchurian Campaign, August 1945: Prototype for the Soviet Offensive." *Military Review*, LVI (May 1976), 65–73.

530. Ekman, Michael E. "The 1945 Soviet Manchurian Campaign: A Model for Sino-Soviet War." *Naval War College Review*, XXVII (July–August 1974), 81–89.

531. Garthoff, Raymond L. "Marshal Malinovsky's Manchurian Campaign." *Military Review*, XLVI (October 1966), 50–61.

532. ———. "Soviet Operations in the War with Japan, August 1945." *U.S. Naval Institute Proceedings*, XCII (May 1966), 50–63.

533. Grayson, Benson L. "Soviet Military Operations in the Far East, 1945." *Military Engineer*, L (January–February 1958), 41–45.

534. Ivanov, S. "Victory in the Far East." *Soviet Military Review*, no. 8 (August 1975), 2–5.

535. MacCaskill, Douglas C. "The Soviet Union's Second Front: Manchuria." *Marine Corps Gazette*, LIX (January 1975), 18–26.

536. Plotnikov, G. "The Far East: Liberation Mission." *Soviet Military Review*, no. 9 (September 1978), 2–5.

537. "Russian Fighters Over Japan." *RAF Flying Review*, XV (October 1959), 47–48.

Documents, Papers, and Reports

538. Despres, John H. *Timely Lessons of History: The Manchurian Model for Soviet Strategy.* RAND Report R-1825-NA. Santa Monica, Calif.: RAND Corporation, 1976. 84p.

539.   Dzirkals, Lilita. *'Lightning War' in Manchuria: Soviet Military Analysis of the 1945 Far East Campaign.* RAND Paper P-5589. Santa Monica, Calif.: RAND Corporation, 1976. 116p.

540.   Hagerty, James J., Jr. "The Soviet Share in the War with Japan." Unpublished Ph.D. Dissertation, University of California at Los Angeles, 1966.

3. Lend-Lease and Foreign Air Cooperation

a. Lend-Lease

Books

541.   Beitzel, Robert. *The Uneasy Alliance: America, Britain, and Russia, 1941–1943.* New York: Knopf, 1972. 404p.

542.   Jones, Robert H. *The Roads to Moscow: United States Lend-Lease to the Soviet Union.* Norman: University of Oklahoma Press, 1969. 326p.

543.   Jordan, George A. *From Major Jordan's Diaries.* New York: Harcourt, 1952. 284p.

544.   Lukas, Richard C. *Eagles East: The Army Air Forces and the Soviet Union, 1941–1945.* Tallahassee: Florida State University Press, 1970. 256p.

545.   Matloff, Maurice and Edwin M. Snell. *Strategic Planning for Coalition Warfare, 1941–1944.* United States Army in World War II: The War Department. 2 vols. Washington, D.C.: Office of the Chief of Military History, Department of the Army, 1953–1959.

546.   Vail-Motter, T. H. *The Persian Corridor and Aid to Russia.* United States Army in World War II: The Middle East Theater. Washington, D.C.: Office of the Chief of Military History, Department of the Army, 1952. 544p.

Articles

547.   Baldwin, Hanson W. "Contributions of Britain and the United States to Russia's Campaign." *Foreign Affairs,* XXII (January 1944), 209–212.

548.   Brandon, Deane R. "ALSIB: The Northwest Ferrying Route Through Alaska, 1942–1945." *American Aviation Historical Society Journal,* XX (Spring 1975), 18–28.

549.   Cook, Charles M. "The Truth About Russian Plane Production." *Flying,* XLIII (October 1948), 18–20.

550. DuPre, Flint O. "Remember When They Were Allies?" *Air Force,* XXXVI (August 1953), 65.

551. Ford, Corey. "Arctic Rendezvous: Russian Pilot Heroes Fly Lend-Lease Planes from Alaska to Siberia." *Collier's,* CXIV (August 12, 1944), 13.

552. Jordan, George A. "We Gave the Reds Everything." *Reader's Digest,* LXI (December 1952), 55-61.

553. "Kingcobras to Alaska." *Air Classics,* X (November 1974), 33-41.

554. Lukas, Richard C. "Aircraft Commitments to Russia: The Moscow Conference, September-October 1941." *Air University Review,* XVI (July-August 1965), 44-53.

555. _____. "The Impact of 'Barbarossa' on the Soviet Air Force and the Resulting Commitment of United States Aircraft, June-October 1941." *Historian,* XXIX (March 1966), 60-80.

556. _____. "The Middle East Corridor to Russia: Lend-Lease Aircraft to the Soviets, 1941-1942." *Air Power Historian,* XII (July 1965), 78-84.

557. _____. "Soviet Stalling Tactics in the Forties." *Aerospace Historian,* XIV (Spring 1967), 51-56.

558. Manning, Stephen O., 3rd. "Red Stars Over America." *Airman,* XX (April 1976), 35-37.

559. "Photo Visit in a Soviet Warplane Plant." *Aviation,* XLIV (May 1945), 156-158.

560. Ringold, Herbert. "Lifeline to the U.S.S.R." *Air Force,* XXVII (November 1944), 24-27.

561. Rogers, Leighton W. "The Russians Like Our Planes." *Harper's,* CLXIX (September 1944), 305-314.

Documents, Papers, and Reports

562. Kravchenko, G. S. *War (Military) Economy of the U.S.S.R., 1941-1945.* Translation, no. 20701. Arlington, Va.: Joint Publications Research Service, 1963. 340p.

563. Lukas, Richard C. "Air Force Aspects of American Aid to the Soviet Union: The Critical Years, 1941-1942." Unpublished Ph.D. Dissertation, Florida State University, 1963.

b. British Assistance

Book

564.   Griffith, Herbert F. *RAF* [No. 151 Wing] *in Russia*. London: Hammond, 1942. 96p.

Articles

565.   Bowyer, Chaz. "Russian Episode." In: *Hurricane at War*. New York: Scribner's, 1978. Chpt. 3.

566.   Jackets, L. A. "Hurricanes in Russia: The Story of No. 151 Wing." *Royal Air Forces Quarterly*, XI (Autumn 1971), 203–206.

c. American Bombers and "Operation Frantic"

Book

567.   Infield, Glenn B. *The Poltava Affair*. New York: Macmillan, 1973. 265p.

Articles

568.   Bowman, Marvin S. "Stopping Over at Ivan's Airdrome." *Air Force Magazine*, LIV (April 1972), 51–55.

569.   Bradshaw, Russell. "To Russia: One Way." *Aerospace Historian*, XXV (Winter 1978), 198–205.

570.   Green, Herschal. "The Russian Shuttle." *Collier's*, CXIV (September 16, 1944), 58.

571.   Hicks, Edmund. "Soviet Sojourn: The First Shuttle-Bombing Mission to Russia." *Air Power Historian*, XI (January 1964), 1–5.

572.   Infield, Glenn B. "Shuttle Raiders to Russia." *Air Force Magazine*, LV (April 1972), 46–50.

573.   Johnson, Gerald E. "How Our Air Force Invaded Russia." *Look*, XXIII (March 17, 1959), 98.

574.   Johnston, Robert E. "Flight to Poltava." *Flying*, XXXVII (July 1945), 24–25.

575.   Lukas, Richard C. "The Velvet Project: Hope and Frustration." *Military Affairs*, XXVIII (1964), 145–162.

576.   Rust, Kenneth C. "Black Night at Poltava." *RAF Flying Review*, XIV (September 1959), 16–17.

577. Stevens, Edmund. "Yankees on the Steppes: The Fighters of Our Eastern Bomber Command." *Saturday Evening Post,* CCXVII (August 5, 1944), 22–23.

578. Walsh, Robert L. "Eastern Command Fact Book." In: Glenn B. Infield. *The Poltava Affair.* New York: Macmillan, 1973. pp. 240–255.

Documents, Papers, and Reports

579. Julian, Thomas A. "'Operation Frantic' and the Search for American-Soviet Military Collaboration, 1941–1944." Unpublished Ph.D. Dissertation, Syracuse University, 1968.

4. Biographies

a. GENERAL STUDIES

Books

580. Bialer, Seweryn. *Stalin and His Generals: Soviet Military Memoirs of World War II.* New York: Pegasus Books, 1969.

581. Burroughs, E. G. *Who's Who in the Red Army.* Hertfordshire, England: Farleigh, 1944. 20p.

582. *Fame of the Falcon.* Translated from the Russian. London: Hutchinson, 1946. 104p.

583. Hess, William N. *Famous Airmen: The Allied Aces of World War II.* New York: Arco, 1966. 64p.

584. Jackson, Robert. *Air-Heroes of World War II.* New York: St. Martin's Press, 1978. 128p.

585. Shores, Christopher F. *Fighter Aces.* London: Hamlyn, 1975. 160p.

586. Sims, Edward H. *The Greatest Aces.* New York: Harper & Row, 1967. 294p.

Articles

587. "How Women Flyers Fight Russia's Air War." *Aviation,* XLIII (July 1944), 116–117.

588. "Leading World War II Russian Aces." *RAF Flying Review,* XIII (January 1958), 23–25.

The leading aces, with victories, were: Ivan N. Kuzhedub 62, Aleksandr I. Pokryshkin 59, Grigori A. Rechkalov 58, Nikolai D.

Gulayev 57, Arsenii V. Vorozheikin 52, Kirill A. Yevstigneyev 52, Dmitri B. Glinka 50, Aleksandr F. Klubov 50, Ivan M. Pilipenko 48, and Vasilii N. Kubarev 46.

589.   Meos, Edgar. "Russian Women Fighter Pilots." *Flight,* LXXXII (December 27, 1962), 1010–1020.

590.   Zabavskaya, L. "Women Fighter Pilots." *Soviet Military Review,* no. 3 (March 1977), 61–62.

b. SPECIFIC PERSONALITIES

Books

591.   Grey, Ian. *Stalin: Man of History.* Garden City, N.Y.: Doubleday, 1979. 600p.

592.   Pokryshkin, Aleksandr I. *Red Air Ace.* New York: Soviet News, 1945. 55p.

593.   Seaton, Albert. *Stalin as Military Commander.* New York: Praeger, 1976.

594.   Toliver, Raymond F. and Trevor J. Constable. *The Blond Knight of Germany: A Biography of Erich Hartmann, Greatest Fighter Pilot of All Times.* Garden City, N.Y.: Doubleday, 1970. 318p.

Articles

595.   "Alexsandr I. Pokryshkin." *RAF Flying Review,* XIII (January 1958), 24–26.

596.   _____. *U.S. Air Services,* II (August 1944), 40.

597.   Blond, Georges. "Ivan Kozedoub." In: *Born to Fly: Exploits of the War's Greatest Aces.* Translated from the French. London: Souvenir Press, 1956. Chpt. 9.

598.   "Ivan N. Kozedub." *RAF Flying Review,* XIII (January 1958), 23–24.

599.   Jackson, Robert. "Ivan N. Kozhedub." In: *Fighter Pilots of World War II.* New York: St. Martin's Press, 1976. pp. 163–176.

600.   Lee, Asher. "He [Pierre Pouyade] Fought for Russia." *RAF Flying Review,* XIII (November 1956), 21–22.

601.   Meos, Edgar. "Russia's Suicide Girl [Eugenie Rudneva]." *RAF Flying Review,* XV (May 1960), 34–36.

602.   "Pokryshkin Wins." *Time,* XLII (November 22, 1943), 22–23.

603. Walker, Wayne T. "The Black Devil [Erich Hartmann] of the Ukraine." *World War II Magazine,* II (August 1972), 60–63.

5. *Aircraft: Soviet and Lend-Lease*

a. GENERAL STUDIES

Books

604. *Aeroplane Spotter.* 9 vols. in 3. London: Aeroplane Magazine, 1941–1948.

605. *Aircraft of the Fighting Powers.* 3 vols. London: Harborough, 1944–1946.

606. Alexander, Jean. *Russian Aircraft Since 1940.* Putnam Aeronautical Books. Totowa, N.J.: Roman and Littlefield, 1976. 555p.

607. Bavousett, Glenn B. *World War II Aircraft in Combat.* New York: Arco, 1976. 144p.

608. Cooke, David C. *The Planes the Allies Flew in World War II.* New York: Dodd, Mead, 1969. 63p.

609. Cross, Roy. *Military Aircraft, 1939–1945.* Greenwich, Conn.: New York Graphic, 1971. 43p.

610. *Fifty Famous Fighters, 1938–1945.* Aircam Aviation Series. New York: Arco, 1972. 96p.

611. Law, Bernard A. *Fighting Planes of the World.* New York: Random House, 1940. 60p.

612. _____. _____. Rev. ed. New York: Random House, 1942. 72p.

613. Munson, Kenneth G. *Aircraft of World War II.* London: Ian Allan, 1962. 256p.

614. _____. _____. 2nd ed. Garden City, N.Y.: Doubleday, 1972. 272p.

615. Nowarra, Heinz J. and G. R. Duval. *Russian Civil and Military Aircraft, 1884–1969.* Fallbrook, Calif.: Aero Publishers, 1976. 288p.

616. Sargent, Eric, comp. *Fighting Planes of the World.* London: Low, 1940. 627p.

617. Talbot-Booth, Eric, ed. *Aircraft of the World.* London: Low, 1942. 1,018p.

618. ———. *Fighting Planes of the World*. 4th ed. London: Low, 1943. 624p.

619. Taylor, John W. R. *Aircraft of World War II*. London: Longacre Press, 1963. 124p.

620. *Warplanes, 1939–1945*. Purnell's History of the Second World War Special. London: Purnell, 1972. 64p.

621. Weal, Elke C., comp. *Combat Aircraft of World War II*. New York: Macmillan, 1977. 238p.

622. Windrow, Martin C., ed. *Aircraft in Profile*. 14 vols. Garden City, N.Y.: Doubleday, 1967–1974.

623. Winter, William J. *Warplanes of the Nations*. New York: T. Y. Crowell, 1943. 418p.

Articles

624. "Airplane Descriptions." *Aeronautical Engineering Review*, I (September 1942), 37.

625. "Air Surprise." *Newsweek*, XX (September 21, 1942), 26.

626. Alexander, Jean and Denys J. Voaden. "Foreign Aircraft in Russian Service." *Air Pictorial*, XXI (December 1959), 428–431; XXII (January 1960), 8–11.

627. Arlazorov, Mikhail. "Duel of Designers." *Soviet Military Review*, no. 1 (January 1976), 50–52.

628. " 'Aviation's' Russian Aircraft Specifications." *Aviation*, XLIV (February 1945), 181.

629. Bourdon, M. W. "Russian Military Aircraft." *Automotive and Aviation Industries*, LXXXVII (August 15, 1942), 40–42.

630. "Directory of the World's Leading Aircraft." *Aviation*, XLIII (February 1944), 155–163.

631. "Four Types of U.S. Warplanes Helping the Russians Smash the Nazis." *Aviation News*, I (August 16, 1942), 13–14.

632. "How Planes are Classified." In: William H. Fetridge, ed. *The Navy Reader*. Indianapolis, Ind.: Bobbs-Merrill, 1943. pp. 334–337.

633. "Names of Military Airplanes." In: Norman Carlisle, ed. *The Air Forces Reader*. Indianapolis, Ind.: Bobbs-Merrill, 1944. pp. 389–391.

634. Nekrasov, F. "Aircraft of the Great Patriotic War." *Soviet Military Review,* no. 7 (July 1978), 16–18.

635. Nemecek, N. "Soviet Stratospheric Aircraft, 1935–1945." *Air Pictorial,* XXVIII (April 1966), 133–135.

636. "New Airplanes of the Red Air Force." *Automotive and Aviation Industries,* LXXXVI (June 15, 1942), 38–39.

637. "Russian Planes: Brief Descriptions, Diagrams, and Illustrations." *Aviation,* XLIV (February 1945), 160–166.

638. "Russian Planes: Brief Descriptions and Illustrations." *Aviation,* XLIII (February 1944), 193–205.

639. "Russian Planes: Brief Descriptions, Illustrations, and Specifications." *Aviation,* XLII (February 1943), 221–227, 259.

640. "The Soviet Air Force Using a Wide Range of Aircraft Types." *Aviation,* XLII (July 1943), 229–230.

641. Stevens, J. H. "Russia's Modern Military Aircraft." *Aviation,* XLI (October 1942), 157–158, 161.

642. "Typical Soviet Aircraft."*Aviation,* XLI (September 1942), 100.

643. "Winged Power of Russia: Aeroplanes of the Red Air Fleet." *Illustrated London News,* CXCIX (August 16, 1941), 196.

644. "Yak, LaGG, Stormovik." *Time,* XLII (August 30, 1943), 30.

Documents, Papers, and Reports

645. *Recognition Journal.* 24 pts. Washington, D.C.: U.S. War and Navy Departments, with the Assistance of Time, Inc., September 1943–August 1945.

646. United States. War Department. Training Division. *Identification Manual.* FM 30-30. Washington, D.C.: U.S. Government Printing Office, 1943.

b. Fighters

(1) General Studies

Books

647. Cooper, Bryan and John Bachelor. *Fighter: A History of Fighter Aircraft.* New York: Scribner's, 1974. 153p.

648.   Green, William. *Famous Fighters of the Second World War.* 2 vols. Garden City, N.Y.: Doubleday, 1960.

649.   _____. _____. 2nd rev. ed. Garden City, N.Y.: Doubleday, 1976. 276p.

650.   _____. *Fighters.* War Planes of the Second World War, vols. 1–4. 4 vols. Garden City, N.Y.: Doubleday, 1961–1962.

651.   _____ and F. Gordon Swanborough. *Soviet Air Force Fighters.* World War II Fact Files. 2 vols. New York: Arco, 1977–1978.

652.   Gunston, William T. *Night Fighters: A Development and Combat History.* New York: Scribner's, 1976. 192p.

653.   Hawks, Ellison. *War in the Air: Fighters of the Present War.* London: Real Photo, 1943. 83p.

654.   _____. *War in the Air: More Fighters of the Present War.* London: Real Photo, 1944. 58p.

655.   Mason, Herbert M., Jr. *Duel for the Sky: Fighter Planes and Fighting Pilots of World War II.* Adventures in Flight Series. New York: Grosset and Dunlap, 1970. 148p.

656.   Munson, Kenneth G. *Fighters, 1939–1945: Attack and Training Aircraft.* The Pocket Encyclopedia of World Aircraft in Color Series. New York: Macmillan, 1969. 163p.

Articles

657.   "Russian Fighter Evolution, 1922–1952." *Skyways,* X (September 1952), 12–15.

658.   Walker, Wayne T. "Fighter Planes of World War II." *World War II Magazine,* II (April 1973), 62–66.

(2) Specific Aircraft

Bell P-39 Airacobra

659.   "America's Airacobra." *Popular Science,* CXL (February 1942), 72D–72E.

660.   "The Bell Airacobra." *Aero Digest,* XLII (March 1943), 256–257.

661.   _____. *Popular Science,* CXLIV (May 1944), 88–89.

662.   "The Bell P-39 Airacobra." *Western Flying,* XIII (October 1943), 84–85.

663. "The Bell P-39 Airacobra in Russian Service." *Western Flying*, XIII (July 1943), 52.

664. "The Cobra." *Flying*, XXXI (November 1942), 61.

665. "Cobras With Wings." *Popular Mechanics*, LXXX (August 1943), 1–5.

666. Dial, Jay F. *Bell P-39 Airacobra*. Aircraft in Profile, no. 165. Windsor, England: Profile Publications, 1967. 12p.

667. Miller, Edward E. "Design Analysis of the Bell Airacobra from Cannon to Tail." *Aviation*, XLII (May 1943), 126–155.

668. Ownes, Rasher. "The Killer Cobra Strikes Again." *Air Classics*, VIII (May 1972), 26–29, 44.

669. Rice, Michael S., ed. *Pilot's Manual for the Bell P-39 Airacobra*. Glendale, Calif.: Aviation Book Company, 1972. 72p.

670. "The Russian P-39 Airacobra." *Air Pilot*, XXIX (August 1943), 16.

Bell P-63 Kingcobra

671. "The Bell P-63 Kingcobra in Russian Service." *RAF Flying Review*, XVI (September 1961), 22–23.

672. "The P-63 Bell Kingcobra Fighter." *Popular Science*, CXLV (December 1944), 98–99.

Lavochkin

673. Liss, Witold. *Lavochkin La-5 and -7*. Aircraft in Profile, no. 149. Windsor, England: Profile Publications, 1967. 12p.

674. "The Russian LaGG-3 Fighter." *Automotive and Aviation Industries*, LXXXIX (October 1, 1943), 30–32.

MIG

675. Green, William. "The First MIG." *Flying Review International*, XXII (January 1967), 327–329.

Polikarpov

676. Green, William. "Polikarpov's 'Little Hawk.'" *Flying Review International*, XXV (November–December 1969), 58–63, 60–64; XXVI (January 1970), 62–66.

677. Liss, Witold. *Polikarpov I-16*. Aircraft in Profile, no. 122. Windsor, England: Profile Publications, 1967. 12p.

Yak

678. Green, William. "Yak-9: Russia's Spitfire." *RAF Flying Review,* XIV (December 1958), 26–30.

679. Liss, Witold. *Yak-9 Series.* Aircraft in Profile, no. 185. Windsor, England: Profile Publications, 1967. 12p.

680. "Yak-1 Fighters." *Automotive and Aviation Industries,* LXXXVIII (March 1, 1943), 37.

681. "Yak-3: Russia's Light Fighter." *RAF Flying Review,* XIX (June 1964), 60–63.

c. BOMBERS

(1) General Studies

682. Ayling, Keith. *Bombers.* New York: T. Y. Crowell, 1944. 194p.

683. Green, William. *Bombers and Reconnaissance Aircraft.* Warplanes of the Second World War, vols. 7, 8, and 10. 3 vols. Garden City, N.Y.: Doubleday, 1968.

684. _____. *Famous Bombers of the Second World War.* 2 vols. Garden City, N.Y.: Doubleday, 1960.

685. Hawks, Ellison. *War in the Air: Bombers of the Present War.* London: Real Photo, 1944. 104p.

686. Munson, Kenneth G. *Bombers, Patrol, and Transport Aircraft, 1939–1945.* The Pocket Encyclopedia of World Aircraft in Color Series. New York: Macmillan, 1969. 163p.

(2) Specific Aircraft

Douglas A-20 Boston

687. Gann, Harry. *Douglas A-20 (7A to Boston III).* Aircraft in Profile, no. 202. Windsor, England: Profile Publications, 1971. 15p.

688. Gault, Owen. "The Amazing 'Coconut Bomber.'" *Air Classics,* IX (July 1973), 26–37.

689. Lodge, J. E. "Name Your Job, the A-20 Does It: The Boston Renamed Havoc." *Popular Science,* CXLV (July 1944), 77–80.

690. Powell, Hickman. "Porcupine Squadron: The A-20 Attack Bomber, Famous Abroad as the Boston and Havoc." *Popular Science,* CXL (May 1942), 82–87.

Ilyushin Il-2 Shturmoviki

691.   Green, William. "Ilyushin's Shturmoviki." *Flying Review International,* XX (September 1965), 51–54; XXI (September 1966), 51–54.

692.   "The Ilyushin Il-2 Stormovik Ground Attack Aircraft." *Flight,* XXXV (March 18, May 20, 1943), 276–277, 526a.

693.   Liss, Witold. *Ilyushin Il-2.* Aircraft in Profile, no. 88. Windsor, England: Profile Publications, 1966. 12p.

694.   Snow, Edgar. "The Red Army's Flying Tank: The Il-2 Stormovik." *Saturday Evening Post,* CCXVII (March 10, 1945), 18–19.

North American B-25 Mitchell

695.   Gault, Owen. "Anatomy of a Killer: The Mitchell." *Air Classics,* VIII (December 1972), 32–59.

696.   Houston, N. S. "North American's B-25C and -D Bomber." *Automotive and Aviation Industries,* XC (February 1–15, 1944), 26–31, 34–37.

697.   McDowell, Ernest R. *B-25 Mitchell in Action.* Warren, Mich.: Squadron/Signal Publications, 1978. 48p.

698.   "The North American Aircraft B-25." *Air Classics,* IV (April 1968), 28–44.

699.   "The North American B-25 Mitchell Medium Bomber." *Aeronautics,* IV (October 1943), 34–37.

700.   _____. *Air Tech,* III (November 1943), 21–33.

701.   _____. *Skyways,* III (May 1944), 18–23.

702.   "The North American Mitchell, B–25H." *Flying,* XXXV (December 1944), 59–63.

703.   United States. Army Air Forces. Training Division. *Pilot Training Manual for the Mitchell Bomber, B-25.* AAF Manual 51-126-4. Washington, D.C., 1944.

704.   Wagner, Ray. *North American B-25 A-G Mitchell.* Aircraft in Profile, no. 59. Windsor, England: Profile Publications, 1966. 12p.

Petlyakov Pe-2

705.   Passingham, Malcolm and Waclaw Klepacki. *Petlyakov Pe-2 Variants.* Aircraft in Profile, no. 216. Windsor, England: Profile Publications, 1971. 24p.

706. "The Petlyakov Pe-2 Buck." *Aircraft Engineering,* XV (May 1944), 124–127.

707. _____ . *Flight,* XXXIII (March 18, July 22, 1943), 276–277, 96; XXXIV (February 10, 1944), 142–144.

708. _____ . *Flying Review International,* XX (December 1964), 50.

709. "The Russian Pe-2 Dive Bomber." *Automotive and Aviation Industries,* XC (April 15, 1944), 22–23.

Petlyakov Pe-8

710. Green, William. "The Petlyakov Pe-8." *Flying Review International,* XX (April 1964), 57–58.

Tupolev SB-2

711. Green, William. "Tupolev's Frontal Bomber, the SB-2." *Flying Review International,* XXII (March 1967), 449–451.

d. Transports

712. Ott, Lester. *Transport Aircraft of the World.* New York: Watts, 1944. 107p.

3 / The Soviet Economy and Defense Establishment

Introduction

Defense Establishment Organization

THE MINISTER OF Defense exercises immediate control of the Soviet military. Within the Russian government, the defense chief is a member of the Council of Ministers, appointed by and technically answerable to the Supreme Soviet or to the Presidium. In practice, the Minister of Defense is responsible to the Central Committee of the Communist Party (CPSU) and its Politburo.

The current Minister of Defense, Marshall of the Soviet Union (MSU) D. F. Ustinov, is a member of the Politburo, as was his predecessor, MSU A. A. Grechko. Politburo control is streamlined by the presence of the Defense Council, successor organization to the World War II State Defense Committee, chaired by the General Secretary of the CPSU. In 1976 General Secretary Leonid Brezhnev was awarded the rank of Marshall of the Soviet Union—Russia's highest award—which indicated to Western analysts that ultimate operational and policymaking control of the armed forces was being vested in the Defense Council.

MSU Ustinov as head of the Ministry of Defense heads a broad spectrum of activities involving both administrative and operational functions. He controls and directs the armed forces General Staff, the Warsaw Pact Headquarters, the five major armed forces components—Ground, Navy, Air, Air Defense, and Strategic Rocket Forces—and sixteen military districts, ten air defense districts, four naval fleets, and four groups of forces.

MSU Ustinov exercises control of the armed forces through his deputies. These men form the high command, which currently consists of the Minister of Defense, three first deputy ministers, eleven deputy ministers, and the Chief of the Main Political Directorate. See Chart I for an illustration of this arrangement. The first deputy ministers and the deputy ministers are responsible to Ustinov for policymaking, planning, coordination, and the control of the services. Relationships within the Ministry of Defense vary in the degree of authority delegated among the deputies and also in established mechanisms for coordination.

Chart I shows the responsibilities of all but one of the first deputy ministers and one of the deputy ministers. The exact duties of this first deputy minister are unknown; it is possible that he serves as assistant to the Defense Minister for general affairs. The functions of this deputy minister are also unclear, but may fall in the area of strategic weapons and systems.

Defense Minister Ustinov has operational control of the force components, military districts, groups of forces, and other elements as depicted in Chart II. Presumably, there is close coordination between the Strategic Rocket Forces, Long-Range Aviation elements of the Air Force, and the Navy's ballistic missile submarines, with these forces and elements comprising a strategic strike force.

The Chief of the General Staff is a first deputy minister responsible for overall planning and coordination and for the implementation of all orders emanating from the Minister of Defense. In the operational chain of command, he is between the Minister of Defense and theater force commanders.

The General Staff is composed of the Chief, an assistant to the Chief for Naval Affairs, an executive officer, two first deputy chiefs, five deputy chiefs, and numerous chiefs of directorates (some of whom may be deputy chiefs). One of the first deputy chiefs is also First Deputy Commander and Chief of Staff of the Warsaw Pact Forces. Through its directorates, the members of the General Staff effectively constitute the nerve center of the Soviet Armed Forces, directing all military activities concerned with intelligence, operations, organization, conscription, mobilization, reserve affairs, communications, cryptography, foreign military assistance, external relations, military science, and, possibly, some planning aspects for military transportation and research and development. In addition, the General Staff members exercise administrative and political control over their own personnel and supervise the General Staff Academy.

The Communist Party and the Military

NUMEROUS OTHER ADMINISTRATIVE, technical, and support elements assist the Minister of Defense in nonoperational activities. Among the most important of these is the Main Political Directorate, which is sometimes called the Main Political Administration. This unit is the principal instrument used by the Central Committee members of the CPSU to maintain political control over the armed forces, including rigid adherence to Party policies and directives.

The Directorate's internal structure consists of a chief, a first deputy chief, seven deputy chiefs who head major directorates concerned with political agitation and propaganda, party organization, the administration of political affairs in the five major force components, and five deputy chiefs without known portfolios. An additional directorate handles personnel administration for the Main Political Directorate, and two separate departments exist for Communist Youth League (Komsomol) affairs and military-sociological research.

The members of the Central Committee appoint the members of the Main Political Directorate to serve on the Bureau, the Directorate's executive body, which is responsible for the overall implementation of Party policies in the armed forces. All Bureau actions are based on Central Committee directives and Secretariat instructions. Its decisions are embodied in decrees and orders issued by the Chief of the Main Political Directorate. The most important directives require the signature of both that leader and the Minister of Defense, as well as Central Committee approval.

The political apparatus outlined above extends down through, and is an integral part of, all headquarters throughout the Soviet military forces down to company level. It trains, administers, and directs the political officers responsible for the indoctrination of all personnel, morale-building programs, assurance of political reliability, and the disciplinary and administrative control of members of the CPSU and Komsomol.

Military Policy and Doctrine, Theory and Strategy

"MILITARY DOCTRINE" IS the Soviet state's officially approved system for viewing the problems of war. It covers the nature of future war and the methods of waging war, as well as the organization and preparation of the military for war. In Russia, the basic principles of doctrine are determined by the political leadership of the Politburo. "Military Strategy" is an elaboration of the forms and methods for conducting and directing war, the problems regarding comprehensive strategic support of combat operations, the training objectives for the armed forces as a whole, and the strategic employment of the individual force components in war. Both the political and military leadership are involved in developing strategy.

Strategy is second to doctrine. Military doctrine is the overall policy in principle. Using doctrine as a starting point, military strategists amplify and investigate concrete problems regarding the nature of future war, the methods of warfare, and the organization and preparation of the armed forces for war. Military doctrine is subject to definite changes. In light of shifting conditions or new theories, the state may either alter existing doctrine or, if outdated, replace it with a new one. There have been several stages in the development of Soviet military doctrine since World War II.

From 1945 until Stalin's death in 1953, the Soviets confined their military goals primarily to protecting their western flanks through consolidating control over East European "satellites," which formed a buffer zone between the USSR and Western Europe. Because the Russians lacked any significant atomic weapons during this period, they were forced to include in their doctrine only the possibility of a conventional war with the Western allies, in which the Central European zone would be the primary theater of operations.

With the development of means for delivery of nuclear weapons between 1953 and 1958, expounders of Soviet military doctrine sought to integrate new weapons systems into the military force structure. However, military doctrine during this period was still basically conventional. The Russians continued to emphasize the capabilities of the ground forces, which most likely would be employed in Europe, treating nuclear weapons more as powerful cousins of conventional armaments and holding to traditional principles of war. It was during this time frame that Soviet doctrine became the joint doctrine for the Warsaw Pact, formed in 1955.

During the period from 1958 through the early 1960s, the Soviets reviewed their military doctrine extensively and concluded that the nuclear weapon would be decisive in a future war. War would inevitably be world-wide and would be thermonuclear from the outset, with conventional forces having a secondary role. These aspects of Soviet doctrine, along with emphasis upon offensive operations and strategic surprise, were promulgated in open-press writings in the early 1960s.

While continuing to maintain that the nuclear weapon would be the decisive factor in a future war and that such weapons would be used in great number, Soviet doctrine in the mid-1960s began to reflect the need for more balanced theater and strategic forces. Analysts recognized that a conflict in the theater might begin conventionally, though it would soon escalate to nuclear conflict.

Beginning in the late 1960s and continuing in the 1970s, the Soviets modernized conventional forces and there are indications that they considered the limited use of nuclear weapons. However, no major doctrinal shift was evident. The basic tenets of Soviet military doctrine remain consistent: 1) in a future war, nuclear weapons will be decisive; 2) the element of surprise and the necessity for offensive operations are paramount; 3) war, including thermonuclear war, can be won; and 4) joint efforts of all forces, including large armies, will be required.

While the general nature of Soviet military doctrine and strategy is strongly influenced by the general line of the CPSU, the influence of politics on doctrine and strategy is not limited solely to determining their general nature. The resolution of many concrete problems also depends directly upon state policy. The Soviets have consistently and energetically attempted to reconcile strategic capabilities with the demands of their military doctrine. This has never taken the form of shaping doctrine to existing capabilities but, rather, has been restricted to developing strategic force structures and equipment in line with the requirements of relatively static doctrine.

The essence of the approved doctrine is instilled in Soviet citizens throughout their entire lifetime through such programs as civil defense training, premilitary training, and active and reserve military service. The Soviets, through the overall doctrine, require superiority in personnel, armaments, and training both as a deterrent to war and as a means for winning war should the deterrent fail. They also demand a national organization of human and economic resources to support these requirements.[1]

The Soviet Economy and the Military

SOVIET EXPENDITURES FOR military might, while impressive in the 1970s, have been accomplished at tremendous sacrifice by the Russian citizenry. According to CIA studies, Soviet military spending during the years 1970 to 1979 exceeded that of the United States by thirty percent. In 1979, the Soviets poured $165 billion into defense, almost fifty percent higher than the $108 billion expended by the United States. Pentagon and CIA analysts estimate that the Russians have spent between eleven and fourteen percent of their gross national product on armed forces activities during the 1970s as compared to five to eight percent for the United States. This lopsided allotment of treasure has severely damaged the Russian civilian economy and has the potential of forcing difficult choices on the Kremlin leadership in the near future.

Examples of difficulties within the Soviet economy include agricultural failures, a growing energy problem, labor shortages, and a significant "computer gap." Some of these problems are felt directly by the military, especially in mechanical areas. American intelligence estimates project only a three percent growth of the Russian economy in the 1980s, compared with gains of six percent or more in the 1950s. The rate of capital growth is expected to decline.

Despite these economic worries, the work of the Soviet aerospace industry will continue in high gear. Russian design bureaus, strong

---

1. Material in this section was drawn from U.S. Department of Defense, Defense Intelligence Agency, *Handbook on the Soviet Armed Forces* (Washington, D.C.: U.S. Government Printing Office, 1979), pp. 2/1–2/6, 4/1–4/3.

since World War II, carrying on the traditions of such giants as Tupolev and Ilyushin, are expected to continue the introduction of new aircraft, helicopters, and missiles designed to meet the strategic/doctrinal requirements of the state. The aerospace industry no longer feels an imperative need to demonstrate its warbirds in massive public displays such as the famed Tushino airshows and flybys of the 1950s and early 1960s. Today, new Soviet aircraft and helicopters are most often spotted by spy satellites or by reporters observing maneuvers.[2]

The references in this section are designed to demonstrate the relationship between the Soviet economy and defense establishment, as well as the organization and operational patterns of both. A few additional titles relative to this section may be found in Sections 4 and 5.

---

2. Information in this section was gathered from various sources cited in Section 3:B:1 and 2 as well as from Secretary of Defense Harold Brown's January 29, 1980 report to Congress as noted in the news media, especially Robert P. Martin's "Special Report: How Strong is Russia" in *U.S. News and World Report,* LXXXVIII (February 11, 1980), 18–19.

A. The Soviet Defense Establishment

1. Organization

a. GENERAL STUDIES

Books

713.   Deitchman, Seymour J. *New Technology and Military Power: General Purpose Military Forces for the 1980s and Beyond.* Boulder, Colo.: Westview, 1979. 350p.

714.   Ely, Louis B. *The Red Army Today.* Harrisburg, Pa.: Military Service Publishing Company, 1951. 284p.

715.   Garder, Michel. *A History of the Soviet Army.* Rev. ed. New York: Praeger, 1966. 226p.

716.   Grechko, Andrei A. *The Armed Forces of the Soviet State: A Soviet View.* Translated from the Russian. Soviet Military Thought Series, no. 12. Washington, D.C.: Published under the auspices of the U.S. Air Force by the U.S. Government Printing Office, 1975. 349p.

717.   Mackintosh, Malcolm. *Juggernaut: A History of the Soviet Armed Forces.* New York: Macmillan, 1967. 320p.

718.   O'Ballance, Edgar. *The Red Army.* London: Faber and Faber, 1964. 237p.

719.   Ryabov, V. *The Soviet Armed Forces, Yesterday and Today.* Moscow: Progress Publishers, 1976. 164p.

720.   Scott, Harriett F. and William F. *The Armed Forces of the U.S.S.R.* Boulder, Colo.: Westview, 1978. 400p.

721.   *Soviet Military Organization: A Compilation of Articles from "The Army Information Digest."* Ft. Slocum, N.Y.: Armed Forces Information School, 1951. 64p.

Articles

722.   "The Armed Forces of the U.S.S.R. in the Post-War Period." *Translations on U.S.S.R. Military Affairs,* no. 134 (April 1964), 28–37.

723.   Asprey, Robert B. "Soviet Military Problems: An Informed Assessment." *Marine Corps Gazette,* XLVI (June 1962), 22–26.

724.   Brown, Harold. "Soviet Union Armed Forces: Excerpt from a Report, January 25, 1979." *Congressional Digest,* LVIII (November 1979), 264–266.

725. Copley, Gregory. "The State of the Soviets." *Defense and Foreign Affairs Digest*, VI (1976), 6–9.

726. "The Development of Soviet Military Power in the Past 20 Years." *NATO's Fifteen Nations*, XVI (April–May 1971), 36–42.

727. Garthoff, Raymond L. "The Military Establishment." *Eastern Europe*, XIV (September 1965), 2–16.

728. _____. "The Organization of the Armed Forces of the U.S.S.R." *U.S. Army Combat Forces Journal*, XXXIX (April 1953), 36–39.

729. _____. "The Organization and Posture of the Armed Forces." In: *Soviet Strategy in the Nuclear Age*. New York: Praeger, 1958. pp. 41–60.

730. Heinl, Robert D., Jr. "The Soviet Military Machine." *Sea Power*, XIX (May 1976), 31–34.

731. Hilton, Richard. "The Soviet Armed Forces." *Journal of the Royal United Service Institution*, XCIV (November 1949), 552–566.

732. International Institute for Strategic Studies. "The Soviet Union." *Air Force Magazine*, LVII (December 1974), 47–49; LVIII (December 1975), 49–51; LIX (December 1976), 47–49; LX (December 1977), 68–70; LXI (December 1978), 68–70; LXII (December 1979), 68–70.

733. Kozicharow, E. "Across the Board Gains in Soviet Forces Detailed." *Aviation Week and Space Technology*, CVII (August 29, 1977), 17–18.

734. Krylov, Nikolai. "Guarding Socialism's Gains." *New Times* (Moscow), no. 8 (February 28, 1968), 3–5.

735. Lee, William T. "The Soviet Defense Establishment in the '80s." *Air Force Magazine*, LXIII (March 1980), 100–108.

736. Legvold, Robert. "The Nature of Soviet Power." *Foreign Affairs*, LVI (October 1977), 49–71.

737. London, Kurt. "Soviet Strengths and Weaknesses." In: David M. Abshire and Richard V. Allen, eds. *National Security*. New York: Praeger, 1963. pp. 41–74.

738. Long, J. F. L. "Soviet Armed Forces in the 1970s." *Royal Air Forces Quarterly*, IX (Spring 1969), 33–38.

739. Mackintosh, Malcolm. "The Soviet Military." *Problems of Communism*, XXII (September 1973), 1–26.

740. Mahoney, Shane E. "Posture and Purpose of the Soviet Military." *Problems of Communism,* XXVIII (January–February 1979), 55–58.

741. Manning, Stephen O., 3rd. "The Soviet Armed Forces." *Airman,* XXI (January–March 1977), 2–7, 42–48, 11–15.

742. O'Ballance, Edgar. "A New Look at Soviet Military Forces." *Military Review,* XLI (April 1961), 71–81.

743. "Organization of the Soviet Armed Forces." *Air Force Magazine,* LXI (March 1978), 89–91; LXII (March 1979), 95–97.

744. Schneider, William, Jr. "Soviet General Purpose Forces." *Orbis,* XXI (Spring 1977), 95–106.

745. Smith, W. Y. "The Soviet Armed Forces." *Air Force Policy Letter for Commanders,* no. 8 (August 1978), 12–23.

746. "The Soviet Armed Forces." *Military Review,* XXX (August 1950), 73–79.

747. _____. *Soviet Military Review,* no. 10 (October 1965), 30–55.

748. "Soviet Armed Forces: Facts and Figures." *Air Force Magazine,* LVIII (March 1975), 76–77; LIX (March 1976), 108–109; LX (March 1977), 109–110.

749. "Soviet Military Organization." *Canadian Army Journal,* V (April–September 1951), 40–57, 5–6, 27–39, 5–17, 15–22, 43–49.

750. "Soviet Military Organization: Its Heritage and Development." *Army Information Digest,* V (October 1950–March 1951), 2–20, 53–64, 33–42, 17–28, 57–64, 58–64.

751. Sulimov, Y. "Principles of the Development of the Soviet Armed Forces." *Soviet Military Review,* no. 3 (March 1973), 12–14.

752. Thomson, I. W. "The U.S.S.R.'s Large Conventional Forces." *Royal Air Forces Quarterly,* XIII (Spring 1973), 45–50.

753. Vigor, Peter H. "The Size and Quality of the Soviet Armed Forces and Soviet Military Policy." *NATO's Fifteen Nations,* XXII (October–November 1977), 24–26.

754. _____. "Soviet Military Developments, 1976." *Strategic Review,* V (Spring 1977), 74–82.

755. Viktorov, G. M. and Will W. Groves, Jr. "The Armed Forces of the U.S.S.R." *Infantry,* LII (September–October 1962), 63–66.

756. Wolfe, Thomas W. "The Soviet Military Since Khrushchev." *Current History,* LVII (October 1969), 220–227.

Documents, Papers, and Reports

757. United States. Air Force. *Military Forces Handbook: Military Forces of the U.S.S.R. and People's Republic of China.* Washington, D.C.: Headquarters, U.S. Air Force, 1978.

758. _____. Army. *Handbook on the Soviet Army.* Washington, D.C., 1958. 260p.

759. _____. _____. *Handbook on the Soviet and Satellite Armies, Pt. 1: The Soviet Army.* DA Pam. 30-50-1. Washington, D.C., 1953. 172p.

760. _____. _____. *Soviet Military Power.* Washington, D.C., 1959. 186p.

761. _____. _____. *Understanding Soviet Military Developments.* Washington, D.C., 1977.

762. _____. Department of Defense. Defense Intelligence Agency. *Handbook on the Soviet Armed Forces.* DDB-2680-40-78. Washington, D.C.: U.S. Government Printing Office, 1979. Unpaged.

763. Whiting, Kenneth R. *The Development of the Soviet Armed Forces, 1917–1972.* Air University Documentary Research Study AU-201-72-IPD. Maxwell AFB, Ala.: Directorate of Documentary Research, Air University Institute for Professional Development, 1972. 102p.

764. Zemskov, V. I. *Types of Armed Forces and Combat Arms.* Translated from the Russian. Arlington, Va.: Joint Publications Research Service, 1975. 40p.

b. THE SOVIET HIGH COMMAND

Books

765. Institut zur Erforschung der U.S.S.R., Munich. *Party and Government Officials of the Soviet Union, 1917–1967.* Metuchen, N.J.: The Scarecrow Press, 1969. 214p.

766. _____. *Prominent Personalities in the U.S.S.R.: A Biographic Directory.* Metuchen, N.J.: The Scarecrow Press, 1968. 1,189p.

767. _____. *The Soviet Diplomatic Corps, 1917–1969.* Metuchen, N.J.: The Scarecrow Press, 1970. 240p.

768. _____. *Who Was Who in the Soviet Union.* Metuchen, N.J.: The Scarecrow Press, 1972. 687p.

769. Lewytzkyj, Borys, ed. *Who's Who in the Socialist Countries: A Biographical Encyclopedia of 10,000 Leading Personalities in 16 Communist Countries.* New York: K. G. Saur, 1978. 748p.

Articles

770. Bailer, Severyn. "The Men Who Run Russia's Armed Forces." *New York Times Magazine,* (February 21, 1965), 14–15, 53–54.

771. Erickson, John. "Soviet Command and Control." *Military Review,* LII (January 1972), 41–50.

772. _____. "Toward a 'New' Soviet High Command." *Journal of the Royal United Service Institution,* CXIV (September 1969), 37–44.

773. Galay, Nikolai. "Changes Among the Leaders of the Soviet Armed Forces." *Bulletin of the Institute for the Study of the History and Culture of the U.S.S.R.,* X (June 1963), 36–40.

774. _____. "The New Marshals." *Bulletin of the Institute for the Study of the History and Culture of the U.S.S.R.,* II (March 1955), 7–12.

775. Garthoff, Raymond L. "The High Command and General Staff." In: Basil H. Liddell-Hart, ed. *The Soviet Army.* London: Weidenfeld and Nicolson, 1956. pp. 244–253.

776. Ghebhardt, Alexander O. and William Schneider, Jr. "The Soviet High Command: Recent Changes and Policy Implications." *Military Review,* LIII (May 1973), 3–14.

777. Kruzhin, Petr. "New Appointments in the Soviet Armed Forces." *Bulletin of the Institute for the Study of the History and Culture of the U.S.S.R.,* XIV (July 1967), 35–44.

778. Parrish, Michael. "The New Soviet High Command." *Military Review,* XLIX (February 1969), 22–27.

779. Scott, Harriet F. "The Soviet High Command." *Air Force Magazine,* LX (March 1977), 52–56.

780. _____. "Top Leaders of the Soviet Armed Forces." *Air Force Magazine,* LXII (March 1979), 94; LXIII (March 1980), 109.

781. "Structure of the High Command." *Army Information Digest,* VI (March 1951), 59–64.

782. Wolfe, Thomas W. "The Soviet General Staff." *Problems of Communism,* XXVIII (January–February 1979), 51–54.

Documents, Papers, and Reports

783. "Composition of the Ministry of Defense, 1960–1963." In: U.S. Army. *Soviet Russia: Strategic Survey.* Washington, D.C.: U.S. Government Printing Office, 1963. pp. 175–177.

784. Scribner, Jeffery L. *Organization of the Soviet Ministry of Defense.* Washington, D.C., 1971.

785. Spahr, William J. "The Soviet Military High Command, 1957–1967: Political Socialization, Professionalization, and Modernization." Unpublished Ph.D. Dissertation, George Washington University, 1972.

786. United States. Central Intelligence Agency. Office of Political Research. *Appearances of Soviet Leaders.* Reference aid. Washington, D.C.: Document Expediting Project, Exchange and Gift Division, Library of Congress, 1972–. vol. 1–.

787. ———. ———. ———. *Directory of Soviet Officials.* Reference aid. Washington, D.C.: Document Expediting Program, Exchange and Gift Division, Library of Congress, 1973–. vol. 1–.

788. ———. ———. ———. *Directory of U.S.S.R. Ministry of Defense.* Reference aid. Washington, D.C.: Document Expediting Project, Exchange and Gift Division, Library of Congress, 1972–. vol. 1–.

789. ———. ———. ———. *Directory of U.S.S.R. Ministry of Foreign Affairs Officials.* Reference aid. Washington, D.C.: Document Expediting Service, Exchange and Gift Division, Library of Congress, 1974–. vol. 1–.

2. The Communist Party and the Military

Books

790. Barry, Donald D. and Carol B. *Contemporary Soviet Politics: An Introduction.* Englewood Cliffs, N.J.: Prentice-Hall, 1978. 406p.

791. Colton, Timothy J. *Commissars, Commanders, and Civilian Authority: The Structure of Soviet Military Politics.* Russian Research Center Studies, no. 77. Cambridge, Mass.: Harvard University Press, 1979. 376p.

792. Conquest, Robert. *Power and Policy in the U.S.S.R.: The Study of Soviet Dynastics.* New York: St. Martin's Press, 1961. 485p.

793. Deane, Michael J. *Political Control of the Soviet Armed Forces.* New York: Published for the Strategic Studies Center, Stanford Research Institute, by Crane, Russak, 1977. 297p.

The Soviet Economy and Defense Establishment 69

794. Hough, Jerry F. *How the Soviet Union is Governed.* Cambridge, Mass.: Harvard University Press, 1979. 696p.

795. Kelleher, Catherine, ed. *Political-Military Systems: Comparative Perspectives.* Sage Research Progress Series on War, Revolution, and Peacekeeping, vol. 4. Beverly Hills, Calif.: Sage, 1974. 306p.

796. Kolkowicz, Roman. *The Soviet Military and the Communist Party.* Princeton, N.J.: Princeton University Press, 1967. 429p.

797. Reshetar, John S., Jr. *The Soviet Polity: Government and Politics in the U.S.S.R.* 2nd ed. New York: Harper & Row, 1978. 413p.

798. Warner, Edward L. *The Military in Contemporary Soviet Politics: An Institutional Analysis.* New York: Praeger, 1977. 374p.

Articles

799. "The Army and the Supreme Soviet." *Bulletin of the Institute for the Study of the History and Culture of the U.S.S.R.,* I (April 1954), 23–26.

800. Artemiev, Vyacheslav, P. "The Communist Party and the Soviet Armed Forces." *Military Review,* XLIV (February 1964), 29–37.

801. _____. "Party Political Work in the Soviet Armed Forces." *Military Review,* XLIV (March 1964), 62–68.

802. Barron, John. "The G.R.U.: Soviet Military Intelligence." In: *KGB: The Secret Work of Soviet Secret Agents.* New York: Reader's Digest Press, dist. by E. P. Dutton, 1973. pp. 343–345.

803. Burney, John C. "The Soviet Political Officer: Asset or Liability?" *Marine Corps Gazette,* L (April 1966), 49–52.

804. Deane, Michael J. "The Main Political Administration as a Factor in Communist Party Control Over the Military in the Soviet Union." *Armed Forces and Society,* III (Winter 1977), 295–324.

805. Donnelly, Christopher. "Military/Political Infrastructure." In: Ray Bonds, ed. *The Soviet War Machine: An Encyclopedia of Russian Military Equipment and Strategy.* New York: Chartwell Books, 1976. pp. 30–41.

806. Ermarth, Fritz. "Soviet Military Politics." *Military Review,* XLVIII (January 1968), 32–36.

807. Garthoff, Raymond L. "The Role of the Military in Soviet Politics." In: *Soviet Strategy in the Nuclear Age.* New York: Praeger, 1958. pp. 18–40.

808. _____. "The Soviet Intelligence Services." In: Basil H. Liddell-Hart, ed. *The Red Army.* New York: Harcourt, Brace, 1956. pp. 265–274.

809. Gorchakov, P. "Strategic Missile Forces Use Brezhnev Works for Indoctrination: Translated from *Kommunist Vooruzhennykh*, October 1978." *Translations on U.S.S.R. Military Affairs,* no. 1402 (December 13, 1978), 74–85.

810. Heinlein, Joseph J., Jr. "The Main Political Administration in Today's Soviet Forces." *Military Review,* LIII (November 1973), 55–64.

811. Holloway, David. "The Role of the Military in Soviet Politics." In: Royal United Service Institution for Defence Studies. *The Soviet Union in Europe and the Near East: Her Capabilities and Intentions.* London, 1970. p. 12.

812. Jones, Christopher D. "The 'Revolution in Military Affairs' and Party-Military Relations, 1965–1970." *Survey,* XX (Winter 1974), 84–100.

813. Kalashinik, M. "Political Education in the Soviet Armed Forces." *Soviet Military Review,* no. 10 (October 1965), 12–16.

814. Kime, Steve F. "How the Soviet Union is Ruled." *Air Force Magazine,* LXIII (March 1980), 54–60.

815. Kolkowicz, Roman. "Interest Groups in Soviet Politics: The Military." In: Leonard J. Cohen and Jane P. Shapiro, eds. *Communist Systems in Comparative Perspective.* Garden City, N.Y.: Doubleday-Anchor, 1974. pp. 317–334.

816. Kuban, Boris. "Politics in the Soviet Air Force." In: Asher Lee, ed. *The Soviet Air and Rocket Forces.* New York: Praeger, 1959. pp. 201–216.

817. Kurochkin, P. A. "Unity of Command in the Soviet Armed Forces." *Soviet Military Review,* no. 7 (July 1965), 16–18.

818. Kuzovov, V. "Political Officer Influence on Flight Training Discussed: Translated from *Krasnaya Zvezda*, March 18, 1978." *Translations on USSR Military Affairs,* no. 1365 (July 19, 1978), 15–18.

819. Malinovskiy, Nikolay F. "Political Indoctrination in [a] Long-Range Aviation Unit Described: Translated from *Krasnaya Zvezda*, July 29, 1978." *Translations on USSR Military Affairs,* no. 1385 (October 11, 1978), 29–33.

820. Moroz, Ivan M. "Important Sector of Political Education Work [Soviet Air Force]." *Soviet Military Review,* no. 3 (March 1974), 10–12.

821. "Party Leadership is the Source of Soviet Army and Navy Power." *Translations on USSR Military Affairs,* no 193a (October 1965), 33–47.

822. Prinz zu Loewenstein, H. "A German View: Airpower vs. Soviet Politics." *Air Force,* XLII (January 1958), 52–56.

823. Scott, Harriet F. "The Military Profession in the USSR." *Air Force Magazine,* LIX (March 1976), 76–81.

824. Skrylnik, A. "Discipline in the Armed Forces." *Soviet Military Review,* no. 9 (September 1974), 28–29.

825. Smith, R. G. "Political Controls Within the Structure of the Soviet Armed Forces—Some Problems?" *Royal Air Forces Quarterly,* XVI (Spring 1976), 45–49.

826. Tsymbal, Nikolay A. "Effectiveness of Air Force Political Organizations Discussed: Translated from *Krasnaya Zvezda,* February 3, 1978." *Translations on USSR Military Affairs,* no. 1352 (May 15, 1978), 29–33.

827. Vasil'yev, B. A. "Indoctrination Methods in [an] Air Force Unit Described: Translated from *Krasnaya Zvezda,* April 1, 1978." *Translations on USSR Military Affairs,* no. 1366 (July 20, 1978), 42–46.

828. Wesson, Robert G. "The Military in Soviet Society." *Russian Review,* XXX (April 1971), 139–145.

Documents, Papers, and Reports

829. Deane, Michael J. "The Evolution, Responsibilities, and Influence of the Main Political Administration of the Soviet Army and Navy Under General A. A. Yepishov, May 1962–March 1973." Unpublished Ph.D. Dissertation, University of Miami (Florida), 1974.

830. Kolkowicz, Roman. *Conflicts in Soviet Party-Military Relations, 1962–1963.* RAND Memorandum RM-3760-PR. Santa Monica, Calif.: RAND Corporation, 1963.

831. _____. "The Political Role of the Soviet Military." Unpublished Ph.D. Dissertation, University of Chicago, 1965.

832. McConnell, James M. *Military–Political and Military–Strategic Leadership in the USSR: A Working Paper.* Arlington, Va.: Center for Naval Analysis, Department of the Navy, 1975.

833. Warner, Edward L., 3rd. "The Military in Contemporary Soviet Politics: An Institutional Analysis." Unpublished Ph.D. Dissertation, Princeton University, 1975.

3. Military Policy and Doctrine, Theory and Strategy

Books

834. Baylis, John et al. *Contemporary Strategy, Theories and Practice.* New York: Holmes and Meier, 1975. 324p.

835. Bidwell, Shelford. *Modern Warfare: A Study of Men, Weapons, and Theories.* London: Lane, 1973. 242p.

836. De Huszar, George B. et al. *Soviet Power and Policy.* New York: T. Y. Crowell, 1955. 598p.

837. Emme, Eugene M., ed. *The Impact of Air Power, National Security, and World Politics.* Princeton, N.J.: Van Nostrand, 1959. 914p.

838. Gallagher, Matthew P. and Karl F. Spielmann, Jr. *Soviet Decision-Making for Defense: A Critique of U.S. Perspectives on the Arms Race.* New York: Praeger, 1972. 102p.

839. Garthoff, Raymond L. *The Soviet Image of Future War.* Washington, D.C.: Public Affairs Press, 1959. 240p.

840. _____. *Soviet Military Policy: An Historical Analysis.* New York: Praeger, 1966. 276p.

841. Heilbrunn, Otto. *Conventional Warfare in the Nuclear Age.* New York: Praeger, 1965. 164p.

842. Howard, Michael, ed. *Restraints on War: Studies on the Limitation of Armed Conflict.* Oxford, England: At the Clarendon Press, 1978. 192p.

843. Khrushchev, Nikita S. *Khrushchev Remembers.* Translated from the Russian. Boston: Little, Brown, 1970. 639p.

844. _____. *Khrushchev Remembers: The Last Testament.* Translated from the Russian. Boston: Little, Brown, 1974. 602p.

845. Modrzhinskaya, Ye. D. et al. *Problems of War and Peace.* Moscow: Progress Publishers, 1972. 363p.

846. Rummel, Rudolph J. *Peace Endangered: The Reality of Detente.* Beverly Hills, Calif.: Sage, 1976. 189p.

The Soviet Economy and Defense Establishment 73

847.   Savkin, V. Ye. *The Basic Principles of Operational Art and Tactics: A Soviet View.* Translated from the Russian. Soviet Military Thought Series, no. 4. Washington, D.C.: Published under the auspices of the U.S. Air Force by the U.S. Government Printing Office, 1974. 284p.

848.   Sidorenko, A. A. *The Offensive: A Soviet View.* Translated from the Russian. Soviet Military Thought Series, no. 1. Washington, D.C.: Published under the auspices of the U.S. Air Force by the U.S. Government Printing Office, 1973. 228p.

849.   Sokolovskii, Vasillii D. *Soviet Military Strategy.* 3rd ed. New York: Crane, Russak, 1975. 494p.

850.   Stoessinger, John G. *Why Nations Go to War.* 2nd ed. New York: St. Martin's Press, 1978. 246p.

851.   Vigor, Peter H. *The Soviet View of War, Peace, and Neutrality.* London and Boston: Routledge and Kegan Paul, 1975. 256p.

852.   Whetten, Lawrence L., ed. *The Future of Soviet Military Power.* New York: Crane, Russak, 1976. 190p.

853.   Wolfe, Thomas W. *Soviet Strategy at the Crossroads.* Cambridge, Mass.: Harvard University Press, 1964. 342p.

Articles

854.   Abshire, David M. and Robert D. Crane. "Soviet Strategy in the '60s: An Analysis of the Current Russian Debate Over Strategy." *Army,* XIII (July 1963), 20–21.

855.   Bailey-Cowell, G. M. "Detente in Soviet Strategy." *NATO's Fifteen Nations,* XX (December 1975–January 1976), 86–90.

856.   Barber, Ransom E. "The Conventional Wisdom on Soviet Strategy—Is It Conventional?" *Forum,* no. 17 (Summer 1973), 21–30.

857.   Barrett, Raymond. "Geography and Soviet Strategic Thinking." *Military Review,* L (January 1970), 17–25.

858.   Cade, David J. "Russian Military Strategy: A Fresh Look." *Air University Review,* XXIX (September–October 1978), 18–27.

859.   Candlin, A. H. S. "Contrast in Strategies: USA and USSR." In: James L. Moulton, ed. *Brassey's Annual.* New York: Praeger, 1973. pp. 232–244.

860.   Clark, Donald L. "Soviet Strategy for the Seventies." *Air University Review,* XXII (January–February 1971), 2–18.

861. Douglass, Joseph D., Jr. "Soviet Military Thought." *Air Force Magazine*, LIX (March 1976), 88–91.

862. Dulacki, Leo J. "Soviet Military Strategy." *Marine Corps Gazette*, XLVII (August 1963), 18–22.

863. Erickson, John. "Detente, Deterrence, and 'Military Superiority': A Soviet Dilemma." *World Today*, XXI (August 1965), 337–345.

864. _____. "Detente: Soviet Policy and Purpose." *Strategic Review*, IV (Spring 1976), 37–43.

865. _____. "The 'Military Factor' in Soviet Policy." *International Affairs*, XXXIX (April 1963), 214–226.

866. _____. "Soviet Military Policy in the 1980s." *Current History*, LXXV (October 1978), 97–99.

867. _____. "Soviet Military Policy: Priorities and Perspectives." *Round Table*, no. 256 (October 1974), 369–379.

868. _____. "The Soviet Military, Soviet Policy, and Soviet Politics." *Strategic Review*, I (Fall 1973), 23–36.

869. "Five Keys to Soviet Strategy: A Special Report." *Air Force and Space Digest*, XLIV (October 1961), 29–32.

870. Galay, Nikolai. "Khrushchev's Military Doctrine." *Bulletin of the Institute for the Study of the History and Culture of the USSR*, IX (March 1962), 45–48.

871. _____. "New Trends in Soviet Military Doctrine." *Bulletin of the Institute for the Study of the History and Culture of the USSR*, III (June 1956), 3–12.

872. _____. "Problems of Atomic Warfare and the Soviet Armed Forces." *Bulletin of the Institute for the Study of the History and Culture of the USSR*, II (April 1955), 3–10.

873. Gallagher, Matthew P. "The Military Role in Soviet Decision-Making." In: Michael MccGwire, Ken Booth, and John McDonnell, eds. *Soviet Naval Policy, Objectives and Constraints*. New York: Praeger, 1975. pp. 40–58.

874. Garthoff, Raymond L. "Military Power in Soviet Policy." In: John Erickson, ed. *The Military-Technical Revolution*. New York: Praeger, 1966. pp. 239–258.

875. _____. "Significant Features of Soviet Military Doctrine." *Military Review*, XLIII (March 1955), 3–13.

876. _____. "Military Strategy and Soviet Policy." In: *Soviet Strategy in the Nuclear Age*. New York: Praeger, 1958. pp. 3–17.

877. _____. "Soviet Military Doctrine and the Decisive Factors in Modern War." *Military Review*, XXXIX (July 1959), 3–22.

878. _____. "Soviet Military Theory." *Military Review*, XLII (March 1962), 78–87.

879. _____. "Surprise and Blitzkrieg in Soviet Eyes." *RCAF Staff College Journal*, (1959), 16–29.

880. _____. "War and Peace in Soviet Policy." *Russian Review*, XX (April 1961), 121–133.

881. Gascogne, Alvary. "Russian Policy Since 1945." *Journal of the Royal United Service Institute*, C (February 1955), 24–35.

882. Gasteyger, Curt. "Modern Warfare and Soviet Strategy." *Survey*, no. 57 (October 1965), 46–55.

883. Gordon, Andrew. "Soviet Strategic Crisis Management." *Strategic Review*, III (Spring 1975), 30–40.

884. Gouré, Leon. "Soviet Military Doctrine." *Air Force Magazine*, LX (March 1977), 47–50.

885. Gray, Colin S. "Soviet Strategic Vulnerabilities." *Air Force Magazine*, LXII (March 1979), 60–64.

886. _____. "War and Peace: The Soviet View." *Air Force Magazine*, LIX (October 1976), 28–31.

887. Green, Murray. "Soviet Military Strategy." *Air Force*, XLVI (March 1963), 38–42.

888. Halperin, Morton. "Soviet Military Strategy." In: Morton Halperin, ed. *Contemporary Military Strategy*. Boston: Little, Brown, 1966. pp. 56–65.

889. _____. _____. In: *Defense Strategies for the Seventies*. Boston: Little, Brown, 1971. Chpt. 5.

890. Hinterhoff, Eugene. "The Evolution of Soviet Strategy and of the Armed Forces." *NATO's Fifteen Nations*, VII (June–July 1962), 110–113.

891. Holloway, David. "Foreign and Defense Policy." In: Archibald H. Brown and Michael Kaser, eds. *The Soviet Union Since the Fall of Khrushchev*. New York: Free Press, 1975. pp. 49–76.

892. _____. "Strategic Concepts and Soviet Policy." *Survival,* XIII (November 1971), 364–369.

893. Horelick, Arnold L. "Deterrence and Surprise Attack in Soviet Strategic Thought." *RCAF Staff College Journal,* (1960), 12–20.

894. _____. "Strategic Mind-Set of the Soviet Military." *Problems of Communism,* XXVI (March–April 1977), 80–85.

895. Jacobsen, Carl G. "Deterrence or War Fighting—The Soviet Case: Soviet Military Posture and Its Relevance to Soviet Concepts of Strategy." *Canadian-American Slavic Studies,* VIII (Spring 1975), 18–29.

896. Jonas, Anne M. "New Dimensions in Soviet Strategy." *Air Force and Space Digest,* LI (January 1968), 22–27.

897. Jukes, Geoffrey. "The Military Approach to Deterrence and Defense." In: Michael MccGwire, Ken Booth, and John McDonnell, eds. *Soviet Naval Policy, Objectives and Constraints.* New York: Praeger, 1975. pp. 479–485.

898. Kincade, W. H. "Strategy for All Seasons." *Bulletin of the Atomic Scientists,* XXXIV (May 1978), 14–20.

899. Kolkowicz, Roman. "Strategic Parity and Beyond: Soviet Perspectives." *World Politics,* XXIII (April 1971), 431–451.

900. "The Kremlin's Reliance on Blitzkrieg." *Far Eastern Economic Review,* XC (October 31, 1975), 33–34.

901. Laske, Robert M. "Soviet Strategic Thinking, 1917–1962: Some History Reexamined." *Naval War College Review,* XXIV (February 1972), 24–34.

902. LeCheminant, Pierre. "Soviet Military Doctrine: A Possible Pattern of War." In: James L. Moulton, ed. *Brassey's Annual.* New York: Macmillan, 1959. pp. 210–216.

903. Lee, William T. "Soviet Military Policy: Objectives and Capabilities." *Air Force Magazine,* LXII (March 1979), 54–59.

904. Lellouche, Pierre. "International Nuclear Politics." *Foreign Affairs,* LVIII (Winter 1979), 336–350.

905. Leontin, L. "The Soviet Concept of National Defense." *Military Review,* XXXIV (January 1955), 89–96.

906. Long, J. F. L. "Soviet Policy and the Role of the Military." *Royal Air Forces Quarterly,* IV (Winter 1964), 267–271.

The Soviet Economy and Defense Establishment 77

907.	McDonnell, John. "The Organization of Soviet Defense and Military Policy-Making." In: Michael MccGwire, and John McDonnell, eds. *Soviet Naval Influence, Domestic and Foreign Dimensions.* New York: Praeger, 1977. pp. 61–106.

908.	Mackintosh, Malcolm. "The Development of Soviet Military Doctrine Since 1918." In: Michael Howard, ed. *The Theory and Practice of War: Essays Presented to Capt. Basil H. Liddell-Hart on His Seventieth Birthday.* New York: Praeger, 1966. pp. 78–95.

909.	_____. "The East-West Military Balance and Soviet Defense Policy." In: James L. Moulton, ed. *Brassey's Annual.* New York: Praeger, 1972. pp. 37–49.

910.	_____. "Soviet Military Strategy." In: Michael MccGwire, ed. *Soviet Naval Developments, Capabilities and Context.* New York: Praeger, 1973. pp. 57–69.

911.	_____. "Soviet Strategy in World War III." *Army*, X (May 1960), 23–32.

912.	_____. "Soviet Thinking on War." In: J. M. Mackintosh, ed. *The Strategy and Tactics of Soviet Foreign Policy.* London and New York: Oxford University Press, 1963. pp. 299–315.

913.	Mahoney, Shane E. "Military Decisionmaking in the U.S.S.R.: The Empirical Past and the Conceptual Present." *Armed Forces and Society*, III (Winter 1977), 271–294.

914.	Malinovsky, Rodion Y. "Soviet Defense Policy." *Military Review*, XLVI (October 1966), 85–90.

915.	_____. "Soviet Strategy." *Survival*, IV (September–October 1962), 229–232.

916.	Martin, Robert P. "How Strong is Russia?" *U.S. News and World Report*, LXXXVIII (February 11, 1980), 17–21.

917.	Matsulenko, V. "Surprise: How It is Achieved and Its Role." *Soviet Military Review*, nos. 5–6 (May–June 1972), 37–39, 37–39.

918.	"Military Doctrine and Strategy." *Translations on U.S.S.R. Military Affairs*, no. 143 (June 1964), 14–24.

919.	Monks, Alfred L. "The Evolution of Soviet Military Thinking." *Military Review*, LI (March 1971), 78–93.

920. Mulley, Frederick W. "Soviet Strategy and Forces." In: Frederick W. Mulley, ed. *Politics of Defense.* New York: Praeger, 1962. pp. 32–49.

921. "On Soviet Military Doctrine." *Translations on USSR Military Affairs,* no. 99 (April 1962), 31–44.

922. Onacewicz, Wlodzimier. "Soviet Military Strategy in Brief." In: Robert D. Crane and Wlodzimier Onacewicz, eds. *Soviet Materials on Military Strategy.* Washington, D.C.: Center for Strategic Studies, Georgetown University, 1964. pp. 13–33.

923. Papp, Daniel S. "Toward an Estimate of the Soviet Worldview." *Naval War College Review,* XXXII (November–December 1979), 60–78.

924. Pappageorge, John G. "The Development of Soviet Military Policy." *Military Review,* LII (July 1972), 36–43.

925. Petersen, Philip A. "Flexibility: A Driving Force in Soviet Strategy." *Air Force Magazine,* LXIII (March 1980), 94–99.

926. Pioro, Tadeusz. "Soviet Military Doctrine." *Marine Corps Gazette,* XLVII (March 1963), 18.

927. Rummel, Rudolph J. "Detente and Reality." *Strategic Review,* IV (Fall 1976), 33–43.

928. Scott, William F. "Soviet Military Doctrine and Strategy: Realities and Misunderstandings." *Strategic Review,* III (Summer 1975), 57–66.

929. Shackleton, N. A. "Soviet Strategy in the Cold War: A Reappraisal." *Canadian Army Journal,* XVIII (Fall 1964), 2–15.

930. Shrader, Cecil L. "The New Blitzkrieg." *Armor,* LXXXI (September–October 1972), 12–16.

931. Sidorov, P. "Foundations of Soviet Military Doctrine." *Military Review,* LII (December 1972), 89–91.

932. Sokol, Anthony E. "The Soviets' War Potential." *Military Review,* XXXIII (December 1953), 44–60.

933. Sokolovskii, Vasilii D. "Current Military Strategy." *Survival,* VIII (August 1966), 266–270.

934. _____ and M. I. Cheredichenko. "The Military Revolution." *Survival,* VI (November–December 1964), 280–283.

935. Spahr, William J. "The Soviet Military Decisionmaking Process." *Parameters,* II (Summer 1972), 51–62.

936. Staar, Michael F. "Current Soviet Military Strategy." *Naval War College Review,* XVIII (January 1966), 1–23.

937. Strauz-Hupé, Robert. "The Protracted Conflict." *Air Force,* XLII (April 1959), 56–63.

938. _____. "Soviet Strategy, 1962–1970." In: David M. Abshire and Richard V. Allen, eds. *National Security.* New York: Praeger, 1963. pp. 3–19.

939. Van den Berk, L. J. M. "Strategic Concepts of the Russian High Command." *NATO's Fifteen Nations,* X (December 1965–January 1966), 58–60.

940. Vernon, Graham D. "Soviet Options for War: Nuclear or Conventional?" *Strategic Review,* VII (Winter 1979), 56–66.

941. Vigor, Peter H. "The Semantics of Deterrence and Defense." In: Michael McGwire, Ken Booth, and John McDonnell, eds. *Soviet Naval Policy, Objectives and Constraints.* New York: Praeger, 1975. pp. 471–478.

942. _____. "The Soviet View of War." In: Michael McGwire, ed. *Soviet Naval Developments, Capability and Context.* New York: Praeger, 1972. pp. 16–30.

943. _____ and John Erickson. "The Soviet View of the Theory and Strategy of War." *Journal of the Royal United Service Institution for Defence Studies,* CXV (June 1970), 3–13.

944. Whiting, Kenneth R. "The Past and Present of Soviet Military Doctrine." *Air University Quarterly Review,* XI (Spring 1959), 38–60.

945. _____. "Some Soviet Views of American Strategy." *Air University Quarterly Review,* XIV (Summer 1963), 114–130.

946. Wilson, William T. "The New Vitality in Soviet 'Defense' Posture: Variations to 'Standard' Soviet Military Strategy." *Air University Review,* XX (July–August 1969), 78–86.

947. Wolfe, Thomas W. "The Impact of Khrushchev's Downfall on Soviet Military Policy and Detente." In: Eleanor L. Dulles, ed. *Detente: Cold War Strategies in Transition.* New York: Praeger, 1965. pp. 280–303.

948. _____. "Military Policy: A Soviet Dilemma." *Current History,* XL (October 1965), 201–207.

949. _____. "Problems of Soviet Defense Policy Under the New Regime." *Slavic Review,* XXVII (June 1965), 175–188.

950. _____. "Shifts in Soviet Strategic Thought." *Foreign Affairs*, XLII (April 1964), 475–486.

951. _____. "Some New Developments in the Soviet Military Debate." *Orbis*, VIII (Fall 1964), 550–562.

952. _____. "Trends in Soviet Thinking on Theater Warfare and Limited War." In: John Erickson, ed. *The Military-Technical Revolution*. New York: Praeger, 1966. pp. 52–80.

953. Wolk, Herman S. "Debating Deterrence." *Air University Review*, XXX (July–August 1979), 80–81.

954. Yeuell, Donovan P. "The Shift in Soviet Strategy." *Military Review*, XLV (June 1965), 87–92.

Documents, Papers, and Reports

955. Atkeson, Edward B. *The Dimensions of Military Strategy*. Military Issues Research Memo. Carlisle Barracks, Pa.: Strategic Studies Institute, U.S. Army War College, 1977. 26p.

956. Collins, Edward M. "The Evolution of Soviet Strategy Under Khrushchev." Unpublished Ph.D. Dissertation, Georgetown University, 1966.

957. Goldhamer, Herbert. *Reality and Belief in Military Affairs: A First Draft*. RAND Report R-2448-Na. Santa Monica, Calif.: RAND Corporation, 1979. 196p.

958. Gouré, Leon. *Soviet Commentary on the Doctrine of Limited Nuclear War*. RAND Translation T-82. Santa Monica, Calif.: RAND Corporation, 1958.

959. Green, Murray. *Soviet Military Strategy Brought Up to Date*. Washington, D.C.: Headquarters, U.S. Air Force, 1963. 280p.

960. Institute for Strategic Studies. *Problems of Modern Strategy*. Adelphi papers, no. 54. 2 vols. London, 1969.

961. Jones, Isaac R. *Soviet Military Strategy*. Professional Paper. Maxwell AFB, Ala: Air War College, Air University, 1974. 51p.

962. Lambeth, Benjamin S. *How to Think About Soviet Military Doctrine*. RAND Paper P-5939. Santa Monica, Calif.: RAND Corporation, 1978. 22p.

963. Mackintosh, Malcolm. *Contemporary Soviet Military Doctrine*. Oxford, England: St. Anthony's College, 1959. 18p.

The Soviet Economy and Defense Establishment 81

964. Monks, Alfred L. "Soviet Military Doctrine, 1964 to Armed Forces Day, 1969." Unpublished Ph.D. Dissertation, University of Pennsylvania, 1969.

965. Rehm, Allan S. *An Assessment of Military Operations Research in the USSR.* Professional paper, no. 116. Arlington, Va.: Center for Naval Analysis, Office of Naval Research, U.S. Navy Department, 1973. 19p.

966. Scott, Harriet F. *The Soviet View of the Character and Features of Modern War.* Technical Note SSC-TN-8260-1. Stanford, Calif.: Stanford Research Institute, Stanford University, 1969.

967. _____ . *Soviet Military Doctrine: Its Formulation and Dissemination.* Stanford, Calif.: Stanford Research Institute, Stanford University, 1971.

968. Sonnenfeldt, Helmut and William G. Hyland. *Soviet Perspectives on Security.* Adelphi papers, no. 150. London: International Institute for Strategic Studies, 1979. 24p.

969. United States. Air Force. Air University. *Selected Soviet Writings on Military Power and Strategy.* Maxwell AFB, Ala.: Text Development Division, Air War College, Air University, 1976.

970. _____ . Congress. Senate. Committee on Government Operations. Subcommittee on National Policy Machinery. *National Policy Machinery in the Soviet Union: Report.* 85th Cong., 2nd sess. Washington, D.C.: U.S. Government Printing Office, 1960. 70p.

971. Wolfe, Thomas W. *The Impact of Khrushchev's Downfall on Soviet Military Policy.* RAND Paper P-3025. Santa Monica, Calif.: RAND Corporation, 1964. 38p.

972. _____ . *The Military Dimension in the Making of Soviet Foreign and Defense Policy.* RAND Paper P-6024. Santa Monica, Calif.: RAND Corporation, 1977. 44p.

973. _____ . *Military Power and Soviet Policy.* RAND Paper P-5388. Santa Monica, Calif.: RAND Corporation, 1975. 82p.

974. _____ . *Problems of Soviet Defense Policy Under the New Regime.* RAND Paper P-3098. Santa Monica, Calif.: RAND Corporation, 1965. 27p.

975. _____ . *Soviet Military Policy Trends Under the Brezhnev–Kosygin Regime.* RAND Paper P-3556. Santa Monica, Calif.: RAND Corporation, 1967. 29p.

976. _____. *Soviet Military Policy Under Khrushchev's Successors.* RAND Paper P-3168. Santa Monica, Calif.: RAND Corporation, 1965. 34p.

977. _____. *The Soviet Military Scene: Institutional and Defense Policy Considerations.* RAND Memorandum RM-4913-PR. Santa Monica, Calif.: RAND Corporation, 1966. 180p.

978. _____. *Soviet Military Theory: An Additional Source of Insight Into Its Development.* RAND Paper P-3258. Santa Monica, Calif.: RAND Corporation, 1965. 54p.

979. _____. *Soviet Policy in the Setting of a Changing Power Balance.* RAND Paper P-4055. Santa Monica, Calif.: RAND Corporation, 1969. 36p.

980. _____. *Soviet Strategic Thought in Transition.* RAND Paper P-2906. Santa Monica, Calif.: RAND Corporation, 1964. 21p.

981. _____. *Soviet Strategy at the Crossroads.* RAND Memorandum RM-4085-PR. Santa Monica, Calif.: RAND Corporation, 1964. 338p.

982. _____. *Trends in Soviet Thinking on Theater Warfare, Conventional Operations, and Limited War.* RAND Memorandum RM-4305-PR. Santa Monica, Calif.: RAND Corporation, 1964. 105p.

B. The Soviet Economy and the Military

1. Defense Expenditures

Books

983. Holzmann, Franklyn D. *Financial Checks on Soviet Defense Expenditures.* Boston: D. C. Heath, 1975. 103p.

984. Lee, William T. *Estimation of Soviet Defense Expenditures, 1955–1975: An Unconventional Approach.* New York: Published in Cooperation with the General Electric TEMPO Center for Advanced Studies by Praeger, 1977. 358p.

984a. Menken, Jules. *The Economics of Defence.* London: Ampersand, 1955. 100p.

Articles

985. Bartenev, S. "The Economic Base of Defense Potential." *Soviet Military Review,* no. 8 (August 1973), 2–5.

986. Becker, Abraham S. "The Meaning and Measure of Soviet Military Expenditure." In: U.S. Congress. Joint Economic Committee. *Soviet Economy in a Time of Change: A Compendium of Papers.* 96th Cong., 1st sess. 2 vols. Washington, D.C.: U.S. Government Printing Office, 1979. I, 352–368.

987. Brownlow, Cecil. "Soviet Military Spending Stressed." *Aviation Week and Space Technology,* XCVI (February 21, 1972), 14–16.

988. Foster, John S., Jr. "The U.S.S.R. is Headed Toward Technological Superiority." *Air Force Magazine,* LIV (August 1971), 28–35.

989. Galay, Nikolai. "The Burden of Soviet Military Expenditure." *Bulletin of the Institute for the Study of the History and Culture of the USSR,* VIII (March 1961), 29–34.

990. Gallik, Daniel. "The Military Burden and Arms Control." In: Holland Hunter, ed. *The Future of the Soviet Economy, 1978–1985.* Boulder, Colo.: Westview, 1978. Chpt. 4.

991. Graham, Daniel O. "The Soviet Military Budget Controversy." *Air Force Magazine,* LIX (May 1976), 33–37.

992. Hansen, Philip. "Analysis of Soviet Defense Expenditures." In: Michael MccGwire, Ken Booth, and John McDonnell, eds. *Soviet Naval Policy, Objectives and Constraints.* New York: Praeger, 1975. pp. 123–126.

993. Hardt, John P. "Soviet Economic Capabilities and Defense Resources." In: Grayson Kirk and Nils H. Wessell, eds. *The Soviet Threat: Myths and Realities.* New York: Praeger, 1978. pp. 122–134.

994. International Institute for Strategic Studies. "Comparative Defense Expenditure, Gross National Product, and Manpower Figures, 1952–1972." *Air Force Magazine,* LVI (December 1973), 120–121.

995. Krylov, Konstantin K. "The Soviet Military-Economic Establishment." *Military Review,* LI (November 1971), 89–97.

996. Lee, William T. "Military Economics in the U.S.S.R." *Air Force Magazine,* LIX (March 1976), 48–51.

997. _____. "Soviet Defense Spending: Planned Growth, 1976–1980." *Strategic Review,* V (Winter 1977), 74–79.

998. _____. "Trends in Soviet Military Spending." *Air Force Magazine,* LX (March 1977), 84–87.

999. Leggett, Robert E. and Sheldon T. Rabin. "A Note on the Meaning of the Soviet Defense Budget." *Soviet Studies,* XXX (October 1978), 561.

1000. Schaefer, Henry W. "Soviet Power and Intentions: Military-Economic Choices." In: U.S. Congress. Joint Economic Committee. *Soviet Economy in a Time of Change: A Compendium of Papers.* 96th Cong., 1st sess. 2 vols. Washington, D.C.: U.S. Government Printing Office, 1979. I, 341–351.

1001. "Soviet Defense Expenditures." *Air Force Magazine,* LIX (December 1976), 49–50.

1002. "Soviet Defense Spending Continues to Exceed U.S." *Aviation Week and Space Technology,* CVIII (January 23, 1978), 15–16.

1003. "Soviet Military Spending Found to Top U.S." *Aviation Week and Space Technology,* CXI (October 27, 1979), 67.

Documents, Papers, and Reports

1004. Alexander, Arthur J., Abraham S. Becker, and William E. Hoehn, Jr. *The Significance of Divergent U.S.-U.S.S.R. Military Expenditure.* RAND Note RN-1000-AF. Santa Monica, Calif.: RAND Corporation, 1979. 57p.

1005. Kershaw, J. A. *The Economic War Potential of the U.S.S.R.* RAND Paper P-182. Santa Monica, Calif.: RAND Corporation, 1950. 12p.

1006. United States. Arms Control and Disarmament Agency. *World Military Expenditures and Arms Trade, 1963–1973.* Publication, no. 74. Washington, D.C.: U.S. Government Printing Office, 1975. 123p.

1007. _____. Central Intelligence Agency. National Foreign Assessment Center. *A Dollar Cost Comparison of Soviet and U.S. Defense Activities, 1965–1975.* SR-76-10001. Washington, D.C.: Document Expediting Project, Exchange and Gift Division, Library of Congress, 1976. 8p.

1008. _____. _____. _____. *A Dollar Cost Comparison of Soviet and U.S. Defense Activities, 1966–1976.* SR-77-1000U. Washington, D.C.: Document Expediting Project, Exchange and Gift Division, Library of Congress, 1977. 15p.

1009. _____. _____. _____. *A Dollar Cost Comparison of Soviet and U.S. Defense Activities, 1967–1977.* SR-78-10002. Washington, D.C.: Document Expediting Project, Exchange and Gift Division, Library of Congress, 1978. 15p.

1010. _____ . _____ . _____ . *A Dollar Cost Comparison of Soviet and U.S. Defense Activities, 1968–1978*. SR-79-10004. Washington, D.C.: Document Expediting Project, Exchange and Gift Division, Library of Congress, 1979. 15p.

1011. _____ . _____ . _____ . *Estimated Soviet Defense Spending in Rubles, 1970–1975*. Washington, D.C.: Document Expediting Project, Exchange and Gift Division, Library of Congress, 1976. 17p.

1012. _____ . _____ . _____ . *Estimated Soviet Defense Spending: Trends and Prospects*. SR-78-10121. Washington, D.C.: Document Expediting Project, Exchange and Gift Division, Library of Congress, 1978. 14p.

1013. _____ . _____ . _____ . *The Soviet State Budget Since 1965*. A Research Paper. ER-77-10529. Washington, D.C.: Document Expediting Project, Exchange and Gift Division, Library of Congress, 1977. 40p.

1014. _____ . Congress. Joint Economic Committee. *Economic Basis of the Russian Military Challenge to the United States: Hearings*. 91st Cong., 1st sess. Washington, D.C.: U.S. Government Printing Office, 1969. 55p.

1015. _____ . _____ . _____ . *Economic Performance and the Military Burden in the Soviet Union: Hearings*. 91st Cong., 2nd sess. Washington, D.C.: U.S. Government Printing Office, 1970.

1016. _____ . _____ . _____ . *The Soviet Economy in a New Perspective: A Compendium of Papers*. 94th Cong., 2nd sess. Washington, D.C.: U.S. Government Printing Office, 1976. 821p.

1017. _____ . _____ . _____ . Subcommittee on Economic Statistics. *Comparisons of the United States and Soviet Economies: Supplemental Statements on the Costs and Benefits to the Soviet Union of Its Bloc and Pact System, Prepared by the Central Intelligence Agency*. 81st Cong., 2nd sess. Washington, D.C.: U.S. Government Printing Office, 1960. 50p.

1018. _____ . _____ . _____ . Subcommittee on Priorities and Economy in Government. *Allocation of Resources in the Soviet Union and China, 1977: Hearings*. 95th Cong., 1st sess. 4 pts. Washington, D.C.: U.S. Government Printing Office, 1977.

1019. _____ . _____ . _____ . _____ . *Allocation of Resources in the Soviet Union and China, 1978: Hearings*. 95th Cong., 2nd sess. 4 pts. Washington, D.C.: U.S. Government Printing Office, 1978.

2. Weapons Procurement

a. GENERAL STUDIES

Books

1020.　Baker, David. *Rocket: The History and Development of Rocket and Missile Technology.* New York: Crown, 1978. 276p.

1021.　Basiuk, Victor. *Technology and World Power.* Headline Series, no. 200. New York: Foreign Policy Association, 1970. 63p.

1022.　Langford, David. *War in 2080: The Future of Military Technology.* New York: Morrow, 1979. 232p.

1023.　Lomov, N. A., ed. *Scientific-Technical Progress and the Revolution in Military Affairs: A Soviet View.* Translated from the Russian. Soviet Military Thought Series, no. 3. Washington, D.C.: Published under the auspices of the U.S. Air Force by the U.S. Government Printing Office, 1974. 279p.

1024.　Miller, Ronald and David Sawers. *The Technical Development of Modern Aviation.* New York: Praeger, 1970. 351p.

1025.　Sutton, Anthony C. *Western Technology and Soviet Economic Development, 1917–1965.* 3 vols. Stanford, Calif.: Stanford University Press, 1968–1973.

Articles

1026.　Anureyev, I. "Scientific Progress and Defensive Potential." *Soviet Military Review,* no. 2 (February 1976), 13–15.

1027.　Butz, J. S. "Soviet Union Decentralizes Weapon System Authority." *Aviation Week and Space Technology,* LXIX (November 17–24, 1958), 50–58, 91–104.

1028.　Cane, J. W. "The Technology of Modern Weapons for Limited Military Use." *Orbis,* XXII (Spring 1978), 217–266.

1029.　Deane, Michael J. and Mark E. Miller. "Science and Technology in Soviet Military Planning." *Strategic Review,* V (Summer 1977), 77–86.

1030.　DeVore, Charles. "Trends in Soviet Military Technology." *Signal,* XXX (July 1976), 47–50.

1031.　DeWitt, N. "Soviet Research and Science Reorganized." *Aviation Week and Space Technology,* LXXV (September 11, 1961), 50–73.

1032. Herold, Robert C. and Shane E. Mahoney. "Military Hardware Procurement: Some Comparative Observations on Soviet and American Policy Processes." *Comparative Politics*, VI (July 1974), 571–599.

1033. Hollist, W. L. "Analysis of Arms Processes in the United States and Soviet Union." *International Studies Quarterly*, XXI (September 1977), 503–528.

1034. Holloway, David. "Technological Change and Military Procurement." In: Michael MccGwire and John McDonnell, eds. *Soviet Naval Influence, Domestic and Foreign Dimensions*. New York: Praeger, 1977. pp. 123–132.

1035. ———. "Technology and Political Decision in Soviet Armaments Policy." *Journal of Peace Research*, XI (Fall 1974), 257–279.

1036. Jahn, Egbert. "The Role of the Armaments Complex in Soviet Society." *Journal of Peace Research*, XII (Fall 1975), 179–194.

1037. Konoplyov, Vasilii. "Military Practice and Scientific Foresight." *Soviet Military Review*, no. 5 (May 1974), 5–7.

1038. Krylov, Konstantin K. "Soviet Armaments Project Organization." *Military Review*, LIII (July 1973), 45–50.

1039. Lomov, N. A. "Scientific-Technical Progress and the Revolution in Military Affairs." *Military Review*, LIV (July 1974), 33–39.

1040. "Moscow's Military Machine: The Best of Everything." *Time*, XCV (May 4, 1970), 36–40.

1041. Ralph, John E. "Tactical Air Systems and the New Technologies." In: Geoffrey Kemp et al. *The Other Arms Race*. Lexington, Mass.: D. C. Heath, 1975. pp. 15–33.

1042. Robinson, Clarence A., Jr. "Soviets Press Technology Gains." *Aviation Week and Space Technology*, CIV (February 9, 1976), 12–15.

1043. Schuster, Edward J. "The Impact of Science and Technology on War." *Social Justice Review*, LVIII (January 1966), 360–364.

1044. "Soviets Press Technical Modernization of Military Services." *Aviation Week and Space Technology*, LXXVIII (March 11, 1963), 92–95.

1045. Ulsamer, Edgar. "Russia's Drive for Technical Productivity." *Air Force Magazine*, LVIII (August 1975), 68–69.

1046. ———. "Soviet Objective: Technological Supremacy." *Air Force Magazine*, LVII (June 1974), 22–27.

1047. _____. "Technological Initiative: A Priceless Asset." *Air Force Magazine,* LVIII (June 1975), 26–31.

1048. _____. "The U.S.S.R. Lifts the Technological Curtain." *Air Force Magazine,* LVI (August 1973), 24–29.

1049. Vorona, Jack. "The Soviet March Toward Technological Superiority." *Defense 80,* no. 3 (March 1980), 1–12.

1050. Warner, Edward L., 3rd. "The Bureaucratic Politics of Weapons Procurement." In: Michael MccGwire, Ken Booth, and John McDonnell, eds. *Soviet Naval Policy, Objectives and Constraints.* New York: Praeger, 1975. pp. 66–86.

Documents, Papers, and Reports

1051. Albritton, Britt L. "Weapons Development as Catalyst in Elite Transformation: The Case of the Soviet Military." Unpublished Ph.D. Dissertation, University of Maryland, 1974.

1052. Alexander, Arthur J. *The Process of Soviet Weapons Design.* RAND Paper P-6137. Santa Monica, Calif.: RAND Corporation, 1978. 37p.

1053. _____. *Weapons Acquisition in the Soviet Union, United States, and France.* RAND Paper P-4989. Santa Monica, Calif.: RAND Corporation, 1973. 33p.

1054. Holloway, David. *Technology, Management, and the Soviet Military Establishment.* Adelphi papers, no. 76. London: International Institute for Strategic Studies, 1971. 44p.

1055. Kassel, Simon. *The Relationship Between Science and the Military in the Soviet Union.* RAND Report R-1457. Santa Monica, Calif.: RAND Corporation, 1974. 46p.

1056. Kolkowicz, Roman. *The Impact of Technology on the Soviet Military: A Challenge to Traditional Military Professionalism.* RAND Memorandum RM-4198-PR. Santa Monica, Calif.: RAND Corporation, 1964.

1057. United States. Central Intelligence Agency. National Foreign Assessment Center. *Directory of Soviet Research Organizations.* A Reference Aid. Washington, D.C.: Document Expediting Project, Exchange and Gift Division, Library of Congress, 1978. 290p.

The Soviet Economy and Defense Establishment 89

b. The Aircraft and Missile Industry

Books

1058. *The Soviet Aircraft Industry.* Soviet Planning Study, no. 4. Chapel Hill: Institute for Research in Social Science, University of North Carolina, 1955. 228p.

1059. Zaehringer, Alfred J. *Soviet Space Technology.* New York: Harper & Row, 1961. 179p.

Articles

1060. Alexeyev, N. "Scientific and Technological Progress and the Armed Forces." *Soviet Military Review,* no. 2 (February 1979), 2–7.

1061. Anderton, David A. "Producing Soviet Fighters the Easy Way." *Aviation Week and Space Technology,* LXIV (April 2, 1956), 50–51.

1062. Astashenkov, P. "Work of Ilyushin Aircraft Design Bureau Described: Translated from *Aviatsiya I Kosmonavtika,* March 1979." *Translations on USSR Military Affairs,* no. 1442 (May 25, 1979), 22–27.

1063. Bird, H. "Technical Developments in the Soviet Air Force." *RCAF Staff College Journal,* (1962), 72–79.

1064. "Capability and Location of Soviet Aircraft Plants." *Aviation Age,* XVII (March 1952), 6–17.

1065. Chaney, Otto P., Jr. and John T. Greenwood. "Patterns in the Soviet Aircraft Industry." In: Robin Higham and Jacob W. Kipp, eds. *Soviet Aviation and Air Power: A Historical View.* Boulder, Colo.: Westview, 1977. pp. 265–288.

1066. "Europe's Major Military Aircraft Programmes." *Interavia,* XXX (May 1975), 478–481.

1067. Glushko, Valentin. "Rocket Engines in the U.S.S.R." *Spaceflight,* VI (March 1974), 115–116.

1068. Green, William. "Czechs Build Jets for Russia." *Flying,* XLVIII (February 1951), 16–17, 45.

1069. ———. "Mikoyan Quarter Century." *Flying Review International,* XXI (November 1965), 155.

1070. ———. "Red Russia's Remarkable Aircraft Industry." *Air Trails,* XL (June 1963), 24–25.

1071. _____. "The Development of Jet Fighter-Bombers." In: Asher Lee, ed. *Soviet Air and Rocket Forces*. New York: Praeger, 1959. pp. 130–146.

1072. _____. "The Soviet Aircraft Industry." *Ordnance*, XXXVII (November–December 1952), 429–433.

1073. _____. "Tupolev's Early Jet Designs." *Flying Review International*, XXV (April 1969), 58–61.

1074. Head, Robert G. "Technology and the Military Balance: U.S. and Soviet R & D Systems." *Foreign Affairs*, LVI (April 1978), 544–563; LVII (Fall 1978), 207–213.

1075. Hotz, Robert. "Soviets Test IRBM, Mach-2 Fighters, Operate Jet Transports." *Aviation Week and Space Technology*, LXVI (February 25, 1957), 288–292.

1076. "How the Russians Stormed the Sonic Barrier." *Aviation Week and Space Technology*, LXIII (September 12, 1955), 21–22.

1077. "Kuibysher: Soviet Aircraft Center." *American Aviation*, XVIII (Janaury 17, 1955), 27–28.

1078. McDonnell, John A. "Defense Industry." In: David R. Jones, ed. *Soviet Armed Forces Review Annual, 1977*. Gulf Breeze, Fla.: Academic International Press, 1978. pp. 94–99.

1079. _____. "The Soviet Defense Industry as a Pressure Group." In: Michael MccGwire, Ken Booth, and John McDonnell, eds. *Soviet Naval Policy, Objectives and Constraints*. New York: Praeger, 1975. pp. 87–122.

1080. Mikoyan, Artom I. "Mikoyan Analyzes Russian Design Trends: Translation of a Russian Article." *Aviation Week and Space Technology*, LXI (September 20, 1954), 30–32.

1081. "Military Production in the U.S.S.R." *NATO's Fifteen Nations*, XXI (June–July 1976), 46–47.

1082. "Outline of the Organization and Production of the Russian Aircraft Industry." *Interavia*, X (May 1955), 324–330.

1083. Petrovich, G. V. "The Development of Soviet Rocket Engines." *Soviet Review*, III (November 1962), 53–61.

1084. Porter, Richard W. "Red Rocket Know-how Matches Ours." *Nation's Business*, XLIII (February 1955), 34–35, 78–79.

1085. "Red Round-up: A Synthesis of the Postwar Development of Russian Aircraft Design." *Flight*, LXX (August 3, 1956), 185–188.

The Soviet Economy and Defense Establishment 91

1086. "Revolution in the Development of Aircraft." *Translations on USSR Military Affairs*, no. 146 (June 1964), 16–20.

1087. Ritchie, Donald J. "Soviet Rockets Exploit German Technology." *Missiles and Rockets*, V (December 7, 1959), 17–19.

1088. Rizika, J. Wilford. "The Development of the Aircraft Industry in the Union of Soviet Socialist Republics." *Journal of the Royal Aeronautical Society*, LIX (March 1955), 209–219.

1089. "Russian Plane Builders Stress Functionalism." *American Aviation*, XX (October 22, 1956), 151–152.

1090. Shtoda, A. "Aircraft Engine Development." *Soviet Military Review*, no. 5 (May 1974), 28–29.

1091. Simpson, John. "The Military Aircraft Procurement Process in the USSR." In: Royal United Service Institution for Defence Studies at Southampton University. *The Soviet Union in Europe and the New East: A Report of a Seminar*. London, 1970. Chpt. 11.

1092. "Soviet Design Bureau Chiefs Meet." *Aviation Week and Space Technology*, CXI (July 2, 1979), 63.

1093. "Soviets May be Shifting Design Emphasis." *Aviation Week and Space Technology*, LXXXIX (August 5, 1968), 32–33.

1094. Spielmann, Karl F. "Defense Industrialists in the U.S.S.R." In: Dale R. Herspring and Ivan Volgyes, eds. *Civil-Military Relations in the Communist System*. Boulder, Colo.: Westview, 1978. Chpt. 5.

1095. Stockwell, Richard E. "The German Legacy." In: Asher Lee, ed. *The Soviet Air and Rocket Forces*. New York: Praeger, 1959. pp. 229–241.

1096. ———. "Soviet Aircraft Production." In: Asher Lee, ed. *The Soviet Air and Rocket Forces*. New York: Praeger, 1959. pp. 241–256.

1097. Taylor, John W. R. "An Industry to Envy." *NATO's Fifteen Nations*, XIV (April–May 1969), 42–45.

1098. ———. "Made in Russia." *Royal Air Forces Quarterly*, III (Winter 1963), 257–265.

1099. Trilling, Leon. "Soviet Aeronautical Scientists: How They Work and Where They Publish." *Aerospace Engineering*, XX (July 1961), 12–13.

1100. Ulsamer, Edgar. "Soviet Engine Technology." *Air Force Magazine*, LVI (September 1973), 12–19.

1101.   Vandyk, Anthony. "Bomber Output Gets Top Russian Priority." *American Aviation,* XVII (August 1953), 13–15.

1102.   Voadan, Denys J. "Aeronautical Research in the U.S.S.R." *Aeronautics,* XL (May 1959), 33.

Documents, Papers, and Reports

1103.   Alexander, Arthur J. *R & D in Soviet Aviation.* RAND Report R-589-PR. Santa Monica, Calif.: RAND Corporation, 1970. 48p.

1104.   *The Design and Testing of Ballistic Missiles.* Translation, no. 51810. Arlington, Va.: Joint Publications Research Service, 1970. 409p.

1105.   Hrubiak, H. *Soviet Launch-Vehicle Tests in the Pacific Ocean [1960–1965]: A Comprehensive Report.* Washington, D.C.: Aerospace Technology Division, Library of Congress, 1965. 36p.

1106.   Yakovlev, Aleksandr S. *New Achievements in Soviet Aviation Designs: Translated from Krasnaya Zvezda, April 17, 1964.* Translation, no. 24731. Arlington, Va.: Joint Publications Research Service, 1964. 4p.

c. Air/Missile Shows and Displays

Articles

1107.   "Algerian MIG-25 Flyby." *Aviation Week and Space Technology,* CXI (November 12, 1979), 24.

1108.   Brownlow, Cecil. "Russian Air Show." *Aviation Week and Space Technology,* LXXXVII (July 17, 1967), 26–39.

1109.   _____. "Tushino Stresses U.S.S.R. Aircraft Priority." *Aviation Week and Space Technology,* LXXV (July 17, 1961), 31–34.

1110.   Cain, Charles W. "Soviet Aviation Day." *Aircraft,* XXXIV (August 1956), 22–28.

1111.   Coleman, Herbert J. "Moscow Parade Features Solid, Liquid-Fueled ICBMs and New Battlefield-Class Missiles." *Aviation Week and Space Technology,* LXXXII (May 17, 1965), 28–31.

1112.   Coughlin, William. "Russians Will Show Off More Aircraft." *Aviation Week and Space Technology,* LXII (June 13, 1955), 15–16.

1113.   "Curtain Up [Soviet Aviation Day]." *RAF Flying Review,* X (June 1955), 25–26.

1114.   "Eye-Popping Show of Red Airpower." *Life,* LI (July 21, 1961), 40–41.

1115. Galay, Nikolai. "Air Force Day [1954]." *Bulletin of the Institute for the Study of the History and Culture of the USSR,* I (June 1954), 19–22.

1116. ——— . "Air Force Day [1955]." *Bulletin of the Institute for the Study of the History and Culture of the USSR,* II (July 1955), 39–44.

1117. Gunston, William T. "Russian Revelation." *Flight,* LXXX (July 27, 1961), 109–112.

1118. Hotz, Robert. "An-22, SST Model Climax Soviet Display." *Aviation Week and Space Technology,* LXXXII (June 21, 1965), 28–31.

1119. "Moscow Air Show." *Military Review,* XLVII (October 1967), 106–107.

1120. "New Air-to-Surface, Air-to-Air Missile Types are Identified on Soviet Bombers and Fighters at Tushino." *Aviation Week and Space Technology,* LXXV (July 24, 1961), 26–31.

1121. "New Soviet Missiles on Parade." *Flight International,* LXXXVII (May 20, 1965), 794–795.

1122. "Red Square Parade." *Flight International,* LXXXIII (January 17, 1963), 98–101.

1123. "Russia Shows Off New Aircraft." *Aviation Week and Space Technology,* LXV (July 9, 1956), 30–32.

1124. "Soviet Aviation Day, 1949: And What It Means." *Interavia,* IV (October 1949), 594–597.

1125. "Soviet Jet Review." *Flight,* LXVII (February 4, 1955), 142–143.

1126. "Soviet May Day Review Reveals Shaddock, Galosh, Scud Details." *Aviation Week and Space Technology,* LXXXIV (May 16, 1966), 30–31.

1127. "Soviets Display Five New Missiles in Red Square Anniversary Parade." *Missiles and Rockets,* XV (November 16, 1964), 16–18.

1128. "Soviets Display Missile Arsenal in Moscow." *Aviation Week and Space Technology,* LXXVIII (May 20, 1963), 52–57.

1129. "Soviets Display Tactical and Anti-Aircraft Missiles." *Aviation Week and Space Technology,* LXXVI (January 1, 1962), 60–61.

1130. "Soviets Parade New Supersonic Bombers, Mach-2 Fighters, Jet Seaplanes, VTOL Aircraft at Tushino." *Aviation Week and Space Technology,* LXXV (July 17, 1961), 26–30.

94   *The Soviet Economy and the Military*

1131.   "Those New Russian Planes [Shown at Tushino]: Just How New are They?" *U.S. News and World Report,* LI (July 24, 1961), 38–39.

1132.   "Whoosh, Tushino Air Show." *Time,* LXXVIII (July 21, 1961), 19.

d. Famous Designers

(1) General Studies

1133.   Cain, Charles W. "The Men Behind the Red Air Force." *Flying,* XLV (November 1949), 13–16.

1134.   Novikov, M. "Russian Rocket Designers." *Soviet Military Review,* no. 3 (March 1966), 34–35.

1135.   "Russia's Top Aircraft Designers." *Time,* LVIII (August 20, 1951), 24.

(2) Specific Individuals

Oleg K. Antonov

1136.   Antonov, Oleg K. "I Design for Russia." *RAF Flying Review,* XII (November 1956), 17–18.

1137.   _____. "Interview." *Aviation Week and Space Technology,* CXI (July 2, 1979), 9.

Mikhail S. Arlazorov

1138.   Arlazorov, Mikhail. *Man on Wings.* Translation, no. 1423-N. Arlington, Va.: Joint Publication Research Service, 1959. 56p.

Mikhail I. Gurevich

1139.   Gurevich, Mikhail I. "I Designed the MIG-15" *Aero Digest,* LXIII (July 1951), 17–19.

1140.   "Mikhail I. Gurevich." *Newsweek,* LXXXVIII (December 6, 1976), 49.

Sergei V. Ilyushin

1141.   Rebrov, M. "Outstanding Aircraft Designer." *Soviet Military Review,* no. 3 (March 1969), 48–51.

1142.   "Sergei V. Ilyushin." *New York Times Biographical Service,* VIII (February 1977), 257–258.

1143.   _____. *Newsweek,* LXXXIX (February 21, 1977), 44.

1144.   _____. *Time,* CIX (February 21, 1977), 76.

The Soviet Economy and Defense Establishment 95

Artom I. Mikoyan

1145. Lebedev, V. "The MIG Designer." *Soviet Military Review,* no. 8 (August 1975), 36–37.

1146. "People of the Week: Artom I. Mikoyan." *U.S. News and World Report,* XXXVII (July 2, 1954), 16.

1147. "Russian Designer." *Aviation Age,* XVI (July 1951), 6–18, 23–26.

Pavel Sukhoi

1148. Rebrov, M. "A Dream Come True." *Soviet Military Review,* no. 7 (July 1975), 28–29.

Andrei N. Tupolev

1149. "Andrei Nikolaevich Tupolev." In: *Current Biography Yearbook.* New York: H. W. Wilson, 1958. pp. 560–562.

1150. "Dean of the Red Bombers: Andrei Tupolev." *Wings,* II (February 1972).

1151. Gladych, Michael. "Andrei Tupolev, Soviet Airpower's Rugged Individualist." *Air Force,* XLI (July 1958), 40–42.

1152. Gunston, William T. "Tupolev." *Flying,* CI (September 1977), 272.

1153. Hotz, Robert. "Memories of Andrei Tupolev." *Aviation Week and Space Technology,* XCVIII (January 8, 1973), 9.

1154. "People of the Week: Andrei N. Tupolev." *U.S. News and World Report,* XXXVI (May 14, 1954), 14.

1155. Volkov, L. "Tupolev, Red Bomber Designer, a Traitor and a Hero." *Newsweek,* XLIV (August 23, 1954), 32–33.

Aleksandr S. Yakovlev

1156. Yakovlev, Aleksandr S. *The Aim of a Lifetime.* Moscow: Progress Publishers, 1972.

1157. _____. *Fifty Years of Soviet Aircraft Construction.* Translated from the Russian. Jerusalem: Published for NASA and the NSF by the Israeli Program for Scientific Translation, 1970.

1158. _____. "Interview: Translated from *Voyenno-Istoricheskiy Zhurnal,* August 1978." *Translations on USSR Military Affairs,* no. 1392 (November 2, 1978), 5–14.

4 / Soviet Aerospace Forces, 1946 to the Present

Introduction

THE SOVIET AIR FORCE (Voyenno-Vozdushnyye Sily–VVS), Air Defense Force (Voyska Protivovozdushnoy Oborony Strany–PVO-Strany), and Strategic Rocket Force (Raketnyye Strategicheskogo Naznacheniye–SRF) comprise three of the five components of the Russian armed forces. Each is led by a Deputy Soviet Defense Minister, who is responsible for organization, manning, training, and logistics. Operational control of these aerospace units varies from the Minister of Defense down to the commanders of districts, groups of forces, or army divisions.

The Soviet Air Force is comprised of three distinct components, each with a separate mission. Long Range Aviation is a heavy- and medium-bomber force which forms, together with the SRF and Soviet Navy's missile submarines, the Russian strategic capability. Front or Tactical Aviation, the largest VVS component, is made up of fighter, fighter-bomber, light bomber, and helicopter units which are designed to provide counterair, interdiction, ground attack, and air mobile support of the Russian Army. Military Transport Aviation with its heavy- and light-aircraft and helicopters is charged with providing airlift support to all elements of the armed forces. The relationship of the VVS to the Ministry of Defense can be seen in Chart III while the Air Force High Command is noted in Chart IV.

All means of air defense of Soviet and Warsaw Pact territory—early warning networks, interceptor aircraft, surface-to-air missiles—are combined in a single, self-contained system under the centralized control of PVO-Strany. The territory to be defended is divided into sixteen air defense districts, including ten in Russia. The operational branches of PVO-Strany are fighter aviation, the antiaircraft rocket troops, and the radiotechnical troops. Although defensively oriented, the first two branches lend themselves to offensive action if called upon. In addition, the Soviet Army is equipped with antiaircraft missile and artillery capability. The composition of the PVO-Strany High Command can be viewed in Chart V while this force's territorial organization is outlined in Chart VI.

The SRF constitutes the main strategic force of the Soviet Union although the youngest service is given first rank among supposed equals. The ICBMs, MRBMs, and IRBMs of this force are organized on the basis of army, division, regiment, and battery with the former deployed in silos along the Trans-Siberian Railroad and the latter two located mainly in the Baltic States and western/southwestern USSR. The Soviet Army, in addition, deploys a large number of short-range battlefield tactical missiles. SRF personnel are well trained and the force is maintained in a continuous state of combat readiness. Organization of Headquarters, Strategic Rocket Forces, is presented in Chart VII.

The references in this section are designed to provide information on the Soviet aerospace forces. A few additional titles relative to this section may be found in Sections 2 and 3.

A. General Studies

Books

1159. Berman, Robert P. *Soviet Air Power in Transition.* Studies in Defense Policy. Washington, D.C.: The Brookings Institution, 1978. 82p.

1160. Erickson, John. *Soviet Military Power.* London: Royal United Service Institution for Defence Studies, 1971. 117p.

1161. _____ and E. J. Feuchtwanger, eds. *Soviet Military Power and Performance.* Hamden, Conn.: Shoe String Press, 1979. 219p.

1162. Feuchtwanger, E. J. and R. A. Mason. *Air Power in the Next Generation.* New York: Simon and Schuster, 1979.

1163. Green, William and D. I. Punnett. *Macdonald World Airpower Guide.* Garden City, N.Y.: Doubleday, 1964. 72p.

1164. Lee, Asher, ed. *The Soviet Air and Rocket Forces.* New York: Praeger, 1959. 311p.

1165. Petersen, Phillip A. *Soviet Air Power and the Pursuit of New Military Options.* Studies in Communist Affairs, no. 3. Washington, D.C.: Published under the auspices of the U.S. Air Force by the U.S. Government Printing Office, 1979. 71p.

1166. Taylor, John W. R. and Kenneth G. Munson. *History of Aviation.* New York: Crown, 1976. 511p.

Articles

1167. Anderton, David A. "Airpower Behind the Iron Curtain." *Aviation Week and Space Technology,* LX (February 15, 1954), 12–13.

1168. "Battlefield of the 1990s: It's Not Sci-Fi, It's Real." *U.S. News and World Report,* LXXXIII (July 4, 1977), 48–50.

1169. Brewster, Owen. "Soviet Air Power: An Address to the American Legion's First National Aeronautics Conference, March 21, 1947." *Congressional Record,* XCIII (April 10, 1947), A1519–A1600.

1170. Cohen, Samuel T. "A Comparison of U.S.–Allied and Soviet Tactical Nuclear Force Capabilities and Policies." *Orbis,* XIX (Spring 1975), 72–92.

1171. Cross, Roy and William Green. "Facets of Soviet Airpower." *Aircraft,* XXIX (February 1951), 14–15.

1172. _____. "Soviet Air Power." *Aircraft,* XXIX (March 1951), 21–23.

1173. Crozier, Brian. "Russia's Balance Sheet, 1974–1975." In: Royal United Service Institution for Defence Studies. *RUSI and Brassey's Defence Yearbook, 1975/76.* Boulder, Colo.: Westview, 1975. pp. 84–98.

1174. Erickson, John. "Soviet Air Power." *Conflict Studies,* IV (January 20, 1973), 4–16.

1175. _____. "Soviet Military Capabilities." *Current History,* LXXI (October 1976), 97–100.

1176. _____. "The Soviet Military Effort in the 1970s: Perspectives and Priorities." In: Royal United Service Institution for Defence Studies. *RUSI and Brassey's Defence Yearbook, 1976/77.* Boulder, Colo.: Westview, 1976. pp. 84–110.

1177. _____. "Soviet Military Power." *Strategic Review,* I (Spring 1973), 1–127.

1177a. Foster, John S. "The Growing Soviet Threat: A Sobering Picture." *Air Force and Space Digest,* LIII (November 1970), 77–81.

1178. "A Glance at Soviet Air Capabilities." *Naval Aviation News,* (October 1954), 13–15.

1179. Kennedy, W. V. "Soviet Air Strength." *Ordnance,* XLIII (May–June 1959), 911–914.

1180. Krasovskiy, S. A. "Aviation and Cosmonautics in the U.S.S.R." In: Joseph D. Douglass, Jr. *The Soviet Theater Nuclear Offensive.* Studies in Communist Affairs, no. 1. Washington, D.C.: Published under the auspices of the U.S. Air Force by the U.S. Government Printing Office, 1976. pp. 60–68.

1181. Lee, Asher. "The Future of Soviet Air Power." In: Asher Lee, ed. *The Soviet Air and Rocket Forces.* New York: Praeger, 1959. pp. 287–301.

1182. _____. "A Review of Red Air Power." *Contact,* II (March 1954), 3–5.

1183. _____. "Soviet Air Power." *19th Century,* CXLV (June 1949), 354–362; CLII (November 1952), 404–407.

1184. Loosbrock, John F. "What's So New About the Red Air Power Threat?" *Air Force,* XXXVIII (July 1955), 22–23.

1185. "A Military Analysis of Russian Preparedness." *Aviation Age*, XVII (February 1952), 6–18, 23.

1186. "Organization of Soviet Aerospace Forces." *Air Force Magazine*, LX (March 1977), 104–106.

1187. "The Role of Aerospace Forces." In: Robert D. Crane, ed. *Soviet Nuclear Strategy: A Critical Appraisal.* Washington, D.C.: Center for Strategic Studies, Georgetown University, 1963. pp. 56–67.

1188. Schneider, Mark B. "The Soviet Capability in Strategic Offensive Forces." *Ordnance*, LVII (March–April 1973), 370–373.

1189. Scott, Fraser. "Three Dimensional Warfare." *Journal of the Royal United Service Institution for Defence Studies*, CXVI (September 1971), 43–47.

1190. Scott, William F. "Soviet Aerospace Forces and Doctrine." *Air Force Magazine*, LVIII (March 1975), 33–43.

1191. _____. "Soviet Aerospace Forces: Continuity and Contrast." *Air Force Magazine*, LIX (March 1976), 38–47.

1192. "Second Annual Soviet Aerospace Almanac." *Air Force Magazine*, LIX (March 1976), 37–120.

1193. "Soviet Aerospace Almanac." *Air Force Magazine*, LVIII (March 1975), 33–120; LX (March 1977), 35–120; LXI (March 1978), 34–120; LXII (March 1979), 39–120; LXIII (March 1980), 35–120.

1194. "Soviet Air Power." *Congressional Record*, XCIX (July 11, 1961), 11734–11738.

1195. "The Soviet Drive for Air Power." *Aeronautics*, XXXIV (August 1956), 52–53.

1196. "Special Report: USSR Aerospace." *Aviation Week and Space Technology*, XCVIII (June 25, 1973), 12–21.

1197. Staar, Richard F. "Strategic Power of the U.S.S.R." *Congressional Record*, CXV (June 12, 1969), E4854–E4857.

1198. Taylor, John W. R. "The Push-Button Age." In: *A History of Aerial Warfare*. London and New York: Hamlyn, 1974. pp. 221–237.

1199. _____. "Soviet Air Power." *NATO's Fifteen Nations*, XII (June–July 1967), 16–23.

1200. _____. _____. *Military Review*, XLVII (December 1967), 16–21.

1201. "The Threat and the Challenge of Soviet Air Power." *Armed Forces Journal*, CVII (September 13, 1969), 26–27.

1202. Ulsamer, Edgar. "The Soviet Drive for Aerospace Superiority." *Air Force Magazine*, LVIII (March 1975), 44–49.

1203. "What's New With Red Air Power?" *Air Force and Space Digest*, XLIV (October 1961), 14–15.

1204. "The Wide Spectrum of Soviet Air Power." *Interavia*, XVII (November 1962), 1453–1459.

1205. Wolfe, Thomas W. "Russia's Forces Go Mobile." *Interplay of European-American Affairs*, I (March 1968), 28, 33–37.

Documents, Papers, and Reports

1206. Wolfe, Thomas W. *The Soviet Quest for More Globally Mobile Military Power.* RAND Memorandum RM-5554-PR. Santa Monica, Calif.: RAND Corporation, 1967. 21p.

B. The Soviet Air Force (Voyenno-Vozdushnyye Sily—VVS)

1. General Studies

Books

1207. Erickson, C. T., ed. *The Red Air Force, 1918–1963.* Michom, England: G. M. Smith, 1963. 64p.

1208. Green, William and John E. Fricker. *The Air Forces of the World: Their History, Development, and Present Strength.* New York: Hanover House, 1958. 336p.

1209. Hewish, Mark et al. *Air Forces of the World: An Illustrated Directory of All the World's Military Air Powers.* New York: Simon and Schuster, 1979. 264p.

1210. Krivinyi, Nikolaus, ed. *World Military Aviation: Aircraft, Air Forces, and Weaponry.* Translated from the German. New York: Arco, 1973. 224p.

1211. Lee, Asher. *The Soviet Air Force.* London: Duckworth, 1951. 207p.

1212. _____. _____. New York: Stein and Day, 1962. 288p.

1213. Stockwell, Richard E. *Soviet Air Power.* New York: Praeger, 1956. 238p.

1214. Wragg, David W. *The World's Air Forces.* New York: Hippocrene Books, 1974. 232p.

Articles

1215. "Air Forces of the World–1979." *Interavia,* XXXIV (January 1979), 51–66.

1216. Brownlow, Cecil. "Soviets Spur Modernized [Air] Force." *Aviation Week and Space Technology,* CIV (April 5, 1976), 14–15.

1217. Brunicardi, D. N. P. "Soviet Air Strength." *An Cosantoir,* X (April 1950), 184–188.

1218. Butz, J. S. "How Far is the Red Air Force Ahead?" *Air Force,* XLIV (September 1961), 52–56.

1219. Chapman, W. C. "The Soviet Air Forces." In: Frank Uhlig, Jr., ed. *The Naval Review, 1965.* Annapolis, Md.: U.S. Naval Institute, 1965. pp. 166–199.

1220. Clark, Donald L. "Who are Those Guys?" *Air University Review,* XXX (May–June 1979), 47–65.

1221. Douglas, Albert. "How Strong is the Red Air Force?" *Reporter,* III (August 29, 1950), 20–23.

1222. Edmonds, Martin. "The Future of Manned Aircraft." In: John Erickson, ed. *The Military-Technical Revolution.* New York: Praeger, 1966. pp. 170–187.

1223. Fullerton, John. "The Dynamic Changes in Soviet Military Aviation." *Defense and Foreign Affairs Digest,* VII (May 1979), 54–56.

1224. Garthoff, Raymond L. "How the Soviets Organize Their Air Power." *Air Force,* XLI (February 1958), 58–60, 63.

1225. ———. "How They Organize the Soviet Air Forces." *RAF Flying Review,* XIII (July 1958), 13–15, 20–21.

1226. ———. "Organization and Staff Work." In: Asher Lee, ed. *The Soviet Air and Rocket Forces.* New York: Praeger, 1959. pp. 170–188.

1227. "A Glimpse of Soviet Aviation." *Naval Aviation News,* (January 1956), 20–23.

1228. Green, William. "The Red Air Force is Ready." *Air Trails,* XL (April–June 1953), 19–21, 58–59, 20–21, 60–61, 24–25.

1229. _____. "The Red Luftwaffe." *RAF Flying Review,* VIII (March 1953), 11–13, 28.

1230. _____. "Red Star Air Force." *Skyways,* X (May 1951), 18–19, 43.

1231. _____. "These are Russia's Air Forces." *RAF Flying Review,* XIII (July 1958), 28–30; XIV (February 1959), 20–23.

1232. _____ and Roy Cross. "This is the Russian Air Force." *Skyways,* X (January 1951), 10–12, 34–36.

1233. Haddaway, George E. "A Look at the Russians." *Flight Management,* XLVIII (August 1959), 20–23.

1234. Hotz, Robert. "Soviets Press Air Force Modernization." *Aviation Week and Space Technology,* LXXVI (March 12, 1962), 271–273.

1235. "Inside the Russian Air Force." *Royal Air Force Review,* VI (June 1951), 7–10.

1236. Key, William G. "A New Look." *Pegasus,* (September 1952), 1–8.

1237. Kutakhov, Pavel. "Interview: Translated from *Sovetskiy Voin,* August 1978." *Translations on USSR Military Affairs,* no. 1388 (October 23, 1978), 1–7.

1238. _____. "Kutakhov on Air Forces Combat Readiness: Translated from *Aviatsiya I Kosmonavtika,* November 1977." *Translations on USSR Military Affairs,* no. 1328 (February 2, 1978), 130–134.

1239. _____. "Marshal Kutakhov on Air Force Combat Readiness: Translated from *Aviatsiya I Kosmonavtika,* February 1979." *Translations on USSR Military Affairs,* no. 1439 (May 21, 1979), 13–20.

1240. _____. "Marshal Kutakhov on Air Force Development: Translated from *Soviet Military Review,* July 1978." *Translations on USSR Military Affairs,* no. 1380 (September 27, 1978), 44–48.

1241. _____. "Marshal Kutakhov on Victory Day: Translated from *Aviatsiya I Kosmonavtika,* May 1978." *Translations on USSR Military Affairs,* no. 1364 (July 18, 1978), 38–44.

1242. _____. "Mighty Wings of the Motherland: Translated from *Voyenno-Istoricheskiy Zhurnal,* August 1978." *Translations on USSR Military Affairs,* no. 1392 (November 2, 1978), 1–5.

1243. _____. "The Soviet Air Force: An Interview." *Soviet Military Review,* no. 8 (August 1975), 9–14.

1244. _____. _____. *Soviet Military Review,* no. 7 (July 1978), 11–15.

1245. Lee, Asher. "Air Headaches at the Kremlin." *RAF Flying Review,* XII (August 1957), 9–11.

1246. _____. "Communist Air Forces." In: James Moulton, ed. *Brassey's Annual.* New York: Macmillan, 1954. pp. 82–91.

1247. _____. "How Good is the Russian Air Force?" *Science Digest,* XXVIII (December 1950), 21–25.

1248. _____. "The Russian and Chinese Air Forces." In: James Moulton, ed. *Brassey's Annual.* New York: Praeger, 1963. pp. 92–100.

1249. _____. "The Threat in the East." *RAF Flying Review,* XI (April 1956), 27–29.

1250. Mallon, Lloyd. "The Big Red Lie." *True,* XXII (June 1959), 41–51.

1251. Menaud, S. W. B. "The Soviet Air Force." In: Ray Bonds, ed. *The Soviet War Machine: An Encyclopedia of Russian Military Equipment and Strategy.* New York: Chartwell Books, 1976. pp. 64–85.

1252. Monks, Alfred L. "The Soviet Air Forces." In: David R. Jones, ed. *Soviet Armed Forces Review Annual, 1977.* Gulf Breeze, Fla.: Academic International Press, 1977. pp. 48–65.

1253. O'Doherty, John K. "Rise of the Red Star." *TAF Review,* II (July 1956), 7–11.

1254. "Organization of Subordinate Soviet Aviation Units." *Air Force Magazine,* LX (March 1977), 107.

1255. Phillips, Thomas R., Jr. "The Growing Power of the Soviet Air Force." *Reporter,* XII (June 30, 1955), 16–19.

1256. "Presentation of Arms in the East: Soviet Russia's Modern Air Force." *Interavia,* V (October 1950), 511–516.

1257. Price, Wesley. "How Strong is Stalin's Air Force?" *Saturday Evening Post,* CCXXI (August 1948), 26–27.

1258. "Red Air Buildup." *Aviation Age,* XVIII (August 1952), 46–47.

1259. "The Red Air Force." *Fortune,* XLVII (February 1953), 120–121.

1260. "The Red Air Force: Our Equal?" *Air Training,* IV (February 1955), 8–11.

1261. "Red Air Power." *An Cosantoir,* XIV (March 1954), 124–128.

1262. "Reviewing the Achievements of Soviet Aviation." *Translations on USSR Military Affairs,* no. 329a (October 1966), 14–24.

1263. "Russia: Colossus of the Air." *Air Trails,* LXXV (May–June 1951), 19–25, 22–23.

1264. "The Russian Air Force." *Air Power,* III (April 1956), 171–181.

1265. _____ . *Contact,* I (September 1952), 55–56.

1266. "The Second Best Air Force is Now Official." *Air Force,* XXXIX (June 1956), 34–35.

1267. Silant'yev, A. P. "Interview: Translated from *Komsomol'skaya Pravda,* August 20, 1978." *Translations on USSR Military Affairs,* no. 1389 (October 24, 1978), 34–40.

1268. Skorikov, G. "Combat Wings of the Motherland: Translated from *Izvestiya,* August 19, 1978." *Translations on USSR Military Affairs,* no. 1377 (September 14, 1978), 54–55.

1269. "The Soviet Air Force." *Aeroplane,* LXXV (August 7 and 20, 1948), 159–161, 220–223.

1270. _____ . *Aviation Age,* XVI (July 1951), 1–89.

1271. "Soviet Air Forces." *Naval Aviation News,* (September 1948), 13–15.

1272. "Soviet Air Power." *Naval Aviation News,* (November 1950), 10–13.

1273. "The Soviet Union Modernizes Its Air Force." *Interavia,* XXII (September 1967), 1372–1376.

1274. Spaatz, Carl. "Red Air Force: The World's Biggest." *Newsweek,* XLIV (August 23, 1954), 28.

1275. Swanborough, F. Gordon. "Aviation in Russia." *Aeroplane,* LXXX (March 1951), 295–297.

1276. _____ . "Aviation in the Soviet Union." *Canadian Army Journal,* V (December 1951), 44–47.

1277. Taylor, John W. R. "How Good is the Soviet Air Force?" *Air Power,* III (April 1956), 170–181.

1278. _____. "The Soviet Air Force: Fact and Fiction." *Royal Air Forces Quarterly,* I (Winter 1961), 267–276.

1279. "The Truth About the Soviet Air Force." *U.S. News and World Report,* XXVII (October 21, 1949), 11–13.

1280. Twining, Nathan F. "Report From Moscow." *Air Force,* XXXIX (August 1956), 60–65.

1281. Vershinin, Konstantin A. "The Soviet Air Forces: Translated and Condensed from Volume 5 of the *Great Soviet Encyclopedia,* 3rd Edition, 1971." *Air Force Policy Letter for Commanders,* no. 11 (November 1975), 32–34.

1282. _____. "USSR is Big Air Power: Translated from *Pravda,* July 9, 1961." *Current Digest of the Soviet Press,* XIII (August 2, 1961), 32.

1283. Whiting, Kenneth R. "The Peacetime Air Force at Home and Abroad, 1945–1976." In: Robin Higham and Jacob W. Kipp, eds. *Soviet Aviation and Air Power: A Historical View.* Boulder, Colo.: Westview, 1977. pp. 289–315.

1284. Winchester, James H. "Is the Soviet Air Force Number 1?" *Reader's Digest,* CIII (September 1973), 86–90.

Documents, Papers, and Reports

1285. United States. Department of Defense. Defense Intelligence Agency. "The Air Force." In: *Handbook of the Soviet Armed Forces.* DDB-2680-40-78. Washington, D.C.: U.S. Government Printing Office, 1979. pp. 10-1—10-10.

1286. *The Winged Shield of the Motherland: Translated from Pravda, August 18, 1974.* Wright Patterson AFB, Ohio: Foreign Technology Division, U.S. Air Force, 1974. 13p.

2. Mission and Doctrine, Strategy and Tactics—VVS

Book

1287. Sims, Edward H. *Fighter Tactics and Strategy, 1914–1970.* New York: Harper & Row, 1972. 266p.

Articles

1288. Agal'tsov, Filipp A. "Air Force of the Soviet Union." *Moscow News,* (August 15, 1964), 3–12.

1289. Arnold, Joseph C. "Current Soviet Tactical Doctrine: A Reflection on the Past." *Military Review,* LVII (July 1977), 16–24.

1290. Beck, Leonard N. "Soviet Military Literature and Soviet Air Doctrine." *Air University Quarterly Review,* VIII (Spring 1956), 93–102.

1291. Blesse, Frederick C. "The Changing World of Air Combat." *Air Force Magazine,* LX (October 1977), 34–37.

1292. Boman, Truman R. "Current Soviet Tactics." *Military Review,* XLII (March 1962), 41–46.

1293. Bowman, "Buddy." "To Fly and Fight." *U.S. Air Force Fighter Weapons Newsletter,* no. 4 (Winter 1970), 10–11.

1294. Brog, David. "Defense Suppression as a Basic Operational Mission." *Air University Review,* XXIX (March–April 1978), 9–12.

1295. Caldwell, Cy. "Air Power and the Russian Octopus." *Aero Digest,* LXI (October 1950), 56.

1296. Clause, D. M. "Soviet Concepts of Air Power." In: Royal United Service Institution for Defence Studies at Southampton University. *The Soviet Union in Europe and the Near East: A Report of a Seminar.* London, 1970. Chpt. 7.

1297. Deitchman, Seymour J. "The Implications of Modern Technological Developments for Tactical Air Tactics and Doctrine." *Air University Review,* XXIX (November–December 1977), 23–45.

1298. Deutscher, Isaac. "New Soviet Strategy." *Reporter,* XVII (October 3, 1957), 10–12.

1299. Dubrov, V. "Changes in Combat Tactics of Fighter Aircraft Discussed: Translated from *Aviatsiya I Kosmonavtika,* March–April 1978." *Translations on USSR Military Affairs,* no. 1362 (July 12, 1978), 56–68.

1300. _____. _____: Translated from *Aviatsiya I Kosmonavtika,* May 1978." *Translations on USSR Military Affairs,* no. 1377 (September 14, 1978), 1–14.

1301. Garthoff, Raymond L. "Air Power and Soviet Strategy." *Air University Quarterly Review,* IX (Winter 1957–1958), 80–97.

1302. _____. _____. In: *Soviet Strategy in the Nuclear Age.* New York: Praeger, 1958. pp. 170–195.

1303. _____. "Soviet Attitudes Toward Modern Air Power." *Military Affairs,* XIX (Summer 1955), 76–80.

1304. Ivanov, B. "Soviet Fighter Tactics." *Marine Corps Gazette,* XLVII (April 1963), 10.

1305. Karikh, A. "Initiative in Air Combat." *Soviet Military Review*, no. 3 (March 1973), 24–27.

1306. Krasnov, A. "Air Combat Control." *Soviet Military Review*, no. 10 (October 1975), 26–27.

1307. Lee, Asher. "Rethinking in Soviet Air Policy." In: James L. Moulton, ed. *Brassey's Annual*. New York: Praeger, 1965. pp. 137–147.

1308. Mastro, Joseph P. "The Lessons of World War II and the Cold War." In: Robin Higham and Jacob W. Kipp, eds. *Soviet Aviation and Air Power: A Historical View*. Boulder, Colo.: Westview, 1977. pp. 195–212.

1309. Mishuk, M. "Roles and Tasks of Military Aviation Discussed: Translated from *Sotsialisticheskaya Industriya*, February 19, 1978." *Translations on USSR Military Affairs*, no. 1349 (May 2, 1978), 77–84.

1310. Possony, Stefan T. "Communism and Air Power." *Air University Quarterly Review*, VII (Winter 1954–1955), 43–54, 106–109.

1311. Savosin, S. and B. Ivanov. "Soviet Fighter Tactics, Pro and Con: Translated from *Red Star*, May 19 and July 18, 1962." *Marine Corps Gazette*, XLVII (April 1963), 10.

1312. "The Soviet Air Forces: An Offensive Posture and Expanding Capabilities." *Air International*, XII (June 1976), 277–281.

1313. Steiger, George. "A Dilemma in Studying Soviet Tactics." *Military Review*, LVI (June 1976), 76–79.

1314. "The Symington Subcommittee's Airpower Findings." *Air Force*, XL (February 1957), 41–45.

1315. Tuzov, N. "Air Combat Analysis." *Soviet Military Review*, no. 3 (March 1977), 18–20.

1316. _____. "Manoeuvre and Fire in Air Combat." *Soviet Military Review*, no. 7 (July 1978), 19–21.

1317. Uryuzhnikov, V. "Element Leader and Wingman." *Soviet Military Review*, no. 10 (October 1976), 24–25.

1318. _____. "Fighter Sweep Tactics." *Soviet Military Review*, no. 4 (April 1969), 25–26.

1319. _____. "Speed in Attack." *Soviet Military Review*, no. 2 (February 1976), 20–21.

1320. Vazhin, F. "Air to Surface." *Soviet Military Review*, no. 8 (August 1965), 29–31.

1321. Vershinin, Konstantin A. "Air Force Chief Stresses Soviet Retaliatory Power: An Interview." *Current Digest of the Soviet Press,* IX (October 16, 1957), 6–8.

1322. _____. "Aviation in Modern War." *Survival,* V (March–April 1963), 83–85.

1323. Whiting, Kenneth R. "Post-War Strategy." In: Asher Lee, ed. *The Soviet Air and Rocket Forces.* New York: Praeger, 1959. pp. 89–101.

1324. _____. "The Search for a Soviet Air Doctrine." *Air University Quarterly Review,* VIII (Spring 1956), 102–107.

Documents, Papers, and Reports

1325. Drane, Leslie. *Soviet Tactical Air Doctrine.* Professional paper. Maxwell AFB, Ala.: Air War College, Air University, 1976.

1326. Leonidov, N. *Aircraft Avoidance of Missiles Discussed, USSR.* Translation, no. 47926. Arlington, Va.: Joint Publications Research Service, 1969. 7p.

1327. Meyer, John C. *Air Strategy in the Cold War.* Maxwell AFB, Ala.: Air War College, Air University, 1956. 95p.

1328. Snow, R. N. *An Effectiveness Model for Multiple Attacks Against an Airbase Area Complex.* RAND Report R-1639-PR. Santa Monica, Calif.: RAND Corporation, 1975. 120p.

1329. United States. Air Force. *Tactical Air Operations–Counter Air, Close Air Support, and Air Interdiction.* AFM 2–1. Washington, D.C.: Headquarters, U.S. Air Force, 1969.

1330. _____. Congress. Senate. Committee on Armed Services. *Airpower: Report.* 84th Cong., 1st sess. Washington, D.C.: U.S. Government Printing Office, 1957. 128p.

1331. _____. _____. _____. _____. *Study on Airpower: Hearings.* 24 pts. 84th Cong., 1st sess. Washington, D.C.: U.S. Government Printing Office, 1957.

3. Specific VVS Air Arms

a. FRONTAL AVIATION (FRONTOVAYA AVIATSIYA—FA)

(1) General Studies

Book

1332. Halley, James J. *The Role of the Fighter in Air Warfare.* New York: Ziff-Davis, 1978. 151p.

Articles

1333.   Ely, Louis B. "Air Support for the Red Army." In: *The Red Army Today.* Harrisburg, Pa.: Military Service Publishing Company, 1949. Chpt. 5.

1334.   Erickson, John. "Some Developments in Soviet Tactical Aviation." *Journal of the Royal United Service Institution for Defence Studies,* CXX (September 1975), 70–74.

1335.   Fullerton, John. "Soviet Frontal Aviation." *Defense and Foreign Affairs Digest,* VI (September 1978), 56–59.

1336.   Geiger, George J. "Russian Attack Aviation." *Marine Corps Gazette,* XLIV (November 1960), 37–39.

1337.   Gorokhov, K. "Aviation Ground Support Operations Described: Translated from *Aviatsiya I Kosmonavtika,* March 1978." *Translations on USSR Military Affairs,* no. 1351 (May 12, 1978), 63–68.

1338.   Gray, Colin S. "Soviet Tactical Airpower." *Air Force Magazine,* LX (March 1977), 62–64.

1339.   _____. _____. *NATO's Fifteen Nations,* XXIII (August–September 1978), 46–48.

1340.   Green, William. "PVO: Russia's Fighter Force." *RAF Flying Review,* XIV (February 1959), 20–23.

1341.   _____. "Russia's Fighter Force." *RAF Flying Review,* XVIII (February 1963), 21–25.

1342.   Hansen, Lynn M. "The Resurgence of Soviet Frontal Aviation." *Strategic Review,* VI (Fall 1978), 71–81.

1343.   Holmes, R. L. "Battlefield Air Power: The Right Lines?" *Royal Air Forces Quarterly,* XVII (Autumn 1977), 230–235.

1344.   Nekhoroshkov, L. "Aircraft Ground Support Effectiveness Discussed: Translated from *Aviatsiya I Kosmonavtika,* September 1978." *Translations on USSR Military Affairs,* no. 1392 (November 2, 1978), 49–52.

1345.   Riccardelli, Richard F. and Gary L. Jackson. "Soviet Close Air Support: An Indispensable Comrade in Combined Arms Operations." *Military Review,* LIX (May 1979), 11–20.

1346.   Schneider, William, Jr. "Trends in Soviet Frontal Aviation." *Air Force Magazine,* LXII (March 1979), 76–81.

1347.   Seamans, Robert. "TacAir: A Look at the Late 1970s." *Air Force Magazine,* LVI (January 1973), 32–37.

1348.   "Soviets Continue Stress on Tactical Air." *Aviation Week and Space Technology,* XCIV (March 8, 1971), 27–28.

1349.   Van Veen, E. "The Soviet Tactical Air Force and Tactical Nuclear Weapons." *NATO's Fifteen Nations,* XVII (August–September 1972), 42–44.

(2) Airmobile

Book

1350.   Galvin, John R. *Air Assault: The Development of Airmobile Warfare.* New York: Hawthorn, 1969. 365p.

Articles

1351.   Backoften, Joseph E. "A Legacy from Lenin." *Armor,* LXXXVIII (January–February 1979), 10–12.

1352.   Belov, M. "Air Landing Forces." *Soviet Military Review,* no. 1 (January 1979), 22–23.

1353.   _____. "Air Mobilization of Modern Armies." *Soviet Military Review,* no. 10 (October 1975), 13–15.

1354.   _____. "Helicopters and Land Force Tactics." *Soviet Military Review,* no. 12 (December 1976), 22–24.

1355.   _____. "Helicopters Used by Ground Troops." *Soviet Military Review,* no. 4 (April 1976), 30–31.

1356.   Blake, Peter J. "Soviet Airmobile Tactics." *U.S. Army Aviation Digest,* XXIII (April 1977), 1–3.

1357.   Bramlett, David A. "Soviet Airmobility: An Overview." *Military Review,* LVII (January 1977), 14–25.

1358.   Butz, J. S. "Soviet Army Airmobility." *Army,* XII (September 1961), 86–88.

1359.   Daschke, Carl E. "The Threat: How to Fight Helicopters—Soviet Style." *U.S. Army Aviation Digest,* XXVI (January 1980), 45–48.

1360.   Erickson, John. "Trends in the Soviet Combined-Arms Concept." *Strategic Review,* V (Winter 1977), 38–53.

1361. Fullerton, John. "The New Charioteers: Soviet Assault Helicopter Planning." *Defense and Foreign Affairs Digest,* VI (August 1978), 34–35.

1362. Myers, Joe B. "Soviet Airmobility." *U.S. Army Aviation Digest,* XVII (September 1971), 1–5.

1363. Sidorenko, A. A. "The Offensive, a Glimpse of Modern Soviet Artillery Tactics." *Field Artillery Journal,* XLII (July–August 1978), 32–45.

1364. Tolstoy, S. "Role of the Helicopter in Combat Discussed: Translated from *Pravda,* August 20, 1978." *Translations on USSR Military Affairs,* no. 1389 (October 24, 1978), 45–49.

1365. Turbiville, Graham H., Jr. "The Attack Helicopter's Growing Role in Russian Combat Doctrine." *Army,* XXVII (December 1977), 28–33.

1366. _____ . "A Soviet View of Heliborne Assault Operations." *Military Review,* LV (October 1975), 3–15.

1367. Wargo, Peter M. "The Evolution of Soviet Airmobility: Impact on the Seventies." *Military Review,* LV (November 1975), 3–13.

Documents, Papers, and Reports

1368. Minnehan, Thomas J. *The Role of Airmobility in Soviet Military Doctrine.* New York: Army Institute for Advanced Russian and East European Studies, 1975. 31p.

1369. Phillips, Richard L. *Air-to-Air Helicopter Combat (USMC Helicopters vs. Russian [Mi–24] HIND).* Study Project. Carlisle Barracks, Pa.: U.S. Army War College, 1979. 58p.

b. Long-Range Aviation (Dal'nyaya Aviatsiya—DA)

1370. "Aviatsiia Dalnego Deistviia." *Interavia,* IX (August 1954), 520–521.

1371. "Bombers Over the Range." *Translations on USSR Military Affairs,* no. 31 (September 1960), 10–13.

1372. Friedman, William S. "How Strong is Russia's A-bomb Fleet?" *Air Force,* XXXIV (February 1951), 25–29, 55–56.

1373. Gladych, Michael. "In Russian, ADD Means SAC." *Air Force,* XXXVIII (May 1955), 31–32.

1374. Green, William. "Strategic Bombing Aviation." *RAF Flying Review,* XIII (June 1958), 28–30.

1375. _____. "The Threat of Russia's Bombers." *RAF Flying Review,* X (March 1955), 17–21.

1376. "How Russia Can Strike." *Life,* XXX (January 22, 1951), 78–79.

1377. Joubert, Philip. "Long-Range Air Attack." In: Asher Lee, ed. *The Soviet Air and Rocket Forces.* New York: Praeger, 1959. pp. 101–117.

1378. Monks, Alfred L. "The Soviet Strategic Air Force and Civil Defense." In: Robin Higham and Jacob W. Kipp, eds. *Soviet Aviation and Air Power: A Historical View.* Boulder, Colo.: Westview, 1977. pp. 213–238.

1379. "A New Soviet Air Force Threat." *Life,* XXXIV (June 6, 1955), 143–149.

1380. "Reds Put Muscle on Strategic Air Arm." *Aviation Week and Space Technology,* LX (March 15, 1954), 90–93.

1381. "Russia Forging Trans-Polar Striking Force." *Aviation Age,* XXII (September 1954), 16–23.

Documents, Papers, and Reports

1382. Moore, Robert P. *Executive Summary of 'Long-Range, Missile-Equipped': A Soviet View by Major General of Aviation B. A. Vasil'yev.* Washington, D.C.: U.S. Government Printing Office, 1979. 6p.

1383. Vasil'yev, B. A. *Long-Range, Missile-Equipped: A Soviet View.* Translated from the Russian. Soviet Military Thought Series, no. 15. Washington, D.C.: Published under the auspices of the U.S. Air Force by the U.S. Government Printing Office, 1979. 79p.

c. Military Transport Aviation (Voyenno-Transportnaya Aviatsiya—VTA)

Book

1384. MacDonald, Hugh. *Aeroflot: Soviet Air Transport Since 1923.* Putnam Aeronautical Series. London: Putnam, 1975. 323p.

Articles

1385. Brehat, Victor. "Air Transport Logistical Capabilities Discussed: Translated from *Defense Nationale,* October 1978." *Translations on USSR Military Affairs,* no. 1399 (December 4, 1978), 61–63.

1386. Friedman, William S. "Air Transportation, a Key Factor in Soviet Strength," *Pegasus,* (April 1951), 4–7.

1387. Fullerton, John. "Expanding Airlift Capacity." *Defense and Foreign Affairs Digest*, VI (March 1978), 34–35.

1388. Izgarshev, V. "Operations of Military Transport Aviation Discussed: Translated from *Pravda*, January 4, 1979." *Translations on USSR Military Affairs*, no. 1419 (March 15, 1979), 85–87.

1389. Passingham, Malcolm. "Red Star Transport." In: Anthony Robinson, ed. *Wings: The Complete Encyclopedia of Aviation*. 25 vols. London: Osprey, 1977. I, 77–80.

1390. "The Red Army Air Transport Fleet." *Interavia*, XII (February 1957), 11–12.

1391. Reitz, James T. "Soviet Civil Aviation in Peace and War." *East Europe*, XXIII (July 1974), 10–13.

1392. Schneider, William, J. "Soviet Military Airlift: Key to Rapid Power Projection." *Air Force Magazine*, LXIII (March 1980), 80–87.

1393. Scott, William F. "The U.S.S.R.'s Growing Global Mobility." *Air Force Magazine*, LX (March 1977), 57–61.

1394. Sin'kevich, V. "Transport Aircraft Air Drop Mission Described: Translated from *Krasnaya Zvezda*, January 25, 1978." *Translations on USSR Military Affairs*, no. 1347 (April 19, 1978), 38–40.

1395. Underhill, Garrett. "Soviet Air Transport." *Ordnance*, XLII (January–February 1958), 624–628.

C. The Soviet National Air Defense Forces (Voyska Protivovozdushnoy Oborony Strany—PVO-Strany)

1. General Studies

Articles

1396. "Airplane and Rocket." *Translations on USSR Military Affairs*, no. 74 (November 1961), 25–29.

1397. Amelchenko, V. "Guardsmen in the Air: Keeping up Traditions of Courage." *Soviet Military Review*, no. 4 (April 1975), 56–59.

1398. Beregovoy, M. T. "Beregovoy on the National Air Defense Command: Translated from *Sovetskaya Latviya*, April 9, 1978." *Translations on USSR Military Affairs*, no. 1358 (June 21, 1978), 34–36.

1399. Bobylev, Sergey A. "Defenders of the Motherland's Peaceful Sky: Translated from *Izvestia,* April 8, 1979." *Translations on USSR Military Affairs,* no. 1440 (May 24, 1979), 11–13.

1400. Bochkov, B. V. "Bochkov on Moscow Air Defense: Translated from *Pravda,* April 9, 1978." *Translations on USSR Military Affairs,* no. 1358 (June 21, 1978), 31–34.

1401. "Building of a Stable Air Defense System." *Translations on USSR Military Affairs,* no. 198a (August 1965), 38–44.

1402. Cobb, Tyrus W. "Tactical Air Defense: A Soviet–U.S. Net Assessment." *Air University Review,* XXX (March–April 1979), 18–39.

1403. Frisbee, John L. "Air Defense: Weakest Link in the Deterrent Chain." *Air Force and Space Digest,* LIII (December 1970), 35–39.

1404. "Generals' Comments on Air Defense Force's Capabilities." *Translations on USSR Military Affairs,* no. 1352 (May 15, 1978), 151–155.

1405. Henk, Daniel W. "The Thrust of Air Assault Operations." *U.S. Army Aviation Digest,* XXII (February 1976), 6–7.

1406. Jones, David R. "The National Air Defense Forces." In: David R. Jones, ed. *Soviet Armed Forces Review Annual, 1977.* Gulf Breeze, Fla.: Academic International Press, 1978. pp. 40–47.

1407. Koldunov, Aleksandr I. "Koldunov on the Air Defense Forces: Translated from *Kommunist,* April 9, 1978." *Translations on USSR Military Affairs,* no. 1358 (June 21, 1978), 27–30.

1408. Kuban, Boris. "Russia Prepares Her Defenses." *RAF Flying Review,* XIII (November 1957), 11–12.

1409. Lee, Asher. "Strategic Air Defense." In: Asher Lee, ed. *The Soviet Air and Rocket Forces.* New York: Praeger, 1959. pp. 117–130.

1410. Mackintosh, Malcolm. "Russia's Defense: A Question of Quality." *Interplay,* IV (February 1971), 14–17.

1411. McQueen, Arthur D. "The Ever–Expanding Umbrella." *Air Defense Magazine,* (July–September 1976), 8–17.

1412. "Materials on Air Defense." *Translations on USSR Military Affairs,* no. 49 (January 1961), 1–21.

1413. _____. *Translations on USSR Military Affairs,* no. 122 (June 1963), 1–21.

1414. Menaud, S. W. B. "Air Defense of the Homeland." In: Ray Bonds, ed. *The Soviet War Machine: An Encyclopedia of Russian Military Equipment and Strategy.* New York: Chartwell Books, 1976. pp. 52–63.

1415. Mil'chenko, N. "Staff Work in the Moscow Air Defense District: Translated from *Kommunist Vooruzhennykh Sil,* March 1978." *Translations on USSR Military Affairs,* no. 1355 (May 30, 1978), 30–40.

1416. Molchan, G. "In an Air Defense Interceptor Unit: Translated from *Krasnaya Zvezda,* March 1, 1978." *Translations on USSR Military Affairs,* no. 1366 (July 20, 1978), 1–8.

1417. Orlov, Yu. "Commander of Outstanding Air Defense Missile Regiment Interviewed: Translated from *Kommunist Vooruzhennykh Sil,* November 1978." *Translations on USSR Military Affairs,* no. 1413 (February 28, 1979), 160–171.

1418. Phillips, Thomas R., Jr. "Air Defense More Difficult for Russia Than for the U.S." *Antiaircraft Journal,* XCV (March–April 1952), 11–12.

1419. Podgornyy, Ivan D. "Podgornyy Notes Combat Readiness of Air Defense Forces: Translated from *Sovetskaya Rossiya,* April 8, 1978." *Translations on USSR Military Affairs,* no. 1348 (April 27, 1978), 98–100.

1420. Polyakov, A. "At Maximum Range." *Soviet Military Review,* no. 1 (January 1976), 21–22.

1421. "The Role of the Air Force in National Defense." *Translations on USSR Military Affairs,* no. 310 (August 1966), 1–3.

1422. Savitskiy, Yevgeny Y. "Air Border Guards: Translated from *Sotsialisticheskaya Industrya,* April 8, 1979." *Translations on USSR Military Affairs,* no. 1440 (May 24, 1979), 7–8.

1423. _____. "Defending the Soviet Skies: An Interview." *Soviet Military Review,* no. 3 (March 1977), 11–14.

1424. Scott, William F. "Troops of National Air Defense." *Air Force Magazine,* LXI (March 1978), 56–58.

1425. Sidelnikov, I. "Soviet Defense Power: Why It is Impregnable." *Soviet Military Review,* no. 4 (April 1966), 9–10.

1426. Yudin, I. "Guarding the Skies." *Soviet Military Review,* no. 4 (April 1965), 20–22.

1427. Zimin, G. "Guards of the Soviet Skies." *Soviet Military Review,* no. 5 (May 1965), 28–30.

Documents, Papers, and Reports

1428. United States. Department of Defense. Defense Intelligence Agency. "The Air Defense Forces." In: *Handbook of the Soviet Armed Forces.* DDB-2680-40-78. Washington, D.C.: U.S. Government Printing Office, 1979. pp. 11–1, 11–17.

2. Mission and Doctrine, Strategy and Tactics—PVO-Strany

Book

1429. Haselkorn, Avigdor. *The Evolution of Soviet Security Strategy, 1965–1975.* Study paper, no. 31. New York: Crane, Russak, 1978. 139p.

Articles

1430. Bearden, Thomas E. "River Crossings as a Matter of Course: SA-8 Tactical Operations and Philosophy." *Air Defense Magazine,* (July–September 1977), 16–22.

1431. ———. "Soviet Air Defense Concepts." *Air Defense Magazine,* (January–March 1976), 6–11.

1432. Bobylev, Sergey A. "Air Defense Forces Political Chief on Capabilities: Translated from *Krasnaya Zvezda,* April 9, 1978." *Translations on USSR Military Affairs,* no. 1348 (April 27, 1978), 68–70.

1433. Borgart, Peter. "The Vulnerability of the Manned Airborne Weapon System." *International Defense Review,* X (August and October 1977), 667–671, 860–866.

1434. Britt, Randolph. "The Threat to United States Airmobile Operations." *U.S. Army Aviation Digest,* XX (September 1974), 1.

1435. Broekmeijer, M. W. J. M. "The Role of Aircraft in Future Warfare." *NATO's Fifteen Nations,* X (June–July 1965), 64–66.

1436. Bystry, N. "Helicopters Over the [AA] Battery." *Soviet Military Review,* no. 1 (January 1975), 28–29.

1437. "Concepts in Air Defense." *Air University Quarterly Review,* XIII (Summer 1961), 34–62.

1438. Gray, Colin S. "Air Defense: A Sceptical View." *Queen's Quarterly,* LXXIX (Spring 1972), 3–13.

1439. Hiestand, Harry H. "Military Intelligence and Enemy [Soviet] Air Defense." *U.S. Army Aviation Digest,* XX (September 1974), 2–3.

1440. Karikh, A. "Fighting Against Low-Flying Targets." *Soviet Military Review,* no. 12 (December 1974), 16–19.

1441. Krasnov, A. "Defense Tactics Against Surprise Air Attacks Discussed: Translated from *Krasnaya Zvezda*, October 18, 1977." *Translations on USSR Military Affairs,* no 1329 (February 10, 1978), 48–51.

1442. Malone, Daniel K. "Air Defense of Soviet Ground Troops." *Air Force Magazine,* LXI (March 1978), 78–83.

1443. Ponamarev, A. N. "Air-to-Air, Air-to-Ground." *Survival,* IV (March–April 1962), 88–89.

1444. Popkov, V. "Ground-Air Combat." *Soviet Military Review,* no. 4 (April 1965), 23–25.

1445. Pretty, Ronald T. "The Growing Threat." *Electronic Warfare,* VIII (March–April 1976), 43.

1446. "Problems of Contemporary Air Defense." *Translations on USSR Military Affairs,* no. 49 (January 1961), 18–21.

1447. Rose, John P. "The Battlefield Threat: Soviet Concepts, Doctrine, and Strategy." *Air Defense Magazine,* (July–September 1978), 24–29.

1448. Shesterin, F. "Air Defense in Local Wars Discussed: Translated from *Voyenno-Istoricheskiy Zhurnal,* October 1977." *Translations on USSR Military Affairs,* no. 1320 (January 5, 1978), 105–114.

1449. Thomas, John R. "The Role of Missile Defense in Soviet Strategy." *Military Review,* XLIV (May 1964), 46–58.

1450. Wells, Norman E. "Air Superiority Comes First." *Air University Review,* XXIV (November–December 1972), 10–25.

Documents, Papers, and Reports

1451. Crawford, Natalie W. *Low-Level Attack of Armored Targets.* RAND Paper P-5982. Santa Monica, Calif.: RAND Corporation, 1977. 25p.

1452. Jones, Chester G. *Attrition of Bomber as a Function of Weapon Load and Grouping of the Airborne Defense.* Report, no. ASD/XRO-73-6. Wright Patterson AFB, Ohio: Directorate of Advanced Systems Analysis, Aeronautical Systems Division, U.S. Air Force, 1973. 33p.

1453. Turchenko, V. V. and M. V. Fedulov. *Defensive Operations During an Offensive.* Translated from the Russian. Report, no. FSTC-HT-23-69-75. Charlottesville, Va.: Army Foreign Service and Technology Center, 1974. 249p.

120   *The Soviet National Air Defense Forces (PVO-Strany)*

1454.   Union of Soviet Socialist Republics. PVO-Strany. *Air Defense Subunits in Combat.* Translated from the Russian. Arlington, Va.: Joint Publications Research Service, 1975. 115p.

1455.   United States. Department of the Army. *Aircraft Battlefield Countermeasures and Survivability.* FM 1-2. Washington, D.C.: U.S. Government Printing Office, 1978. 184p.

3. Incidents of Home Defense

a. The U-2 Incident, 1960

Books

1456.   Asanov, D. et al., comps. *No Return for U-2: Truth About the Provocative Penetration of Soviet Air Space by an American Plane.* Moscow: Prepared for Publication by the Union of Journalists of the USSR and Published by the Foreign Languages Publishing House, 1960. 174p.

1457.   Cook, Fred J. *The U-2 Incident.* New York: Franklin Watts, 1973. 64p.

1458.   Powers, Francis G. *Operation Overflight: The U-2 Pilot Tells His Story For the First Time.* New York: Holt, 1970. 375p.

1459.   Wise, David and Thomas B. Ross. *The U-2 Affair.* New York: Random House, 1962. 269p.

Articles

1460.   Alsop, Joseph. "The Dulles Testimony: Reprinted from the *Washington Post,* February 5, 1960." *Congressional Record,* CVI (February 9, 1960), 2297.

1461.   Anderson, Jack. "United States Heard Russians Chasing the U-2: Reprinted from the *Washington Post,* May 12, 1960." *Congressional Record,* CVI (June 23, 1960), 13937–13938.

1462.   "Chronological Account of U.S. Reports on the U-2." *Congressional Record,* CVI (May 23, 1960), 10792.

1463.   "Cold War." *Newsweek,* LV (May 20, 1960), 21–28.

1464.   "Cold War Candor: The Flight to Sverdlovsk." *Time,* LXXV (May 23, 1960), 15–18.

1465.   "Flight of the U-2." *Newsweek,* LV (May 16, 1960), 27–29.

1466.   "The Flight to Sverdlovsk." *Time,* LXXV (May 16, 1960), 15–18.

1467.   Green, William. "U-2: Fact (and Fiction)." *RAF Flying Review,* XV (August 1960), 18–19, 22.

1468.   Herter, Christian A. "Official Account of the U-2 and the Summit Breakup: Testimony Before the Senate Foreign Relations Committee." *U.S. News and World Report,* XLVIII (June 6, 1960), 68–70.

1469.   Hotz, Robert. "Lockheed U-2 Over Sverdlovsk: A Study in Fabrication." *Aviation Week and Space Technology,* LXXII (May 16, 1960), 20–21.

1470.   "Khrushchev's Pre-Summit Spy Cry." *Life,* XLVIII (May 16, 1960), 38–41.

1471.   Nathan, James A. "A Fragile Detente: The U-2 Incident Reexamined." *Military Affairs,* XXXIX (October 1975), 97–104.

1472.   Powers, Francis G. "Flight and Capture of the U-2." *U.S. News and World Report,* LII (March 19, 1962), 48–51.

1473.   _____ . "Francis Gary Powers Tells His Story." *New York Times Magazine,* (April 19, 1970), 36–37.

1474.   _____ . "Here is Powers' Own Story—As Told by the Russians." *U.S. News and World Report,* XLIX (August 22, 1960), 53–55.

1475.   Randle, Kevin D. "What Really Happened to Gary Powers and His U-2?" *Air Classics,* XV (April 1979), 64–67.

1476.   Ransom, Harry H. "How Intelligent is Intelligence?" *New York Times Magazine,* (May 22, 1960), 26, 80–83.

1477.   "Tracked Toward Trouble." *Time,* LXXV (May 23, 1960), 12–13.

1478.   "Was Powers Shot Down?" *Time,* LXXVI (October 3, 1960), 28.

1479.   Willoughby, Charles A. "Khrushchev and the Flight to Sverdlovsk." *American Mercury,* XCI (August 1960), 34–43.

1480.   Wise, David and Thomas B. Ross. "The Secret History of the U-2." *Look,* XXVI (May 8 and 22, 1962), 128, 101–102.

Documents, Papers, and Reports

1481.   Eisenhower, Dwight D. and Christian A. Herter. *President Eisenhower's Report to the Nation, May 25, 1960* [and] *Secretary Herter's Report to the Senate Foreign Relations Committee.* Department of State Publication, no. 7010, General Foreign Policy Series, no. 151. Washington, D.C.: Department of State, 1960. 25p.

1482. Khrushchev, Nikita S. *Statement and Replies to Questions, Gorky Park, Moscow, May 11, 1960: The U-2 Incident.* New York: Crosscurrents Press, 1960. 32p.

1483. Mezerik, Avraham G., ed. *U-2 and Open Skies: Overflights, U.N. Action, Chronology.* New York: International Review Service, 1960. 46p.

1484. *Soviet Booklets,* Editors of. *The Powers Case.* Soviet Booklet, no. 79. London, 1960. 92p.

1485. *Soviet Weekly,* Editors of. *American Spy Plane on Exhibition in Moscow.* London: Soviet Weekly, 1960. 7p.

1488. Union of Soviet Socialist Republics. Soviet Information Bureau. *Caught in the Act.* Moscow, 1960. 83p.

1489. United States. Congress. Senate. Committee on Foreign Relations. *Events Incident to the Summit Conference: Hearings.* 86th Cong., 2nd sess. Washington, D.C.: U.S. Government Printing Office, 1960.

b. OTHER INCIDENTS

Book

1490. White, William L. *The Little Toy Dog: The Story of Two RB-47 Flyers, Captain John R. McKone and Captain Truman B. Olmstead.* New York: E. P. Dutton, 1962. 304p.

Articles

1491. "Nikita and the RB-47." *Time,* LXXVI (July 25, 1960), 21–22.

1492. Norman, L. B. "Mystery of the RB-47." *Newsweek,* LVI (July 25, 1960), 36–37.

1493. "Russians Stir Up a Phony Spy Crisis: Shooting Down an RB-47 Over the Barents Sea." *Life,* XLIX (July 25, 1960), 30–31.

1494. "Soviet Fighters Down USAF RB-66 Over East Germany." *Air Force and Space Digest,* XLVII (April 1964), 23–24.

D. The Strategic Rocket Forces (Raketnyye Voyska Strategicheskogo Naznacheniya—SRF)

1. General Studies

Book

1495. Stoiko, Michael. *Soviet Rocketry: Past, Present and Future.* New York: Holt, 1970. 272p.

Articles

1496. Ackley, Richard T. "Strategic Rocket Forces." In: David R. Jones, ed. *Soviet Armed Forces Review Annual, 1977.* Gulf Breeze, Fla.: Academic International Press, 1978. pp. 13–27.

1497. Boman, Truman R. "Soviet Guided Missile Deployment." *Military Review,* XLII (November 1962), 75–79.

1498. Brown, George S. "Strategic Missile Forces." *National Defense,* LXI (July–August 1976), 36–38.

1499. Currie, Malcolm R. "Currie Cautions on Soviet Missile Gains." *Aviation Week and Space Technology,* CIV (May 24, 1976), 55–57.

1500. Dornan, James E., Jr. "Strategic Rocket Forces." In: Ray Bonds, ed. *The Soviet War Machine: An Illustrated Encyclopedia of Russian Military Equipment and Strategy.* New York: Chartwell Books, 1976. pp. 200–211.

1501. "G-2 Chief Reports on New Soviet Rocket Command." *Army, Navy, Air Force Journal,* XCVIII (March 4, 1961), 18–19.

1502. Garthoff, Raymond L. "How the Soviets Run Their Missile Program." *Air Force,* XL (December 1957), 53–54.

1503. Gorchakov, P. "Loyal Sons of the Fatherland." *Air Force Policy Letter for Commanders,* no. 12 (December 1974), 24–26.

1504. Gray, Colin S. "Soviet Rocket Forces: Military Capability, Political Utility." *Air Force Magazine,* LXI (March 1978), 49–55.

1505. Grigor'yev, Mikhail G. "Combat Readiness of the Strategic Rocket Forces Praised: Translated from *Znamenosets,* October 1977." *Translations on USSR Military Affairs,* no. 1323 (January 11, 1978), 35–39.

1506. _____. "Powerful Strike Force: Translated from *Izvestia,* November 20, 1969." *Current Digest of the Soviet Press,* XXI (December 17, 1969), 7.

1507. Krylov, Nikolai I. "Rocket Might of the Country: Translated from *Pravda,* November 19, 1967." *Daily Review,* XIII (November 20, 1967), 1–4.

1508. _____. "Soviet Strategic Rocket Forces." *Soviet Military Review,* no. 6 (June 1965), 7–10.

1509. Laird, Melvin R. "Strategic Forces." *Defense Industries Bulletin,* VI (April 1970), 7–20.

1510. Long, J. F. L. "New Emphasis on the U.S.S.R.'s Strategic Rocket Force." *Royal Air Forces Quarterly,* II (Winter 1962), 263–267.

1511. Malinovsky, Rodion Y. "Mighty Shield of the Homeland: Translated from *Pravda,* February 23, 1966." *Current Digest of the Soviet Press,* LXXVIII (March 16, 1966), 39–40.

1512. Melekhin, Aleksey D. "The Motherland's Reliable Shield: Translated from *Sovetskiy Patriot,* November 19, 1978." *Translations on USSR Military Affairs,* no. 1416 (March 7, 1979), 72–74.

1513. Moskalenko, Kirill S. "Rocket Troops are Mounting Guard Over the Motherland's Security: Translated from *Krasnaya Zvezda,* September 13, 1961." *Current Digest of the Soviet Press,* XIII (October 11, 1961), 12–13.

1514. Petersen, Philip A. "Strategic Missile Forces and Cosmic Research." In: Robin Higham and Jacob W. Kipp, eds. *Soviet Aviation and Air Power: A Historical View.* Boulder, Colo.: Westview, 1977. pp. 239–264.

1515. "Russia's Guided Missile Program." *Missiles and Rockets,* II (February 1957), 33–41.

1516. Ulsamer, Edgar. "The Soviet ICBM Threat is Mounting." *Air Force Magazine,* LVI (November 1973), 34–37.

1517. Zaehringer, Alfred J. "Soviet Rocket Forces." *Ordnance,* XLVI (September–October 1961), 216–219.

Documents, Papers, and Reports

1518. Gray, Colin S. *The Future of Land-Based Missile Forces.* Adelphi papers, no. 140. London: International Institute for Strategic Studies, 1977. 32p.

1519. Lucas, Stevan R. *Soviet Strategic Rocket Forces: An Analysis.* Report, no. 02985. Washington, D.C.: Defense Intelligence School, 1977. 55p.

1520. United States. Department of Defense. Defense Intelligence Agency. "Strategic Rocket Forces." In: *Handbook of the Soviet Armed Forces.* DDB-2680-40-78. Washington, D.C.: U.S. Government Printing Office, 1979. pp. 12–1—12–11.

2. Mission, Doctrine, and Nuclear Strategy

Books

1521. Brodie, Bernard. *Strategy in the Missile Age.* Princeton, N. J.: Princeton University Press, 1959. 423p.

1522. Dinerstein, Herbert S. *War and the Soviet Union: Nuclear Weapons and the Revolution in Soviet Military and Political Thinking.* New York: Praeger, 1962. 268p.

1523. Douglass, Joseph D., Jr. *The Soviet Theater Nuclear Offensive.* Studies in Communist Affairs, no. 1. Washington, D.C.: Published under the auspices of the U.S. Air Force by the U.S. Government Printing Office, 1976. 127p.

1524. _____ and Amoretta Hoeber. *Soviet Strategy for Nuclear War.* Stanford, Calif.: Hoover Institution Press, 1979. 138p.

1525. Gompert, David C. et al. *Nuclear Weapons and World Politics: Alternatives for the Future.* New York: McGraw-Hill, 1977. 370p.

1526. Gouré, Leon et al. *The Role of Nuclear Forces in Current Soviet Strategy.* Monographs in International Affairs. Miami, Fla.: Center for Advanced International Studies, University of Miami, 1974. 148p.

1527. Hobbs, Richard. *The Myth of Victory: What is Victory in War?* Boulder, Colo.: Westview, 1979. 450p.

1528. Kintner, William R. and Harriet F. Scott, comps. *The Nuclear Revolution in Soviet Military Affairs.* Norman: University of Oklahoma Press, 1968. 420p.

1529. Parson, Nels A., Jr. *Missiles and the Revolution in Warfare.* Cambridge, Mass.: Harvard University Press, 1962. 245p.

1530. Speed, Roger D. *Strategic Deterrence in the 1980's.* Stanford, Calif.: Hoover Institution Press, 1979. 174p.

1531. Spielmann, Karl F. *Analyzing Soviet Strategic Arms Decisions.* Boulder, Colo.: Westview, 1978. 184p.

Articles

1532. Allen, Luther, Jr. "The Strategic Nuclear Scene: An Address, October 27, 1978." *Vital Speeches,* XLV (January 1, 1979), 185–188.

1533. Atkeson, Edward B. "Hemisphere Denial: Geo-Political Imperatives and Soviet Strategy." *Strategic Review,* IV (Spring 1976), 29.

1534. "Ballistic Missiles and Military Strategy." *Interavia,* XVII (November 1962), 434–436.

1535. Barber, Ransom E. "The Myth of Soviet Nuclear War Strategy." *Army,* XXV (June 1975), 10–17.

1536. Barnett, Frank R. "Overview of Soviet Strategy." *Naval War College Review,* XXIII (June 1971), 16–21.

1537. Barnett, Roger W. "Trans-SALT Soviet Strategic Doctrine." *Orbis,* XIX (Summer 1975), 533–561.

1538. Biörklund, E. "A Space-Missile Strategy in Development." *NATO's Fifteen Nations,* X (April–May 1965), 58–63.

1539. Burke, Gerald K. "Fighting the Unthinkable: Nuclear War in the 1980s." *Military Review,* LVIII (June 1978), 9–19.

1540. Crane, Robert D. "Soviet Military Policy During the Era of Ballistic Missile Defense." In: Denis Dirscherl, ed. *The New Russia.* Dayton, Ohio: Pflaum Press, 1968. pp. 157–170.

1541. Dinerstein, Herbert S. "Revolution in Soviet Strategic Thinking." *Foreign Affairs,* XXXVI (January 1958), 241–252.

1542. Dornberger, Walter R. "Can Russian Missiles Strike the United States?" *Collier's,* CXXXV (January 7, 1955), 22–25.

1543. Douglass, Joseph D., Jr. "Soviet Nuclear Strategy in Europe." *Strategic Review,* V (Fall 1977), 19–32.

1544. Dupuy, Trevor N. "Tactical Nuclear Combat." *Ordnance,* LIII (November–December 1968), 292–296.

1545. Erickson, John. "Nuclear Strategy, World Dilemma." In: John Erickson, ed. *The Military–Technical Revolution.* New York: Praeger, 1966. pp. 1–20.

1546. Ermarth, Fritz W. "Contrasts in American and Soviet Strategic Thought." *International Security,* III (Fall 1978), 138–155.

1547. Frank, Lewis A. "Soviet Power After SALT I: A Strategic-Coercive Capability?" *Strategic Review,* II (Spring 1974), 54–60.

1548. Galay, Nikolai. "Guided Missiles and Soviet Military Doctrine." *Bulletin of the Institute for the Study of the History and Culture of the USSR,* (October 1957), 14–21.

1549. Gareau, Frederick H. "Nuclear Deterrence: The Soviet Position." *Orbis,* VIII (Winter 1965), 922–936.

1550. Garthoff, Raymond L. "Missiles in Soviet Strategy." *Air Force,* XLI (July 1958), 91–92.

1551. _____. _____. In: *Soviet Strategy in the Nuclear Age.* New York: Praeger, 1958. pp. 221–240.

1552. _____. "Strategic Concepts and Doctrines for the Nuclear Era." In: *Soviet Strategy in the Nuclear Age.* New York: Praeger, 1958. pp. 61–96.

1553. Gray, Colin S. "Theater Nuclear Weapons: Doctrines and Posture." *World Politics,* XXVIII (January 1976), 300–314.

1554. Hahn, Walter F. "Ballistic Missile Defense and Soviet Strategy." *Orbis,* IX (Summer 1965), 316–337.

1555. Jacobs, Walter D. "Marshal Malinovskii and Missiles." *Military Review,* XL (June 1960), 14–20.

1556. _____. "Soviet Strategic Effectiveness." *Journal of International Affairs,* XXVI (Spring 1972), 60–72.

1557. Jenson, John W. "Nuclear Strategy: Differences in Soviet and American Thinking." *Air University Review,* XXX (March–April 1979), 2–17.

1558. Jörgensen, K. "The Rocket and Military Strategy (of the U.S.S.R.). *Military Review,* XXXVII (July 1957), 101–103.

1559. Kohler, Foy D. "Role of Nuclear Forces in Current Soviet Strategy." *Atlantic Community Quarterly,* XII (Fall 1974), 283–299.

1560. Lee, William T. "Soviet Targeting Strategy and SALT." *Air Force Magazine,* LXI (September 1978), 120–122.

1561. Long, J. F. L. "The Missile vs. the Bomber: Khrushchev's Choice." *Air Power,* VII (Summer 1960), 277–281.

1562. MccGwire, Michael. "Soviet Strategic Weapons Policy, 1955–1970." In: Michael MccGwire, Ken Booth, and John McDonnell, eds. *Soviet Naval Policy, Objectives and Constraints.* New York: Praeger, 1975. pp. 486–504.

1563. Mackintosh, Malcolm. "The Soviet Defense Debate." In: J. M. Mackintosh, ed. *The Strategy and Tactics of Soviet Foreign Policy.* London and New York: Oxford University Press, 1963. pp. 88–105.

1564. _____. "Soviet Strategic Policy." *World Today,* XXVI (July 1970), 269–276.

1565. Malyanchikov, S. V. "The Character and Features of Nuclear Rocket War: Translated from *Kommunist Vooruzhennykh Sil,* November 1965." In: William R. Kintner and Harriet F. Scott. *The Nuclear Revolution in Soviet Strategy.* Norman: University of Oklahoma Press, 1968. pp. 78–80.

1566. Martin, Glen W. "The Deterrent Role of Strategic Forces." *Signal,* XXVI (March 1972), 18–20.

The Strategic Rocket Forces (SRF)

1567. Miller, Martin J., Jr. "Soviet Nuclear Tactics." *Ordnance,* LV (May–June 1970), 624–627.

1568. "Missiles and Methods." *Translations on USSR Military Affairs,* no. 142 (May 1964), 47–56.

1569. "Missiles and Nuclear Weapons Protect Socialist Nations." *Translations on USSR Military Affairs,* no. 130 (April 1964), 35–45.

1570. Monks, Alfred L. "Soviet Strategic Claims, 1964–1970." *Orbis,* XVI (Summer 1972), 520–544.

1571. Muckerman, Joseph E., 2nd. "Hedging on a Strategic Gamble." *Army,* XXI (September 1971), 10–16.

1572. Nevskii, N. A. "Modern Armaments and Problems of Strategy." *World Marxist Review,* VI (March 1963), 28–34.

1573. Nitze, Paul. "The Relationship of Strategic and Theater Nuclear Forces." *International Security,* II (Fall 1977), 122–132.

1574. Pipes, Richard. "Why the Soviet Union Thinks It Could Fight and Win a Nuclear War." *Air Force Magazine,* LX (September 1977), 54–66.

1575. Reinhordt, G. C. "Atomic Weapons and Warfare." In: Basil H. Liddell-Hart, ed. *The Soviet Army.* London: Weidenfeld and Nicolson, 1956. pp. 420–438.

1576. Reznichenko, Vasilii. "Soviet Tactics on the Nuclear Battlefield." *Military Review,* XLV (June 1965), 76–80.

1577. Richelson, J. T. "Soviet Strategic Doctrine and Limited Nuclear Operations: A Metagame Analysis." *Journal of Conflict Resolution,* XXIII (June 1979), 326–336.

1578. Ross, Dennis. "Rethinking Soviet Strategic Policy: Inputs and Implications." In: Wolfram F. Hanrieder, ed. *Arms Control and Security: Current Issues.* Boulder, Colo.: Westview, 1979. Chpt. 7.

1579. Schneider, Mark B. "Soviet Nuclear Doctrine." *National Defense,* LXIII (January–February 1979), 51–53.

1580. Schneider, William, Jr. "Survivable ICBMs." *Strategic Review,* VI (Fall 1978), 13–28.

1581. Simpson, Benjamin M., 3rd. "Current Strategic Theories." *Naval War College Review,* XXIV (May 1972), 76–85.

1582. Skirdo, M. P. "Nuclear Missile War." In: *The People, the Army the Commander: A Soviet View.* Translated from the Russian. Soviet Military Thought Series, no. 14. Washington, D.C.: Published under the auspices of the U.S. Air Force by the U.S. Government Printing Office, 1977. pp. 16–23.

1583. "Soviet Nuclear and Rocket Policy." *Aeroplane,* CI (November 16, 1961), 650–651.

1584. "Strategic Warfare." *Space/Aeronautics,* LIII (January 1970), 59–69.

1585. Thomas, John R. "Limited Nuclear War in Soviet Strategic Thinking." *Orbis,* X (Spring 1966), 184–212.

1586. Tolubko, Vladimir F. "Tolubko on the Mission and Readiness of the Strategic Missile Forces: Translated from *Kommunist Vooruzhennykh Sil,* December 1977." *Translations on USSR Military Affairs,* no. 1330 (February 15, 1978), 12–21.

1587. Whiting, Kenneth R. "The Debate Between Khrushchev and His Marshals." *Air University Quarterly Review,* XVI (March–April 1965), 68–79.

1588. Wolfe, Thomas W. "Soviet Strategic Policy." In: Michael MccGwire, ed. *Soviet Naval Developments, Capabilities and Context.* New York: Praeger, 1973. pp. 70–81.

Documents, Papers, and Reports

1589. Dinerstein, Herbert S. *The Revolution in Soviet Strategic Thinking.* RAND Paper P-1927. Santa Monica, Calif.: Rand Corporation, 1957. 24p.

1590. Douglass, Joseph D., Jr. *The Soviet Theater Nuclear Offensive.* Research Note, no. 201. Arlington, Va.: Systems Planning Corporation, 1975. 88p.

1591. Gray, Colin S. *The Geopolitics of the Nuclear Era: Heartland, Rimlands, and the Technological Revolution.* New York: Published for the National Strategy Information Center by Crane, Russak, 1977. 70p.

1592. Horelick, Arnold and Myron Rush. *The Political Use of Soviet Strategic Power.* RAND Memorandum RM-2831-PR. Santa Monica, Calif.: RAND Corporation, 1962. 139p.

1593. Intriligator, Michael D. *Strategy in a Missile War: Targets and Rates of Fire.* Security Studies Paper, no. 10. Los Angeles, Calif.: University of California, 1967. 77p.

1594. Kang, Young H. "The Relationship Between the Development of Strategic Nuclear Weapons Systems and Deterrence Doctrine in the Soviet Union and China." Unpublished Ph.D. Dissertation, University of Southern California, 1973.

1595. Kolkowicz, Roman. *The Soviet Strategic Debate: An Important Recent Addendum.* RAND Paper P-2936. Santa Monica, Calif.: RAND Corporation, 1964. 38p.

1596. Khrushchev, Nikita S. *Key Khrushchev Missile Statements.* Washington, D.C.: Bureau of Intelligence and Research, Department of State, 1960. 50p.

1597. Lambeth, Benjamin S. *Selective Nuclear Options in American and Soviet Strategic Policy.* RAND Report R-2034-DDRE. Santa Monica, Calif.: RAND Corporation, 1976. 56p.

1598. Luttwak, Edward. *Strategic Power: Military Capabilities and Political Utility.* Washington Papers, vol. 4, no. 38. Beverly Hills, Calif.: Sage, 1976. 70p.

1599. Scianna, Philip P. *Soviet Strategic Doctrine: Toward an Effective Military Posture.* Alexandria, Va.: Army Military Personnel Center, 1978. 146p.

1600. Snyder, Jack L. *The Soviet Strategic Culture: Implications for Limited Nuclear Operations.* RAND Report R-2154-AF. Santa Monica, Calif.: RAND Corporation, 1977. 40p.

1601. United States. Congress. House. Committee on Armed Services. Subcommittee on Intelligence and the Military Application of Nuclear Energy. *Land-Based ICBM Forces Vulnerability and Options: A Staff Report.* 95th Cong., 2nd sess. Washington, D.C.: U.S. Government Printing Office, 1978. 14p.

1602. _____. _____. Senate. Committee on Armed Services. *U.S.-U.S.S.R. Strategic Policies: Hearings.* 93rd Cong., 2nd sess. Washington, D.C.: U.S. Government Printing Office, 1974. 57p.

1603. _____. _____. _____. Committee on Foreign Relations. *Nuclear Weapons and Foreign Policy: Hearings.* 93rd Cong., 2nd sess. Washington, D.C.: U.S. Government Printing Office, 1974. 316p.

1604. _____. _____. _____. _____. Subcommittee on Arms Control, Oceans, and International Environment. *United States/Soviet Strategic Options: Hearings.* 95th Cong., 1st sess. Washington, D.C.: U.S. Government Printing Office, 1977. 187p.

1605. Wolfe, Thomas W. *Some Recent Signs of Reaction Against Prevailing Soviet Doctrinal Emphasis on Missiles.* RAND Paper P-2929. Santa Monica, Calif.: RAND Corporation, 1964. 11p.

E. Personnel, Training, and Exercises

1. Personnel

a. GENERAL STUDIES

Books

1606. Babenko, I. *Soviet Officers*. Moscow: Progress Publishers, 1976. 133p.

1607. Kozlov, S. N., ed. *The Officer's Handbook: A Soviet View*. Translated from the Russian. Soviet Military Thought Series, no. 13. Washington, D.C.: Published under the auspices of the U.S. Air Force by the U.S. Government Printing Office, 1977. 358p.

Articles

1608. "The Beauty of Rocketeer Service." *Translations on USSR Military Affairs*, no. 153a (September 1964), 28–32.

1609. Bialer, Seweryn. "Konstantin Andreevich Vershinin." In: George W. Simmonds, ed. *Soviet Leaders*. New York: T. Y. Crowell, 1967. pp. 138–141.

1610. Chopovskiy, V. "Role of the Chief of Staff in a Missile Unit Described: Translated from *Krasnaya Zvezda*, September 22, 1977." *Translations on USSR Military Affairs*, no. 1325 (January 19, 1978), 12–15.

1611. "Discussion on the Style of Work of the Chief of Staff (PVO)." *Translations on USSR Military Affairs*, no. 40 (December 1960), 1–5.

1612. Dokuchayev, I. "Career of Missile Officer Described: Translated from *Krasnaya Zvezda*, April 14, 1978." *Translations on USSR Military Affairs*, no. 1368 (August 3, 1978), 18–20.

1613. Drozdov, V. "The Soviet Officer Corps." *Soviet Military Review*, nos. 1–2 (January–February 1977), 5–9, 5–9.

1614. Erickson, John. "Soviet Military Manpower Policies." *Armed Forces and Society*, I (November 1974), 29–47.

1615. Fast, Harriet F. "A New Chief [Marshal of Aviation Pavel S. Kutakov] for the Soviet Air Force." *Air University Review*, XX (September–October 1969), 73–76.

1616. Friedman, William S. "The Story of a Russian Bomber Pilot." *Air Force*, XXXIV (April 1951), 28–31.

1617. Ghebhardt, Alexander O. and William Schneider, Jr. "The Soviet Air Force High Command." *Air University Review,* XXIV (May–June 1973), 75–83.

1618. Grigor'yev, Mikhail G. "Service in Strategic Missile Forces Described: Translated from *Voyennyye Znaniya,* March 1978." *Translations on USSR Military Affairs,* no. 1352 (May 15, 1978), 81–86.

1619. Hawkins, D. G. "The Soviet Pilot." *Hawk,* no. 39 (Winter 1978–1979), 61–65.

1620. Jarecki, Franciszek. "What It Means to be a Red Jet Pilot." *Air Force,* XXXVI (July 1953), 30–31.

1621. Krylov, Nikolai I. "Strategic Missile Troops: An Interview as Translated from *Pravda,* November 19, 1969." *Current Digest of the Soviet Press,* XXI (December 17, 1969), 6–7.

1622. Kuban, Boris. "Daily Life in the Soviet Air Force." In: Asher Lee, ed. *The Soviet Air and Rocket Forces.* New York: Praeger, 1959. pp. 216–229.

1623. _____. "How the Red Air Force Lives." *Air Force,* XLII (October 1959), 42.

1624. Leonard, George B., Jr. "Meet the Soviet Pilot." *Air Training,* II (May 1953), 8–12.

1625. Loosbrock, John F. "Red Pilots Never Had It So Good." *Air Force,* XXXVII (August 1954), 21–24.

1626. "Materials on PVO Rocket Units." *Translations on USSR Military Affairs,* no. 47 (November 1960), 1–27.

1627. "Materials on PVO Troops." *Translations on USSR Military Affairs,* nos. 102–103 (September–October 1962), 1–47, 2–15.

1628. "Materials on Rocket, PVO, and Ground Troops." *Translations on USSR Military Affairs,* no. 112 (December 1962), 2–35.

1629. "The Men Who Guide the Rockets." *Translations on USSR Military Affairs,* no. 50 (March 1961), 17–21.

1630. "Missilemen." *Soviet Military Review,* no. 9 (September 1974), 8–9.

1631. "People of the Week: Marshal Konstantin Andreevich Vershinin." *U.S. News and World Report,* XLIII (September 20, 1957), 12.

1632.   Schlieper, Fritz. "Life in the Soviet Forces." *Military Review*, XLII (June 1962), 74–86.

1633.   Selyodkin, V. "Maturing of Soldiers: Experience in Work with Young Soldiers [Missilemen] of the Air Defense Forces." *Soviet Military Review*, no. 8 (August 1976), 36–37.

1634.   "Shakeups in Soviet Air Commands." *Air Force*, XL (September 1957), 20.

1635.   Smith, David A. "Soviet Military Manpower." *Air Force Magazine*, LX (March 1977), 78–81.

1636.   Stockwell, Richard D. "The Soviet Pilot is Quite a Fellow." *Flying*, LXIII (September 1961), 34–35.

1637.   Tapman, Thomas F. "I Met a MIG-19 Squadron Commander." *TAC Attack*, XVII (July 1977), 24–26.

1638.   Williams, E. S. "The Soviet Airman." *Royal Air Forces Quarterly*, XIII (Spring–Winter 1973), 17–22, 109–114, 193–199, 297–302; XV (Spring 1975), 17–22.

Documents, Papers, and Reports

1639.   Tsyganov, Nikolay G. *Air Defense Troops, U.S.S.R.* Translation, no. 40227. Arlington, Va.: Joint Publication Research Service, 1967. 6p.

b. Defectors

Books

1640.   Barron, John. *MIG Pilot: The Final Escape of Lt.* [Viktor] *Belenko*. New York: Reader's Digest Press; dist. by McGraw-Hill, 1980. 217p.

1641.   Pirogov, Petr. *Why I Escaped*. New York: Duell, 1950. 336p.

Articles

1642.   Barron, John. "MIG Pilot." *Reader's Digest*, CXVI (January 1980), 187–226.

1643.   "Lieutenant Belenko's [MIG-25] Gift." *Time*, CVIII (September 20, 1976), 24–25.

1644.   "MIG-25 Pilot Lands Fighter at Hakodate." *Aviation Week and Space Technology*, CV (September 20, 1976), 26–27.

1645.   "Plucking Out a Thorn [Grisha I. Feigin]." *Newsweek*, LXXVII (February 15, 1971), 38.

1646.	Taylor, John W. R. "The Freedom Flight of Kum Suk No." *Airman,* XX (January 1976), 38–40.

1647.	"Unexpected Gift: MIG-25." *Science Digest,* LXXX (December 1976), 10–11.

1648.	Willenson, K. "Bagging a Foxbat: Defector Viktor Belenko Landing MIG-25 in Japan." *Newsweek,* LXXXV (September 20, 1976), 63.

2. Training

a. AVIATION

Books

1649.	Danchenko, A. M. and I. F. Vydrin. *Military Pedagogy: A Soviet View.* Translated from the Russian. Soviet Military Thought Series, no. 7. Washington, D.C.: Published under the auspices of the U.S. Air Force by the U.S. Government Printing Office, 1976. 363p.

1650.	Trilling, Leon. *Soviet Education in Aeronautics.* Cambridge: MIT Center for International Studies, Massachusetts Institute of Technology, 1956. 112p.

Articles

1651.	Adrianov, A. "Problems Involving Flight Instructors Discussed: Translated from *Aviatsiya I Kosmonavtika,* July 1978." *Translations on USSR Military Affairs,* no. 1387 (October 18, 1978), 21–25.

1652.	Agal'tsov, Filipp A. "Fewer Excuses, Higher Combat Readiness." *Translations on USSR Military Affairs,* no. 39 (November 1960), 5–10.

1653.	Barmin, V. "Methods of Training on New Aircraft Described: Translated from *Aviatsiya I Kosmonavtika,* November 1978." *Translations on USSR Military Affairs,* no. 1417 (March 9, 1979), 1–6.

1654.	Bazanov, Petr V. "Veteran Advises on the Training of Young Pilots: Translated from *Krasnaya Zvezda,* December 3, 1977." *Translations on USSR Military Affairs,* no. 1338 (March 16, 1978), 27–32.

1655.	Biryuzov, S. "Training the Soviet Forces." *Survival,* VI (July–August 1964), 188–192.

1656.	Borovykh, A. "A Pilot's Combat Readiness." *Soviet Military Review,* no. 1 (January 1974), 15–17.

Soviet Aerospace Forces, 1946 to the Present 135

1657. Borsuk, A. "Training of Flight Commanders Described: Translated from *Aviatsiya I Kosmonavtika*, November 1977." *Translations on USSR Military Affairs*, no. 1328 (February 2, 1978), 134–139.

1658. Cherednichenko, V. "Outstanding Air Defense Unit Training Activities: Translated from *Krasnaya Zvezda*, November 16, 1977." *Translations on USSR Military Affairs*, no. 1333 (February 27, 1978), 23–26.

1659. Denisenko, P. "Mastering Advanced Flying." *Soviet Military Review*, no. 6 (June 1978), 26–28.

1660. "Doctrine and Training." *Translations on USSR Military Affairs*, no. 99 (September 17, 1962), 2–62.

1661. Duncan, Charles W., Jr. "Air Force Higher Education." *Air Force Policy Letter for Commanders*, no. 3 (March 1979), 31–33.

1662. "The Educational Background and Training of Soviet Air Force Officers." *Royal Air Forces Quarterly*, XVI (Winter 1976), 333–335.

1663. Fedorov, P. "Methods of Training for Firing from Helicopters Described: Translated from *Znamenosets*, April 1978." *Translations on USSR Military Affairs*, no. 1367 (July 25, 1978), 40–48.

1664. "Fighter Pilot Training in the Soviet Air Force." *Interavia*, XX (October 1965), 1612.

1665. Fil'chenko, L. "Instruction Quality in [Gagarin] Air Force Academy Praised: Translated from *Krasnaya Zvezda*, September 3, 1977." *Translations on USSR Military Affairs*, no. 1328 (February 2, 1978), 9–11.

1666. Garanin, Viktor. "Learning to Fly: An Interview." *Soviet Military Review*, no. 8 (August 1977), 11–14.

1667. Gnusar'kov, V. "Retraining on New Aircraft—Factors Involved: Translated from *Aviatsiya I Kosmonavtika*, January 1978." *Translations on USSR Military Affairs*, no. 1346 (April 13, 1978), 51–55.

1668. Green, William. "Training—Red Weakness?" *Flying*, LI (October 1952), 12–13, 40.

1669. Gudymenko, Yu. "Helicopter Ground Support Training Described: Translated from *Aviatsiya I Kosmonavtika*, May 1978." *Translations on USSR Military Affairs*, no. 1364 (July 18, 1978), 44–49.

1670. Head, Richard G. "Russian Military Education." *Military Review*, LIX (February 1979), 14–16.

1671. _____. "Soviet Military Education." *Air University Review,* XXX (November–December 1978), 45–57.

1672. Ivanov, B. "Procedures for Improving Flight Combat Training Discussed: Translated from *Aviatsiya I Kosmonavtika,* June 1978." *Translations on USSR Military Affairs,* no. 1376 (September 12, 1978), 1–6.

1673. Izgarshev, V. "Military Transport Aviation Training Described: Translated from *Pravda,* January 4, 1979." *Translations on USSR Military Affairs,* no. 1435 (May 15, 1979), 1–6.

1674. _____. "Training Activities in an Outstanding Helicopter Regiment: Translated from *Krasnaya Zvezda,* August 26, 1978." *Translations on USSR Military Affairs,* no. 1404 (December 21, 1978), 42–55.

1675. Kadyshev, V. "Interceptor Pilots' Navigational Training." *Soviet Military Review,* no. 11 (November 1976), 28–29.

1676. Kalinayev, S. "Training Activities in Yeysk Aviation School Described: Translated from *Krasnaya Zvezda,* October 26, 1978." *Translations on USSR Military Affairs,* no. 1413 (February 28, 1979), 89–93.

1677. Kharlamov, S. "Effectiveness of DOSAAF Aviation Training Debated: Translated from *Sovetskiy Patriot,* August 6, 1978." *Translations on USSR Military Affairs,* no. 1381 (October 2, 1978), 68–72.

1678. Kirsanov, P. "Tactical Training of Fighter Pilots: Translated from *Aviatsiya I Kosmonavtika,* January 1978." *Translations on USSR Military Affairs,* no. 1346 (April 13, 1978), 20–26.

1679. Klochikhin, L. "Advanced Flight Training—Definition and Purpose: Translated from *Aviatsiya I Kosmonavtika,* July 1978." *Translations on USSR Military Affairs,* no. 1388 (October 23, 1978), 35–40.

1680. Konkov, N. "Air Force Engineers' School [Yakov Alksnis Higher Aviation Engineering School at Riga]." *Soviet Military Review,* no. 7 (July 1976), 42–43.

1681. Konyukhov, A. "The Training of Air Snipers." *Soviet Military Review,* no. 3 (March 1974), 16–17.

1682. Kulikov, N. "A Pilot's Activity and Resolve." *Soviet Military Review,* no. 11 (November 1974), 11–13.

1683. Kuts, S. "Helicopter Regiment Training Results Described: Translated from *Krasnaya Zvezda,* November 15, 1977." *Translations on USSR Military Affairs,* no. 1334 (March 2, 1978), 55–58.

1684. Kuznetsov, V. "Special Flight Conditions." *Soviet Military Review*, no. 7 (July 1971), 23–24.

1685. Makarov, V. "Effectiveness of Officer Schools Discussed: Translated from *Krasnaya Zvezda*, September 14, 1977." *Translations on USSR Military Affairs*, no. 1328 (February 2, 1978), 38–42.

1686. Malinovsky, Rodion Y. "Soviet Military Education." *Military Review*, XLVII (February 1967), 30–37.

1687. "Military Air Training." *Aviation Age*, XVI (July 1951), 55–57.

1688. Moroz, Ivan M. "Interview: Translated from *Kryl'ya Rodiny*, August 1978." *Translations on USSR Military Affairs*, no. 1388 (October 23, 1978), 7–13.

1689. Murphy, Paul J. and Margaret, comps. "Higher Soviet Naval and Related Military Schools." In: Paul J. Murphy, ed. *Naval Power in Soviet Policy*. Studies in Communist Affairs, no. 2. Washington, D.C.: Published under the auspices of the U.S. Air Force by the U.S. Government Printing Office, 1978. pp. 307–311.

1690. Murray, Michael P., Jr. "The Education and Training of Soviet Air Force Officers." *Strategic Review*, V (Spring 1977), 83–88.

1691. New, George. "Nikolai is Ready." *Air Training*, IV (October 1954), 7–10.

1692. Novikov, A. "Fighter Pilot Training Procedures Described: Translated from *Aviatsiya I Kosmonavtika*, October 1977." *Translations on USSR Military Affairs*, no. 1322 (January 9, 1978), 29–34.

1693. Odom, William E. "The Soviet Military-Educational Complex." In: Dale R. Herspring and Ivan Volgyes, eds. *Civil-Military Relations in the Communist System*. Boulder, Colo.: Westview, 1978. Chpt. 4.

1694. Oleynik, A. "Transport Aircraft Crew Training for Paradrop Described: Translated from *Krasnaya Zvezda*, May 30, 1978." *Translations on USSR Military Affairs*, no. 1370 (August 17, 1978), 86–89.

1695. Puzanov, A. "Fighter-Interceptor Squadron Training Described: Translated from *Krasnaya Zvezda*, September 6, 1977." *Translations on USSR Military Affairs*, no. 1327 (January 27, 1978), 1–4.

1696. "Red Air Force Training Schools Accused of Instruction Deficiencies." *Aviation Week and Space Technology*, LXVI (February 11, 1957), 75.

1697. Ryzhov, V. "Need for Combat Pilot Independence and Initiative Stressed: Translated from *Aviatsiya I Kosmonavtika*, January 1978." *Translations on USSR Military Affairs*, no. 1346 (April 13, 1978), 34–40.

1698. Safronov, P. "Methods of Tactical Flight Training Discussed: Translated from *Krasnaya Zvezda*, November 26, 1977." *Translations on USSR Military Affairs*, no. 1334 (March 2, 1978), 108–112.

1699. _____. "Training Procedures in an Outstanding Air Regiment: Translated from *Aviatsiya I Kosmonavtika*, December 1977." *Translations on USSR Military Affairs*, no. 1333 (February 27, 1978), 97–102.

1700. Schatunowskii, George. "The Training of Personnel." In: Asher Lee, ed. *The Soviet Air and Rocket Forces*. New York: Praeger, 1959. pp. 21–47.

1701. Schleicher, Rolf. "Activities at Yuri Gagarin Military Air Academy: Translated from *Volksarmee*, no. 2, 1978." *Translations on USSR Military Affairs*, no. 1336 (March 10, 1978), 115–118.

1702. Scott, Harriet F. "Educating the Soviet Officer Corps." *Air Force Magazine*, LVIII (March 1975), 57–60.

1703. _____. "Universal Military Training in the U.S.S.R." *Air Force Magazine*, LXI (March 1978), 84–88.

1704. Sergeyev, O. "Training Progress of Young Pilots Discussed: Translated from *Krasnaya Zvezda*, May 4, 1978." *Translations on USSR Military Affairs*, no. 1370 (August 17, 1978), 15–19.

1705. Seymov, P. "Parachute Rescue Training for Pilots: Translated from *Aviatsiya I Kosmonavtika*, September 1978." *Translations on USSR Military Affairs*, no. 1391 (October 30, 1978), 94–98.

1706. Shchitov, G. "Training Procedures of a Guards Air Regiment Described: Translated from *Krasnaya Zvezda*, May 18, 1978." *Translations on USSR Military Affairs*, no. 1373 (August 29, 1978), 107–111.

1707. Smirnov, Aleksandr V. "Fighter Ace Views on Training Described: Translated from *Rabochaya Gazeta*, February 15, 1978." *Translations on USSR Military Affairs*, no. 1359 (June 25, 1978), 1–5.

1708. Sorokin, A. "Aviation Regiment Training Activities Discussed: Translated from *Krasnaya Zvezda*, September 7, 1978." *Translations on USSR Military Affairs*, no. 1382 (October 3, 1978), 29–33.

1709. _____. "Long-Range Bomber Training Mission Described: Translated from *Krasnaya Zvezda*, January 25, 1978." *Translations on USSR Military Affairs*, no. 1347 (April 19, 1978), 40–44.

1710. "The Soviet Air Force Engineering Academy." *RAF Flying Review*, XIII (July 1958), 41.

1711. "Soviet Military Air Training." *Canadian Army Journal*, V (November 1951), 44–48.

1712. Sulyanov, A. "Pilots' Navigational Training." *Soviet Military Review*, no. 10 (October 1974), 38–39.

1713. "Tactical Training for Fighter Pilots." *Translations on USSR Military Affairs*, no. 128 (October 1963), 18–21.

1714. "Training Activities in Air Defense Units: Translated from *Krasnaya Zvezda*." *Translations on USSR Military Affairs*, no. 1401 (December 13, 1978), 104–113.

1715. _____. *Translations on USSR Military Affairs*, no. 1414 (March 1, 1979), 8–26.

1716. _____. *Translations on USSR Military Affairs*, no. 1423 (March 26, 1979), 3–17.

1717. _____. *Translations on USSR Military Affairs*, no. 1428 (April 13, 1979), 1–12.

1718. _____. *Translations on USSR Military Affairs*, no. 1433 (May 4, 1979), 8–20.

1719. _____. *Translations on USSR Military Affairs*, no. 1449 (June 25, 1979), 53–73.

1720. "Training Activities in Aviation Units: Translated from *Krasnaya Zvezda*." *Translations on USSR Military Affairs*, no. 1401 (December 13, 1978), 83–92.

1721. _____. *Translations on USSR Military Affairs*, no. 1404 (December 21, 1978), 27–41.

1722. _____. *Translations on USSR Military Affairs*, no. 1423 (March 26, 1979), 66–76.

1723. _____. *Translations on USSR Military Affairs*, no. 1428 (April 13, 1979), 27–34.

1724. _____. *Translations on USSR Military Affairs*, no. 1431 (April 30, 1979), 1–9.

1725. _____. *Translations on USSR Military Affairs*, no. 1433 (May 4, 1979), 20–33.

1726. _____ . *Translations on USSR Military Affairs,* no. 1448 (June 21, 1979), 1–13.

1727. "Training of Helicopter Pilots." *Translations on USSR Military Affairs,* no. 192a (November 1965), 42–47.

1728. Trusov, V. "Helicopter Squadron Training Activities Described: Translated from *Krasnaya Zvezda,* July 13, 1978." *Translations on USSR Military Affairs,* no. 1382 (October 3, 1978), 42–45.

1729. Uryuzhnikov, V. "Criteria for Flight Training Objectives Discussed: Translated from *Krasnaya Zvezda,* April 18, 1978." *Translations on USSR Military Affairs,* no. 1369 (August 9, 1978), 24–28.

1730. Walen, W. W. "The Russian Air Force Academy." *Talon,* IV (March 1959), 8–9.

1731. Yefimov, Aleksandr. "Equipment + Aerodynamics + Tactics: An Interview." *Soviet Military Review,* no. 8 (August 1971), 13–15.

1732. Yurkin, A. "Helicopter Unit Tasks and Training Activities Considered: Translated from *Krasnaya Zvezda,* November 5, 1977." *Translations on USSR Military Affairs,* no. 1331 (February 16, 1978), 3–6.

1733. Zhal'nerauskas, R. "Status of DOSAAF Aviation Training in the Lithuanian SSR: Translated from *Sovetskiy Patriot,* November 20, 1977." *Translations on USSR Military Affairs,* no. 1323 (January 11, 1978), 23–26.

1734. Zharko, V. "Fighter-Interceptor Tactical Training Described: Translated from *Krasnaya Zvezda,* September 21, 1977." *Translations on USSR Military Affairs,* no. 1328 (February 2, 1978), 71–73.

1735. Zhukov, A. "Training of Long-Range Bomber Crews Described: Translated from *Aviatsiya I Kosmonavtika,* November 1977." *Translations on USSR Military Affairs,* no. 1328 (February 2, 1978), 140–144.

1736. Zhuravlev, V. "Far East Military District Aviation Training Results Discussed: Translated from *Krasnaya Zvezda,* June 14, 1978." *Translations on USSR Military Affairs,* no. 1378 (September 21, 1978), 36–41.

Documents, Papers, and Reports

1737. Olmstead, William S. *Current Aspects of the Combat Training of Soviet National Air Defense Troops.* New York: Army Institute for Advanced Russian and East European Studies, 1976. 43p.

Soviet Aerospace Forces, 1946 to the Present 141

b. Missiles

1738. Bud'ko, A. "Mobile Missile Crew Training Described: Translated from *Znamenosets*, November 1978." *Translations on USSR Military Affairs*, no. 1417 (March 9, 1979), 18–21.

1739. "Combat Training of Rocket Troops." *Translations on USSR Military Affairs*, no. 263 (May 1966), 39–45.

1740. Dobrov, G. "Training Procedures for Air Defense Missile Troops Compared: Translated from *Krasnaya Zvezda*, August 18, 1978." *Translations on USSR Military Affairs*, no. 1398 (November 29, 1978), 37–41.

1741. Dokuchayev, I. "Training Procedures in an Air Defense Missile Unit Described: Translated from *Krasnaya Zvezda*, July 15, 1978." *Translations on USSR Military Affairs*, no. 1385 (October 11, 1978), 6–10.

1742. Fedorov, A. "Training Results in Strategic Missile Forces: Translated from *Kommunist Vooruzhennysk Sil*, October 1977." *Translations on USSR Military Affairs*, no. 1321 (January 9, 1978), 12–21.

1743. "Greater Combat Readiness for PVO Soldiers." *Translations on USSR Military Affairs*, no. 50 (March 1961), 10–13.

1744. Ivanov, V. "Complex Training of a Launching Battery." *Soviet Military Review*, no. 3 (March 1978), 19–20.

1745. Konnov, A. "Missile Control Officers' Training." *Soviet Military Review*, no. 4 (April 1977), 18–19.

1746. Lavreichuk, V. "Training of AA Gunners." *Soviet Military Review*, no. 3 (March 1977), 21–22.

1747. Lebedev, L. "Improvement of Training in Air Defense Missile Unit Described: Translated from *Krasnaya Zvezda*, May 20, 1978." *Translations on USSR Military Affairs*, no. 1372 (August 24, 1978), 38–41.

1748. "Methods Lesson with Officers of a Missile Unit." *Soviet Military Review*, no. 4 (April 1974), 40–41.

1749. "Missile Training and Indoctrination." *Translations on USSR Military Affairs*, no. 146 (June 1964), 32–36.

1750. "Missile Units—Training Activities and Results." *Translations on USSR Military Affairs*, no. 1327 (January 27, 1978), 28–39.

1751. Obukhov, V. "Improving Missilemen's Proficiency." *Soviet Military Review*, no. 2 (February 1978), 34–35.

1752. Petrov, A. "Training Activities in a Tactical Missile Battery: Translated from *Krasnaya Zvezda,* May 21, 1978." *Translations on USSR Military Affairs,* no. 1372 (August 24, 1978), 42–45.

1753. Polezhayev, V. "Combat Training of Air Defense Crews: Translated from *Izvestia,* February 19, 1978." *Translations on USSR Military Affairs,* no. 1344 (April 7, 1978), 168–171.

1754. Pryadko, P. "Air Defense Missile Crew Training Described: Translated from *Krasnaya Zvezda,* September 20, 1977." *Translations on USSR Military Affairs,* no. 1328 (February 2, 1978), 64–67.

1755. "A Report on Training for Launching Ground-Air Rockets." *Translations on USSR Military Affairs,* no. 161a (October 1964), 1–12.

1756. Sinyutin, V. "Training Objectives in an Air Defense Missile Unit: Translated from *Krasnaya Zvezda,* November 29, 1977." *Translations on USSR Military Affairs,* no. 1331 (February 16, 1978), 29–32.

1757. Tkachenko, N. "Training of Missilemen Described: Translated from *Krasnaya Zvezda,* April 11, 1978." *Translations on USSR Military Affairs,* no. 1366 (July 20, 1978), 63–67.

1758. "Training Activities in Air Defense Missile Units: Translated from *Krasnaya Zvezda.*" *Translations on USSR Military Affairs,* no. 1353 (May 22, 1978), 12–24.

1759. _____ . *Translations on USSR Military Affairs,* no. 1357 (June 14, 1978), 37–45.

1760. "Training Activities in Missile Units: Translated from *Krasnaya Zvezda.*" *Translations on USSR Military Affairs,* no. 1371 (August 21, 1978), 1–12.

1761. _____ . *Translations on USSR Military Affairs,* no. 1378 (September 21, 1978), 18–29.

1762. "The Training of Missilemen." *Translations on USSR Military Affairs,* no. 152a (September 1964), 32–37.

1763. Vishenkov, Vladimir M. "Training and Readiness of Strategic Rocket Forces Discussed: Translated from *Sotsialisticheskaya Industriya,* February 21, 1978." *Translations on USSR Military Affairs,* no. 1348 (April 27, 1978), 114–118.

1764. Zakharov, A. "Air Defense Battery Training for Low-Flying Targets: Translated from *Znamenosets,* January 1978." *Translations on USSR Military Affairs,* no. 1344 (April 7, 1978), 112–115.

Documents, Papers, and Reports

1765.   Shevchenko, N. A. *Advice on Mastering Small Arms and Rocket Launchers.* Translated from the Russian. Report, no. FSTC-HT-23-0462-75. Charlottesville, Va.: Army Foreign Science and Technology Center, 1975. 146p.

3. Exercises

Articles

1766.   Bazanov, Petr V. "Air Operations at the 'Berezina' Exercise." *Soviet Military Review,* no. 11 (November 1978), 18–19.

1767.   ———. "Aircraft Operations at the 'Berezina' Field Exercise Discussed: Translated from *Aviatsiya I Kosmonavtika,* April 1978." *Translations on USSR Military Affairs,* no. 1364 (July 18, 1978), 27–33.

1768.   "'Berezina' Field Training Exercise." *Translations on USSR Military Affairs,* no. 1350 (May 8, 1978), 32–83.

1769.   Berlovskiy, N. "Problems of Flights Away from Home Base Discussed: Translated from *Aviatsiya I Kosmonavtika,* November 1978." *Translations on USSR Military Affairs,* no. 1417 (March 9, 1979), 6–11.

1770.   Dudnik, A. "Long-Range Overwater Air Intercept Exercise Described: Translated from *Krasnaya Zvezda,* December 7, 1977." *Translations on USSR Military Affairs,* no. 1342 (March 29, 1978), 17–20.

1771.   Gukasov, G. "Troop Carrier Aircraft in Airborne Exercise: Translated from *Izvestia,* January 26, 1978." *Translations on USSR Military Affairs,* no. 1344 (April 7, 1978), 164–168.

1772.   Ivanov, G. "Helicopter-Motorized Infantry Landing Exercise: Translated from *Krasnaya Zvezda,* August 2, 1978." *Translations on USSR Military Affairs,* no. 1407 (December 19, 1978), 9–12.

1773.   Meehan, James F., 3rd. "Soviet Maneuvers: Summer 1971." *Military Review,* LII (April 1972), 14–21.

1774.   "Missile Crew Field Training." *Translations on USSR Military Affairs,* no. 130 (November 1963), 15–19.

1775.   Pryadko, Y. "Tactical Air Exercises of a Squadron." *Soviet Military Review,* no. 9 (September 1975), 24–26.

1776.   Robinson, Clarence A., Jr. "Soviets Test Cold-Launch ICBM Firings." *Aviation Week and Space Technology,* XCIX (September 24, 1973), 20.

1777. "The 'Sever' Maneuvers." *Soviet Military Review*, no. 10 (October 1976), 17–19.

1778. "Soviet Crews Simulate Scud [SS-lc] Firing." *Aviation Week and Space Technology*, XCII (April 20, 1970), 54–55.

1779. "Soviets Display Cold Launch SS-11 [Sego]." *Aviation Week and Space Technology*, XCIX (November 26, 1973), 18–19.

1780. Tolstoy, S. "Pilot Error in Bombing Exercise Discussed: Translated from *Aviatsiya I Kosmonavtika*, October 1977." *Translations on USSR Military Affairs*, no. 1321 (January 9, 1978), 47–50.

1781. Turbiville, Graham H., Jr., "Warsaw Pact Exercise: 'Shield '72'" *Military Review*, LIII (July 1973), 17–24.

1782. Vetrovoy, P. "Bomber Crew Training Exercises Described: Translated from *Aviatsiya I Kosmonavtika*, February 1979." *Translations on USSR Military Affairs*, no. 1439 (May 21, 1979), 30–34.

1783. Vigor, Peter H. "Soviet Military Exercises." *Journal of the Royal United Service Institution for Defence Studies*, CXVI (September 1971), 23–29.

Documents, Papers, and Reports

1784. Stadnyuk, Ivan. *Dnepr War Games in Ukraine and Belorussia*. Translation, no. 43324. Arlington, Va.: Joint Publication Research Service, 1967. 4p.

F. Logistics, Bases, and Technical Support

Book

1785. Dickson, Paul. *The Electronic Battlefield*. Bloomington: Indiana University Press, 1976. 256p.

Articles

1786. Amelchenko, V. "Flying from Non-Metalled Airfields." *Soviet Military Review*, no. 1 (January 1966), 1–3.

1787. "Aviation Ground Service Operations Described: Translated from *Znamenosets*, August 1978." *Translations on USSR Military Affairs*, no. 1392 (November 2, 1978), 30–35.

1788. *Aviation Week and Space Technology*, Editors of. "Electronic Counter-measures Symposium: A Special Report." *Aviation Week and Space Technology*, XCVI (February 21, 1972), 33–40.

1789. _____. "Special Report on Electronic Warfare." *Aviation Week and Space Technology*, XCIV (January 27, 1975), 41–144.

1790. Baar, James and William E. Howard. "Russia's Big Missile Bases." *Missiles and Rockets*, VI (February 15, 1960), 25–29.

1791. Balabolin, M. "Aircraft Service Operations in Winter Described: Translated from *Znamenosets*, January 1979." *Translations on USSR Military Affairs*, no. 1438 (May 18, 1979), 58–61.

1792. Chupov, V. "Air Force Logistics." *Soviet Military Review*, no. 8 (August 1979), 8–9.

1793. "Equipment and Its Use so that Rockets Strike Their Targets Accurately." *Translations on USSR Military Affairs*, no. 168 (December 1964), 5–9.

1794. Gastello, V. "Preflight Preparation of Armament." *Soviet Military Review*, no. 11 (November 1978), 24–25.

1795. Gusev, V. "Training of Aviation Maintenance Personnel Noted: Translated from *Aviatsiya I Kosmonavtika*, July 1978." *Translations on USSR Military Affairs*, no. 1387 (October 18, 1978), 26–31.

1796. Kondioglo, A. "Need for Supply Economy in Air Force Units Noted: Translated from *Aviatsiya I Kosmonavtika*, February 1979." *Translations on USSR Military Affairs*, no. 1444 (June 4, 1979), 1–5.

1797. Mamayev, V. "Flight Control Officers—Good and Bad Examples Described: Translated from *Aviatsiya I Kosmonavtika*, October 1977." *Translations on USSR Military Affairs*, no. 1321 (January 9, 1978), 41–46.

1798. Nikitin, V. "Aviation Weather Forecasting Operations Described: Translated from *Krasnaya Zvezda*, August 4, 1978." *Translations on USSR Military Affairs*, no. 1399 (December 4, 1978), 24–27.

1799. Orlov, V. "Winter Airfield Service Operations Described: Translated from *Aviatsiya I Kosmonavtika*, February 1979." *Translations on USSR Military Affairs*, no. 1444 (June 4, 1979), 5–10.

1800. Ponamaryov, A. N. "Aircraft Equipment and Its Development." *Soviet Military Review*, no. 8 (August 1979), 2–5.

1801. Prikhodchenko, G. "Aircraft Maintenance Procedures: Translated from *Znamenosets*, November 1977." *Translations on USSR Military Affairs*, no. 1329 (February 10, 1978), 72–74.

1802. "Soviet Air Force Equipment." *Air Pictorial*, XIV (January–February 1952), 8–11, 42–44.

1803. Stepanov, V. "Air Base Maintenance in Winter Described: Translated from *Aviatsiya I Kosmonavtika*, December 1977." *Translations on USSR Military Affairs*, no. 1330 (February 15, 1978), 57–60.

1804. "Successes and Shortcomings in Modernizing Air Rear Services." *Translations on USSR Military Affairs*, no. 150 (July 1964), 9–13.

1805. Tolstoy, S. "Helicopter Maintenance Procedures Described: Translated from *Aviatsiya I Kosmonavtika*, September 1978." *Translations on USSR Military Affairs*, no. 1391 (October 30, 1978), 89–94.

1806. Vysotskiy, V. "Activities in an Aviation Technical Maintenance Unit: Translated from *Aviatsiya I Kosmonavtika*, October 1977." *Translations on USSR Military Affairs*, no. 1321 (January 9, 1978), 33–36.

1807. Zheltov, V. "Supply Economy in Air Defense Units Described: Translated from *Krasnaya Zvezda*, March 21, 1978." *Translations on USSR Military Affairs*, no. 1366 (July 20, 1978), 18–22.

1808. Zhukov, B. "Training of Aviation Maintenance Personnel Described: Translated from *Aviatsiya I Kosmonavtika*, December 1977." *Translations on USSR Military Affairs*, no. 1330 (February 15, 1978), 53–56.

Documents, Papers, and Reports

1809. Trapans, A. *Organizational Maintenance in the Soviet Air Force*. RAND Memorandum RM-4382-PR. Santa Monica, Calif.: RAND Corporation, 1965. 49p.

G. Soviet Satellite Reconnaissance

Books

1810. Heaps, Leo. *"Operation Morning Light": Terror in the Skies, the True Story of Cosmos 954*. New York: Paddington Press, 1978. 208p.

1811. Hochman, Sandra and Sybil Wong. *Satellite Spies: The Frightening Impact of a New Technology, an Investigation*. Indianapolis, Ind.: Bobbs-Merrill, 1976. 212p.

1812. Klass, Philip J. *Secret Sentries in Space*. New York: Random House, 1971. 236p.

1813. Porter, Richard W. *The Versatile Satellite*. London and New York: Oxford University Press, 1977. 173p.

1814. Taylor, John W. R. and David Mondey. *Spies in the Sky*. New York: Scribner's, 1972. 128p.

Articles

1815. Bates, E. Asa. "National Technical Means of Verification." *Journal of the Royal United Service Institution for Defence Studies*, CXXII (June 1978), 64–72.

1816. Beecher, William. "Spy Satellites Will Monitor [SALT] Pacts." *Sea Power*, XV (July–August 1972), 20–24.

1817. Brown, Neville. "Reconnaissance from Space." *World Today*, XXVII (February 1971), 68–76.

1818. Butz, J. S. "New Vistas in Reconnaissance from Space." *Aviation Week and Space Technology*, LI (March 1968), 46–56.

1819. Davies, Merton E. and Bruce C. Murray. "Inspection of Earth from Orbit." In: *The View from Space*. New York: Columbia University Press, 1971. pp. 9–33.

1820. DeWeerd, Harvey A. "Verifying the SALT Agreements." *Army*, XXVIII (August 1978), 15–18.

1821. Gatland, Kenneth W. "Espionage from Orbit." *Flight International*, XCV (April 10–17, 1969), 604, 642.

1822. Greenwood, Ted. "Reconnaissance and Arms Control." *Scientific American*, CCXXVIII (February 1973), 14–25.

1823. Jasani, Bhupendra. "Verification Using Reconnaissance Satellites." In: Stockholm International Peace Research Institute. *SIPRI Yearbook of World Armament and Disarmament*. New York: Humanities Press, 1973. pp. 60–101.

1824. Klass, Philip J. "Keeping the Nuclear Peace: Spies in the Sky." *New York Times Magazine*, (September 3, 1972), 6–7, 31–36.

1825. _____. "Reconnaissance Satellite Assumes Dual Role." *Aviation Week and Space Technology*, XCV (August 30, 1971), 12–13.

1826. Kolcum, Edward H. "Operational Russian Satellites Scan U.S." *Aviation Week and Space Technology*, LXXXIX (February 22, 1965), 22.

1827. Latour, Charles. "Ocean Reconnaissance from the Sky." *NATO's Fifteen Nations*, XIX (October–November 1974), 34–43.

1828. Lord, Carnes. "Verification and the Future of Arms Control." *Strategic Review*, VI (Spring 1978), 24–32.

1829. Marriott, John. "[Spy] Satellites." *Army Quarterly*, CVII (July 1977), 291–297.

1830. Moore, Otis C. "No Hiding Place in Space." *Air Force Magazine,* LVII (August 1974), 43–48.

1831. "More Spies in the Sky: How the U.S. and Russia Watch Each Other." *U.S. News and World Report,* LXXV (August 13, 1973), 27–28.

1832. Morrison, Philip. "The Role of Reconnaissance Satellites in the Arms Race." *Scientific American,* CCXXV (September 1971), 229–230.

1833. Perry, Geoffrey E. "Cosmos Observation." *Flight International,* XCIII (July 1, 1971), 29–32.

1834. _____. "The Cosmos Programme." *Flight International,* XC (December 26, 1968), 1077–1079; XCI (May 8, 1969), 773–776.

1835. _____. "Reconnaissance Aspects of Eight-Day Cosmos Satellites." *Spaceflight,* X (June 1978), 204–206.

1836. _____. "Recoverable Cosmos Satellites for Military Reconnaissance." In: Vol. I of U.S. Library of Congress, Science Policy Research Division, Congressional Research Service. *Soviet Space Programs, 1971–1975.* 2 vols. Washington, D.C.: U.S. Government Printing Office, 1976. pp. 457–478.

1837. _____. "Russian Ocean Surveillance Satellites." *Royal Air Forces Quarterly,* XVIII (Spring 1978), 60–67.

1838. "Reconnaissance Satellites." *Interavia,* XX (January 1965), 104–107.

1839. Sheldon, Charles S., 2nd. "Program Details of Unmanned Flights: The Cosmos Program, Military Observation Recoverable Satellites." In: U.S. Library of Congress, Science Policy Research Division, Congressional Research Service. *Soviet Space Programs, 1966–1970.* Washington, D.C.: U.S. Government Printing Office, 1971. pp. 180–186.

1840. _____. "Soviet Military Space Activities." In: Vol. I of U.S. Library of Congress, Science Policy Research Division, Congressional Research Service. *Soviet Space Programs, 1971–1975.* 2 vols. Washington, D.C.: U.S. Government Printing Office, 1976. pp. 12–15.

1841. Sorahan, Joseph R. "Reconnaissance Satellites: Legal Characteristics and Possible Utilization for Peacekeeping." *McGill Law Journal,* XIII (Fall 1967), 458–493.

1842. "Spies Above." *Time,* XCIX (August 30, 1971), 20.

1843.   Spurr, Robert. "Sky Spies." *Far Eastern Economic Review*, XCV (February 25, 1977), 24–28.

1844.   "Spy Race in the Sky." *U.S. News and World Report*, LXIX (October 12, 1970), 24–26.

1845.   Steeg, George F. "The Military Characteristics of Reconnaissance and Surveillance." *Electronic Warfare*, VIII (September–October 1976), 71.

1846.   Taylor, John W. R. "Reconnaissance, 1972." *Royal Air Forces Quarterly*, XII (Spring 1972), 7–14.

1847.   Ulsamer, Edgar. "The Question of Soviet Orbital Bombs." *Air Force Magazine*, LV (April 1972), 74–75.

1848.   Vigor, Peter H. and Christopher Donnelly. "Soviet Reconnaissance." *Journal of the Royal United Service Institution for Defence Studies*, CXX (December 1975), 41–45; CXXI (March 1976), 68–75.

Documents, Papers, and Reports

1849.   Greenwood, Ted. *Reconnaissance, Surveillance, and Arms Control*. Adelphi papers, no. 88. London: International Institute for Strategic Studies, 1972. 30p.

5 / Soviet Aerospace Weapons Systems

Introduction

THE AEROSPACE WEAPONS systems of the Soviet Union have undergone impressive changes since the end of World War II. Russian engineers, utilizing local and Western technology, have developed a full range of aerospace weapons.

For many years Western observers have paid close attention to Russian air and missile developments. Yet there have been frequent unexpected developments or complete surprises. These have included, for example, the MIG-15 encountered by Allied pilots over Korea, the SS-6 ICBM which placed Sputnik I into orbit in 1957, and the Mi-24 helicopter gunship first noted on East German maneuvers in the mid-1970s. Today the Soviet Air Force, National Air Defense Force, and the Strategic Rocket Forces possess formidable weapons, as the following will demonstrate.

VVS: Frontal Aviation

FRONTAL AVIATION HAS more than forty-five hundred combat aircraft, some one hundred fifty transports, and some three thousand helicopters in its inventory. The MIG-21 Fishbed remains the mainstay while newer models of aircraft such as the MIG-25 Foxbat B, MIG-23 Flogger, Su-17 Fitter C, and the Su-19 Fencer A make up a growing segment of FAs fixed-wing combat assets. The MIG-25 Foxbat B provides excellent reconnaissance capability.

In addition to transports such as the An-12 Cub, Frontal Aviation has lately been adding large numbers of helicopters. The introduction of the Mi-24 Hind helicopter gunship demonstrates the commitment of FA to rotary wing airmobile and air support missions.

VVS: Long-Range Aviation

SOVIET LONG-RANGE Aviation (DA) units are presently equipped with five types of bomber aircraft: the Tu-95 Bear, M-4 Bison, Tu-22 Blinder, Tu-16 Badger, and Tu-26 Backfire. These warplanes have as their primary mission the performance of intercontinental and peripheral strike operations, long-range reconnaissance, strikes against naval forces, and support for theater forces.

VVS: Military Transport Aviation

THE COMPOSITION OF Military Transport Aviation's (VTA) inventory of about seventeen hundred aircraft and four hundred helicopters reflects both its primary historical role and its evolving new responsibilities.

The mainstay of the VTA is its fleet of medium-range An-12 Cub transports, each of which can carry twenty-two tons of ramp-loaded cargo or one hundred soldiers. Other light- and medium-range aircraft in service include the Il-14 Crate, An-8 Camp, An-24 Coke, An-26 Curl, and Il-18 Coot. A significant number of helicopters also play a growing role.

Until the mid-1970s, VTA's long-range airlift capability was limited to the turboprop An-22 Cock, which is no longer in production. In the mid-1970s, the Il-76 Candid was introduced—an almost look-alike for the U.S. C-141. Capable of transporting 88,200 pounds of ramp-loaded cargo or 145 troops, the Candid has given VTA globally significant airlift potential—potential which has thus far been demonstrated in the Middle East and Africa. The civilian airliners of the state line Aeroflot continue to represent an important reserve for use in crisis operations.

PVO-Strany: IA

APROXIMATELY THREE THOUSAND fighter-interceptors are assigned to the National Air Defense Forces. The current inventory is a mixture of older and newer types, which historically have had a limited low-intercept capability.

Aircraft currently in service include the MIG-17 Fresco, MIG-19 Farmer, Su-9 Fishpot B, the Yak-28P Firebar, the Tu-28 Fiddler, MIG-23 Flogger, the Su-15 Flagon A-D-E, and the MIG-25 Foxbat A.

Only a few of the first two mentioned warbirds remain in service and these may have been replaced by the time this book is published.

PVO-Strany: SAM

SOVIET SURFACE-TO-AIR MISSILE (SAM) systems for strategic defense consist of approximately ten thousand launchers located at over a thousand sites. Four major systems comprise these defenses: the SA-1 Guild, the SA-2 Guideline, the SA-3 Goa, and the SA-5 Gammon. In addition to these long-range missiles, the Red Army possesses certain tactical mobile SAMs which could be employed within the USSR to meet a strategic threat. These systems include the SA-4 Ganef, the SA-6 Gainful, the SA-8 Gecko, and the SA-9 Gaskin. Both strategic and tactical SAM missiles have been sent to friendly or client states overseas and many were expended in such wars as those in Indochina and the Middle East.

SRF

THE STRATEGIC ROCKET Forces (SRF) control intercontinental-, intermediate-, and medium-range ballistic missiles; the Red Army possesses a number of battlefield tactical missiles.

The SRF now have about fourteen hundred operational ICBM launchers. Most of the missiles use liquid propellants and are launched from silos. The older missiles, which carry single warheads, are being replaced by a new generation that possesses greater targeting flexibility and accuracy and which carries multiple reentry vehicles (MIRVs) capable of being targeted independently. The SS-9 hard-target killer is currently being phased out in favor of the SS-18, while the bulk of the inventory continues to consist of the SS-11, SS-17, and SS-19 soft-target destroyers. The only solid-fueled Russian ICBM, the SS-13, is expected to be replaced by the SS-16.

The SRF, IRBM, and MRBM missiles are designed for peripheral attack and now number about six hundred launchers, SS-4s and SS-5s, deployed in mobile- and fixed-configurations. These missiles will be supplemented by increasing numbers of solid-fueled SS-20s, which can carry three MIRVs.

The Red Army employed large numbers of battlefield rockets during World War II and has maintained its interest in this weaponry ever since. Today, large numbers of battlefield-support missiles are deployed with Soviet ground forces, including the unguided "Frog" artillery rocket, the SS-1 Scud A-B and SS-12 Scaleboard battlefield-support missiles. In addition, the AT-1, AT-2, and AT-3 anti-tank missiles are in common usage.

The references in this section address the literature which has been developed, primarily by Western writers, on Soviet aerospace weapons which have been tested or placed in inventory over the past thirty-five years. Certain general citations relative to this section will be found in Section 1:D, 2:B:5, 3:B:2, and 4 above.

A. Aircraft

1. General Studies

Books

1850.   Anderton, David A. and John Batchelor. *Jet Fighters and Bombers*. London: Phoebus Publishing Company, 1976. 127p.

1851.   Cain, Charles W. and Denys J. Voaden. *Military Aircraft of the U.S.S.R.* London: Jenkins, 1952. 72p.

1852.   Colby, Carrol B. *Jets of the World: New Fighters, Bombers, and Transports*. Rev. ed. New York: Coward-McCann, 1966. 48p.

1853.   Cornwell, E. L. *Aircraft Annual, 1978*. London: Ian Allan, 1978. 127p.

1854.   Desoutter, Denis M. *Aircraft and Missiles*. 2nd ed. New York: J. deGraff, 1959. 213p.

1855.   Gilbert, James. *Great Planes*. New York: Grosset and Dunlap, 1970. 251p.

1856.   Green, William. *The Aircraft of the World*. Garden City, N.Y.: Doubleday, 1965, 360p.

1857.   _____. *The World Guide to Combat Planes*. 2 vols. Garden City, N.Y.: Doubleday, 1967.

1858.   _____. *The World's Fighting Planes*. 4th rev. ed. Garden City, N.Y.: Doubleday, 1965. 216p.

1859.   _____ and Roy Cross. *The Jet Aircraft of the World*. New York: Hanover House, 1955. 176p.

1860.   _____ and Gerald Pollinger. *The Aircraft of the World*. New York: Hanover House, 1955. 211p.

1861.   _____. _____. 3rd ed. Garden City, N.Y.: Doubleday, 1965. 360p.

1862.   _____. *The World's Fighting Planes*. London: Macdonald, 1954. 204p.

1863.   _____ and F. Gordon Swanborough, comps. *The Observer's Soviet Aircraft Directory*. New York: Frederick Warne, 1975. 256p.

1864.   _____ and Derek Wood. *Russia's Jets and Other Aircraft*. Sevenoaks, England: Smith, 1951. 59p.

1865. Hooftman, Hugo. *Russian Aircraft*. Fallbrook, Calif.: Aviation and Space Books, 1965. 158p.

1866. Munro, Colin. *Soviet Air Forces: Fighters and Bombers*. Modern Aircraft Series. New York: Sports Car Press, 1973. 121p.

1867. Munson, Kenneth. *Famous Aircraft of All Time*. New York: Arco, 1977. 192p.

1868. _____. *Record-Breaking Aircraft*. London: Macdonald and Jane's, 1978. 264p.

1869. Perlmutter, Tom, ed. *War Machines, Air*. New York: Crown, 1975. 140p.

1870. Polmar, Norman, ed. *World Combat Aircraft Directory*. Garden City, N.Y.: Doubleday, 1976. 373p.

1871. Robertson, Bruce. *Aircraft Camouflage and Markings, 1907–1954*. Letchworth, England: Harleyford Books, 1961. 232p.

1872. _____. *Aircraft Markings of the World, 1912–1967*. Letchworth, England: Harleyford Books, 1967. 232p.

1873. Squarlato, Nico. *Soviet Aircraft of Today*. Warren, Mich.: Squadron/Signal Publications, 1978. 80p.

1874. Swanborough, F. Gordon. *Combat Aircraft of the World*. New York: Taplinger, 1962. 122p.

1875. _____. *Military Transport and Training Aircraft of the World*. London: Temple Press, 1965. 128p.

1876. Taylor, John W. R. *Military Aircraft of the World*. New York: Scribner's, 1971. 230p.

1877. _____. *Military Aircraft Recognition, 1969*. London: Ian Allan, 1969. 81p.

1878. _____. *Warplanes of the World*. New York: Simmons-Boardman, 1960. 96p.

1879. _____. _____. Rev. ed. New York: Arco, 1966. 203p.

1880. _____, ed. *Combat Aircraft of the World From 1909 to the Present*. New York: Putnam, 1969. 647p.

1881. _____. *Milestones of the Air: Jane's 100 Significant Aircraft*. New York: McGraw-Hill, 1969, 158p.

1882. ____ and F. Gordon Swanborough. *Military Aircraft of the World*. Rev. ed. New York: Scribner's, 1973. 240p.

1883. ____. ____. 3rd ed. New York: Scribner's, 1978. 240p.

1884. ____. ____. Rev. ed. New York: Scribner's, 1979. 224p.

1885. ____ and Kenneth G. Munson, eds. *The History of Aviation Aircraft Identification Guide*. London: New English Library, 1973. 192p.

1886. ____. *Jane's Pocket Book of Major Combat Aircraft*. New York: Macmillan, 1974. 263p.

1887. ____. *Jane's Pocket Book of Military Transport and Training Aircraft*. New York: Macmillan, 1975. 262p.

Articles

1888. "Air Armaments in the East." *Interavia*, VI (Winter 1951), 209–210.

1889. "The Air Forces of the U.S.S.R." *Joint Services Recognition Journal*, X (December 1955), 318–319.

1890. Davis, R. J. "What the Reds Have." *Newsweek*, XLIV (August 23, 1954), 31–33.

1891. "First-Line Military Production Aircraft." *Aeroplane*, XCII (May 31, 1957), 785–794.

1892. "Front-Line Military Aircraft." *Aeroplane*, XCVIII (March 25, 1960), 375–389.

1893. Geiger, George J. "Russia's Aerospace Arsenal: Aircraft, Missiles, and Spacecraft." *Aerospace Management*, V (March 1962), 92–110.

1894. Gilson, Charles M. and Bill Sweetman. "Military Aircraft of the World." *Flight International*, XCVIII (March 6, 1976), 549–606.

1895. Green, William. "Behind the Iron Curtain: Three New Russian Jets." *Flying*, XLVIII (January 1951), 23–24, 50–51.

1896. ____. "Transports and Trainers." *RAF Flying Review*, XVIII (April 1963), 21–25.

1897. ____ and Roy Cross. "Russia's Jet Aircraft." *Ordnance*, XXXV (January–February 1951), 287–292.

1898. Griswold, W. S. "How Soviet Warplanes Look Alongside Ours." *Popular Science*, CXVI (January 1955), 116–118.

1899. Gunston, William T. "Military Aircraft." *Flight International,* LXXXVI (August 20, 1964), 280–295.

1900. _____. "New Developments in Aircraft and Missiles." In: James L. Moulton, ed. *Brassey's Annual.* New York: Praeger, 1965. pp. 156–168.

1901. _____. _____. _____. New York: Praeger, 1968. pp. 78–95.

1902. _____. "Soviet Aircraft." In: Roy Bonds, ed. *The Soviet War Machine: An Illustrated Encyclopedia of Russian Military Equipment and Strategy.* New York: Chartwell Books, 1976. pp. 86–111.

1903. Hotz, Robert. "Russian Air Force Now Gaining in Quality." *Aviation Week and Space Technology,* LXIV (March 12, 1956), 286–291.

1904. _____. Russian Jet Airpower Gains Fast on U.S." *Aviation Week and Space Technology,* LXII (May 23, 1955), 12–13.

1905. *Interavia* Study Group. "New Soviet Military Aircraft." *Interavia,* XVI (October–November 1961), 1434–1435, 1520–1521.

1906. Kneble, Fletcher. "Red Jets Can Rule the Skies." *Look,* XVII (April 7, 1953), 31–35.

1907. "Main Combat Aircraft of the Soviet Air Force." *International Defense Review,* VIII (April 1975), 180–181.

1908. Meller, R. "Europe's New Generation of Combat Aircraft, Part 1: The Increasing Threat." *International Defense Review,* VIII (April 1975), 175–179, 182–186.

1909. "Military Aircraft." *Flight,* LXIX (June 8, 1956), 699–758; LXXIII (June 20, 1958), 833–876; LXXVIII (July 8, 1960), 43–74.

1910. "Military Aircraft of the World." *Aeroplane,* C (March 17, 1961), 285–298.

1911. "Modern Planes Dominate Soviet Airpower." *American Aviation,* XIX (March 12, 1956), 26–27.

1912. Moore, John. "Soviet Military Aircraft." *NATO's Fifteen Nations,* XVIII (April–May 1973), 24–25.

1913. Morton, I. "Russia's Jet Warplanes." *Mechanical Engineering,* LXXIV (May 1952), 398–400.

1914. "New Russian Aircraft Revealed." *Aviation Week,* L (April 18, 1949), 20–21.

1915. Petersen, Phillip A. "Index of NATO Code Names for Soviet Aircraft." In: *Soviet Air Power and the Pursuit of New Military Options.* Studies in Communist Affairs, no. 3. Washington, D.C.: Published under the auspices of the U.S. Air Force by the U.S. Government Printing Office, 1979. pp. 70–71.

1916. "Red Stars in the Blue." *Flying,* LVI (January 1955), 14–15.

1917. "Red Stars in the Sky." *Interavia,* IV (November 1949), 641–649.

1918. "Russia is Well Armed." *Air Force,* XXXII (December 1949), 20–21.

1919. "Russian Air Strength." *Air Pictorial,* XII (May 1950), 138–140.

1920. "Russian Aircraft Given New [NATO] Codenames." *American Aviation,* XVIII (April 11, 1955), 30.

1921. "Russian Aircraft Today Under the Red Star." *Naval Aviation News,* (May 1956), 20–23.

1922. "Russian Line-Up (Codenames and Characteristics of Russian Aircraft)." *RAF Flying Review,* XII (April 1957), 23–26.

1923. "Russian Planes Show Improvement." *Aviation Week,* LI (August 1, 1949), 24–25.

1924. "Russian Round-Up." *Flight,* LXX (July 6, 1956), 2–4.

1925. "Russian Revolution." *Flying Review International,* XXI (May 1966), 507.

1926. "Russia's Line-Up." *RAF Flying Review,* XVIII (February–April 1963), 21–25, 21–25, 21–25.

1927. "Russia's Wings: A Pictorial Review of Soviet Aircraft." *RAF Flying Review,* XII (October 1956), 37–39.

1928. "Silhouette Digest." *Joint Services Recognition Journal,* X (January 1955), 2–27.

1929. "Soviet Aircraft." *Mechanical Engineering,* LXXI (May 1949), 416–417.

1930. ———. *Military Review,* XLIII (October 1963), 104–107.

1931. "Soviet Aircraft Edition." *Joint Services Recognition Journal,* XI (January 1956), 1–28.

1932. "Soviet Military Aircraft." *Naval Aviation News*, (March 1957), 38–39.

1933. Swanborough, F. Gordon. "Russian Aircraft Review." *Aeroplane*, LXXX (March 23, 1951), 349–353.

1934. _____ and William T. Gunston. "Technical Directory." In: *Soviet Air Power: An Illustrated Encyclopedia of the Warsaw Pact Air Forces Today*. London: Salamander Books, 1978. pp. 102–188.

1935. Taylor, John W. R. "Gallery of Soviet Aerospace Weapons." *Air Force Magazine*, LIX (March 1976), 93–107; LX (March 1977), 93–106; LXI (March 1978), 93–109; LXII (March 1979), 99–114; LXIII (March 1980), 119–135.

1936. _____ . "Jane's Aerospace Review." *Air Force Magazine*, LV (January 1972), 24–33; LVI (January 1973), 24–31; LVII (January 1974), 24–31; LVIII (January 1975), 28–36; LIX (January 1976), 22–29; LX (January 1977), 30–39.

1937. Ulsamer, Edgar. "SALT II's Gray Area Weapon Systems." *Air Force Magazine*, LIX (July 1976), 80–82.

1938. "U.S. Tags Combat Names to Red Planes." *Aviation Week and Space Technology*, LXI (October 4, 1954), 15–16.

1939. Vandyk, Anthony. "What's in the Air Behind the Iron Curtain?" *American Aviation*, XVI (February 16, 1953), 24–27.

1940. Wilson, Gill R. and Chalmers H. Goodlin. "Soviet Fighting Planes." *National Air Review*, II (May 1951), 10–13.

1941. Wood, Derek H. "[Soviet] Aircraft Recognition." *Air Pictorial*, XIV (January 1952), 8–11.

1942. Zharko, V. "At Supersonic Speed." *Soviet Military Review*, no. 1 (January 1970), 24–26.

1943. Zhigarev, V. "Soviet Winged Craft and Helicopters." *Soviet Military Review*, no. 3 (March 1972), 36–37.

2. *Specific Systems*

a. FIGHTERS

(1) General Studies

Books

1944. King, Horace F. *The World's Fighters*. Chicago: Follett Publishing Company, 1973. 127p.

1945. Munson, Kenneth G. *Fighters in Service: Attack and Training Aircraft Since 1960.* Pocket Encyclopedia of World Aircraft in Color. Rev. ed. New York: Macmillan, 1975. 175p.

Articles

1946. Anderton, David A. "Russia's Answers." *Air Trails,* XXXIII (February 1950), 21–23.

1947. Archer, Robert D. "The Soviet Fighters." *Space/Aeronautics,* L (July 1968), 64–72.

1948. Brownlow, Cecil. "Soviets Push Advances in Fighters." *Aviation Week and Space Technology,* XCV (October 18, 1971), 34–37.

1949. Fricker, John E. "Russian Fighter Strength." *Aeroplane,* LXXV (August 20, 1948), 211–212.

1950. Froelich, David V. "The Threat: Mig-17, -19, and -21." *Interceptor,* XVIII (October 1976), 20–23.

1951. "Gallery of Soviet Aerospace Weapons: Attack Aircraft." *Air Force Magazine,* LVIII (March 1975), 67; LIX (March 1976), 98–99; LX (March 1977), 93–94; LXI (March 1978), 99–100; LXII (March 1979), 105; LXIII (March 1980), 125.

1952. "Gallery of Soviet Aerospace Weapons: Fighters." *Air Force Magazine,* LVIII (March 1975), 64–66; LIX (March 1976), 96–98; LX (March 1977), 90–93; LXI (March 1978), 96–99; LXII (March 1979), 102–105; LXIII (March 1980), 122–124.

1953. Gladych, Michael. "How the New Red Fighters Stack Up." *Air Force,* XXXVIII (March 1955), 25–29.

1954. Goodlin, Chalmers H. "Evolution of Russia's Fighters." *Aviation Age,* XVI (August 1951), 15–20.

1955. Green, William. "How Hot are Soviet Jets?" *Canadian Aviation,* XXIV (March–April 1951), 14–15, 20–21.

1956. Miller, Jay N. "About the MIG." *Air Force Times,* XL (September 24–October 8, 1979), 8, 38, 56.

1957. Rebrov, M. "The MIG Dynasty." *Soviet Military Review,* no. 8 (August 1970), 40–43.

1958. Robinson, Clarence A., Jr. "Soviets to Field Three New Fighters in Aviation Modernization Drive." *Aviation Week and Space Technology,* CX (March 26, 1979), 14–16.

1959. "Soviet Fighters." *Space/Aeronautics,* LI (July 1968), 64–72.

1960. "Sukhoi Aircraft." *Flying Review International,* XXII (February–April 1966), 351–354, 373–375, 435–437, 490–492.

(2) Specific Types

Lavochkin La-17

1961. Green, William. "Russia's Newest Jet Fighter, the La-17." *Skyways,* X (September 1951), 10–11.

1962. "Last of the Lavochkins." *Flying Review International,* XXIII (April–June 1968), 220–222, 289–291, 349–351.

1962a. "Lavochkin La-17." *Aviation Age,* XV (May 1951), 21–22.

Mikoyan/Gurevich MIG-15 "Fagot"

1963. "Air Force Report Sizes Up Russia's MIG." *Business Week,* (July 12, 1952), 30–31.

1964. "Allies Get Look at Intact MIG." *Aviation Week,* LVIII (March 16, 1953), 16–17.

1965. Anderton, David A. "Red MIG-15: Air Force Test Pilots Analyze Captive Fighter." *Aviation Week,* LIX (November 30, 1953), 16–17.

1966. Baldwin, Hanson W. "Russia's MIG—World's Best Jet?" *Science Digest,* XXXI (March 1952), 43–47.

1967. Braybrook, Roy M. "The First Step: The MIG-15." *Flying Review International,* XX (January–February 1965), 24–31, 35, 31–33.

1968. "Captured Russian MIG Shows Top Notch Engineering." *Product Engineering,* XXIII (August 1952), 194–195.

1969. "Design Detail: Russia's MIG-15." *Aviation Week,* LIV (April 1951), 32.

1970. Friedman, William S. "How Deadly are the Russian Jets?" *Popular Science,* CLVIII (January 1951), 90–95.

1971. "Fugitive MIG Closeup Shows New Details." *Aviation Week,* LVIII (April 13, 1953), 17–19.

1972. Goodlin, Chalmers H. "The MIG-15." *Aviation Age,* XV (February 1951), 21–25.

1973. Green, William. "The MIG-15." *Aircraft,* XXIX (May 1951), 17–18.

1974. _____. "Russia's Secret Sonic Fighters." *Flying,* XLVII (August 1950), 15–17.

1975. "How Good is the MIG?" *Time,* LXIII (December 21, 1953), 47.

1976. "How Good is Russia's Superjet?" *U.S. News and World Report,* XXXVI (May 14, 1954), 32.

1977. Jarecki, Franciszek. "Flying a MIG." *RAF Flying Review,* VIII (June 1953), 11–14.

1978. Jessup, Alpheus W. "Russians Can Make Good Planes." *Aviation Week,* LIV (February 19, 1951), 15–16.

1979. Lee, Benjamin S. "Secrets of Russia's MIG Revealed." *Aviation Week,* LVII (July 1, 1952), 10–15.

1980. "MIG-15." *Aeroplane,* LX (August 1, 1952), 160–162; LXI (November 13, 1953), 656–657.

1981. _____. *Flight,* LXII (July 1952), 102–104.

1982. _____. *Naval Aviation News,* (January 1951), 14–15.

1983. _____. *RAF Flying Review,* VIII (December 1953), 21; IX (January 1954), 12–13.

1984. Retalliata, J. T. "Jet Fighter." *Mechanical Engineering,* LXXIII (June 1951), 505.

1985. "Russia's MIG-15." *RAF Flying Review,* XI (May 1956), 31–34.

1986. Vandyk, Anthony. "Technical Data on MIG-15 Revealed." *American Aviation,* XVII (October 12, 1953), 38–47.

Mikoyan/Gurevich MIG-17 "Fresco"

1987. "A Battlefield Fresco." *Flying Review International,* XIX (February 1964), 42–43.

1988. Braybrook, Roy M. "The Perennial MIG-17." *Flying Review International,* XIX (September 1964), 20–23.

1989. "The MIG-17." *Air Pictorial,* XXI (July 1959), 260–261.

1990. _____. *RAF Flying Review,* XIII (August 1958), 8–9.

1991. "The New Fresco: Familiar Falcon." *Naval Aviation News,* (February 1955), 20–21.

Mikoyan/Gurevich MIG-19 "Farmer"

1992. Braybrook, Roy M. "The MIG-19 Farmer." *Flying Review International*, XIX (February 1964), 22–25.

1993. Geiger, George J. "MIG-19." *Marine Corps Gazette*, XLVIII (June 1964), 15.

1994. "Red's MIG-19 Interceptor Designed for Top Climb Performance." *Aviation Age*, XXVIII (October 1957), 36–45.

1995. "Russian Delta: The MIG-19." *Flying*, LIV (February 1954), 20–21.

1996. Taylor, John W. R. "MIG-19 Farmer." *Air Pictorial*, XXV (August 1963), 244–245.

1997. Vandyk, Anthony. "Those Russian Delta Fighters are Good." *American Aviation*, XX (October 8, 1956), 27–28.

Mikoyan/Gurevich MIG-21 "Fishbed"

1998. Braybrook, Roy M. "Fishbed in Focus." *Flying Review International*, XXII (November 1966), 195–198.

1999. _____. "The MIG-21 Fishbed." *Flying Review International*, XIX (November 1963), 20–22.

2000. "A Close Look at Fishbed: How the Soviet Air Force's MIG-21 Stacks Up." *Air Force*, XLII (April 1959), 54–55.

2001. Lambert, Mark. "How Good is the MIG-21?" *U.S. Naval Institute Proceedings*, CII (January 1976), 98–101.

2002. "MIG and [F-4] Phantom: How They Compare." *U.S. News and World Report*, LX (May 9, 1966), 6.

2003. "The MIG-21 Fishbed." *Air Progress*, XXII (May–June 1966), 6–8.

2004. _____. *RAF Flying Review*, XVI (March 1961), 15–16.

2005. "The MIG 21PF [Fishbed D]." *Flight*, XCVI (April 24, 1969), 664.

2006. Panyalev, Georg. "MIG-21bis and F-16A Air Combat Potential: A Comparison." *International Defense Review*, XI (September 1978), 1429–1434.

2007. Taylor, John W. R. "The MIG-21 Mystery." *Air Pictorial*, XXIV (December 1962), 384–385.

2008. Wetmore, Warren C. "Israelis Class MIG-21C as Efficient, High Altitude Fighter." *Aviation Week and Space Technology,* XCI (July 31, 1967), 50–51.

Mikoyan/Gurevich MIG-23 "Flogger"

2009. Braybrook, Roy M. "The MIG-23 Flogger." *Flying Review International,* XIX (June 1964), 28–29.

2010. "Fighter Capabilities: Effectiveness of U.S. F-14 Fighter Versus the Russian MIG-23 Flogger." *Aviation Week and Space Technology,* XCV (September 13, October 11–18, 1971), 64, 62, 54.

2011. Froehlich, David V. "The Threat: Flogger MIG-23." *Interceptor,* XVIII (November 1976), 20–21.

2012. Holford, D. J. "Russian MIG-23 Unbeatable?" *Popular Mechanics,* CXXXVI (November 1971), 90–94.

2013. Panyalev, Georg. "The MIG-23 Flogger: A Versatile Family of Soviet Combat Aircraft." *International Defense Review,* X (February 1977), 48–53.

2014. _____. "The Mikoyan MIG-23 Combat Aircraft Family." *Interavia,* XXXII (March 1977), 247–249.

2015. "The Soviet Flogger in Close-Up." *Interavia,* XXXII (January 1977), 27–29.

Mikoyan/Gurevich MIG-25 "Foxbat"

2016. Allward, Maurice. "Mikoyan MIG-25 Foxbat." *Air Pictorial,* XXXIX (February 1977), 48–51.

2017. Awanohara, S. "Dogfight Over Moscow's MIG." *Far Eastern Economic Review,* XCIV (October 8, 1976), 15–16.

2018. Bennett, Ralph K. "Outfoxed by Foxbat." *Data,* XIII (August 1968), 11–12.

2019. "Bonanza or Bust?: MIG-25." *Time,* CVIII (November 1, 1976), 59–60.

2020. Brownlow, Cecil. "MIG-25 Based on Technology Spinoffs." *Aviation Week and Space Technology,* CV (October 11, 1976), 16–17.

2021. Eaker, Ira C. "And How Good is the MIG-25?" *Air Force Times,* XXXVII (October 4, 1976), 13–14.

2022. _____. "What We Learned from the MIG-25." *Air Force Times,* XXXVII (October 25, 1976), 13–14.

2023. "Foxbat: Demythologizing a Superplane." *Science Newsletter*, CX (October 9, December 11, 1976), 231–371.

2024. "Foxbat, Flogger Increase Soviet Offensive Potential." *Aviation Week and Space Technology*, CIV (March 22, 1976), 18–20.

2025. Froelich, David V. "The Threat: MIG-25 Foxbat." *Interceptor*, XVIII (December 1976), 5–7.

2026. North, D. M. "Soviets Test Two-Seat MIG-25 Version." *Aviation Week and Space Technology*, CVI (March 28, 1977), 17–18.

2027. Panyalev, Georg. "The MIG-25 Foxbat Weapon System: Underestimated in the West." *International Defense Review*, X (April 1977), 255–260.

2028. Rubenstein, Murray. "MIG: The Ultimate Airplane Killer." *Popular Mechanics*, CL (July 1978), 72–75.

2029. Sayle, Murray. "Quick Red Foxbat." *New Statesman and Nation*, XCII (October 15, 1976), 502–503.

2030. Winston, D. C. "New MIG Imperils U.S. Superiority." *Aviation Week and Space Technology*, LXXXVIII (June 3, 1968), 22–23.

Mikoyan/Gurevich MIG-27 "Flogger D"

2031. MIG-27 Flogger D Attack Version Equipped for Rough Terrain." *Aviation Week and Space Technology*, CXI (October 22, 1979), 17.

Sukhoi Su-7 "Fitter"

2032. Braybrook, Roy M. "The Sukhoi Su-7 Fitter." *Flying Review International*, XIX (December 1963), 22–25.

2033. "Fitter C: Link Between Second and Third Generation Soviet Attack Aircraft." *International Defense Review*, IX (April 1976), 167–169.

2034. "Sukhoi Su-7." *Flight*, XCII (December 30, 1965), 1120–1121.

2035. Turner, Thomas. "Russia's Answer to the F-104 Starfighter: Sukhoi." *Popular Mechanics*, CVII (May 1957), 110–111.

Sukhoi Su-9 "Fishpot"

2036. Froelich, David V. "The Threat: Fishpot Su-9, Flagon Su-15." *Interceptor*, XIX (February 1977), 20–21.

2037. Taylor, John W. R. "Sukhoi Su-9 Fishpot." *Air Pictorial*, XXV (May 1963), 140–141.

Sukhoi Su-15 "Flagon"

2038.   "Design Details of Flaggon Fighter Shown." *Aviation Week and Space Technology,* CVII (July 4, 1977), 17.

2039.   "New Features of the Su-15 Flagon." *International Defense Review,* X (August 1977), 610–611.

2040.   "Sukhoi Su-15 Flagon." *Flying Review International,* XXV (June 1969), 33–35.

Sukhoi Su-19 "Fencer"

2041.   Panyalev, Georg. "The Su-19 Fencer: Threat to Western Europe." *International Defense Review,* IX (February 1976), 67–69.

2042.   Sweetman, Bill. "Su-19 Fencer." *Flight International,* CXIV (July 29, 1978), 350–352.

Tupolev Tu-28 "Fiddler"

2043.   Braybrook, Roy M. "The Tupolev Tu-28 Fiddler." *Flying Review International,* XX (April 1964), 28–30.

2044.   Taylor, John W. R. "The Tupolev Tu-28." *Air Pictorial,* XXIV (May 1962), 140–141.

Yakovlev Yak-15

2045.   Green, William. "Russia's First Jet Fighter." *RAF Flying Review,* XVI (May 1961), 20–21.

Yakovlev Yak-19

2046.   Cain, Charles W. "Russia's Answer to the F-86." *Flying,* XLVI (June 1950), 28–29, 44.

Yakovlev Yak-25 "Flashlight"

2047.   Braybrook, Roy M. "The Yak-25." *Flying Review International,* XIX (March 1964), 19–21.

2048.   "Soviet Yak-25 All-Weather Fighter Operational." *Aviation Week and Space Technology,* LXX (April 13, 1959), 72–73.

2049.   "The Curious Beast: The Russian Yak-25." *Air Force,* XLI (May 1958), 50–51.

2050.   "Yakovlev Yak-25 Flashlight." *RAF Flying Review,* XIV (January 1959), 20–21.

Yakovlev Yak-28 "Firebar"

2051. Braybrook, Roy M. "Variations on a Theme: The Firebar." *Flying Review International*, XIX (January 1964), 24–26.

2052. Froehlich, David V. "The Threat: Fiddler Tu-28, Firebar Yak-28." *Interceptor*, XIX (March 1977), 20–21.

2053. Taylor, John W. R. "Yakovlev's Firebar." *Air Pictorial*, XXV (March 1963), 76–77.

b. BOMBERS

(1) General Studies

Books

2054. Cross, Roy, ed. *The Bomber Aircraft Pocket Book*. London: Batsford, 1964. 256p.

2055. King, Horace F. *The World's Bombers*. Chicago: Follett Publishing Co., 1973. 112p.

2056. Munson, Kenneth G. *Bombers in Service: Patrol and Transport Aircraft Since 1960*. The Pocket Encyclopedia of Aircraft in Color Series. New York: Macmillan, 1973. 155p.

Articles

2057. "*Air Pictorial*'s Bomber and Reconnaissance Aircraft Guide." *Air Pictorial*, XXI (June–July 1959), 208–214, 251–256.

2058. Anderton, David A. "Pictures Reveal Red's New Sunday Punch." *Aviation Week and Space Technology*, LX (February 15, 1954), 12–13.

2059. Archer, Robert D. "The Soviet Bombers." *Space/Aeronautics*, LI (April 1969), 52–59.

2060. "Bombers Next." *Aviation Week*, LIV (February 26, 1951), 174–180.

2061. Day, Bonner. "Soviet Bombers: A Growing Threat." *Air Force Magazine*, LXI (November 1978), 84–87.

2062. "Gallery of Soviet Aerospace Weapons: Bomber and Maritime." *Air Force Magazine*, LVIII (March 1975), 62–64; LIX (March 1976), 94–95; LX (March 1977), 88–90; LXI (March 1978), 93–95; LXII (March 1979), 99–101; LXIII (March 1980), 119–121.

2063. Green, William. "New Generation of Soviet Bombers." *Aircraft*, XXX (June 1952), 34–36.

2064. _____. "Russia Concentrates on Tactical Jet Bombers." *Aircraft*, XXIX (August 1951), 25–26.

2065. _____. "The Threat: Russia's Bombers." *RAF Flying Review*, X (March 1955), 17–21.

2066. Long, J. F. L. "U.S.S.R. Long-Range Aircraft." *Royal Air Forces Quarterly*, V (Winter 1965), 291–295.

2067. "New Details on Red's Jet Bombers." *Aviation Age*, XXIII (April 1955), 134–135.

2068. Robinson, Clarence A., Jr. "Soviets Developing Two Bombers, Extending Range of Backfire." *Aviation Week and Space Technology*, CX (February 19, 1979), 14–18.

2069. "Russian Long-Range Bombers." *Interavia*, IX (April 1954), 236.

(2) Specific Types

Ilyushin IL-12

2070. Pcrhal, E. M. "I Flew Russia's IL-12." *Flying*, XLIX (September 1951), 16–17, 53.

2071. Peck, J. L.H. "Russia's New Storm Bomber." *Flying*, L (February 1952), 12–13.

Ilyushin IL-28 "Beagle"

2072. Anderton, David A. "Curtain is Raised on Red Ilyushin Jet." *Aviation Week*, LVIII (March 30, 1953), 30–32.

2073. Braybrook, Roy M. "The Ilyushin Il-28 Beagle." *Flying Review International*, XIX (July 1964), 42–45.

2074. Green, William. "Soviet Jet Bomber." *Skyways*, X (October 1951), 13–38.

2075. Nemecek, Vaclav. "Ilyushin's Experimentals." *Flying Review International*, XXII (December 1960), 267–270.

Myasishchev M-4 "Bison"

2076. "Bison Details Shown by Navy Model." *Aviation Week and Space Technology*, LXIII (August 8, 1955), 16–17.

2077. "Myasishchev M-4." *Air Force*, XXXVIII (May 1955), 31–32.

2078. "The Threat: Bison, M-4." *Interceptor*, XVIII (July 1976), 20–21.

Myasishchev M-52 "Bounder"

2079. "A Look at the Bounder: Russia's Delta-Wing Bomber." *Air Force*, XLIII (January 1960), 46–47.

Tupolev Tu-4 "Bull"

2080. Kappel, Lon C. "The American Legacy to Russian Air Power." *Aviation Age*, XVIII (December 1952), 12–15.

2081. Phillips, Reynolds. "Russia's Intercontinental Bomber." *Boeing Magazine*, XXII (March 1952), 3–5.

Tupolev Tu-16 "Badger"

2082. Braybrook, Roy M. "The Tupolev Tu–16 Badger." *Flying Review International*, XIX (May 1964), 21–25; XXIV (August 1969), 46–47.

2083. "The Russian Badger." *Naval Aviation News*, (May 1955), 16–17.

2084. Taylor, John W. R. "Tupolev's Badger." *Air Pictorial*, XXV (January 1963), 10–11.

2085. "The Threat: Badger, Tu–16." *Interceptor*, XVIII (June 1976), 20–21.

2086. "Tupolev's Badger." *Aeroplane*, XCVI (January 23, 1959), 106–107.

Tupolev Tu-20 (Tu-95) "Bear A-F"

2087. Allward, Maurice. "Tupolev Tu-95 Bear." *Air Pictorial*, XXXIX (October 1977), 400–402.

2088. Braybrook, Roy M. "The Unique Tu–20 Bear." *Flying Review International*, XX (October 1964), 46–49.

2089. Cain, Charles W. "Russia's Incredible Bear." *Aircraft*, XXXIV (September 1956), 60.

2090. "How Good is Russia's Long-Range Turboprop Bear Bomber?" *Aviation Age*, XXVII (May 1957), 42–49.

2091.   Taylor, John W. R. "Tupolev's Tu-20 Bear." *Air Pictorial,* XXV (July 1963), 212–213.

2092.   "The Threat: Bear, Tu-95." *Interceptor,* XVIII (August 1976), 20–21.

2093.   "The Tupolev Tu-20 Bear." *Aviation Week and Space Technology,* LVII (April 8, 1957), 53–57.

2094.   "The Tupolev Tu-95 Bear." *Aviation Week,* XC (June 10, 1968), 58–59.

Tupolev Tu-22 "Blinder"

2095.   Braybrook, Roy M. "The Tupolev Tu-22 Blinder." *Flying Review International,* XX (August 1964), 28–31.

2096.   Taylor, John W. R. "Tupolev's Blinder." *Air Pictorial,* XVII (October 1962), 318–319.

2097.   "The Threat: Blinder, Tu-22." *Interceptor,* XVIII (May 1976), 12–13.

Tupolev Tu-26 "Backfire A-B"

2098.   Bradsher, Henry S. "Backfire Flights Support Strategic Weapons Theory: Reprinted from the *Washington Star,* July 28, 1976." *U.S. Naval Institute Proceedings,* CII (October 1976), 146.

2099.   "New Soviet Swing-Wing Bomber." *Interavia,* XXVI (February 1971), 113–114.

2100.   O'Neil, William D. "Backfire: Long Shadow on the Sea-Lanes." *U.S. Naval Institute Proceedings,* CIII (March 1977), 26–35.

2101.   Panyalev, Georg. "Backfire—Soviet Counter to the American B-1." *International Defense Review,* VII (October 1975), 639–642.

2102.   "Soviet Backfire Strategic Bomber Revealed." *Armed Forces Journal,* CIX (November 1971), 23–24.

2103.   Sweetman, Bill. "Backfire: The Bogeyman Bomber." *Flight International,* CXII (December 17, 1977), 1810–1815.

Yakovlev Yak-42 "Backfin"

2104.   "Red's Yak-42 Bomber." *Space/Aeronautics,* XXX (October 1958), 40–46.

2105.   "Yak-42 Backfin: Soviet High-Performance Fighter-Bomber." *Air Force,* XLIII (May 1960), 44–45.

c. Reconnaissance/Liaison/ECM

(1) General Studies

Articles

2106. "Gallery of Soviet Aerospace Weapons: Reconnaissance, ECM, and Early Warning Aircraft." *Air Force Magazine,* LVIII (March 1975), 67–68; LIX (March 1976), 99; LX (March 1977), 94; LXI (March 1978), 100–101; LXII (March 1979), 106; LXIII (March 1980), 126.

2107. Logvinenko, B. "Reconnaissance of Enemy Air Targets." *Soviet Military Review,* no. 1 (January 1974), 22–23.

2108. Losev, G. "The Skill of a Reconnaissance Pilot." *Soviet Military Review,* no. 2 (February 1979), 18–19.

2109. "Reconnaissance and Bomber Forces, U.S.S.R." *RAF Flying Review,* XVIII (March 1963), 21–25.

2110. Trofimov, R. "Tactical Reconnaissance." *Soviet Military Review,* no. 5 (May 1976), 13–16.

2111. Zhuplatov, N. "In the Air—Reconnaissance Pilots: Translated from *Aviatsiya I Kosmonavtika,* April 1975." *Translations on USSR Military Affairs,* no. 1150 (June 5, 1975), 1–3.

(2) Specific Types

Antonov An-2 "Colt"

2112. "The Antonov An-2." *Flight,* LXX (July 13, 1956), 97.

2113. Braybrook, Roy M. "The Ubiquitous Antonov." *RAF Flying Review,* XI (August 1956), 22–25; XIV (February 1959), 8–9.

2114. Fricker, John E. "Flying Russia's Biggest Biplane." *Aeroplane,* XCI (September 7, 1956), 385–388.

2115. Taylor, John W. R. "Antonov's Colt." *Air Pictorial,* XXV (April 1963), 108–109.

2116. "A Versatile Russian Biplane." *Aeroplane,* XCV (December 5, 1958), 828–829.

Tupolev Tu-126 "Moss"

2117. Cherikow, Nikolai. "Moss: AWACS With a Red Star." *International Defense Review,* VIII (October 1975), 677–678.

d. Transport

(1) General Studies

Books

2118.   Stroud, John. *Soviet Transport Aircraft Since 1945*. Putnam Aeronautical Books. London: Bodley Head, 1975. 318p.

2119.   Taylor, John W. R. *Civil Aircraft of the World*. Rev. ed. New York: Scribner's, 1978. 177p.

Articles

2120.   Borgart, Peter. "The Soviet Transport Air Force: Aircraft and Capabilities." *International Defense Review*, XII (June 1979), 945–950.

2121.   "Gallery of Soviet Aerospace Weapons: Transports." *Air Force Magazine*, LVIII (March 1975), 118–120; LIX (March 1976), 100–101; LX (March 1977), 95–96; LXI (March 1978), 100–103; LXII (March 1979), 107–108; LXIII (March 1980), 127–128.

2122.   "Russian Transport Aircraft." *RAF Flying Review*, XII (April 1957), 27.

(2) Specific Types

Antonov An-8 "Camp"

2123.   "The An-8: New Soviet Assault Transport." *Air Force*, XL (July 1957), 82–83.

Antanov An-12 "Cub"

2124.   "The Antanov An-12." *Air Progress*, XXI (November–December 1965), 22–23.

Antonov An-22 "Cock"

2125.   "Details of An-22 Logistics Transport Shown." *Aviation Week and Space Technology*, LXXXIII (July 12, 1965), 94–97.

2126.   "Soviets Demonstrate Vertical Envelopment Capability with An-22 Heavy Transport." *Aviation Week and Space Technology*, LXXXVII (August 14, 1967), 52–55.

Antonov An-24 "Coke"

2127.   Gregory, W. G. "Soviets Add Two New Versions to Growing An-24 Family." *Aviation Week and Space Technology*, LXXXVII (July 10, 1967), 54–55.

Ilyushin Il-76 "Candid"

2128. Winston, D. C. "Soviet Il-76 to Have Remote Supply Role." *Aviation Week and Space Technology,* XCVIII (June 11, 1973), 57–59.

Ilyushin Il-86

2129. Borgart, Peter. "U.S.S.R. Develops New Il-86 [Tanker] Variants." *International Defense Review,* XI (July 1978), 1015–1016.

e. TRAINING

(1) General Studies

Book

2130. Taylor, Michael J. H. and Kenneth Munson, comps. *Jane's Pocket Book of Light Aircraft.* New York: Collier Books, 1976. 260p.

Articles

2131. "Gallery of Soviet Aerospace Weapons: Trainers." *Air Force Magazine,* LVIII (March 1975), 69–70; LIX (March 1976), 101–102; LX (March 1977), 96–97; LXI (March 1978), 104; LXII (March 1979), 108–109; LXIII (March 1980), 128–129.

2132. "New Jet Trainers in Eastern Europe." *Interavia,* XVIII (July 1963), 1080–1082.

2133. "U.S.S.R. Small Aircraft." *U.S. Army Aviation Digest,* V (May 1959), 16–17.

(2) Specific Types

Aero L-39 "Albatros"

2134. Braybrook, Roy M. "The Aero L-39 Albatros." *Interavia,* XXXII (November 1977), 1136–1138.

Mikoyan/Gurevich MIG-15UTI "Midget"

2135. "The MIG-15UTI." *Flight,* XCVI (April 24, 1969), 669–672.

Yakovlev Yak-18 "Max"

2136. Cain, Charles W. "How Good is Russia's Best Light Plane, Yak-18?" *Flying,* XLIX (October 1951), 22–23.

f. Helicopters

(1) General Studies

Books

2137.   Adwill, James. *Helicopters in Action.* New York: Meredith, 1969. 92p.

2138.   Ahnstrom, D. Newell. *The Complete Book of Helicopters.* Rev. ed. Cleveland, Ohio: World Publishing Company, 1968. 175p.

2139.   Bradbrooke, Joan. *The World's Helicopters.* Putnam World Aeronautical Library. Rev. ed. London: Bodley Head, 1975. 111p.

2140.   Fay, John. *Helicopter: History, Piloting, and How It Flies.* 3rd ed. New York: David and Charles, 1976. 96p.

2141.   Gablehouse, Charles. *Helicopters and Autogiros: A Chronicle of Rotating-Wing Aircraft.* Philadelphia: Lippincott, 1967. 254p.

2142.   Hellman, Harold. *Helicopters and Other VTOLs.* Garden City, N.Y.: Doubleday, 1970. 140p.

2143.   Jackson, Robert. *The Dragonflies: The Story of Helicopters and Autogiros.* London: Barker, 1971. 204p.

2144.   Lambermont, Paul M. and Anthony Pirie. *Helicopters and Autogiros of the World.* Rev. ed. Cranbury, N.J.: A. S. Barnes, 1970. 446p.

2145.   Munson, Kenneth G. *Helicopters and Other Rotorcraft Since 1907.* Pocket Encyclopedia of World Aircraft in Color Series. New York: Macmillan, 1969. 178p.

2146.   Swanborough, F. Gordon. *Vertical Flight Aircraft of the World.* Fallbrook, Calif.: Aero Publishers, 1964. 120p.

2147.   Taylor, John W. R. *Helicopters and VTOL Aircraft.* Garden City, N.Y.: Doubleday, 1968. 96p.

2148.   Taylor, Michael J. H. *Helicopters.* London: Macdonald and Jane's, 1978. 260p.

2149.   _____ and John W. R. *Helicopters of the World.* New York: Scribner's, 1976. 128p.

2150.   _____ . _____ . 2nd ed. New York: Scribner's, 1978. 112p.

Articles

2151. Alex, Ralph. "A Technician Looks at Russia—and Especially at Soviet Helicopters." *Flight,* LXXVI (December 11, 1959), 713–714.

2152. Barshevsky, Vasilii. "Russia's 'Copters." *RAF Flying Review,* XII (March 1957), 41–42.

2153. Fricker, John E. "Soviet Helicopters Surveyed." *Aeroplane,* XCII (March 15–22, 1957), 382–384, 415–417.

2154. "Gallery of Soviet Aerospace Weapons: Helicopters." *Air Force Magazine,* LVIII (March 1975), 70–72; LIX (March 1976), 102–103; LX (March 1977), 97–98; LXI (March 1978), 105–106; LXII (March 1979), 110–111; LXIII (March 1980), 130–131.

2155. Geiger, George J. "Soviet Helicopters." *Marine Corps Gazette,* XLV (January 1961), 48–50.

2156. George, Theodore. "The Soviet Helicopter Program." *U.S. Army Aviation Digest,* VIII (September 1958), 4–9.

2157. _____. "Soviet Helicopters." *Ordnance,* XLIV (September–October 1959), 225–230.

2158. Hansen, Lynn M. "Soviet Combat Helicopter Operations." *International Defense Review,* XI (August 1978), 1242–1246.

2159. "Helicopter Operations in the U.S.S.R." *Interavia,* XX (March 1965), 364–367.

2160. "Helicopters for Combat." *Flying Review International,* XXII (November 1966), 171–176, 181–187.

2161. "Helicopters for Military Mobility." *Interavia,* XVIII (September 1963), 1314.

2162. "How the Soviet Helicopters Stack Up." *Air Force,* XLII (December 1959), 15.

2163. Liberatare, E. K. "Russian Helicopter Activities." *U.S. Army Aviation Digest,* II (December 1956), 27–30.

2164. _____. "A Summary of Russian Helicopter Activities." *Marine Corps Gazette,* XL (December 1956), 20–21.

2165. Matwiczak, Kenneth M. "Soviet Helicopters, A Threat to the Forward Army Area." *Air Defense Magazine,* (October–December 1977), 26–29.

2166. "MIL Helicopters." *Flying Review International,* XXI (October 1965), 69–73.

2167. "Military Helicopters." *Flight International,* CXI (July 17, 1976), 183.

2168. "New Russian Rotorcraft." *Flight,* LXXI (January 4, 1957), 18–22.

2169. "Russian Army Helicopters." *Army,* VII (February 1957), 28–29.

2170. "Soviet Helicopters." *Data,* V (February 1960), 30–33.

2171. _____. *Military Review,* XL (October 1960), 71–74.

2172. "Twenty-Five Years of Russian Helicopter Development." *Flying Review International,* XX (February, April, October 1965), 16–20, 37–38, 69–73.

(2) Specific Types

Mil Mi-1 "Hare"

2173. Fricker, John E. "Flying the Mi-1 Helicopter." *Aeroplane,* XCI (August 17, 1956), 204–205.

2174. "The Mil Mi-1 Hare." *Flight,* LXXXIII (April 20, 1956), 444–445.

2175. _____. *Skyways,* XI (June 1952), 13.

2176. "Russia's Mi-1." *RAF Flying Review,* XI (May 1956), 36–37.

2177. Taylor, John W. R. "Hares and Hounds, The Mi-1/Mi-4 Family." *Air Pictorial,* XXV (November 1963), 358–359.

Mil Mi-6 "Hook"

2178. "The Mil Mi-6 Hook." *Air Progress,* XXI (November–December 1965), 24–25.

2179. _____. *Flying Review International,* XXIV (December 1968), 34–35.

2180. _____. *U.S. Army Aviation Digest,* XI (November 1965), 30–32.

2181. Taylor, John W. R. "Mil's Mi-6." *Air Pictorial,* XXVI (March 1964), 76–77.

Mil Mi-8 "Hip"

2182. "The Threat: Mi-8." *U.S. Army Aviation Digest*, XXIV (November 1978), 41.

Mil Mi-10 "Harke"

2183. "The Mil Ni-10 Harke." *Air Progress*, XXI (November–December 1965), 18–20.

2184. _____. *U.S. Army Aviation Digest*, XI (November 1965), 30–32.

Mil Mi-12 "Homer"

2185. Bigler, William B., 2nd. "Russia's Super Chopper." *Army*, XXIII (April 1973), 29–35.

Mil Mi-24 "Hind"

2186. Daschke, Carl. "The Threat: The Hind, Myth and Facts." *U.S. Army Aviation Digest*, XXV (December 1979), 42–46.

2187. "Is This Russia's Tank Killer?" *Armor*, LXXXVI (March–April 1977), 40–41.

2188. Malzeyev, Alexander. "The Mil Mi-24: The First Soviet Combat Helicopter." *Interavia*, XXXI (January 1976), 44–45.

2189. _____. "Soviet Mi-24 Combat Helicopter." *International Defense Review*, VIII (December 1975), 879–881.

2190. "Mi-24 Attack Version Can Fly Troops." *Aviation Week and Space Technology*, CVI (January 31, 1977), 16–17.

2191. "The Threat: Mi-24 Hind." *U.S. Army Aviation Digest*, XXV (April 1979), 23.

2192. Urbach, Walter, Jr. "Behind the Hind." *U.S. Army Aviation Digest*, XXIII (April 1977), 4–5.

g. V/STOL and Experimental

Books

2193. Myles, Bruce. *Jump Jet, The Revolutionary V/STOL Fighter*. San Rafael, Calif.: Presidio Press, 1978. 263p.

2194. Taylor, John W. R. and Kenneth G. Munson, eds. *Jane's Pocket Book of RPVs, Robot Aircraft Today*. New York: Macmillan, 1977. 239p.

Articles

2195. Arkill, Basil. "V/STOL." In: David Monday, ed. *The International Encyclopedia of Aviation*. New York: Crown, 1977. pp. 358–365.

2196. "Gallery of Soviet Aerospace Weapons: Experimental Aircraft." *Air Force Magazine*, LVIII (March 1975), 70; LIX (March 1976), 102.

2197. "STOL and VTOL Aircraft in the Soviet Air Force." *Interavia*, XXIV (May 1969), 602–603.

2198. Taylor, Peter P. W. "The Impact of V/STOL on Tactical Air Warfare." *Air University Review*, XXIX (November–December 1977), 65–81.

3. Aircraft Armament and Munitions

Books

2199. Lumsden, Malvern. *Incendiary Weapons*. A SIPRI Monograph. Cambridge, Mass., Published for the Stockholm International Peace Research Institute by MIT Press, 1976. 255p.

2200. Olmstead, Merle. *Aircraft Armament*. Modern Aircraft Series. New York, Sports Car Press, 1970. 112p.

Articles

2201. "Gallery of Soviet Aerospace Weapons: Airborne Tactical and Defense Missiles." *Air Force Magazine*, LVIII (March 1975), 73–74; LIX (March 1976), 105–106; LX (March 1977), 100–101; LXI (March 1978), 108; LXII (March 1979), 113; LXIII (March 1980), 133–134.

2202. Marriott, John. "Modern Tactical Air-to-Ground Weapons." *NATO's Fifteen Nations*, XX (April–May 1975), 40–45.

2203. Marsh, Roger. "Russian Aircraft Guns." *Aviation Age*, XVII (May–June 1952), 34–35, 40–41.

2204. Proskuryakov, V. "Air-to-Air Missiles." *Soviet Military Review*, no. 10 (October 1966), 27–29.

2205. Sorokin, V. "Soviet Aircraft Cannons and Machine Guns." *Soviet Military Review*, no. 2 (February 1973), 36–38.

2206. "Three New Soviet Air-to-Air Missiles in Service." *International Defense Review*, IX (September 1976), 400.

2207. Wetmore, Warren C. "Israelis Display Soviet-Built [AA-2] Atoll Missile." *Aviation Week and Space Technology*, LXXXVII (July 24, 1967), 65.

B. Missiles

1. AA Missile Systems

a. GENERAL STUDIES

Articles

2208. "Air Defense Missile Development." *Military Review,* XLVI (March 1966), 104–105.

2209. Crabb, Merle L. "The Low Altitude SAM Threat." *Marine Corps Gazette,* LV (February 1971), 48–49.

2210. Ellis, Paul and Mark Hewish. "World Missile Market and Air Defense Systems." *Flight International,* CI (May 11, 1972), 670–693.

2211. "Gallery of Soviet Aerospace Weapons: Surface-to-Air Missiles." *Air Force Magazine,* LVIII (March 1975), 74–75; LIX (March 1976), 106–107; LX (March 1977), 101–103; LXI (March 1978), 109; LXII (March 1979), 114; LXIII (March 1980), 134–135.

2212. Hines, Kerry L. "Defense Against Airmobility." *Air Defense Magazine,* (April–June 1978), 26–29.

2213. Maney, Rhoi M. "Man-Portable Air Defense Systems: A Comparison." *Air Defense Magazine,* (October–December 1977), 19–23.

2214. Marriott, John. "Land-Based Surface-to-Air Weapons." *NATO's Fifteen Nations,* XXIII (August–September 1978), 32–34.

2215. "Russian AA Rocket Development." *Aviation Age,* XX (October 1953), 6–9.

2216. "SAM the Sham: Antiaircraft Weapons." *Time,* LXXXVI (December 17, 1965), 29.

2217. Scoville, Herbert. "Upgrading the Soviet SAM." *New Republic,* CLXV (October 9, 1971), 19–20.

2218. Tanin, Ye. "Soviet Anti-Aircraft Defense." *Bulletin of the Institute for the Study of the History and Culture of the U.S.S.R.,* VII (June 1960), 33–38.

2219. Vershinin, Konstantin A. "Rocket Vehicles: The Basis of the Combat Might of the Soviet Air Force." *Survival,* IV (March–April 1962), 90–91.

Documents, Papers, and Reports

2220. Clemow, John. *Short Range Guided Weapons*, Temple Press Monograph on Rockets and Missiles, no. 1. London: Temple Press, 1961. 64p.

2221. Neupokoev, F. *Self-Guidance System of an Anti-Aircraft Guided Missile*. Translated from the Russian. Report, no. FSTC-HT-23-0680-74. Charlottesville, Va.: Army Foreign Science and Technology Center, 1974. 14p.

b. SPECIFIC TYPES

SA-2 "Guild"

2222. Brownlow, Cecil. "Anti-SAM Weapon Development Stressed." *Aviation Week and Space Technology*, LXXXIV (March 21, 1966), 26–28.

2223. "Soviets Unveil New Air Defense Missile." *Aviation Week and Space Technology*, LXXIX (November 18, 1963), 28–29.

SA-3 "Goa"

2224. "How to Cope with SAM-3." *Newsweek*, LXXV (April 6, 1970), 40.

SA-6 "Gainful"

2225. "SA-6: Arab Ace in the 20-Day War." *International Defense Review*, VI (December 1973), 779–781.

2226. "SA-6 Shows Soviet Technology Gains." *Aviation Week and Space Technology*, XCIX (October 2, 1973), 21.

2227. "U.S. Finds SA-6 to be Simple, Effective." *Aviation Week and Space Technology*, XCIX (December 3, 1973), 22.

SA-7 "Strella"

2228. Brown, Michael J. et al. "Missile, Missile, Missile." *U.S. Army Aviation Digest*, XXI (April 1975), 30–33.

2229. "North Vietnamese Use Shoulder-Fired, Infrared, Homing SAMS in the South: Soviet-Built Strella Missiles." *Aviation Week and Space Technology*, XCVI (May 18, 1972), 24.

SA-8 "Gecko"

2230. "SA-8: The Latest Soviet Mobile SAM System." *International Defense Review*, VIII (December 1975), 805–806.

SA-9 "Gaskin"

2231. "SA-9 Gaskin at Launch." *Air Defense Magazine*, (April–June 1979), 55–56.

2232. "The Threat: SA-9 Gaskin." *U.S. Army Aviation Digest*, XXIV (August 1978), 44.

2. Strategic and Battlefield Missile Systems

a. GENERAL STUDIES

Books

2233. Allward, Maurice and John W. R. Taylor. *ABC Rockets and Missiles*. New Rochelle, N.Y.: Sportshelf, 1960. 36p.

2234. Bowman, Norman J. *The Handbook of Rockets and Guided Missiles*. Chicago: Perastadion Press, 1957. 328p.

2235. Cox, John. *Overkill: Weapons of the Nuclear Age*. New York: T. Y. Crowell, 1978. 208p.

2236. Davis, C. E. *The Book of Missiles*. New York: Dodd, 1959. 96p.

2237. Gatland, Kenneth W. *Missiles and Rockets*. Pocket Encyclopedia of Spaceflight in Color Series. New York: Macmillan, 1975. 256p.

2238. Howard, William E. and James Baar. *Spacecraft and Missiles of the World*. New and rev. ed. New York: Harcourt, 1966. 104p.

2239. Ordway, Frederick I. and Ronald C. Wakeford. *International Missile and Spacecraft Guide*. New York: McGraw-Hill, 1960. 277p.

2240. Parry, Albert. *Russia's Rockets and Missiles*. Garden City, N.Y.: Doubleday, 1960. 382p.

2241. Polmar, Norman. *Strategic Weapons: An Introduction*. New York: Crane, Russak, 1975. 164p.

2242. Pretty, Ronald, ed. *Jane's Pocket Book of Missiles*. New ed. London: Macdonald and Jane's, 1978. 256p.

2243. Taylor, John W. R. *Rockets and Missiles*. All Color Guide Series, no. 17. New York: Grosset and Dunlap, 1970. 159p.

2244. Taylor, Michael J. H. and John W. R. *Missiles of the World*. London: Ian Allan, 1973. 167p.

2245. _____. _____. Rev. ed. New York: Scribner's, 1976. 159p.

2246. Van Cleave, William R. *Tactical Nuclear Weapons: An Examination of the Issues.* New York: Crane, Russak, 1978. 119p.

Articles

2247. "Already in Service: The Second Generation of Soviet Anti-Tank Missiles." *International Defense Review,* XI (January 1978), 15–17.

2248. Ashmore, Edward B. "Guided Missiles: Faction and Reality." *NATO's Fifteen Nations,* XVII (February–March 1972), 54–55, 57–60.

2249. "The Battlefield Missile Tables." *Defense and Foreign Affairs Digest,* no. 2 (February 1976), 15–17.

2250. "Battlefield Rockets for the Red GI." *Popular Science,* CLXXXI (October 1962), 104–105.

2251. Boman, Truman R. "Soviet Guided Missile Deployment." *Military Review,* XLIII (November 1962), 75–79.

2252. Breitkopf, Hans. "Soviet Long Range Missiles." *Military Review,* XXXV (May 1955), 77–83.

2253. Brownlow, Cecil. "Growing Threat: The Soviet Union's New Military Hardware." *Aviation Week and Space Technology,* XCV (October 4, 1971), 12–15.

2254. _____. "Soviets Deploy New, Larger ICBMs." *Aviation Week and Space Technology,* XCIV (March 15, 1971), 16–17.

2255. _____. "Soviets Developing New ICBMs" *Aviation Week and Space Technology,* XCVIII (April 2, 1973), 14–15.

2256. Butz, J. S. "New Soviet Missiles: Technological Storm Warning or False Alarm?" *Air Force and Space Digest,* XLVIII (July 1965), 32–39.

2257. "Collection on Strategic Missiles." *Translations on USSR Military Affairs,* no. 116 (March 1963), 1–21.

2258. Currie, Malcolm R. "Future Tactical Missiles." *National Defense,* LXI (July–August 1976), 32–35.

2259. "Gallery of Soviet Aerospace Weapons: Strategic Missiles." *Air Force Magazine,* LVIII (March 1975), 72–73; LIX (March 1976), 103–105; LX (March 1977), 98–100; LXI (March 1978), 106–108; LXII (March 1979), 111–113; LXIII (March 1980), 131–133.

2260. Garthoff, Raymond L. "Russia Leading the World in ICBM and Satellite Development?" *Missiles and Rockets,* II (October 1957), 72–76.

2261. Gatland, Kenneth W. "New Missiles in Moscow." *Flying Review International,* XXIII (January 1968), 32–33.

2262. _____. "Russia's Guided Weapons." *RAF Flying Review,* XIII (July 1958), 42.

2263. _____. "Soviet Ballistic Strength." *Flying Review International,* XXIII (April 1968), 208; XXVI (July 1970), 56.

2264. _____. "Soviet Missiles." In: Ray Bonds, ed. *The Soviet War Machine: An Illustrated Encyclopedia of Russian Military Equipment and Strategy.* New York: Chartwell Books, 1976. pp. 212–231.

2265. _____. "Within the Shadow of Russian Missiles." *Interavia,* VIII (November 1953), 632–634.

2266. Geiger, George J. "Russia's Missiles and Space Boosters." *Aerospace Management,* V (March 1962), 98–107.

2267. _____. "Soviet Battlefield Rockets." *Infantry,* LIII (January–February 1963), 62–64.

2268. Getler, Michael. "Soviets Trying to Close Strategic Gap." *Technology Weekly,* XVIII (June 27, 1966), 14–15.

2269. Gunston, William T. "Missiles, 1962." *Flight International,* LXXXII (November 8, 1962), 743–766.

2270. Harvey, David. "Missile Muscle: A Report on Battlefield Missiles." *Defense and Foreign Affairs Digest,* no. 2 (February 1976), 12–14.

2271. Heiman, Leo. "In the Soviet Arsenal." *Ordnance,* LII (January–February 1968), 366–373.

2272. International Institute for Strategic Studies. "Nuclear Delivery Vehicles: Comparative Strengths and Characteristics." *Air Force Magazine,* LV (December 1972), 100–102; LVIII (December 1975), 90–92.

2273. "Ivan Gets a New Bomb: MIRV." *Newsweek,* LXXXII (August 27, 1973), 33.

2274. Kaplan, Fred. "The Arms of Armageddon: The Doomsday Weapons that SALT II is All About." *Washington Post Magazine,* (July 15, 1979), 20–25.

2275. "Khrushchev's Missile Threat." *RAF Flying Review,* XVI (January 1961), 13–15.

2276. Krylov, Nikolai I. "Strategic Rockets." *Military Review,* XLIV (December 1964), 33–35.

2777. _____. _____. *NATO's Fifteen Nations,* IX (April–May 1964), 98–103.

2278. Lee, Asher. "Soviet Missiles." In: Asher Lee, ed. *The Soviet Air and Rocket Forces.* New York: Praeger, 1959. pp. 146–160.

2279. _____. "To Set You Straight on Russia's Rockets: An Interview." *U.S. News and World Report,* XLVII (July 20, 1959), 46–49.

2280. McGuire, Frank G. "Soviet Troops Get New Missiles." *Missiles and Rockets,* II (December 1957), 37.

2281. McGuire, James D. "Soviet Rocket Weapons." *Army,* XI (August 1960), 45–49.

2282. Marriott, John. "Anti-Tank Missiles." *Army Quarterly,* CVII (April 1977), 147–153.

2283. Mataxis, Theodore C. "The Soviets Forge Ahead." *Infantry,* XLVIII (April 1958), 14–27.

2284. "Missiles of the U.S.S.R." *Missiles and Rockets,* IV (July 28, 1958), 142–148.

2285. "Modern Weapons of the Soviet Army." *Interavia,* XXI (May 1966), 590–593.

2286. "The New-Look Soviet Weapons." *Army Information Digest,* XIII (March 1958), 24–33.

2287. "Nuclear Missiles: The Backbone of Defenses." *Translations on USSR Military Affairs,* no. 173a (June 1965), 17–23.

2288. "Nuclear Weapons." *Interavia,* XVII (November 1962), 1421–1436.

2289. Parry, Albert. "What the Russians Tell—and What They Don't Tell." *Missiles and Rockets,* II (February 1957), 70–72.

2290. Ritchie, Donald J. "A Russian ICBM." *Ordnance,* XLIX (November–December 1964), 325–327.

2291. Robinson, Clarence A., Jr. "Soviets Boost ICBM Accuracy." *Aviation Week and Space Technology,* CVIII (April 3, 1978), 14–16.

Missiles

2292. "Russia Revamps Its Missile Might." *Business Week*, (November 20, 1965), 138.

2293. "Russia's Guided Missile Program." *Missiles and Rockets*, II (February 1957), 33–41.

2294. "Scare Over Russian Missiles: What It's About." *U.S. News and World Report*, LXXV (September 3, 1973), 59–60.

2295. "Second Annual Encyclopedia of U.S. and Russian Missiles." *Missiles and Rockets*, IV (July 28, 1958), 105–148.

2296. Shafter, Richard A. "On Target: Rockets—Red Russia's Most Secret Weapons?" *Our Navy*, XLV (January 1951), 7–8.

2297. Sherman, Robert. "A Manual of Missile Capability." *Air Force Magazine*, LX (February 1977), 35–39.

2298. "Soviet Missile Inventory." *Interavia*, XX (March 1965), 377–381; XXI (February 1966), 188–189.

2299. "Soviet Missiles." *Aviation Week and Space Technology*, CX (March 12, 1979), 98–99.

2300. ———. *Missile Engineering*, II (January 1958), 6–7.

2301. "Soviet Union Modernizes IRBM." *International Defense Review*, IX (October 1976), 709.

2302. "Soviets Show Details of Various Missiles." *Aviation Week and Space Technology*, LXXXV (November 28, 1966), 58–59.

2303. Sutton, George P. "Evaluation of Russian Rocket Developments." *British Interplanetary Society Journal*, XIII (September 1954), 262–268.

2304. ———. "Rockets Behind the Iron Curtain." *American Rocket Society Journal*, XXIII (May–June 1953), 186–191.

2305. Taylor, John W. R. "World Missiles, 1971." *Flight International*, XCIX (March 18, 1971), 374–393.

2306. Tsipis, Kosta. "The Calculus of Nuclear Counterforce." *Technology Review*, LXXV (October–November 1974), 34–47.

2307. Ulsamer, Edgar. "A New Family of Soviet Strategic Weapons." *Air Force Magazine*, LIX (October 1976), 24–27.

2308. "U.S.S.R. Surface-to-Surface Missiles." *Military Review*, XLVI (November 1966), 106–107.

2309. "U.S.S.R. Unveils New Anti-Tank Missiles." *Aviation Week and Space Technology,* CVII (December 5, 1977), 19.

2310. "What Does Russia Have?" *American Aviation,* XVIII (October 25, 1954), 33-37.

2311. Wilson, Peter A. "Battlefield Guided Weapons: The Big Equalizer." *U.S. Naval Institute Proceedings,* CI (February 1975), 18-25.

2312. Zaehringer, Alfred J. "Missiles of the U.S.S.R." *Ordnance,* XLII (Janaury-February 1958), 639-642.

Documents, Papers, and Reports

2313. Digby, James F. *Precision-Guided Munitions: Capabilities and Consequences.* RAND Paper P-5257. Santa Monica, Calif.: RAND Corporation, 1974. 19p.

2314. Mikhaylov, V. A. *Nuclear Weapons.* Translated from the Russian. Report, no. FTD-MT-24-1271-71. Wright Patterson AFB, Ohio: Foreign Technology Division, U.S. Air Force, 1972. 63p.

2315. *Rocket Weapons of Modern Armies, U.S.S.R.* Translation, no. 12045. Arlington, Va.: Joint Publications Research Service, 1962. 11p.

2316. Smart, Ian. *Advanced Strategic Missiles: A Short Guide.* Adelphi papers, no. 63. London: Institute for Strategic Studies, 1969. 31p.

2317. Tinajero, A. A. *Projected Strategic Offensive Weapons Inventories of the U.S. and U.S.S.R.* Multilith, no. 77-59F. Washington, D.C.: Foreign Affairs and National Defense Division, Library of Congress, 1977. 180p.

2318. Tsipis, Kosta. *Offensive Missiles.* Stockholm Paper, no. 5. Stockholm: Stockholm International Peace Research Institute, 1974. 34p.

b. Specific Types

FROG 3-7

2319. Geiger, George J. "Russian Frogs." *Ordnance,* XLIX (May-June 1965), 644-646.

SS-lc "Scud"

2320. Geiger, George J. "Russia's Scud Missile." *Ordnance,* LI (May-June 1967), 610-611.

SS-16

2321. "SS-16 Raises Questions." *Aviation Week and Space Technology*, CXI (September 24, 1979), 24.

2322. "Soviets Deploy SS-16 ICBM." *Aviation Week and Space Technology*, CVIII (February 27, 1978), 15.

SS-18

2323. "Significance of SS-18 Questioned." *Aviation Week and Space Technology*, CXI (July 16, 1979), 24.

SS-20

2324. Hoffman, Hubertus. "SS-20 Multiplies U.S.S.R.'s Nuclear Superiority." *NATO's Fifteen Nations*, XXIII (December 1978–January 1979), 42–44.

2325. "SS-20 Depicted." *Aviation Week and Space Technology*, CXI (November 12, 1979), 18.

6/ *Arms Competition, Arms Control, and the Balance of Power*

Introduction

THE NATURE OF war has been forever changed by the atomic bomb. By the late 1950s when Russia obtained the capability to deliver these weapons by plane and missile, a new and deadly arms race with the United States was begun—a race which has accelerated in recent months.

The sources cited in the three parts of this section deal with the arms race and delivery systems of nuclear weapons, efforts to halt or slow the arms race contest by disarmament agreements, and the balance of potential atomic devastation maintained between East and West.

Additional citations regarding this section appear in Sections 3:A:3 and 4:D:2 above.

A. Arms Competition

Books

2326. Baldwin, Hanson W. *The Great Arms Race: A Comparison of U.S. and Soviet Power Today.* New York: Praeger, 1958. 116p.

2327. Barnaby, Frank and Ronald Huisken. *Arms Uncontrolled.* Cambridge, Mass.: Published for the Stockholm International Peace Research Institute by Harvard University Press, 1975. 232p.

2328. Bertram, Christopher, ed. *New Conventional Weapons and East-West Security: Based on a 1977 Conference of the International Institute for Strategic Studies.* New York: Praeger, 1979. 97p.

2329. Bottome, Edgar M. *The Missile Gap* [1958–1961]: *A Study of the Formulation of Military and Political Policy.* Rutherford, N.J.: Farleigh Dickinson University Press, 1971. 265p.

2330. Carlton, David and Carlo Schaerf, eds. *The Dynamics of the Arms Race.* London: Halsted Press, 1975. 244p.

2331. Chodes, John J. *The Myth of America's Military Power.* New York: Brandon House, 1973. 224p.

2332. Cline, Ray S. *World Power Assessment: A Calculus of Strategic Drift.* Boulder, Colo.: Westview, 1975. 173p.

2333. _____ . _____ . Rev. ed. Boulder, Colo.: Westview, 1977. 206p.

2334. DeSeversky, Alexander P. *America: Too Young to Die.* New York: McGraw-Hill, 1961. 237p.

2335. Graham, Daniel O. *Shall America Be Defended?: SALT II and Beyond.* New Rochelle, N.Y.: Arlington House, 1979. 267p.

2336. Holbrand, Carsten. *Superpowers and International Conflict.* New York: St. Martin's Press, 1979. 178p.

2337. Holst, Johan J. and Uwe Nerlich, eds. *Beyond Nuclear Deterrence: New Aims, New Arms.* New York: Crane, Russak, 1977. 314p.

2338. Kemp, Geoffrey et al., eds. The *Superpowers in a Multi-Nuclear World.* Lexington, Mass: Lexington Books, 1974. 300p.

2339. Kirk, Grayson and Nils Wessell, eds. *The Soviet Threat: Myths and Realities.* New York: Praeger, 1978. 192p.

2340. Larson, Thomas B. *Soviet-American Rivalry.* New York: Norton, 1978.

2341.   LeMay, Curtis E. *Mission With LeMay.* Garden City, N.Y.: Doubleday, 1965. 581p.

2342.   Lens, Sidney. *The Day Before Doomsday: An Anatomy of the Nuclear Arms Race.* Garden City, N.Y.: Doubleday, 1977. 274p.

2343.   Lowe, George E. *The Age of Deterrence* [1952–1963]. Boston: Little, Brown, 1964. 324p.

2344.   Marriott, John, comp. *International Weapons Developments.* San Rafael, Calif.: Presidio Press, 1979. 157p.

2345.   Middleton, Drew. *Can America Win the Next War?* New York: Scribner's, 1975. 271p.

2346.   Moulton, Harland B. *From Superiority to Parity: The United States and the Strategic Arms Race, 1961–1971.* Westport, Conn.: Greenwood Press, 1973. 333p.

2347.   Myrdal, Alva. *The Game of Disarmament: How the United States and Russia Run the Arms Race.* New York: Pantheon, 1976. 397p.

2348.   Peckman, Joseph A., ed. *Setting National Priorities: The 1980 Budget.* Washington, D.C.: Brookings Institution, 1979. 229p.

2349.   *Prospects of Soviet Power in the 1980s: Papers from the International Institute for Strategic Studies' 20th Annual Conference.* Adelphi papers, nos. 151–152. 2 vols. London, 1979.

2350.   Schurmann, Franz. *The Logic of World Power: An Inquiry Into the Origins, Currents, and Contradictions of World Politics.* New York: Pantheon, 1974. 593p.

2351.   Scoville, Herbert and Robert C. Osborn. *Missile Madness.* Boston: Houghton, Mifflin, 1970. 93p.

2352.   Thomson, Jeffrey R. *U.S./U.S.S.R. Strategic Forces, Asymmetrical Developments: A Net American Assessment.* Washington, D.C.: University Press of America, 1977. 591p.

2353.   Whetten, Lawrence L., ed. *The Political Implications of Soviet Military Power.* New York: Crane, Russak, 1976. 183p.

Articles

2354.   "The Arms Race—Marathon to Madness: A Symposium." *America,* CXL (June 30, 1979), 525–537.

2355.   Blechman, Barry M. "Handicapping the Arms Race: Are the Soviets Ahead?" *New Republic,* CLXXIV (January 3, 1976), 19–21.

Arms Competition, Arms Control, Balance of Power

2356. Brown, George S. "If the Soviets Insist, There Will Be an Arms Race: An Interview." *U.S. News and World Report,* LXXVI (February 25, 1974), 62–65.

2357. Brown, Harold. "The Growing Soviet Threat, Even With an Arms Pact." *U.S. News and World Report,* LXXXVI (February 5, 1979), 33–34.

2358. Brownlow, Cecil. "The Growing Threat." *Aviation Week and Space Technology,* XCV (October 4–November 8, 1971), 12–15, 36–40, 34–37, 40–43, 38–43.

2359. _____ . "Soviets Challenge U.S. for Strategic Lead." *Aviation Week and Space Technology,* LXXXVIII (March 4, 1968), 51.

2360. Burke, Gerald K. "The Metaphysics of Power Realities and Nuclear Armaments." *Military Review,* LV (September 1975), 14–24.

2361. Butz, J. S. "How Far is the Red Air Force Ahead?" *Air Force,* XLIV (September 1961), 52–56.

2362. Cady, Steven E. "World Peace and the Soviet Military Threat." *Air University Review,* XXX (January–February 1979), 94–98.

2363. Citizens' Panel on Defense. "U.S. Superiority Has Ended: Summary of a Statement." *U.S. News and World Report,* LXX (April 5, 1971), 49–50.

2364. Constant, James. "The Strategic Conflict." *Countermeasures,* II (March–April 1976), 32–36, 26–30.

2365. Cordes, Harry N. "The Strategic Threat." *Air Force Magazine,* LIV (July 1971), 51–55.

2366. Dick, J. C. "The Strategic Arms Race, 1957–1961: Who Opened a Missile Gap?" *Journal of Politics,* XXXIV (November 1972), 1062–1110.

2367. "Fresh Worry Over Soviet Arms Buildup." *U.S. News and World Report,* LXXII (February 28, 1972), 24–26.

2368. Fromm, Joseph. "Arms Gap: How Russia Stole a March on the U.S." *U.S. News and World Report,* LXXXVII (November 12, 1979), 41.

2369. _____ . "Can U.S. Block Soviet Bid for Nuclear Supremacy?" *U.S. News and World Report,* LXXXI (September 6, 1976), 16–18.

2370. _____ . "New Alarm Over the Russian Threat: A Special Report." *U.S. News and World Report,* LXXXV (October 30, 1978), 47–53.

2371. Garn, Jake. "Soviet Superiority: A Question for National Debate." *International Security Review,* IV (Spring 1979), 1–25.

2372. Gray, Colin S. "Action and Reaction in the Nuclear Arms Race." *Military Review,* LI (August 1971), 16–26.

2373. _____. "How Does the Nuclear Arms Race Work?" *Cooperation and Conflict,* IX (Fall 1974), 285–295.

2374. _____. "The Urge to Compete: Rationales for Arms Racing." *World Politics,* XXVI (Janaury 1974), 595–611.

2375. Green, William. "Does Russia Lead?" *RAF Flying Review,* XI (May 1956), 19–25.

2376. Haig, Alexander M. "Russia's Relentless Arms Buildup: An Interview." *U.S. News and World Report,* LXXXII (January 17, 1977), 35–37.

2377. Hessman, James D. "The Soviet Union Moves Ahead: On Land, on the Sea, and in the Air." *Armed Forces Journal,* CVII (August 17, 1970), 28–37.

2378. Hinterhoff, Eugene. "The Erosion of the Western Deterrent: An Analysis of Russia's Growing 'Position of Strength.'" *NATO's Fifteen Nations,* XIII (June–July 1968), 57–65.

2379. "Is the U.S. Forfeiting the Arms Race to Russia?" *U.S. News and World Report,* LXIX (October 19, 1970), 21–24.

2380. "'Jane's' Sees U.S. Air Power Second to the U.S.S.R.'s and Slipping Further Behind: Reprinted from the *Los Angeles Times,* December 22, 1976." *U.S. Naval Institute Proceedings,* CIII (March 1977), 108.

2381. Keegan, George J., Jr. "New Assessment Put on Soviet Threat: An Address." *Aviation Week and Space Technology,* CVI (March 28, 1977), 38–43.

2382. Laird, Melvin R. "Why Soviet Arms Worry the U.S.: An Interview." *U.S. News and World Report,* LXXII (March 27, 1972), 41–46.

2383. Lambeth, Benjamin S. "The Evolving Soviet Strategic Threat." *Current History,* LXIX (October 1975), 121–125.

2384. _____. "Moscow and the Missile Race." *Current History,* LXI (October 1971), 215–221, 242.

2385. Lemnitzer, Lyman. "Russia's Growing Power: An Interview." *U.S. News and World Report,* LXVI (May 12, 1969), 44–46.

2386. Levine, Isaac D. "Détente and Reality." *Strategic Review,* II (Summer 1974), 44–50.

2387. Lowther, William. "Gathering Storm: Russia's Shift in the Balance of Terror." *Maclean's,* XCI (May 29, 1978), 22–24.

2388. Lucier, C. E. "Changes in Values of Arms Race Parameters." *Journal of Conflict Resolution,* XXIII (March 1979), 17–39.

2389. McBride, James H. "How the Strategic Balance is Shifting, 1961–1972." *Air Force and Space Digest,* LI (October 1968), 36–43.

2390. McWhinnie, A. J. "Air Line-Up: Russia Still Leads the West." *Navy,* LVII (September 1952), 240–242.

2391. Marzari, Frank. "Prospects for Strategic Stability in the 1970s." *Canadian Journal of Political Science,* IV (December 1971), 541–558.

2392. May, M. M. "Nuclear Weapons: An Address, March 10, 1978." *Vital Speeches,* XLIV (June 1, 1978), 486–489.

2393. Murphy, Charles J. V. "The New Air Situation." *Fortune,* LII (September 1955), 86–87.

2394. _____. "Our Strategic Arms Advantage is Fading Fast." *Reader's Digest,* XCVIII (February 1971), 94–98.

2395. Nanes, Allan S. "American-Russian Arms Competition." *Current History,* XXXVII (October 1959), 214–221.

2396. Norman, Lloyd. "What Has Become of the Missile Gap?" *National Guardsman,* XXIV (May 1970), 2–7.

2397. O'Ballance, Edgar. "The Megatonnage and Missile Gaps." *Military Review,* XLIX (March 1969), 65–70.

2398. "Pentagon Size-Up: Where Russia is Outstripping the U.S. in Military Might." *U.S. News and World Report,* LXXX (February 9, 1976), 20–21.

2399. Polmar, Norman. "Is the U.S.S.R. Behind or Ahead?" *Sealift,* XXV (January 1975), 24–27.

2400. Powell, Craig. "Strategic Forces: Second-Guessing Tomorrow." *Armed Forces Management,* XVI (April 1970), 26–29.

2401. Price, William. "How Does Our Air Force Stack Up Against Stalin's?" *Saturday Evening Post,* CCXXV (September 6, 1952), 25.

Arms Competition

2402. Rentschler, Frederick B. "The Jet Air Power Race, 1945–1955." *U.S. Air Services*, XI (August 1955), 6–9.

2403. Robinson, Clarence A., Jr. "Carter Warned on Soviet Nuclear Advantage." *Aviation Week and Space Technology*, CVII (November 7, 1977), 18–21.

2404. ———. "Soviets Grasping Strategic Lead." *Aviation Week and Space Technology*, CV (August 30, 1976), 14–18.

2405. Rosser, Richard F. "The Dangerous Decade." *Air Force Magazine*, LV (January 1972), 44–48.

2406. Rummel, Rudolph J. "Will the Soviet Union Soon Have a First-Strike Capability?" *Orbis*, XX (Fall 1976), 579–594.

2407. Schemmer, Benjamin F. "U.S./U.S.S.R. Military Balance Shifts in Favor of Russia." *Armed Forces Journal International*, CXIII (March 1976), 18.

2408. Schlesinger, James R. "Testing Time for America: The Russian Threat." *Fortune*, XCIII (February 1976), 74–77.

2409. Scowcroft, Brent. "Deterrence and Strategic Superiority." *Orbis*, XIII (Summer 1969), 435–454.

2410. Scribner, Jeffrey L. "The Soviet Military Build-Up: A New Dimension in Foreign Policy." *Military Review*, LI (August 1971), 53–62.

2411. Sherman, Robert. "The Fallacies of Counterforce." *Strategic Review*, III (Spring 1975), 48–57.

2412. "Soviet Global Military Capability Gains." *Aviation Week and Space Technology*, CVIII (May 29, 1978), 60–61.

2413. Stares, John. "The Strategic Nuclear Arms Race." *Impact of Science on Society*, XXVI (January–April 1976), 27–38.

2414. Stratton, Andrew. "Aircraft, Missiles, and Spacecraft: Contests in the Sky." In: Nigel Calder, ed. *Unless Peace Comes: A Scientific Forecast of New Weapons*. New York: Viking, 1968. pp. 64–90.

2415. "That Alarming Soviet Buildup." *Time*, CVII (March 8, 1976), 35–36.

2416. Turner, Roscoe. "Shall America or Russia Rule the Air: An Address." *Congressional Record*, XCV (March 18, 1949), A1560–A1562.

2417. Ulsamer, Edgar. "The Accelerating Momentum of Soviet Military Might." *Air Force Magazine*, LXI (March 1978), 34–41.

2418. _____. "How Russia is Tipping the Strategic Balance." *Air Force Magazine,* LVIII (January 1975), 48–53.

2419. _____. "Increasing Momentum in Soviet Strategic Systems." *Air Force Magazine,* LVI (March 1973), 62–64.

2420. _____. "Nuclear War: The Life and Death Issues." *Air Force Magazine,* LIX (January 1976), 57–59.

2421. _____. "The Soviet ICBM Threat is Mounting." *Air Force Magazine,* LVI (November 1973), 34–37.

2422. _____. "The Soviet Juggernaut: Racing Faster Than Ever." *Air Force Magazine,* LIX (March 1976), 56–58.

2423. _____. "The U.S.S.R's Military Shadow is Lengthening." *Air Force Magazine,* LX (March 1977), 36–46.

2424. _____. "World Hegemony Through Military Superiority." *Air Force Magazine,* LXII (March 1979), 40–47.

2425. "U.S. and Soviet Strategic Capability through the Mid-1980s." *Department of State Bulletin,* LXXVIII (October 1978), 24–28.

2426. Vandyk, Anthony. "Red Aviation Progress Challenges U.S. Airpower Supremacy." *American Aviation,* XIX (June 6, 1955), 21–24.

2427. Vigor, Peter H. "Soviet Military Developments—1976." *Strategic Review,* V (Spring 1977), 74–82.

2428. Wallace, M. D. "Dynamics of the Arms Race: Military R & D and Disarmament." *Journal of Conflict Resolution,* XXIII (March 1979), 3–16.

2429. Weeks, Albert L. "The Growth of Soviet Military Power." *American Legion Magazine,* XCI (November 1971), 6–11.

2430. Winston, D. C. "DOD Warns Congress on Soviet Gains." *Aviation Week and Space Technology,* XCVI (February 28, 1972), 18–19.

2431. _____. "Soviets Press Strategic Military Expansion." *Aviation Week and Space Technology,* XCII (March 9, 1970), 46–47.

2432. Wohstetter, Albert. "Legends of the Strategic Arms Race." *Strategic Review,* II (Summer 1974), 67–92; V (Winter 1975), 70–86.

Documents, Papers, and Reports

2433. Aspin, Les and Jack F. Kemp. *Realities of Soviet Power: Two Views.* AEI Defense Review, vol. 2, no. 3. Washington, D.C.: American Enterprise Institute for Public Policy Research, 1978. 36p.

2434. Barnett, Frank R. et al. *The Military Unbalance: Is the U.S. Becoming a Second Class Power?* New York: National Strategy Information Center, 1971. 65p.

2435. Blechman, Barry M. et al. *Soviet Military Buildup and U.S. Defense Spending.* Studies in Defense Policy. Washington, D.C.: Brookings Institution, 1977. 61p.

2436. Clemens, Walter C., Jr. *The Arms Race and Sino-Soviet Relations.* Paper P-72. Stanford, Calif.: Hoover Institution Press, 1968. 335p.

2437. Committee on the Present Danger. *Is America Becoming No. 2?* Washington, D.C., 1978. 46p.

2438. Duffy, John J., Jr. and Allen S. Merritt. *Nuclear Parity or Nuclear Sufficiency: The U.S.-Soviet Strategic Competition.* Research Project. Carlisle Barracks, Pa.: U.S. Army War College, 1975. 60p.

2439. Georgetown University, Center for Strategic Studies. *The Soviet Military Technological Challenge.* Special Report Series, no. 6. Washington, D.C., 1967. 98p.

2440. Goldhamer, Herbert. *The Soviet Union in a Period of Strategic Parity.* RAND Report R-889-PR. Santa Monica, Calif.: RAND Corporation, 1971. 71p.

2441. Holst, Johan J. *Comparative U.S. and Soviet Deployments, Doctrines, and Arms Limitations.* An Occasional Paper. Chicago: Center for Policy Study, University of Chicago, 1971. 60p.

2442. Hood, Joseph W., Jr. "Strategic Arms Interactions, 1945–1961." Unpublished thesis, U.S. Naval Postgraduate School, 1974.

2443. Jennings, Richard M. "U.S./Soviet Arms Competition, 1945–1972: Aspects of Its Nature, Control, and Results." Unpublished Ph.D. Dissertation, Georgetown University, 1975.

2444. Kintner, William R. and Robert L. Pfalzgraff, Jr. *Soviet Military Trends: Implications for U.S. Security.* Special Analysis, no. 6. Washington, D.C.: American Enterprise Institute for Public Policy Research, 1971. 50p.

2445. Korb, Laurence J. *The FY 1980–1984 Defense Program: Issues and Trends.* Washington, D.C.: American Enterprise Institute for Public Policy Research, 1979. 53p.

2446. Lambeth, Benjamin S. *The Evolving Soviet Strategic Threat.* RAND Paper P-5493. Santa Monica, Calif: RAND Corporation, 1975. 20p.

Arms Competition, Arms Control, Balance of Power 199

2447. Pauker, Guy J. *Military Implications of a Possible World Order Crisis in the 1980s.* RAND Report R–2003–AF. Santa Monica, Calif.: RAND Corporation, 1977. 101p.

2448. Thompson, W. Scott. *Power Projection: A Net Assessment of U.S. and Soviet Capabilities.* New York: National Strategy Information Center, 1978. 39p.

2449. _____ . *The Projection of Soviet Power.* RAND Paper P–5988. Santa Monica, Calif.: RAND Corporation, 1977. 37p.

2450. United States. Congress. House. Committee on Armed Services. *The Soviet Threat: Report.* 91st Cong., 2nd sess. Washington, D.C.: U.S. Government Printing Office, 1970. 33p.

2451. _____ . _____ . Senate. Committee on Foreign Relations. Subcommittee on Arms Control, International Law and Organizations. *ABM, MIRV, SALT and the Nuclear Arms Race: Hearings.* 91st Cong., 2nd sess. Washington, D.C.: U.S. Government Printing Office, 1970.

2452. _____ . _____ . _____ . _____ . Subcommittee on Arms Control, Oceans and International Environment. *United States/Soviet Strategic Options: Hearings.* 95th Cong., 2nd sess. Washington, D.C.: U.S. Government Printing Office, 1977.

2453. _____ . _____ . _____ . Select Committee on Intelligence. *The National Intelligence Estimates, A-B Team Episode Concerning Soviet Strategic Capability and Objectives.* 95th Cong., 2nd sess. Washington, D.C.: U.S. Government Printing Office, 1978.

2454. _____ . Department of Defense. "General Purpose Forces." *Commander's Digest,* XXI (March 23, 1978), 1–20.

2455. Yancey, George P. *Strategic Overkill: Fact or Fancy?* Maxwell AFB, Ala.: Air Command and Staff College, Air University, 1974. 73p.

B. Arms Control

Introduction

THE EFFORT TO control national arms inventories has taken on new significance since the beginning of the atomic era. We are no longer concerned with counting battleships; now we must face the possibility of total nuclear destruction.

The literature on arms control is quite extensive and we can include here only a representative sample of entries, with emphasis on those directly relative to Soviet aerospace forces.

For a comprehensive look at the literature of arms control two works by series editor Richard Burns are recommended:

Burns, Richard Dean. *Arms Control and Disarmament: A Bibliography.* War/Peace Bibliography Series, no. 6. Santa Barbara, Calif.: ABC-Clio, 1977. 416p.

———— and Susan Hoffman, comps. *The SALT Era: A Selected Bibliography.* Political Issues Series, vol. 6, no. 1. Rev. ed. Los Angeles: Center for the Study of Armament and Disarmament, California State University, 1979. 59p.

Books

2456.   Kintner, William R. and Robert L. Pfaltzgraff, Jr., eds. *SALT: Implications for Arms Control in the 1970s.* Pittsburgh, Pa.: University of Pittsburgh Press, 1973. 447p.

2457.   Newhouse, John. *Cold Dawn: The Story of SALT.* New York: Holt, 1973. 302p.

2458.   Talbot, Strobe. *Endgame: The Inside Story of SALT II.* New York: Harper & Row, 1979. 288p.

2459.   Willrich, Mason and John B. Rhinelander, eds. *SALT: The Moscow Agreements and Beyond.* New York: Free Press, 1974. 361p.

Articles

2460.   "Backfire Boggles SALT II." *Astronautics and Aeronautics,* XIV (July–August 1976), 21–23.

2461.   Brennan, Donald G. "The Soviet Military Buildup and Its Implications for the Negotiations on Strategic Arms Limitations." *Orbis,* XXI (Spring 1977), 117–120.

2462.   Brindel, Charles L. "The Implications of SALT Agreements in the 1970s." *Military Review,* LV (June 1975), 39–48.

2463.   Buckley, James L. "On SALT II." *National Review,* XIX (March 15, 1974), 312–317.

2464.   Clemens, Walter C., Jr. "How the Russians Look at SALT." *Worldview,* XXII (September 1979), 13–18.

2465.   Coffey, Joseph I. "Strategy, Strategic Forces, and Arms Control." *Orbis,* IX (Spring 1965), 98–115.

2466.   "Conventional Arms Control." *Stanford Journal of International Studies,* XIV (Spring 1979), 3–159.

Arms Competition, Arms Control, Balance of Power 201

2467. Davis, Jacquelyn K. "SALT and the Balance of Superpower Strategic Forces." *NATO's Fifteen Nations,* XXIII (February–March 1978), 56–61.

2468. Doty, Paul et al. "The Race to Control Nuclear Arms." *Foreign Affairs,* LV (October 1976), 119–132.

2469. Frank, Lewis A. "Soviet Power After SALT I: A Strategic-Coercive Capability." *Strategic Review,* II (Spring 1974), 54–60.

2470. Garthoff, Raymond L. "Mutual Deterrence and Strategic Arms Limitation in Soviet Policy." *International Security,* III (Summer 1978), 112–147.

2471. _____. "SALT and the Soviet Military." *Problems of Communism,* XXIV (January–February 1975), 21–37.

2472. _____. "SALT I: An Evaluation." *World Politics,* XXXI (October 1978), 1–25.

2473. Gray, Colin S. "Arms Control in Soviet Policy." *Air Force Magazine,* LXIII (March 1980), 66–71.

2474. _____. "Defense and Negotiation: The Strategic Arms Limitations Talks." *Air Force Magazine,* LVII (January 1974), 32–36.

2475. _____. "A Problem Guide to SALT II." *Survival,* XVII (September–October 1975), 230–234.

2476. _____. "SALT I Aftermath: Have the Soviets Been Cheating?" *Air Force Magazine,* LVIII (November 1975), 28–33.

2477. Hamlett, Bruce. "SALT: The Illusion and the Reality." *Strategic Review,* III (Summer 1975), 67–78.

2478. Hughes, Peter. "SALT and the Emerging Strategic Threat." *Air Force Magazine,* LXII (March 1979), 48–53.

2479. Jackson, William D. "The Soviets and Strategic Arms: Toward an Evaluation of the Record." *Political Science Quarterly,* XCV (Summer 1979), 243–262.

2480. "Judging SALT II." Orbis, XXIII (Summer 1979), 251–260.

2481. Kolkowicz, Roman. "SALT and the Kremlin: The Policy of Hold-and-Explore." *Interplay,* III (November 1970), 33–36.

2482. Lambeth, Benjamin S. "The Soviet Strategic Challenge Under SALT I." *Current History,* LXIII (October 1972), 150–155.

2483. Luck, Edward C. "The Soviet Union and Conventional Arms Control." In: Grayson Kirk and Nils H. Wessell, eds. *The Soviet Threat: Myths and Realities.* New York: Praeger, 1978. pp. 57–65.

2484. Metcalf, Arthur G. "SALT II: Some Principles." *Strategic Review,* I (Summer 1973), 6–16.

2485. _____ . "SALT II and Offensive Force Levels." *Orbis,* XVIII (Summer 1974), 465–481.

2486. Milstein, Michael A. "Strategic Arms Limitations and Military Strategic Concepts." In: David Carlton and Carlo Schaerf, eds. *Arms Control and Technological Innovation.* New York: Wiley, 1978. pp. 198–209.

2487. Nunn, Sam. "Mutual and Balanced Force Reductions: A Need to Shift Our Focus." *Atlantic Community Quarterly,* XVI (Spring 1978), 18–21.

2488. Ognibene, Peter J. "Upsetting SALT II: Unruly Bombers, Unseen Missiles." *New Republic,* LXXVIII (January 24, 1976), 8–11.

2489. Payne, Samuel B., Jr. "The Soviet Debate on Strategic Arms Limitation, 1969–1972." *Soviet Studies,* XXVII (January 1975), 27–45.

2490. Pfaltzgraff, Robert L., Jr. "The SALT II Issues." *Astronautics and Aeronautics,* XII (February 1974), 18–24.

2491. Potter, W. C. "Coping with MIRV in a Mad World." *Journal of Conflict Resolution,* XXII (December 1978), 599–626.

2492. Reed, Thomas C. "The Soviet Backfire and SALT II: An Appraisal." *International Security Review,* IV (Spring 1979), 60–73.

2493. Reppert, John C. "The Soviet Military and Force Reductions." *Military Review,* LIV (October 1974), 24–29.

2494. Robinson, Clarence A., Jr. "Another SALT Violation Spotted: Deployment of SS-20 Nuclear Missiles to Kamchatka." *Aviation Week and Space Technology,* CIV (May 31, 1976), 12–14.

2495. _____ . "Backfire Draws Focus in SALT." *Aviation Week and Space Technology,* CIII (August 25, 1975), 14–15.

2496. "SALT II: A Brief Guide." *Department of State Bulletin,* LXXIX (July 1979), 58–65.

2497. Schneider, Mark B. "Red Missiles and SALT." *Ordnance,* LV (November–December 1970), 254–256.

2498. _____. "SALT and the Strategic Balance, 1974." *Strategic Review,* II (Fall 1974), 41–47.

2499. Scoville, Herbert. "The Limitation of Offensive Weapons." *Scientific American,* CCXXIV (January 1971), 15–25.

2500. Shulman, Marshall D. "SALT and the Soviet Union." In: Mason Willrich and John B. Rhinelander, eds. *SALT: The Moscow Agreements and Beyond.* New York: Free Press, 1974. pp. 101–121.

2501. Sienkiewicz, Stanley. "SALT and Soviet Nuclear Doctrine." *International Security,* II (Spring 1978), 84–100.

2502. Slominski, Martin J. "SALT Facets." *Military Review,* LIV (January 1974), 82–88.

2503. Stone, Jeremy J. "Bomber Disarmament." *World Politics,* XVII (October 1964), 13–39.

2504. Sullivan, David S. "The Legacy of SALT I: Soviet Deception and U.S. Retreat." *Strategic Review,* VII (Winter 1979), 26–41.

2505. United States, Department of State. Bureau of Public Affairs. "SALT II Agreement, Vienna, June 18, 1979." *Department of State Bulletin,* LXXIX (July 1979), 1–65.

2506. Wolfe, Thomas W. "Soviet Approaches to SALT." *Problems of Communism,* XIX (September 1970), 1–10.

2507. _____. "The Soviet Union and SALT." *World Today,* XXVII (April 1971), 162–173.

2508. York, Herbert F. "Reducing the Overkill." *Survival,* XVI (March–April 1974), 70–74.

Documents, Papers, and Reports

2509. Bell, Robert G. and Mark M. Lowenthal. *SALT II: Major Issues.* CRS Report, no. 78-249F. Washington, D.C.: Congressional Research Service, Library of Congress, 1978. 137p.

2510. Caldwell, Lawrence T. *Soviet Attitudes to SALT.* Adelphi papers, no. 75. London: Institute for Strategic Studies, 1971. 27p.

2511. Foreign Policy Association. *SALT II, Toward Security or Danger: A Balanced Account of the Key Issues in the Debate.* New York, 1979. 32p.

2512. Frank, Lewis A. *Soviet Nuclear Planning: A Point of View on SALT.* Defense Policy Studies, no. 1. Washington, D.C.: American Enterprise Institute for Public Policy Research, 1977. 63p.

2513. Klare, Michael T. *Conventional Arms Restraint: An Unfulfilled Promise*. Washington, D.C.: Institute for Policy Studies, 1978. 8p.

2514. Miko, Francis T. *Soviet Strategic Options and SALT II: American Perspectives*. CRS Report, no. 78–119F. Washington, D.C.: Congressional Research Service, Library of Congress, 1978. 64p.

2515. Mitchell, Douglas D. *SALT II: A Glossary*. CRS Report, no. 78–167F. Washington, D.C.: Congressional Research Service, Library of Congress, 1978. 29p.

2516. Pfaltzgraff, Robert L., Jr. and Jacquelyn K. Davis. *SALT II: Promise or Precipice?* Miami, Fla.: Center for Advanced International Studies, University of Miami, 1976. 45p.

2517. Prendergast, William. *Mutual and Balanced Force Reduction: Issues and Prospects*. AEI Study, no. 196. Washington, D.C.: American Enterprise Institute for Public Policy Research, 1978. 75p.

2518. Slocombe, Walter B. *Controlling Strategic Nuclear Weapons*. Headline Series, no. 226. New York: Foreign Policy Association, 1975. 63p.

2519. Stukel, Donald J. *Technology and Arms Control*. NSA Monograph 78–5. Washington, D.C.: Research Directorate, National Defense University, 1978. 40p.

2520. United States. Congress. Senate. Committee on Foreign Relations. *The SALT II Treaty: Hearings, Pt. 1*. 96th Cong., 1st sess. Washington, D.C.: U.S. Government Printing Office, 1979. 615p.

2521. Wolfe, Thomas W. *The SALT Experience: Its Impact on U.S. and Soviet Strategic Policy and Decisionmaking*. RAND Report R–1686–PR. Santa Monica, Calif.: RAND Corporation, 1975. 248p.

C. The Balance of Power

Books

2522. Bottome, Edgar M. *The Balance of Terror: A Guide to the Arms Race*. Boston: Beacon Press, 1971. 215p.

2523. Buchan, Alastair F. *Power and Equilibrium in the 1970s*. Russell C. Leffingwell Lectures, 1972. New York: Praeger, 1972. 120p.

2524. Collins, John M. *American and Soviet Military Trends—Since the Cuban Missile Crisis*. Washington, D.C.: Center for Strategic and International Studies, Georgetown University, 1978. 496p.

Arms Competition, Arms Control, Balance of Power

2525. _____ and Anthony H. Cordesman. *Imbalance of Power: Shifting U.S.–Soviet Military Strength.* San Rafael, Calif.: Presidio Press, 1978. 316p.

2526. Daniel, Donald C., ed. *International Perceptions of the Superpower Military Balance.* New York: Praeger, 1978. 198p.

2527. Legault, Albert and G. R. Lindsey. *The Dynamics of the Nuclear Balance.* Rev. ed. Ithaca, N.Y.: Cornell University Press, 1976. 283p.

2528. Liddell-Hart, Basil H. *Deterrent or Defense.* New York: Praeger, 1960. 257p.

2529. Liska, George. *Quest for Equilibrium: America and the Balance of Power on Land and Sea.* Baltimore, Md.: Johns Hopkins University Press, 1977. 256p.

2530. Martin, Laurence W. *Arms and Strategy: The World Power Structure Today.* New York: McKay, 1973. 320p.

2531. Rosecrance, Richard N., ed. *The Future of the International Strategic System.* San Francisco, Calif.: Published under the auspices of the Institute for International Studies, University of California at Berkeley, by Chandler Publications, 1972. 219p.

Articles

2532. Adams, D. "The Balance of Power." *Flight,* LXXV (April 3, 1959), 452–453.

2533. American Enterprise Institute for Public Policy Research. "Who's First in Defense: The U.S. or the U.S.S.R.?" *AEI Round Table,* (June 3, 1976), 1–39.

2534. "An Appraisal of the Tactical Balance." *Aeronautics,* XXXV (February 1957), 54–57.

2535. Aspaturian, Vernon V. "Détente and the Strategic Balance." In: Michael MccGwire and John McDonnell, eds. *Soviet Naval Influence, Domestic and Foreign Dimensions.* New York: Praeger, 1977. pp. 3–30.

2536. Aspin, Les. "Comparing Soviet and American Defense Efforts." *NATO's Fifteen Nations,* XXI (June–July 1976), 34–36.

2537. _____. "How to Look at the Soviet–American Balance." *Foreign Policy,* no. 22 (Spring 1976), 96–106; no. 23 (Summer 1976), 32–52.

2538. Barrett, Raymond J. "A Balance of Powers." *U.S. Naval Institute Proceedings,* XCVIII (April 1972), 18–24.

2539. Bellamy, Ian. "The Central Balance: Arms Race and Arms Control." In: Carsten Holbraad, ed. *Super Powers and World Order.* Canberra: Australian National University Press, 1971. pp. 41–63.

2540. Bennett, Ralph K. "U.S.–Soviet Military Balance: Who's Ahead?" *Reader's Digest,* CIX (September 1976), 79–83.

2541. Brock, William E. "The Shifting Balance." *Ordnance,* LVI (March–April 1972), 366–368.

2542. Brown, George S. "Appraising the Strategic Nuclear Balance." *Commanders Digest,* XX (February 3, 1977), 2–24.

2543. Brown, Harold. "The Balance Between the United States and the Soviet Union: An Address, June 23, 1978." *Vital Speeches,* XLIV (July 15, 1978), 581–589.

2544. _____. "The Strategic Nuclear Balance." *Commanders Digest,* XXI (March 9, 1978), 2–19.

2545. Brown, Neville. "The Balance Between the Superpowers: Into Strategic Deadlock." *Journal of the Royal United Service Institute,* CXI (August 1966), 243–247.

2546. Brown, Thomas A. "Number Mysticism, Rationality, and the Strategic Balance." *Orbis,* XXI (Fall 1977), 479–496.

2547. Cameron, Neil. "The Strategic Balance." *Royal Air Forces Quarterly,* XI (Autumn–Winter 1971), 169–175; XII (Spring 1972), 1–5.

2548. Clarke, Bruce C. The Balance of Power in Europe." *NATO's Fifteen Nations,* VII (June–July 1962), 58–62.

2549. Cobb, Tyrus W. "The Military Imbalance: Soviet Military Expansion During the Era of Détente." *Military Review,* LVII (March 1977), 79–85.

2550. _____. "Who's Out in Front?" *Army,* XXV (January 1975), 12–18.

2551. Collins, John M. "American and Soviet Armed Services: Strengths Compared, 1970–1976." *Congressional Record,* CXXII (August 5, 1976), S14064–S14104.

2552. Erickson, John. "The European Military Balance." *Academy of Political Science Proceedings,* XXIII (Janaury 1978), 110–121.

2553. _____. "The World Strategic Balance." In: George W. Keeton and Georg Schwarzenberger, eds. *Yearbook of World Affairs, 1969.* New York: Praeger, 1969. pp. 1–19.

2554. Foster, John S., Jr. "The Balance of Security." *Ordnance*, LVII (July–August 1972), 44–47.

2555. Freedman, Laurence. "SALT II and the Strategic Balance." *World Today*, XXXV (August 1979), 315–323.

2556. Galen, Justin. "The Tactical Nuclear Balance." *Armed Forces Journal International*, CXV (December 1977–January 1978), 29–32, 20–24.

2557. Garrett, S. A. "Détente and the Military Balance." *Bulletin of the Atomic Scientists*, XXXIII (April 1977), 10–20.

2558. Garthoff, Raymond L. "The Concept of Balance of Power in Soviet Policy Making." *World Politics*, IV (October 1951), 256–268.

2559. Garwin, Thomas and John Steinbrunner. "Strategic Vulnerability: The Balance Between Prudence and Paranoia." In: U.S. National Defense University. *Long-Range U.S.–U.S.S.R. Competition: National Security Implications*. Washington, D.C., 1976. pp. 54–94.

2560. _____. _____. *International Security*, I (Summer 1976), 138–181.

2561. Gray, Colin S. "Foreign Policy and the Strategic Balance." *Orbis*, XVIII (Fall 1974), 706–727.

2562. _____. "SALT and the Strategic Balance." *Air Force Magazine*, LV (December 1972), 53–55.

2563. _____. "Strategic 'Superiority' in Superpower Relations." *Military Review*, LI (December 1971), 8–21.

2564. Griffiths, D. R. "Future Far East Balance Call Clouded." *Aviation Week and Space Technology*, CXI (August 6, 1979), 45.

2565. Hessman, James D. "Arms, Men, and Military Budgets: Some Grim Facts and Sobering Conclusions About the Present Military 'Balance.'" *Sea Power*, XIX (May 1976), 14–16.

2566. _____. "The Platform War: Ships, Aircraft, Missiles, Numbers Sometimes Do Count." *Sea Power*, XVII (July 1974), 17–21.

2567. Hinterhoff, Eugene. "The Delicate Balance." *Military Review*, XLVIII (December 1968), 78–85.

2568. _____. "The Soviet Threat since Czechoslovakia." *Military Review*, L (June 1970), 68–73.

2569. Hoeber, Amoretta M. "Some Myths About the Strategic Balance." *Air University Review,* XXVI (July–August 1975), 85–91.

2570. _____. "Strategic Stability." *Air University Review,* XIX (July–August 1968), 67–73.

2571. Hoffmann, Stanley. "Weighing the Balance of Power." *Foreign Affairs,* L (July 1972), 618–643.

2572. Holloway, Bruce K. "U.S. and U.S.S.R. Strategic Forces." *Air Force Policy Letter for Commanders,* no. 9 (September 1971), 20–28.

2573. Ilke, Fred C. "What It Means to Be Number Two." *Fortune,* XCVIII (November 20, 1978), 72–74.

2574. International Institute for Strategic Studies. "The Military Balance." *Air Force Magazine,* LV (December 1972), 43–105; LVI (December 1973), 57–121; LIX (December 1976), 41–107.

2575. _____. "Tables of Comparative Strengths." *Air Force Magazine,* LXI (December 1978), 122–127.

2576. _____. "The United States and the Soviet Union." *Air Force Magazine,* LV (December 1972), 46–52; LVI (December 1973), 60–67; LVII (December 1974), 44–49; LVIII (December 1975), 46–51; LIX (December 1976), 44–50; LX (December 1977), 62–65; XLI (December 1978), 64–70; LXII (December 1979).

2577. Jacobsen, Carl G. "Soviet Strategic Capabilities: The Superpower Balance." *Current History,* LXXIII (October 1977), 97–99.

2578. Kaysen, Carl. "Keeping the Strategic Balance." *Foreign Affairs,* LXVI (July 1968), 665–675.

2579. Kemp, Jack. "The Soviet Military Threat to Our National Security: The Real Facts and Figures." *Congressional Record,* CXXII (June 16, 1976), H6008–H6013.

2580. Kolkowicz, Roman. "Strategic Parity and Beyond: Soviet Perspectives." *World Politics,* XXIII (April 1971), 431–451.

2581. "Living With the Soviet Superpower: A Symposium." *Foreign Policy,* no. 32 (Fall 1978), 22–106.

2582. Lowther, W. "Gathering Storm: Russia's Shift in the Balance of Terror." *Macleans,* XCI (May 29, 1978), 22–24.

2583. McBride, James H. and John I. H. Eates. "The Balance of Power." In: *Military Posture: Fourteen Strategic Issues Before Congress, 1964.* New York: Published for the Center for Strategic Studies, Georgetown University, by Praeger, 1965. Chpt. 9.

Arms Competition, Arms Control, Balance of Power

2584. Mackintosh, Malcolm. "Moscow's View of the Balance of Power." *World Today,* XXIX (March 1973), 108–118.

2585. Martin, Laurence W. "The Changing Military Balance." *Annals of the American Academy of Political Sciences,* XXIX (May 1969), 61–74.

2586. "Measuring the Strategic Nuclear Balance." *Air Force Magazine,* LIX (December 1976), 106–107.

2587. Moorer, Thomas H. "The Narrowing Gap." *Ordnance,* LVIII (July–August 1973), 30–32.

2588. Nitze, Paul H. "Assuring Strategic Stability in an Era of Détente." *Foreign Affairs,* LIV (January 1976), 207–232.

2589. ———. "The Global Military Balance." In: Grayson Kirk and Nils H. Wessell, eds. *The Soviet Threat: Myths and Realities.* New York: Praeger, 1978. pp. 4–14.

2590. "Panel Disputes U.S./Soviet Arms Parity." *Aviation Week and Space Technology,* CIV (June 28, 1976), 19–20.

2591. Panofsky, Wolfgang K. H. "The Mutual-Hostage Relationship Between America and Russia." *Foreign Affairs,* LII (October 1973), 109–118.

2592. "Red Air Strength vs. the U.S.A.F." *Aviation Age,* XX (September 1953), 6–9.

2593. Schemmer, Benjamin F. "U.S./U.S.S.R. Military Balance." *Armed Forces Journal International,* CXIII (March–May, 1976), 18, 23–26, 24–28.

2594. Seamans, Robert C. "The Growing Soviet Threat and What to Do About It." *Air Force and Space Digest,* LIII (May 1970), 38–41.

2595. Shakhnazarov, G. "The Question of the World Balance of Strength." *Soviet Military Review,* no. 9 (September 1974), 50–52.

2596. Sienkiewicz, Stanley. "Gambling With the Strategic Balance." *Ripon Forum,* VII (June 1971), 17–19, 22.

2597. "Special Report: U.S./U.S.S.R. Strategic Weapons Shifts." *Aviation Week and Space Technology,* CV (August 30–September 6, 1976), 14–18, 30–34.

2598. Stevenson, Adlai E., 3rd. "Imbalance of Strategic Forces Between the United States and Soviet Union." *Congressional Record,* CXXII (March 11, 1976), S3298–S3309.

2599. "Strategic Arms: Worries and Cold Comfort." *Astronautics and Aeronautics,* XIV (April 1976), 6–11.

2600. "The Strategic Military Balance." *Air Force Policy Letter for Commanders,* no. 9 (September 1979), 10–21.

2601. Sullivan, R. R. "ABM, MIRV, SALT, and the Balance of Power." *Midwest Quarterly,* XIII (October 1971), 11–36.

2602. "Superweapons Race: The Balance of Power Tilts to the United States." *U.S. News and World Report,* XLV (December 12, 1958), 35–37.

2603. "U.S. vs. Soviet Missiles." *Ordnance,* XLVIII (January–February 1964), 388–389.

2604. Vakhramyev, A. "Detente and the World Balance of Forces." *International Affairs* (Moscow), no. 1 (January 1979), 78–86.

2605. Wessell, Nils H. "Soviet Views of Multi-Polarity and the Emerging Balance of Power." *Orbis,* XXII (Winter 1979), 785–813.

2606. Wheeler, Earl G. "Why Defense Planners Worry: An Interview." *U.S. News and World Report,* LXVIII (April 20, 1970), 34–39.

2607. Wohstetter, Albert J. "The Delicate Balance of Terror." *Foreign Affairs,* XXXVII (January 1959), 211–234.

2608. Young, Frederick W. "The Military Balance in Europe." *Military Review,* LVIII (March 1978), 38–45.

Documents, Papers and Reports

2609. American Security Council. National Strategy Committee. *The Changing Strategic Military Balance, U.S.A. vs. U.S.S.R.: A Report Prepared at the Request of the Committee on Armed Services, House of Representatives.* 90th Cong., 1st sess. Washington, D.C.: U.S. Government Printing Office, 1967. 94p.

2610. Buckley, James L. and Paul C. Warnke. *Strategic Sufficience: Fact or Fiction?* Rational Debate Series. Washington, D.C.: American Enterprise Institute for Public Policy Research, 1972. 87p.

2611. Daniel, Donald C. *Perceptions of the Superpower Military Balance: Considerations and Evidence.* Report, no. NPS-56-78-001. Monterey, Calif.: Naval Postgraduate School, 1978. 308p.

2612. Dinerstein, Herbert S. *The United States and the Soviet Union: Standoff or Confrontation?* RAND Paper P-3046. Santa Monica, Calif.: RAND Corporation, 1965. 25p.

Arms Competition, Arms Control, Balance of Power 211

2613. Hoag, Malcolm W. *Superpower Strategic Postures for a Multipolar World.* RAND Paper P-4201. Santa Monica, Calif.: RAND Corporation, 1969. 26p.

2614. Lewis, Jesse W., Jr. *The Strategic Balance in the Mediterranean.* Foreign Affairs Study, no. 29. Washington, D.C.: American Enterprise Institute for Public Policy Research, 1976. 169p.

2615. Nash, Henry T. *Nuclear Weapons and International Behavior.* Atlantic Series, no. 9. The Hague: Sizthoff, 1975. 172p.

2616. Tinazero, A. A. *Projected Strategic Offensive Weapons Inventories of the U.S. and U.S.S.R.: An Unclassified Report.* CRS-77-59F. Washington, D.C.: Congressional Research Service, Library of Congress, 1977.

2617. United States. Blue Ribbon Defense Panel. *Supplemental Statement to Report on the Shifting Balance of Military Power.* Washington, D.C.: U.S. Government Printing Office, 1970. 35p.

2618. _____. Congress. House. Committee on Foreign Affairs. Subcommittee on National Security Policy and Scientific Developments. *National Security Policy and the Changing World Alignment: Hearings.* 92nd Cong., 2nd sess. Washington, D.C.: U.S. Government Printing Office, 1972. 509p.

2619. _____. _____. _____. _____. _____. _____: *Report.* 92nd Cong., 2nd sess. Washington, D.C.: U.S. Government Printing Office, 1972. 22p.

2620. _____. _____. Senate. Committee on Armed Services. *United States/Soviet Military Balance: A Frame of Reference for Congress.* Cmte. Print. 94th Cong., 1st sess. Washington, D.C.: U.S. Government Printing Office, 1976. 86p.

2621. _____. National Defense University. *Continuity and Change in the Eighties and Beyond.* Washington, D.C.: U.S. Government Printing Office, 1979. 222p.

7/ Soviet Aerospace Arms and Assistance around the Globe, 1945–1980

Introduction

SECTIONS 3:A:3, 4:B:2 and C:2, and 6 above treat in some generality the question of aerospace power as it relates to strategic, political, and doctrinal goals of the Soviet Union. The works cited in this section examine by region the role of Russia's aerospace arms as a tool of Kremlin foreign policy.

Until recently the aviation and antiaircraft arms of the Soviet Air and National Air Defense Forces as well as the AA arm of the Red Army have had no declared war experience since 1945. Experience helpful to those forces has been gained, however, under battlefield conditions.

From Korea to Vietnam, from the Middle East to Africa, and from Cuba to South Asia, pilots, missile troops, aircraft, and antiaircraft systems have received extensive testing. Beginning with Nikita Khrushchev, the Soviets have made significant aerospace military assistance available to friendly states or clients, who have often had the chance to test this aid in combat. Usually, Russian advisors have been involved in witnessing such displays for reports back home and have had a valuable role in deployment and operations.

Many of the titles cited here have been prepared by Western writers over the years. Some writers present the problems of Soviet aerospace systems in a particular locale and ponder what was done or could be expected of them in conflict situations. Others examine the policy of Russian arms aid to various countries or regions and question the implications. All are concerned with a growing Soviet capacity to project military power, often through surrogates, to parts of the world usually distant from the continental USSR.

A. General Studies

Books

2622.   Booth, Ken. *The Military Instrument in Soviet Foreign Policy, 1917–1972*. London: Royal United Service Institution for Defence Studies, 1973. 65p.

2623.   Eide, Asbjorn and Marek Thee, eds. *Problems of Contemporary Militarism*. New York: St. Martin's Press, 1980. 336p.

2624.   Frank, Lewis A. *The Arms Trade in International Relations*. New York: Praeger, 1969. 266p.

2625.   Harkavy, Robert E. *The Arms Trade and International Systems*. Boston: Ballinger, 1975. 291p.

2626.   Jacobsen, Carl G. *Soviet Strategic Initiatives: Challenges and Response*. New York: Praeger, 1979. 168p.

2627.   ———. *Soviet Strategy—Soviet Foreign Policy: Military Considerations Affecting Soviet Policy-Making*. Glasgow, Scotland: The University Press, 1972. 232p.

2628.   Joshua, Wynford and Stephen P. Gilbert. *Arms for the Third World: Soviet Military Aid Diplomacy*. Baltimore, Md.: Johns Hopkins University Press, 1969. 169p.

2629.   Kaldor, Mary and Asbjorn Eide, eds. *The World Military Order: The Impact of Military Technology on the Third World*. New York: Praeger, 1979. 350p.

2630.   Neuman, Stephanie G. and Robert E. Harkavy, eds. *Arms Transfers in the Modern World*. New York: Praeger, 1979. 400p.

2631.   Ra'anan, Uri. *The U.S.S.R. Arms the Third World: Case Studies in Soviet Foreign Policy*. Cambridge, Mass.: MIT Press, 1969. 256p.

2632.   Rubinstein, Alvin Z., ed. *Soviet and Chinese Influence in the Third World*. New York: Praeger, 1975. 246p.

2633.   Stern, Ellen, ed. *The Limits of Military Intervention*. Sage Series in Armed Forces and Society, vol. 12. Beverly Hills, Calif.: Sage, 1977. 400p.

2634.   Stockholm International Peace Research Institute. *The Arms Trade With the Third World*. Rev. and abr. ed. New York: Homes and Meier, 1975. 362p.

Articles

2635. Bader, William B. "The Proliferation of Conventional Weapons." In: Vol. 3 of Cyril E. Black and Richard A. Falk, eds. *The Future of the International Legal Order.* Princeton, N.J.: Princeton University Press, 1971. pp. 210–223.

2636. Berry, F. Clifton, Jr. "Military Aircraft Exports: Soviet Foreign Policy Tool." *Air Force Magazine,* LXIII (March 1980), 72–79.

2637. Booth, Ken. "Military Power, Military Force, and Soviet Foreign Policy." In: Michael McGwire, ed. *Soviet Naval Developments, Capability and Context.* New York: Praeger, 1973. pp. 31–56.

2638. Chaudhuri, N. J. "The International Arms Trade: The Recipient's Problem." *Political Quarterly,* XLIII (July–September 1972), 261–269.

2639. Clemens, Walter C. "Soviet Policy in the Third World in the 1970s: Five Alternative Models." *Orbis,* XIII (Summer 1969), 476–501.

2640. Garthoff, Raymond L. "Soviet Views on the Interrelation of Diplomacy and Military Strategy." *Political Science Quarterly,* XCIV (Fall 1979), 391–406.

2641. Gilbert, Stephen P. "Soviet-American Military Aid Competition in the Third World." *Orbis,* XIII (Winter 1970), 1117–1137.

2642. _____. "Wars of Liberation and Soviet Military Aid Policy." *Orbis,* X (Fall 1966), 839–858.

2643. Ginsburgs, George. "The Soviet Quest for Influence and Military Facilities in the Third World." In: Michael MccGwire and John McDonnell, eds. *Soviet Naval Influence, Domestic and Foreign Dimensions.* New York: Praeger, 1977. pp. 445–458.

2644. Haselkorn, Avigdor. "The Expanding Soviet Collective Security Network." *Strategic Review,* VI (Summer 1978), 62–73.

2645. _____. "The Soviet Collective Security System." *Orbis,* XIX (Spring 1975), 231–254.

2646. Hinterhoff, Eugene. "Soviet Military Aid and Its Implications." *NATO's Fifteen Nations,* VI (February–March 1962), 79.

2647. Jacobsen, Carl G. "Soviet Strategic Objectives for the 1980s." *World Today,* XXXV (April 1979), 130–137.

2648. Jones, Christopher D. "Just Wars and Limited Wars: Restraints on the Use of the Soviet Armed Forces." *World Politics,* XXVIII (October 1975), 44–68.

2649. Keep, John. "The Soviet Union and the Third World." *Survey*, no. 72 (Summer 1969), 19–38.

2650. Legvold, Robert. "The Super Rivals: Conflicts in the Third World." *Foreign Affairs*, LVII (Spring 1979), 755–778.

2651. McConnell, James M. and Bradford Dismukes. "The Soviet Diplomacy of Force in the Third World." *Problems of Communism*, XXVIII (January–February 1979), 14–27.

2652. Mackintosh, Malcolm. "The Soviet Military Influence on Foreign Policy." In: Michael MccGwire, Ken Booth, and John McDonnell, eds. *Soviet Naval Policy, Objectives and Constraints*. New York: Praeger, 1975. pp. 23–29.

2653. MccGwire, Michael. "The Overseas Role of a 'Soviet Military Presence.'" In: Michael MccGwire and John McDonnell, eds. *Soviet Naval Influence, Domestic and Foreign Dimensions*. New York: Praeger, 1977. pp. 31–60.

2654. Millar, Thomas B. "Soviet Politics South and East of Suez." *Foreign Affairs*, XLIX (October 1970), 70–80.

2655. Miller, B. "World Air Defense Market Grows." *Aviation Week and Space Technology*, XCIV (January 4, 1971), 38–42.

2656. Ra'anan, Uri. "Soviet Arms Transfers and the Problem of Political Leverage." In: Uri Ra'anan, Robert L. Pfaltzgraff, Jr., and Geoffrey Kemp, eds. *Arms Transfers to the Third World: The Military Buildup in Less-Industrial Countries*. Boulder, Colo.: Westview, 1979. Chpt. 7.

2657. Ramazani, R. K. "Soviet Military Assistance to the Uncommitted Countries." *Midwest Journal of Political Science*, II (November 1959), 356–373.

2658. Scott, William F. "The U.S.S.R.'s Growing Global Mobility." *Air Force Magazine*, LX (March 1977), 57–61.

2659. Scribner, Jeffrey L. "The Soviet Military Buildup: A New Dimension in Foreign Policy." *Military Review*, LI (August 1971), 53–62.

2660. Shulman, Marshall D. "Trends in Soviet Foreign Policy." In: Michael MccGwire, Ken Booth, and John McDonnell, eds. *Soviet Naval Policy, Objectives and Constraints*. New York: Praeger, 1975. pp. 3–22.

2661. "Soviet Global Military Capability Grows." *Aviation Week and Space Technology*, CVIII (May 29, 1978), 60–61.

2662. "Soviet Weapons Exports: Russian Roulette in the Third World." *Defense Monitor,* VIII (January 1979), 1–57.

2663. Staar, Richard F. "Soviet Weapons for the Third World." *Marine Corps Gazette,* LVII (December 1973), 14–22.

2664. Yost, Charles. "Observing [Soviet] Close Encounters in the Third World." *International Security,* III (Summer 1978), 187–192.

2665. Zagoria, Donald. "Into the Breach: New Soviet Alliances in the Third World." *Foreign Affairs,* LVII (Spring 1979), 733–754.

2666. Zorza, Victor. "Arms and the Soviet Union." *New Republic,* CLVI (January 14, 1967), 13–15.

Documents, Papers, and Reports

2667. Brown and Shaw Research Corporation. *The Diffusion of Combat Aircraft, Missiles, and Their Supporting Technologies.* Waltham, Mass., 1966.

2668. Gilbert, Stephen P. and Wynford Joshua. *Guns and Rubles: Soviet Aid Diplomacy in Neutral Asia.* Monograph Series, no. 6. New York: American-Asian Educational Exchange, 1970. 60p.

2669. Hoagland, John H. *World Combat Aircraft Inventories and Production, 1970–1975: Implications for Arms Transfer Policies.* Cambridge, Mass.: Center for International Studies, Massachusetts Institute of Technology, 1970.

2670. McConnell, Robert B. "Conventional Military Force and Soviet Foreign Policy." Unpublished thesis, Naval Postgraduate School, 1978.

2671. Pajak, Roger F. "Soviet Military Aid: An Instrument of Soviet Foreign Policy Toward the Developing Countries." Unpublished Ph.D. Dissertation, American University, 1966.

2672. Shulsky, Abram N. *The Soviet Air Force: Silence About Its Interventionary and Political Uses.* Arlington, Va.: Center for Naval Analysis, Bureau for Naval Research, Department of the Navy, 1976. 7p.

2673. Sutton, John L. *Arms to Developing Countries, 1945–1965.* Adelphi papers, no. 28. London: Institute for Strategic Studies, 1966. 45p.

2674. Thompson, W. Scott. *The Projection of Soviet Power.* RAND Paper P-5988. Santa Monica, Calif.: RAND Corporation, 1977. 37p.

2675. United States. Central Intelligence Agency. *Communist Aid to the Less-Developed Countries of the Free World.* Washington, D.C.: Document Expediting Project, Exchange and Gifts Division, Library of Congress, 1977. 33p.

2676. _____. Congress. House. Committee on International Relations. Subcommittee on Europe and the Middle East. *The Soviet Union—International Dynamics of Foreign Policy, Present and Future: Hearings.* 95th Cong., 2nd sess. Washington, D.C.: U.S. Government Printing Office, 1978. 333p.

2677. _____. _____. _____. _____. _____. *The Soviet Union and the Third World: A Watershed in Great Power Policy.* Cmte. Print. 95th Cong., 1st sess. Washington, D.C.: U.S. Government Printing Office, 1977. 186p.

2678. _____. Government Accounting Office. Logistics and Communications Division. *The Readiness of U.S. Air Forces in Europe: Selected Aspects and Issues: A Report to Congress.* Washington, D.C.: U.S. Government Printing Office, 1979. 111p.

2679. Wolfe, Thomas W. *Worldwide Soviet Military Strategy and Policy.* RAND Paper P-5008. Santa Monica, Calif.: RAND Corporation, 1973. 38p.

B. Soviet Aerospace Arms and Assistance Deployment by Region

1. Europe: The Warsaw Pact vs. the West

a. General Studies

Books

2680. Barnaby, Frank, ed. *Tactical Nuclear Weapons: European Perspectives.* London: Eyre and Francis, 1978. 371p.

2681. Bidwell, Shelford, ed. *World War 3: A Military Projection Founded on Today's Facts.* Englewood Cliffs, N.J.: Prentice-Hall, 1978. 207p.

2682. Coffey, Joseph I. *Arms Control and European Security.* New York: Praeger, 1977. 271p.

2683. DePorte, Anton W. *Europe Between the Superpowers: The Enduring Balance.* New Haven, Conn.: Yale University Press, 1979. 256p.

2684. Douglass, Joseph D., Jr. *Soviet Military Strategy in Europe.* Elmsford, N.Y.: Published as an Institute for Foreign Policy Analysis Book by Pergamon Press, 1978. 350p.

2685. Hackett, John W. *The Third World War: A Future History.* London: Hutchinson, 1978. 368p.

2686. Leebaert, Derek, ed. *European Security: Prospects for the 1980s.* Boston, Mass.: Lexington Books, 1979. 320p.

2687. Mechan, John F. *The Warsaw Treaty Organization.* Boulder: University of Colorado Press, 1970.

2688. Pipes, Richard, ed. *Soviet Strategy in Europe.* New York: Crane, Russak, 1976. 316p.

2689. Stockholm International Peace Research Institute. *Force Reductions in Europe.* New York: Humanities Press, 1974. 105p.

2690. Wolfe, Thomas W. *Soviet Power and Europe, 1945–1970.* Baltimore, Md.: Johns Hopkins University Press, 1970. 534p.

Articles

2691. "Air Power for the Pact." *Flight International,* LXVII (June 5, 1976), 1513–1522.

2692. "All for Peace: Russian Air Power in the Soviet Zone of Germany." *Time,* LV (May 8, 1952), 22.

2693. "Armed Forces of Warsaw Treaty Member Countries." *Soviet Military Review,* no. 9 (September 1968), 22–23.

2694. Armitage, M. J. "Air Power and NATO Options." *Royal Air Forces Quarterly,* XVI (Spring 1976), 17–23.

2695. Betit, Eugene D. "Soviet Tactical Doctrine and Capabilities and NATO's Strategic Defense." *Strategic Review,* IV (Fall 1976), 95–107.

2696. Booda, L. "Soviets Flying Electronic Ferret Missions." *Aviation Week and Space Technology,* LXXVIII (March 25, 1963), 22–23.

2697. Booth, Ken. "NATO Ground Forces and the Soviet Threat." *Army Quarterly,* CI (July 1971), 426–436.

2698. Borawski, John. "Mutual Force Reductions in Europe from a Soviet Perspective." *Orbis,* XXII (Winter 1979), 845–873.

2699. Borgart, Peter. "Increasingly Relevant to MBFR: The Air Attack Potential of the Warsaw Pact." *International Defense Review,* IX (April 1976), 193–197.

2700. Brown, Dallas C., Jr. "Conventional Warfare in Europe: The Soviet View." *Military Review,* LV (February 1975), 58–71.

2701. Brown, Neville. "The Tactical Air Balance in Europe." *World Today,* XXVIII (September 1972), 385–392.

2702. Burt, Richard. "SS-20 and the Eurostrategic Balance." *World Today,* XXXIII (February 1977), 43–51.

2703. Buteux, Pierre. "Theater Nuclear Weapons and European Security." *Canadian Journal of Political Science,* X (December 1977), 781–808.

2704. Bykov, V. L. "The U.S.S.R. and Security in Europe: A Soviet View." *Annals of the American Academy of Political and Social Science,* CDXIV (July 1974), 96–104.

2705. Caldwell, Lawrence T. "The Warsaw Pact: Directions of Change." *Problems of Communism,* XXIV (September–October 1975), 1–18.

2706. "Can Soviet Aircraft Penetrate NATO's Air Defense?" *Electronic Warfare,* IX (May–June 1977), 57–58.

2707. Cohen, Samuel T. "Tactical Nuclear Weapons and U.S. Military Strategy in Europe." *Orbis,* XV (Spring 1971), 178–183.

2708. Cross, Roy and William Green. "If Russia Strikes in Europe." *Aero Digest,* LXI (December 1950), 17–19.

2709. Dyer, Philip W. "Tactical Nuclear Weapons and Deterrence in Europe." *Political Science Quarterly,* XCII (Summer 1977), 245–257.

2710. Erickson, John. "The European Military Balance." In: Grayson Kirk and Nils H. Wessell, eds. *The Soviet Threat: Myths and Realities.* New York: Praeger, 1978. pp. 110–121.

2711. _____. "European Security: Soviet Preferences and Priorities." *Strategic Review,* IV (Winter 1976), 37–43.

2712. _____. "Soviet Military Capabilities in Europe." *Journal of the Royal United Service Institution for Defence Studies,* CXX (March 1975), 65–69.

2713. _____. _____. *Military Review,* LVI (January 1976), 58–65.

2714. _____. "The Warsaw Pact." In: Ray Bonds, ed. *The Soviet War Machine: An Illustrated Encyclopedia of Russian Military Equipment and Strategy.* New York: Chartwell Books, 1976. pp. 232–241.

2715. Goodpaster, Andrew J. "NATO Today: The Russian Threat, an Address, September 2, 1971." *Vital Speeches,* XXXVII (October 1, 1971), 743–749.

2716. International Institute for Strategic Studies. "The Theater Balance Between NATO and the Warsaw Pact." *Air Force Magazine,* LV (December 1972), 68–71.

2717. Johnson, A. Ross. "Soviet-East European Military Relations: An Overview." In: Dale R. Herspring and Ivan Volgyes, eds. *Civil-Military Relations in the Communist System.* Boulder, Colo.: Westview, 1978. Chpt. 12.

2718. Jokel, G. "Soviet-East German Armed Forces Cooperation Recounted: Translated from *Voyenno-Istoricheskiy Zhurnal,* July 1978." *Translations on USSR Military Affairs,* no. 1387 (October 18, 1978), 44–55.

2719. Kock, F. H. C. "Problems of Comparing Force Levels." *NATO's Fifteen Nations,* XIX (March–April 1971), 19–22.

2720. Menaul, Stewart. "The Use of Nuclear Weapons in the European Theater." *NATO's Fifteen Nations,* XX (April–May 1975), 30–38.

2721. Moorer, Thomas H. "An Assessment of NATO and Warsaw Pact Force Capabilities." *Defense Management Journal,* IX (October 1973), 7–11.

2722. "NATO, European Security, and the New Weapons Technology." *Orbis,* XIX (Summer 1975), 461–532.

2723. Nunn, Sam and Dewey F. Bartlett. "NATO and the New Soviet Threat: Excerpts from the Report, January 24, 1977." *Atlantic Community Quarterly,* XV (Spring 1977), 18–32.

2724. Papworth, Peter M. "The Integrity of the Warsaw Pact." *Air University Quarterly,* XXVIII (March–June 1977), 16–23, 47–59.

2725. Patrick, Stephen B. "Red Star, White Star: Warsaw Pact and NATO Forces in the 1970s." *Strategy and Tactics,* (January 1973), 18–34.

2726. Ranger, Robin. "MBFR: Political or Technical Arms Control?" *World Today,* XXX (October 1974), 411–418.

2727. Rattinger, Hans. "Armament, Détente, and Bureaucracy: The Case of the Arms Race in Europe." *Journal of Conflict Resolution*, XIX (December 1975), 571–595.

2728. Schneider, William, Jr. "Changes in the Soviet Defense Posture in Europe." *Journal of Social and Political Studies*, II (Summer 1977), 67–71.

2729. "Soviet Badger Two-Plane Teams Shadows Carrier." *Aviation Week and Space Technology*, LXXVIII (May 27, 1963), 28–29.

2730. "Soviet Bloc Military Integration." *Intelligence Digest*, no. 320 (July 1965), 7–8.

2731. Talbert, Ansel E. "Military Airpower in Europe." *National Air Review*, I (November 1949), 1–8.

2732. Taylor, Peter P. W. "NATO's Dispersal Capability—A Fatal Flaw?" *Royal Air Forces Quarterly*, XVIII (Spring–Summer 1978), 11–17, 173–178.

2733. "Third [MIG-23] Flogger Version in East Germany." *Aviation Week and Space Technology*, CIV (May 31, 1976), 16–17.

2734. "Trends in Warsaw Pact Military Developments." *NATO Review*, XXI (July–August 1973), 8–11.

2735. Turbiville, Graham H. "Invasion in Europe: A Scenario." *Army*, XXVI (November 1976), 16–21.

2736. "The U.S.S.R. and the NATO Powers: The Military Balance." *Air Force*, XLIII (March 1960), 38–45.

2737. Vigor, Peter H. and Christopher N. Donnelly. "The Soviet Threat to Europe." *Journal of the Royal United Service Institution for Defence Studies*, CXX (March 1975), 69–75.

2738. "The Warsaw Pact Air Forces." In: *Royal Air Force Yearbook, 1975*. London, 1975. pp. 46–47.

2739. Whetten, Lawrence L. "The Warsaw Pact Threat in the 1970s." *NATO's Fifteen Nations*, XV (October–November 1970), 20–28.

2740. Wolfe, Thomas W. "The Soviet Union's Strategic Stake in the German Democratic Republic." *World Today*, XXVII (August 1971), 340–350.

2741. York, Herbert F. "The Nuclear Balance of Terror in Europe." *Bulletin of the Atomic Scientists*, XXXII (May 1976), 8–14.

Documents, Papers, and Reports

2742. Brown, Neville. *European Security, 1972–1980.* London: Royal United Service Institution for Defence Studies, 1972.

2743. Buchan, Alastair et al. *The Soviet Threat to Europe: An Analysis of Soviet Potentials and Intentions.* London: Foreign Affairs Publishing Company, 1969. 78p.

2744. Burrell, Raymond E. *Strategic Nuclear Parity and NATO Defense Doctrine.* NSA Monograph 78–4. Washington, D.C.: Defense Directorate, National Defense University, 1978. 34p.

2745. Canby, Steven L. *Tactical Airpower in Europe: Airing the European View.* Santa Monica, Calif.: Technology Service Corporation, 1976.

2746. Cliffe, Trevor. *Military Technology and the European Balance.* Adelphi papers, no. 89. London: International Institute for Strategic Studies, 1972. 58p.

2747. Davis, Jacquelyn K. and Robert L. Pfaltzgraff, Jr. *Soviet Theater Strategy: Implications for NATO.* Washington, D.C.: United States Strategic Institute, 1978. 54p.

2748. Erickson, John. *Soviet Theater Warfare Capability.* Waverly Occasional Papers. Edinburgh, Scotland: Department of Politics, Edinburgh University, 1975.

2749. _____. *Soviet-Warsaw Pact Force Levels.* Washington, D.C.: United States Strategic Institute, 1976.

2750. Foster, R. B. *Soviet Reactions to U.S./NATO Force Modernization.* Report, no. DNA–4265F–1. 2 vols. Arlington, Va.: Strategic Studies Center, SRI International, 1977.

2751. Johnson, A. Ross. *Soviet-East European Military Relations: An Overview.* RAND Paper P–5383–1. Santa Monica, Calif.: RAND Corporation, 1977. 29p.

2752. Korbonski, Andrzej. *The Warsaw Pact.* International Conciliation, no. 69. New York: Carnegie Endowment for International Peace, 1969. 73p.

2753. Mackintosh, Malcolm. *The Evolution of the Warsaw Pact.* Adelphi papers, no. 58. London: Institute for Strategic Studies, 1969.

2754. McPeak, William S., Jr. *Surprise and the New Soviet Threat in Europe.* New York: Army Institute for Advanced Russian and East European Studies, 1977. 40p.

2755. Spier, Hans. *Soviet Atomic Blackmail and the North Atlantic Alliance.* RAND Memorandum RM–1837. Santa Monica, Calif.: RAND Corporation, 1956. 43p.

2756. United States. Army. Intelligence Center and School. *Opposing Forces: Europe.* FM–30–102. Washington, D.C.: U.S. Government Printing Office, 1977. Various pagination.

2757. _____. Congress. Senate. Committee on Armed Services. *NATO and the New Soviet Threat: Report of Senator Sam Nunn and Senator Dewey F. Bartlett.* 95th Cong., 1st sess. Washington, D.C.: U.S. Government Printing Office, 1977. 20p.

2758. Vernon, Graham D. *Soviet Options for War in Europe: Nuclear or Conventional?* NSA Monograph 79–1. Washington, D.C.: Research Directorate, National Defense University, 1979. 27p.

2759. Wolfe, Thomas W. *Soviet Attitudes Toward MBFR and the U.S.S.R.'s Military Presence in Europe.* RAND Paper P–4819. Santa Monica, Calif.: RAND Corporation, 1972. 17p.

2760. _____. *Soviet Military Capabilities and Intentions in Europe.* RAND Paper P–5188. Santa Monica, Calif.: RAND Corporation, 1974. 42p.

b. NORTHERN EUROPE AND THE ATLANTIC

Articles

2761. Araldsen, O. P. "Norwegian Defense Problems." *U.S. Naval Institute Proceedings,* LXXXIV (October 1958), 38–47.

2762. _____. "The Soviet Union and the Arctic." *U.S. Naval Institute Proceedings,* XCIII (June 1967), 48–57.

2763. Breyer, Siegfried. "Soviet Power in the Baltic." *Military Review,* XLII (January 1962), 41–47.

2764. Brundtland, Arne O. "The Nordic Balance." *Co-operation and Conflict,* II (1966), 30–63.

2765. Cabrita-Matias, A. "The Atlantic as an Objective of Soviet Geostrategy." *NATO's Fifteen Nations,* XIV (December 1969–January 1970), 42–44.

2766. Chabanier, A. "Soviet Strength in the Baltic Area." *Military Review,* XXXVII (February 1957), 45–101.

2767. Dewey, Arthur E. "The Nordic Balance." *Strategic Review,* IV (Fall 1976), 49–60.

2768. Dobbs, Theodore. "Baltic Defense." *Marine Corps Gazette*, XLVII (July 1963), 20–24.

2769. Dudley, Harrison G. "The Strategic Importance of the North Atlantic Ocean." *NATO's Fifteen Nations*, XIV (August–September 1969), 33–37.

2770. Erickson, John. "The Northern Theater: Soviet Capabilities and Concepts." *Strategic Review*, IV (Summer 1976), 67–82.

2771. Furlong, R. D. M. "The Strategic Situation in Northern Europe." *International Defense Review*, XII (June 1979), 899–910.

2772. Geisenheyner, Stefan. "NATO's Northern Flank." *Air Force Magazine*, LIV (July 1971), 56–61.

2773. Griswold, Laurence. "The Cold Front: The U.S.S.R. Has the Strategic Advantage Above the Arctic Circle." *Sea Power*, XIV (December 1972), 18–23.

2774. Haworth, David. "Denmark Feels the Heat of Warsaw Pact Baltic Exercises: Reprinted from the *Washington Post*, December 28, 1976." *U.S. Naval Institute Proceedings*, CIII (March 1977), 108–109.

2775. Healey, Denis W. "NATO, Britain, and Soviet Military Policy." *Orbis*, XIII (Spring 1969), 49–58.

2776. Holst, Johan J. "The Soviet Union and Nordic Security." *Cooperation and Conflict*, VII (1971), 137–145.

2777. Lindberg, Folke. "Power Politics and the Baltic." *American-Scandinavian Review*, LIV (June 1966), 158–168.

2778. Mansfield, E. G. N. "The Shifting Strategic Balance in the Atlantic." *Strategic Review*, II (Summer 1974), 16–21.

2779. Morgan, Henry G., Jr. "Soviet Policy in the Baltic." *U.S. Naval Institute Proceedings*, LXXXVI (April 1960), 82–89.

2780. Moulton, James L. "The Defense of NW Europe and the North Sea." In: Frank Uhlig, Jr., ed. *The Naval Review, 1971*. Annapolis, Md.: U.S. Naval Institute, 1971. pp. 80–98.

2781. "NATO's Northern Flank." *Royal Air Forces Quarterly*, X (Summer 1970), 133–143.

2782. Orvik, Nils. "Scandinavia, NATO, and Northern Security." *International Journal*, XX (Summer 1966), 380–396.

2783. _____. "Soviet Approaches to NATO's Northern Flank." *International Journal*, XX (Winter 1964–1965), 54–67.

2784. Romaneski, Albert L. "The Nordic Balance in the 1970s." *U.S. Naval Institute Proceedings,* XCIX (August 1973), 32–41.

2785. Sharp, F. R. "The Threat to North America." *E.M.O. Digest,* IX (December 1969–January 1970), 2–4.

2786. Sjaastad, Anders C. "Security Problems on the Northern Flank." *World Today,* XXXV (April 1979), 137–149.

2787. Sterne, Joseph R. L. "Soviet Forces Strengthened in the Northern Peninsula Area: Reprinted from the *Baltimore Sun,* April 30, 1972." *U.S. Naval Institute Proceedings,* XCVIII (September 1972), 115–116.

2788. Sullivan, William K. "Soviet Strategy and NATO's Northern Flank." *Naval War College Review,* XXXII (June–July 1979), 26–38.

2789. Walker, Walter. "The Defense of the Northern Flank." *Journal of the Royal United Service Institution for Defence Studies,* CXIII (September 1973), 21–30.

2790. _____. "Problems of the Defence of NATO's Northern Flank." *Journal of the Royal United Service Institute,* CXV (September 1970), 13–23.

2791. Wettern, Desmond. "NATO's Northern Flank." *U.S. Naval Institute Proceedings,* XCV (July 1969), 529.

Documents, Papers, and Reports

2792. Hunt, Herman L. "Policy and Posture of NATO on the Northern Flank: An Appraisal." Unpublished thesis, Naval War College, 1972.

2793. Klenberg, Jan. *The Cap and the Straits Problems of Nordic Security.* Occasional Papers in International Affairs, no. 18. Cambridge, Mass.: Center for International Affairs, Harvard University, 1968. 22p.

2794. Nesbitt, Robert L. *Denmark: The Cork in the Baltic Bottle.* Research Study. Maxwell AFB, Ala.: Air Command and Staff College, Air University, 1973. 51p.

2795. Ulstein, Egil. *Nordic Security.* Adelphi papers, no. 81. London: International Institute for Strategic Studies, 1971. 34p.

c. Central Europe

Books

2796. Close, Robert. *Europe Without Defense: 48 Hours That Could Change the Face of the World.* Translated from the French. New York: Pergamon, 1979. 278p.

228   Soviet Aerospace Arms and Assistance Deployment

2797.   Cordier, Sherwood S. *Calculus of Power: The Current Soviet-American Conventional Military Balance in Central Europe*. 3rd ed. Washington, D.C.: University Press of America, 1980. 150p.

Articles

2798.   Cohen, Samuel T. "Western European Collateral Damage from Tactical Nuclear Weapons." *Journal of the Royal United Service Institution for Defence Studies*, CXXI (June 1976), 32–38.

2799.   Coleman, Herbert J. "Soviet Air Probes Testing NATO." *Aviation Week and Space Technology*, XCVI (January 17, 1972), 12–14.

2800.   Davison, Michael S. "The Military Balance in Central Army Group." *Strategic Review*, II (Fall 1974), 13–18.

2801.   DeMaiziere, Ulrich. "A German View of the Strategic Situation in Central Europe." In: Royal United Service Institution for Defence Studies. *R.U.S.I. and Brassey's Defence Yearbook, 1977–1978*. Boulder, Colo: Westview, 1977. pp. 113–123.

2802.   Geneste, Marc. "The Nuclear Land Battle." *Strategic Review*, IV (Winter 1976), 79–85.

2803.   McMichael, Scott R. "The Soviet Theater Nuclear Offensive and the European Battlefield." *Field Artillery Journal*, XLVII (September–October 1979), 24–27.

2804.   Miller, D. M. O. "Strategic Factors Affecting a Soviet Conventional Attack in Western Europe." *International Defense Review*, XI (June 1978), 553–559.

2805.   Polk, James H. "The Realities of Tactical Nuclear Weapons." *Orbis*, XVII (Summer 1973), 439–447.

2806.   Pratt, Clayton A. "The Benelux and Northern German Plains Avenue of Approach." *Military Review*, LVIII (June 1978), 2–8.

2807.   Rasmussen, Robert D. "The Central European Battlefield: Doctrinal Implications for Counterair-Interdiction." *Air University Review*, XXIX (July–August 1978), 2–20.

Documents, Papers, and Reports

2808.   Braddock, J. V. *An Assessment of Soviet Forces Facing NATO—The Central Region—and Suggested NATO Initiatives*. Report, no. DNA-4343F. Alexandria, Va.: Santa Fe Corporation, 1977. 87p.

2809. Fischer, Robert L. *Defending the Central Front: The Balance of Forces.* Adelphi papers, no. 127. London: International Institute for Strategic Studies, 1976. 43p.

2810. Johnson, A. Ross. *Has East Central Europe Become a Liability to the U.S.S.R.? The Military Aspect.* RAND Paper P-5383. Santa Monica, Calif.: RAND Corporation, 1975. 29p.

d. SOUTHERN EUROPE AND THE MEDITERRANEAN

Articles

2811. Brownlow, Cecil. "Il-28, Tu-16 Threaten Sixth Fleet Area." *Aviation Week and Space Technology,* LXXI (August 17, 1959), 101-102.

2812. Geisenheyner, Stefan. "The Growing Threat to NATO's Southern Flank." *Air Force and Space Digest,* LII (January 1969), 40-44.

2813. Heiman, Leo. "Soviet [Czechoslovakia] Invasion Weaknesses." *Military Review,* XLIX (August 1969), 38-45.

2814. Hinterhoff, Eugene. "The Complex Problems of the Southern NATO Flank." *NATO's Fifteen Nations,* XVII (April-May 1972), 32-39.

2815. Honan, W. H. "Playing Chicken Over the Mediterranean." *Reader's Digest,* XCVIII (March 1971), 77-81.

2816. Johnson, Means, Jr. "NATO's Southern Front: Where Soviets Show Big Gains, an Interview." *U.S. News and World Report,* LXXVIII (June 2, 1975), 22-23.

2817. ———. "NATO's Southern Region: Problems and Prospects." *U.S. Naval Institute Proceedings,* CI (January 1975), 47-51.

2818. Kilmarx, Robert A. "The Challenge of the Mediterranean." *Military Review,* L (November 1970), 81-89.

2819. Locksley, Norman. "NATO's Southern Exposure." *U.S. Naval Institute Proceedings,* LXXXVIII (November 1962), 41-54.

2820. Vickery, William W. "The Mediterranean Basin and Soviet Air Power." *Air University Quarterly Review,* IV (Summer 1951), 66-75.

Documents, Papers, and Reports

2821. Gasteyger, Curt W. *Conflict and Tension in the Mediterranean.* Adelphi papers, no. 51. London: Institute for Strategic Studies, 1968. 18p.

2. Cuba

a. GENERAL STUDIES

Books

2822. Levesque, Jacques. *The U.S.S.R. and the Cuban Revolution: Soviet Ideology and Strategic Perspectives.* New York: Praeger, 1978. 220p.

2823. Sobel, Lester A., ed. *Cuba, the U.S. and Russia, 1960–1963.* New York: Facts on File, 1964. 138p.

Articles

2824. Quester, George H. "Missiles in Cuba, 1970." *Foreign Affairs,* XLIX (April 1971), 493–506.

2825. "Russians in Our Back Yard to Stay?" *U.S. News and World Report,* LXXXVII (October 15, 1979), 23–26.

2826. Willenson, K. "New Cuban Crisis?" The Stationing of MIG–23 Jets in Cuba." *Newsweek,* XCII (November 27, 1978), 51–52.

Documents, Papers, and Reports

2827. United States. Central Intelligence Agency. *The Cuban Economy: A Statistical View, 1968–1976.* Research Aid. Washington, D.C.: Document Expediting Project, Exchange and Gift Division, Library of Congress, 1976. 17p.

b. THE CUBAN MISSILE CRISIS, 1962

Books

2828. Abel, Ellie. *The Missile Crisis.* New York: McClelland, 1966. 220p.

2829. Allison, Graham T. *Essence of Decision: Explaining the Cuban Missile Crisis.* Boston: Little, Brown, 1971. 338p.

2830. Daniel, James and John G. Hubble. *Strike in the West: The Complete Story of the Cuban Crisis.* New York: Holt, 1963. 180p.

2831. Detzer, David. *The Brink: The Cuban Missile Crisis, 1962.* New York: Crowell, 1979. 304p.

2832. Divine, Robert A., ed. *The Cuban Missile Crisis.* Chicago: Quadrangle Books, 1971. 248p.

2833. Kennedy, Robert F. *Thirteen Days.* New York: W. W. Norton, 1969. 224p.

2834. Larson, David L., ed. *The "Cuban Crisis" of 1962: Selected Documents and Chronology.* Boston: Houghton, Mifflin, 1963. 333p.

2835. Pachter, Henry M. *Collision Course: The Cuban Missile Crisis and Coexistence.* New York: Praeger, 1963. 261p.

Articles

2836. Bernstein, Barton J. "The Cuban Missile Crisis." In: L. H. Miller and K. W. Pruessen, eds. *Reflections on the Cold War: A Quarter Century of American Foreign Policy.* Philadelphia: Temple University Press, 1974. pp. 130–134.

2837. _____. "The Week We Almost Went to War." *Bulletin of the Atomic Scientists,* XXXII (February 1976), 13–21.

2838. Crane, Robert D. "The Cuban Crisis: A Strategic Analysis of American and Soviet Policy." *Orbis,* VI (Winter 1963), 528–563.

2839. Crosby, Ralph D., Jr. "The Cuban Missile Crisis: A Soviet View." *Military Review,* LVI (September 1976), 58–70.

2840. Hagan, Kenneth. "The Military Value of Missiles in Cuba." *Bulletin of the Atomic Scientists,* XIX (February 1963), 8–13.

2841. Kahan, Jerome H. and Anne K. Long. "The Cuban Missile Crisis: A Study of Its Strategic Context." *Political Science Quarterly,* LXXXVII (December 1972), 564–590.

2842. Knorr, Klaus E. "Failures in National Intelligence Estimates: The Case of the Cuban Missiles." *World Politics,* XVI (April 1964), 455–467.

2843. Pederson, John C. "Soviet Reporting of the Cuban Crisis." *U.S. Naval Institute Proceedings,* XCI (October 1965), 54–63.

2844. Trainor, James. "Cuban Missile Threat Detailed." *Missiles and Rockets,* (October 29, 1962), 12–14, 47.

2845. Waters, H. R. "Fact and Fancy." *Newsweek,* LXXXIV (December 23, 1974), 53–54.

Documents, Papers, and Reports

2846. Horelick, Arnold L. *The Cuban Missile Crisis: An Analysis of Soviet Calculations and Behavior.* RAND Memorandum RM–3779–PR. Santa Monica, Calif.: RAND Corporation, 1963. 60p.

2847. Lantzer, Lawrence A. "The Cuban Missile Crisis: The Soviet View." Unpublished thesis, Naval War College, 1972.

2848. United States. Central Intelligence Agency. National Foreign Assessment Center. *Cuban Chronology.* Reference Aid. Washington, D.C.: Document Expediting Project, Exchange and Gift Division, Library of Congress, 1978. 94p.

2849. _____. Congress. Senate. Committee on Armed Services. Subcommittee on the Cuban Military Buildup. *Interim Report.* 88th Cong., 1st sess. Washington, D.C.: U.S. Government Printing Office, 1963. 18p.

2850. Wohstetter, Roberta. *Cuba and Pearl Harbor: Hindsight and Foresight.* RAND Memorandum RM–4328–ISA. Santa Monica, Calif.: RAND Corporation, 1965. 41p.

3. The Middle East and the Persian Gulf

a. Helping the Arabs

(1) General Studies

Books

2851. Bell, J. Bowyer. *The Long War: Israel and the Arabs Since 1946.* Englewood Cliffs, N.J.: Prentice-Hall, 1969. 467p.

2852. Confino, Michael and Shimon Shamir, eds. *The U.S.S.R. and the Middle East.* Israel Program for Scientific Translations. New York: Wiley, 1973. 441p.

2853. *Congressional Quarterly,* Editors of. *The Middle East: U.S. Policy, Israel, Oil, and the Arabs.* 4th ed. Washington, D.C., 1979. 252p.

2854. Donovan, John, ed. *U.S. and Soviet Policy in the Middle East, 1957–1966.* New York: Facts on File, 1974. 218p.

2855. Dupuy, Trevor N. *Elusive Victory: The Arab–Israeli Wars, 1947–1974.* New York: Harper & Row, 1978. 672p.

2856. Freedman, Robert O. *Soviet Policy Toward the Middle East Since 1970.* Rev. ed. New York: Praeger, 1978. 400p.

2857. _____. *World Politics and the Arab-Israeli Conflict.* New York: Pergamon, 1979. 358p.

2858. Geyer, Georgie A. *The New One Hundred Years War.* Garden City, N.Y.: Doubleday, 1972. 318p.

2859. Glassman, Jon D. *Arms for the Arabs: The Soviet Union and the War in the Middle East.* Baltimore, Md.: Johns Hopkins University Press, 1976. 243p.

2860. Golan, Galia. *Yom Kippur and After: The Soviet Union and the Middle East Crises.* Cambridge, England: Cambridge University Press, 1977. 350p.

2861. Haykal, Muhammad H. *Sphinx and the Commissar: The Rise and Fall of Soviet Influence in the Middle East.* New York: Harper & Row, 1979. 304p.

2862. Jackson, Robert. *The Israeli Air Force Story: The Struggle for Middle East Aircraft Supermacy Since 1948.* London: Stacey, 1970. 256p.

2863. Kass, Ilana. *Soviet Involvement in the Middle East: Policy Formulation, 1966–1973.* Boulder, Colo.: Westview, 1978. 273p.

2864. Klieman, Aaron S. *Soviet Russia and the Middle East.* Baltimore, Md.: Johns Hopkins University Press, 1970. 101p.

2865. Laqueur, Walter Z. *The Struggle for the Middle East: The Soviet Union in the Mediterranean, 1948–1968.* New York: Macmillan, 1969. 360p.

2866. _____. _____, *1958–1973.* Rev. ed. Harmondsworth, England: Penguin Books, 1972. 267p.

2867. Lenczowski, George. *Soviet Advances in the Middle East.* Foreign Affairs Study, no. 2. Washington, D.C.: American Enterprise Institute for Public Policy Research, 1972. 176p.

2868. McLane, Charles B. *Soviet-Middle East Relations.* Soviet–Third World Relations, no. 1. London: Asian Research Centre, 1973. 126p.

2869. McLaurin, Ronald D. *The Middle East in Soviet Policy.* Boston: D. C. Heath, 1975. 206p.

2870. Mangold, Peter. *Superpower Intervention in the Middle East.* New York: St. Martin's Press, 1978. 209p.

2871. Moore, John N., ed. *The Arab-Israeli Conflict: Readings and Documents.* Rev. ed. Princeton, N. J.: Princeton University Press, 1977. 1,285p.

2872. Ro'i, Yaacov. *From Encroachment to Involvement: A Documentary Study of Soviet Policy in the Middle East, 1945–1973.* London: Halsted Press, 1974. 616p.

2873. _____, ed. *Limits to Power: Soviet Policy in the Middle East.* New York: St. Martin's Press, 1979. 376p.

2874. Smolansky, Oles M. *The Soviet Union and the Arab East Under Khrushchev.* Modern Middle East Series, vol. 6. Cranbury, N.J.: Bucknell University Press, 1974. 326p.

2875. Snider, Lewis W. *Arabesque: Untangling the Patterns of Supply of Conventional Arms to Israel and the Arab States and the Implications for United States Policy of Supply of "Lethal" Weapons to Israel.* Monograph Series in World Affairs, vol. 15, no. 1. Denver: Colorado Seminary, University of Denver, 1977. 151p.

2876. Wagner, Abraham R. *Crisis Decision-Making: Israel's Experience in 1967 and 1973.* New York: Praeger, 1974. 186p.

2877. Weizman, Ezer. *On Eagles' Wings: The Personal Story of the Leading Commander of the Israeli Air Force.* New York: Macmillan, 1977. 302p.

2878. Williams, Louis, ed. *Military Aspects of the Arab-Israeli Conflict.* Tel Aviv: University Publishing Projects, 1975. 265p.

Articles

2879. Adomeit, Hannes. "Soviet Policy in the Middle East: Problems of Analysis." *Soviet Studies,* XXVII (April 1975), 288–305.

2880. Allon, Yigel. "The Soviet Involvement in the Arab–Israeli Conflict." In: Michael Confino and Shimon Shamir, eds. *The U.S.S.R. and the Middle East.* Israel Program for Scientific Translations. New York: Wiley, 1973. p. 152.

2881. Alsop, Joseph. "Reading Soviet Intentions." *New Republic,* CLXIII (October 3, 1970), 17–19.

2882. "Arms in the Middle East: A Special Report." *Moment,* II (December 1976), 15–20.

2883. Azar, Edward E. "Soviet and Chinese Roles in the Middle East." *Problems of Communism,* XXVIII (May–June 1979), 18–30.

2884. Beasley, Robert D. "The Arab and Israeli Air Forces." *New Middle East,* no. 12 (September 1969), 44–46.

2885. Blixt, Melvin D. "Soviet Objectives in the Eastern Mediterranean." *Naval War College Review,* XXI (March 1969), 4–24.

2886. Brown, Neville. "The Real Capabilities of Soviet and U.S. Weapons in the Middle East and How the Two Sides Use Them: A New Approach to Assessing the Aerial Power Balance." *New Middle East,* no. 20 (May 1970), 11–14.

2887. Coleman, Herbert J. "Mideast Power Structure Shifting." *Aviation Week and Space Technology,* XCVIII (March 26, 1973), 12–13.

2888. Cordesman, Anthony H. "The Arab-Israeli Balance: How Much is Too Much?" *Armed Forces Journal International,* CXV (October 1977), 32–41.

2889. Cottrell, Alvin J. "The Role of Air Power in the Military Balance of the Middle East." *New Middle East,* no. 19 (April 1970), 12–16.

2890. ———. "The Soviet Union in the Middle East." Orbis, XIV (Fall 1970), 588–589.

2891. Dawisha, Karen. "Soviet Policy in the Middle East: Present Dilemmas and Future Trends." *Journal of International Studies,* VI (Autumn 1977), 182–189.

2892. DeVore, Ronald M. "The Arab-Israeli Arms Race and the Superpowers." *Current History,* LXVI (February 1974), 70–73.

2893. Dimant-Kass, Ilana. "The Soviet Military and Soviet Policy in the Middle East, 1970–1973." *Soviet Studies,* XXVI (October 1974), 502–521.

2894. Forsythe, David P. "The Soviets and the Arab-Israeli Conflict." *World Affairs,* XIV (Fall 1971), 132–142.

2895. Freedman, Robert O. "Soviet Policy Toward the Middle East From the Exodus of 1972 to the Yom Kippur War." *Naval War College Review,* XXVII (January–February 1975), 32–53.

2896. ———. "Soviet Policy Toward the Middle East Since the October 1973 Arab–Israeli War." *Naval War College Review,* XXIX (Fall 1976), 61–103.

2897. ———. "The Soviet Union and the Middle East: The High Cost of Influence." *Naval War College Review,* XXIV (January–February 1972), 15–34.

2898. Gabelic, Andro. "The U.S.S.R.: New Ascent in Strategy." *Review of International Affairs,* XVIII (November 20, 1967), 16–18.

2899. Geisenheyner, Stefan. "The Arab Air Forces: Will They Try Again?" *Air Force and Space Digest,* LI (July 1968), 44–48.

2900. Golan, Galia. "Soviet Policy in the Middle East: Growing Difficulties and Changing Interests." *World Today,* XXXIII (September 1977), 335–342.

2901. Jabber, Fuad. "Not by War Alone: Curbing the Arab–Israeli Arms Race." *Middle East Journal*, XXVIII (Summer 1974), 233–247.

2902. Joshua, Wynfred. "Arms for the Love of Allah." *U.S. Naval Institute Proceedings*, XCVI (March 1970), 30–39.

2903. _____. "The Middle East in Soviet Strategy." *Strategic Review*, II (Spring 1974), 61–67.

2904. Kemp, Geoffrey. "Middle East Strategy and Arms Levels, 1945–1967." *Academy of Political Science Proceedings*, XXIX (Fall 1969), 21–37.

2905. Kilmarx, Robert A. and Alvin J. Cottrell. "The U.S.S.R. in the Middle East." *Air Force Magazine*, LIII (August 1970), 40–46.

2906. Kimche, Jon. "The Superpowers in the Middle East—Backstage." *Midstream*, XXI (June–July 1975), 7–13.

2907. Lenczowski, George. "The Middle East in Soviet Strategy." *Problems of Communism*, XXVII (November–December 1978), 49–53.

2908. "The Middle East: The Military Dimension." *Journal of Palestine Studies*, IV (Summer 1975), 3–25.

2909. Nes, David G. "The Soviets in the Middle East." *Military Review*, LII (June 1972), 80–85.

2910. Ra'anan, Uri. "Soviet Decision-Making in the Middle East, 1969–1973." In: Michael MccGwire, Ken Booth, and John McDonnell, eds. *Soviet Naval Policy, Objectives and Constraints*. New York: Praeger, 1975. pp. 182–210.

2911. _____. "The U.S.S.R. and the Middle East: Some Reflections on the Soviet Decision-Making Process." *Orbis*, XVII (Fall 1973), 946–977.

2912. _____. "Soviet Global Policy and the Middle East." *Naval War College Review*, XXIV (September–October 1971), 19–29.

2913. Rey, Gabriel. "The Arms Balance in the Middle East." *Israel Horizons*, XVII (March 1969), 8–15.

2914. Rosen, Stephen J. "Temptation to Pre-empt in a Fifth Arab-Israeli War." *Orbis*, XX (Summer 1976), 265–285.

2915. _____. "What the Next Arab-Israeli War Might Look Like." *International Security*, II (Spring 1978), 149–174.

2916. Rubinstein, Alvin Z. "The Soviet Union and the Eastern Mediterranean, 1968–1978." *Orbis*, XXIII (Summer 1979), 299–315.

2917. Sella, Amnon. "Patterns of Soviet Involvement in Local War." *Journal of the Royal United Service Institution for Defence Studies*, CXXIV (June 1979), 53–56.

2918. Smolansky, Oles M. "Moscow and the Arab-Israeli Sector." *Current History*, LXXI (October 1976), 105–108.

2919. _____. "The United States and the Soviet Union in the Middle East." In: Grayson Kirk and Nils H. Wessell, eds. *The Soviet Threat: Myths and Realities.* New York: Praeger, 1978. pp. 99–109.

2920. "Soviet–Arab Aircraft Strength in the Mideast Tops Israel's 4 to 1." *Aviation Week and Space Technology*, XCII (June 1, 1970), 16–17.

2921. Stolley, R. B. "Russia in the Middle East." *Life*, LXV (November 29, 1968), 22–31.

2922. _____. "The Struggle for Air Supremacy, October 1973–December 1975." *Journal of the Royal United Service Institution for Defence Studies*, CXXI (December 1976), 31–36.

2923. Whetten, Lawrence L. "The Mediterranean Threat: Has Strategic Parity Been Achieved?" *Survey*, no. 74–75 (Winter–Spring 1970), 270–281.

2924. _____. "The Military Consequences of Mediterranean Super Power Parity." *New Middle East*, no. 38 (November 1971), 14–25.

2925. _____. "Soviet Strategy." *Survival*, XII (August 1970), 252–260.

2926. _____. "Strategic Parity in the Middle East." *Military Review*, L (September 1970), 24–31.

2927. "Who Has Been Arming the Middle East?" *Business Week*, (July 18, 1970), 72–73.

2928. Winston, D. C. "Soviet Mideast Buildup Shows Tactic Shift." *Aviation Week and Space Technology*, LXXXVII (November 6, 1967), 19–20.

2929. Yodfat, Aryeh Y. "Soviet Policy in the Middle East: Before October 1973 and After." *New Outlook*, XVII (November–December 1974), 31–56.

Documents, Papers, and Reports

2930. Becker, Abraham S. *Arms Transfers, Great Power Intervention, and Settlement of the Arab-Israeli Conflict.* RAND Paper P-5901. Santa Monica, Calif.: RAND Corporation, 1978. 25p.

2931. _____. *The Superpowers in the Arab-Israeli Conflict, 1970–1973*. RAND Paper P-5162. Santa Monica, Calif.: RAND Corporation, 1973. 67p.

2932. _____ and Arnold L. Horelick. *Soviet Policy in the Middle East*. RAND Report R-504-FF. Santa Monica, Calif.: RAND Corporation, 1970. 115p.

2933. Chase, Alan C. *Soviet Military Goals in the Middle East*. Research Study. Maxwell AFB, Ala.: Air Command and Staff College, Air University, 1972. 79p.

2934. Churba, Joseph. *Soviet Penetration into the Middle East*. Documentary Research Study AU-203-68-ASI. Maxwell AFB, Ala.: Documentary Research Division, Aerospace Studies Institute, Air University, 1968. 113p.

2935. Glassman, Jon D. "Arms for the Arabs: The Soviet Union and War in the Middle East." Unpublished Ph.D. Dissertation, Columbia University, 1976.

2936. Hunter, Robert E. *The Soviet Dilemma in the Middle East*. Adelphi papers, nos. 59–60. 2 vols. London: Institute for Strategic Studies, 1969.

2937. Kemp, Geoffrey. *Arms and Security: the Egypt–Israel Case*. Adelphi papers, no. 52. London: Institute for Strategic Studies, 1968. 27p.

2938. *The Middle East and the International System*. Adelphi papers, nos. 114–115. 2 vols. London: International Institute for Strategic Studies, 1975.

2939. Milstein, Jeffrey S. *Soviet and American Influences on the Arab-Israeli Arms Race: A Quantitative Analysis*. New Haven, Conn.: Department of Political Science, Yale University, 1970. 27p.

2940. Pajak, Roger F. *Soviet Arms Aid in the Middle East*. Washington, D.C.: Center for Strategic and International Studies, Georgetown University, 1976. 45p.

2941. Pierce, Max R. *Soviet Involvement in Egypt, Syria, and Iraq*. Maxwell AFB, Ala.: Air Command and Staff College, Air University, 1973. 53p.

2942. Tahtinen, Dale R. *The Arab-Israeli Military Balance Since October 1973*. Foreign Affairs Study, no. 11. Washington, D.C.: American Enterprise Institute for Public Policy Research, 1974. 43p.

2943. _____. *The Arab-Israeli Military Status in 1976.* Foreign Affairs Study, no. 30. Washington, D.C.: American Enterprise Institute for Public Policy Research, 1976. 31p.

2944. United States. Central Intelligence Agency. Office of Political Research. *Issues in the Middle East: Atlas.* Washington, D.C.: U.S. Government Printing Office, 1973. 40p.

2945. _____. Congress. House. Committee on Foreign Affairs. Subcommittee on Europe and the Near East. *Soviet Involvement in the Middle East and the Western Response: Hearings.* 92nd Cong., 1st sess. Washington, D.C.: U.S. Government Printing Office, 1971. 219p.

2946. _____. _____. _____. _____. _____. *The Middle East in Crisis—Problems and Prospects: Report.* 92nd Cong., 1st sess. Washington, D.C.: U.S. Government Printing Office, 1971. 28p.

2947. Whetten, Lawrence L. *The Soviet Presence in the Eastern Mediterranean.* New York: National Strategy Information Center, 1971. 50p.

2948. Wolfe, Thomas W. *Soviet Goals and Policies in the Middle East.* RAND Paper P-4472. Santa Monica, Calif.: RAND Corporation, 1970. 27p.

(2) Egypt

Books

2949. Dawisha, Karen. *Soviet Foreign Policy Towards Egypt.* New York: St. Martin's Press, 1979. 276p.

2950. Heikal, Mohamed. *The Road to Ramadan.* New York: Quadrangle Books, 1975. 285p.

2951. Rubinstein, Alvin Z. *Red Star on the Nile: The Soviet–Egyptian Influence Relationship Since the June [1967] War.* Princeton, N.J.: Princeton University Press, 1977. 383p.

2952. Sadat, Anwar. *In Search of Identity: An Autobiography.* New York: Harper & Row, 1978. 360p.

Articles

2953. Alsop, Joseph. "Russia's Menacing New Challenge in the Mideast." *Reader's Digest,* XCVII (August 1970), 47–51.

2954. "Buildup on the Suez: Soviet Missiles." *Time,* XCII (September 14, 1970), 21.

2955.   Cottrell, Alvin J. "Soviet–Egyptian Relations." *Military Review,* XLIX (December 1969), 69–76.

2956.   Cox, Frederick J. "The Russian Presence in Egypt." *Naval War College Review,* XXII (January–February 1970), 45–53.

2957.   DeBorchgrave, André. "The Kremlin's Mideast Gamble." *Newsweek,* LXXV (June 1, 1970), 37–42.

2958.   "Egypt Displays Soviet-Supplied Weapons." *Aviation Week and Space Technology,* CI (August 26, 1974), 14–18.

2959.   "Electronic Summer." *Time,* XCV (April 6, 1970), 38.

2960.   Evron, Yair. "The Soviet Union in Egypt." *Survival,* XII (August 1970), 259–262.

2961.   "Foxbats Again Evade Israeli Intercept." *Aviation Week and Space Technology,* XCV (November 15, 1971), 17.

2962.   Freedman, Robert O. "Soviet Policy Toward Sadat's Egypt." *Naval War College Review,* XXV (November–December 1973), 63–79.

2963.   "The Growing Soviet Commitment: Training Programs and Missile Sites in Egypt." *Time,* XCV (April 13, 1970), 33.

2964.   Hottinger, Arnold. "Cairo's Ties to Moscow." *Swiss Review of World Affairs,* XIX (November 1969), 7–8.

2965.   International Institute for Strategic Studies. "The Soviet Military Presence in the U.A.R." In: *Strategic Survey, 1970.* London, 1971. pp. 46–49.

2966.   Kapeliuk, Amnon. "The Egyptian–Russian Conflict: Origins and Development." *New Outlook,* XV (September 1972), 8–18.

2967.   Kolcum, Edward H. "SAM Changes Force New Strategy on Israelis." *Aviation Week and Space Technology,* XCIII (November 16, 1970), 16–21.

2968.   _____. "Soviets Accelerating Mideast Drive." *Aviation Week and Space Technology,* XCII (May 18, 1970), 9, 14–18.

2969.   _____. "Soviets Shifting Mideast Balance." *Aviation Week and Space Technology,* XCII (May 11, 1970), 18–21.

2970.   _____. "Soviets Spur Arms Flow to Egypt." *Aviation Week and Space Technology,* XCIV (April 19, 1971), 9, 14–16.

2971.   "Latest Gifts From Russia: MIG-21's to Egypt." *Time,* XCVII (April 26, 1971), 40.

Soviet Aerospace Arms and Assistance, 1945–1980 241

2972. "Living on the Brink of War." *U.S. News and World Report,* LXX (March 15, 1971), 78–82.

2973. "Middle East: That Electronic Summer." *Time,* XCVI (July 20, 1970), 18–19.

2974. "Moscow-on-the-Nile." *Time,* XCV (June 22, 1970), 31.

2975. "New Missile Sites a Threat to Israeli Air Superiority." *Aviation Week and Space Technology,* XCIII (August 24, 1970), 20.

2976. "Of Mosques and MIGs: Moscow's Growing Military Role in Egypt." *Time,* XCV (June 1, 1970), 19–20.

2977. Oliver, Luis G. "Tactical Electronic Warfare: ECM are Gold When You Know How to Use Them." *TacAir Warfare Center Quarterly Report,* II (Spring 1971), 4–9.

2978. "On Their Own Turf: Soviet Pilots in Egypt." *Newsweek,* LXXV (May 18, 1970), 58.

2979. Pajak, Roger F. "Soviet Arms and Egypt." *Survival,* XVII (July–August 1975), 166.

2980. "Question of Credence: Buildup of Soviet Missiles." *Newsweek,* LXXVI (September 14, 1970), 50–51.

2981. "Relief for Egypt, Anxiety for Israel." *Time,* XCV (May 11, 1970), 43–44.

2982. "Russians Fly Defense Missions for Egypt in Middle East Conflict." *Aviation Week and Space Technology,* XCII (May 4, 1970), 27.

2983. "SAMs, MIGs, Russians: Soviet Troops in Egypt." *Newsweek,* LXXV (May 11, 1970), 59–60.

2984. Singh, K. Rajendra. "The Soviet-U.A.R. Relations." *India Quarterly,* XXV (April–June 1969), 139–152.

2985. "Soviets Deploy New Suez Defenses." *Aviation Week and Space Technology,* XCIII (July 13, 1970), 14–16.

2986. "Sparring Along the Canal." *Newsweek,* LXXVIII (September 27, 1971), 46.

2987. Whetten, Lawrence L. "June 1967 to June 1971: Four Years of Canal War Reconsidered." *New Middle East,* no. 33 (June 1971), 15–25.

2988. _____. "Sadat's Strategic Options in the Canal War." *World Today,* XXIX (February 1973), 58–67.

2989. "World's Hottest Plane [MIG-21]? Advanced Jet Fighters to Egypt." *Newsweek,* LXXVII (April 26, 1971), 39.

2990. Yodfat, Aryeh. "Arms and Influence in Egypt: The Record of Soviet Military Assistance Since June 1967." *New Middle East,* no. 10 (June 1969), 27–32.

Documents, Papers, and Reports

2991. Horelick, Arnold L. *Moscow's Rift with Sadat: Implications for Soviet Middle East Policy.* RAND Paper P-5666. Santa Monica, Calif.: RAND Corporation, 1976. 29p.

2992. Israel. Ministry of Foreign Affairs. *Policy Background: Russian Military Intervention—The Third Phase—Soviet-Manned SAM-3s Into the Suez Canal Battle Zone.* Washington, D.C.: Embassy of Israel, 1970. 27p.

2993. Preisser, Chester J., Jr. *A Description of the Soviet Role in the Air Defense of Egypt.* Maxwell AFB, Ala.: Air Command and Staff College, Air University, 1971. 62p.

2994. Waltermire, Jacob B., Jr. *Egypt's Shield: Soviet Air Power.* Maxwell AFB, Ala.: Air Command and Staff College, Air University, 1971. 91p.

(3) Syria/Jordan

Articles

2995. "Arab Airpower." *Air International,* XIII (July 1977), 7.

2996. Golan, Galia. "Syria and the Soviet Union Since the Yom Kippur War." *Orbis,* XXI (Winter 1978), 777–801.

2997. Mangold, Peter. "The Soviet–Syrian Military Relationship, 1955–1977." *Journal of the Royal United Service Institution for Defence Studies,* CXXII (September 1977), 27–33.

2998. "Other Fronts: Syrian Border Dogfights." *Newsweek,* XCV (April 13, 1970), 38–40.

2999. Pajak, Roger F. "Soviet Military Aid to Iraq and Syria." *Strategic Review,* IV (Winter 1976), 51–59.

3000. Rudolph, James D. "National Security." In: Richard F. Nyrop, ed. *Syria: A Country Study.* Foreign Area Studies Series. Washington, D.C.: U.S. Government Printing Office, 1978. pp. 191–225.

3001. "Syrian MIGs Downed." *Aviation Week and Space Technology,* CXI (July 2, 1979), 27.

Soviet Aerospace Arms and Assistance, 1945–1980

b. The Arab-Israeli Wars

(1) The Six-Day War, 1967

Books

3002. Barker, Arthur J. *The Six-Day War.* Ballantine's Illustrated History of the Violent Century. New York: Ballantine Books, 1974. 159p.

3003. Dayan, David. *Strike First! A Battle History of Israel's Six-Day War.* Translated from the Hebrew. New York: Pittman, 1968. 292p.

3004. *Kessing's Research Report: The Arab–Israeli Conflict, the 1967 Campaign.* New York: Scribner's, 1968. 96p.

3005. O'Ballance, Edgar. *The Third Arab–Israeli War.* Hamden, Conn.: Archon Books, 1972. 288p.

3006. Young, Peter. *The Israeli Campaign, 1967.* London: Kimber, 1967. 192p.

Articles

3007. Badeau, J. S. "The Arabs, 1967." *Atlantic,* CCXX (December 1967), 102–110.

3008. Hotz, Robert. "Effective Airpower." *Aviation Week and Space Technology,* LXXXVI (June 26, 1967), 11.

3009. "Israeli Thrust." *Life,* LXII (June 16, 1967), 26–38D.

3010. Kotch, W. J. "The Six-Day War of 1967." *U.S. Naval Institute Proceedings,* XCIV (June 1968), 72–81.

3011. "Lightning in the Desert: The Story of the Israeli Victory." *U.S. News and World Report,* LXII (June 19, 1967), 62–63.

3012. Marshall, Samuel L. A. "The Air Strike." In: *Swift Sword: The Historical Record of Israel's Victory, June 1967.* New York: American Heritage, 1967. pp. 21–38.

3013. "Massive [Soviet] Resupply Narrows Israeli Margin in Air Power." *Aviation Week and Space Technology,* LXXXVI (June 19, 1967), 16–19.

3014. "Quickest War." *Time,* LXXXIX (June 16, 1967), 22–28.

3015. Shoemaker, Robert. "The Arab–Israeli War." *Military Review,* XLVIII (August 1968), 56–69.

3016. "Terrible Swift Sword: How the War was Won." *Newsweek,* LXIX (June 19, 1967), 24–29.

3017. "Three-Day Blitz From Gaza to Suez." *U.S. News and World Report,* LXII (June 19, 1967), 33–37.

3018. Tuchman, Barbara W. "Israel's Swift Sword." *Atlantic,* CCXX (September 1967), 56–62.

3019. Wetmore, Warren C. "Israeli Mirage Pilot Describes MIG Kills." *Aviation Week and Space Technology,* LXXXVII (July 17, 1967), 76–77.

3020. _____. "Israel's Air Punch Major Factor in the War." *Aviation Week and Space Technology,* LXXXVII (July 3, 1967), 18–23.

3021. Yost, Charles W. "The Arab–Israeli War." *Foreign Affairs,* XLVI (January 1968), 304–346.

(2) The Yom Kippur War, 1973

Books

3022. Barker, Arthur J. *Yom Kippur War.* Ballantine's Illustrated History of the Violent Century. New York: Ballantine Books, 1974. 159p.

3023. Bullock, John. *The Making of a War.* London: Longmans, 1974.

3024. El-Badri, Hassan. *Ramadan War, 1973.* Translated from the Arabic. New York: Hippocrene Books, 1978. 239p.

3025. Herzog, Chaim. *The War of Atonement, October 1973.* Boston: Little, Brown, 1975. 300p.

3026. Kohler, Foy D. et al. *The Soviet Union and the October 1973 Middle East War: The Implications for Détente.* Miami, Fla.: Center for Advanced International Studies, University of Miami, 1974. 127p.

3027. *London Sunday Times* Insight Team. *The Yom Kippur War.* Garden City, N.Y.: Doubleday, 1974. 514p.

3028. O'Ballance, Edgar. *No Victor, No Vanquished: The Yom Kippur War.* San Rafael, Calif.: Presidio Press, 1979. 383p.

3029. Palit, Dharitri K. *Return to Sanai: The Arab Offensive, October 1973.* New Delhi, India: Palit & Palit, 1974. 172p.

3030. Schiff, Zeev. *October Earthquake: Yom Kippur, 1973.* Tel Aviv: University Publishing Projects, 1974.

3031. Sobel, Lester A., ed. *Israel and the Arabs: The October 1973 War.* New York: Facts on File, 1974. 185p.

3032. Williams, Louis, ed. *Military Aspects of the Israeli–Arab Conflict.* Tel Aviv: University Publishing Projects, 1975. 265p.

Articles

3033. Alberts, Donald J. "A Call From the Wilderness." *Air University Review,* XXVIII (November–December 1976), 35–45.

3034. Barker, Arthur J. "Aspects of the October 1973 War." *Royal Air Forces Quarterly,* XIV (Winter 1974), 301–307.

3035. "Both Sides Continue Mideast Cargo Airlift." *Aerospace Daily,* LXIII (October 30, 1973), 306–307.

3036. Crump, Roger L. "The October War: A Postwar Assessment." *Military Review,* LIV (August 1974), 12–26.

3037. "Deadly New Weapons: Use in Israel–Arab War." *Time,* CII (October 22, 1973), 37–38.

3038. "The Desert as a Proving Ground: Use of Newest Weapons." *Time,* CII (October 29, 1973), 43–44.

3039. Dixon, Robert J. "The Range of Tactical Air Operations." *Strategic Review,* II (Spring 1974), 21–26.

3040. Eaker, Ira C. "The Fourth Arab–Israeli War." *Strategic Review,* II (Winter 1974), 18–25.

3041. Greenhut, Jeffrey. "Air War Middle East: A Report From the International Symposium on the Military Aspects of the Arab–Israeli Conflict, Jerusalem, 12–17 October 1975." *Aerospace Historian,* XXIII (March 1976), 21–23.

3042. Handel, Michael I. "Yom Kippur and the Inevitability of Surprise." *International Studies Quarterly,* XXI (September 1977), 461–502.

3043. Herzog, Chaim. "The Middle East War, 1973." *Journal of the Royal United Service Institution for Defence Studies,* CXX (March 1975), 3–13.

3044. "History's Biggest Airlift: Israel-Arab War." *Time,* CII (October 29, 1973), 52.

3045. "Israeli Aircraft, Arab SAMs in Key Battle." *Aviation Week and Space Technology,* XCIX (October 22, 1973), 14–17.

3046. Latter, B. "Lessons for NATO From the Yom Kippur War." *Royal Air Forces Quarterly,* XVI (Winter 1976), 380–385.

3047. "Looking Back in Anger: The Report of the Agranat Commission of Inquiry." *Time,* CIII (April 15, 1974), 42.

3048. McKenzie-Smith, Robert H. "Crisis Decisionmaking in Israel: The Case of the October 1973 Middle East War." *Naval War College Review,* XXIX (Summer 1976), 39–52.

3049. Meir, Golda. "The Yom Kippur War." In: *My Life.* New York: Dell, 1975. pp. 405–437.

3050. Middleton, Drew. "Who Lost the Yom Kippur War?" *Atlantic,* CCXXXIII (March 1974), 45–47.

3051. O'Neill, Bard E. "The October War: A Political–Military Assessment." *Air University Review,* XXV (July–August 1974), 27–35.

3052. Perimutter, Amos. "Israel's Fourth War, October 1973: Political and Military Misperceptions." *Orbis,* XIX (Summer 1975), 434–460.

3053. Quant, William B. "Soviet Policy in the October Middle East War." *International Affairs,* LIII (July and October 1977), 377–389, 587–603.

3054. Record, Jeffrey. "The October War: Burying the Blitzkrieg." *Military Review,* LVI (April 1976), 19–21.

3055. Rodwell, Robert R. "The Mideast War: A Damned Close-Run Thing." *Air Force Magazine,* LVII (February 1974), 36–41.

3056. Ropelewski, R. R. "Egypt Assesses Lessons of October War." *Aviation Week and Space Technology,* XCIX (December 17, 1973), 14–17.

3057. Sagan, S. D. "Lessons of the Yom Kippur Alert." *Foreign Policy,* no. 36 (Fall 1979), 160–177.

3058. Shlaim, Avi. "Failures in National Intelligence Estimates: The Case of the Yom Kippur War." *World Politics,* XXVIII (April 1976), 348–380.

3059. Singh, K. Rajendra. "Ground Attack vs. Anti-Aircraft Defense." *India Quarterly,* (April–June 1975).

3060. "Soviet Aid Sparks Arab Gains." *Aviation Week and Space Technology,* XCIX (October 15, 1973), 12–14.

3061. Timmons, Richard F. "Anti-Tank Missiles in the Yom Kippur War." *Infantry,* LXIV (January–February 1974), 18–21.

3062. Toyne-Sewell, T. P. "The War of Atonement and Its Lessons." *Army Quarterly*, CVI (January 1976), 67–71.

3063. Turley, G. H. "Time of Change in Modern War." *Marine Corps Gazette*, LVIII (December 1974), 16–20.

3064. "U.S., Soviets Boost Mideast Airlift." *Aviation Week and Space Technology*, XCIX (October 22, 1973), 18–21.

3065. Viksne, J. "The Yom Kippur War in Retrospect: Electronic Warfare." *Army Journal*, no. 324 (May 1976), 25–28.

3066. Wakebridge, Charles. "A Tank Myth or a Missile Mirage? *Military Review*, LVI (August 1976), 3–11.

3067. Whetten, Lawrence. "Military Lessons of the Yom Kippur War." *World Today*, XXX (March 1974), 101–110.

3068. Williams, Philip. "Detente and the Yom Kippur War: From Crisis Management to Crisis Prevention." *Royal Air Forces Quarterly*, XVI (Autumn 1976), 227–233.

Documents, Papers, and Reports

3069. Israel. Agranant Commission of Inquiry. *Interim Report.* Jerusalem, 1974.

3070. Mergien, A. *Military Lessons of the October War.* Adelphi papers, no. 114. London: International Institute for Strategic Studies, 1975. 28p.

3071. Monroe, Elizabeth. *The Arab–Israeli War, October 1973: Background and Events.* Adelphi papers, no. 111. London: International Institute for Strategic Studies, 1975.

3072. Quandt, William B. *Soviet Policy in the October 1973 War.* RAND Research Study RS-1864-ISA. Santa Monica, Calif.: RAND Corporation, 1976. 39p.

3073. United States. Department of Defense. Defense Intelligence Agency. *A Summary of Lessons Learned in the Arab-Israeli War of 1973.* DI-646-71-74. Washington, D.C.: U.S. Government Printing Office, 1974. 47p.

3074. Van Creveid, Martin. *Military Lessons of the Yom Kippur War: Historical Perspectives.* Washington Papers, vol. 3, no. 4. Los Angeles, Calif.: Sage, 1975. 60p.

c. The Persian Gulf Region

Books

3075. Mughisuddin, Mohammed, ed. *Conflict and Co-operation in the Persian Gulf.* New York: Praeger, 1976. 192p.

3076. Noyes, James H. *Clouded Lens: Persian Gulf Security and U.S. Policy.* Publication, no. 206. Stanford, Calif.: Hoover Institution Press, 1979. 165p.

3077. Page, Stephen. *The U.S.S.R. and Arabia: The Development of Soviet Policies and Attitudes Toward the Countries of the Arabian Peninsula, 1955–1970.* London: Central Asian Research Centre, in Association with the Canadian Institute of International Affairs, 1971. 149p.

3078. Yodfat, Aryeh and Mordechai Abir. *In the Direction of the Persian Gulf: The Soviet Union and the Persian Gulf.* London: Cass, 1977. 167p.

Articles

3079. Becker, Abraham S. "Oil and the Persian Gulf in Soviet Policy in the 1970's." In: Michael Confino and Shimon Shamir, eds. *The U.S.S.R. and the Middle East.* New York: Wiley, 1973. pp. 173–214.

3080. Croizat, Victor J. "Stability in the Persian Gulf." *U.S. Naval Institute Proceedings,* XCIX (July 1973), 48–59.

3081. Griswold, Laurence. "The Bear on the Roof: Soviet Power Encircles the Persian Gulf." *Sea Power,* XV (June 1972), 20–25.

3082. Harrigan, Anthony. "Security Interests in the Persian Gulf and Western Indian Ocean." *Strategic Review,* I (Fall 1973), 13–22.

3083. Hurewitz, J. C. "The Persian Gulf: British Withdrawal and Western Security." *Annals of the American Academy of Political and Social Sciences,* CDI (May 1972), 106–115.

3084. Price, David L. "Moscow and the Persian Gulf." *Problems of Communism,* XXVIII (March–April 1979), 1–13.

3085. Smolansky, Oles M. "Moscow and the Persian Gulf: An Analysis of Soviet Ambitions and Potential." *Orbis,* IV (Spring 1970), 92–108.

3086. Standish, J. F. "The Pursuit of Peace in the Persian Gulf." *World Politics,* XXXII (December 1969), 235–244.

3087. Wright, Denis. "The Changing Balance of Power in the Persian Gulf." *Asian Affairs,* LX (October 1973), 255–262.

3088. Yodfat, Aryeh Y. "The U.S.S.R. and the Persian Gulf Area." *Australian Outlook*, XXXIII (April 1979), 60–72.

Documents, Papers, and Reports

3089. Becker, Abraham S. *Oil and the Persian Gulf in Soviet Policy in the 1970s*. RAND Paper P-1743. Santa Monica, Calif.: RAND Corporation, 1971. 45p.

3090. Center for Strategic and International Studies, Georgetown University. *The Gulf: Implications of British Withdrawal*. Special Report Series, no. 8. Washington, D.C., 1969. 107p.

3091. Hensel, Howard M. "Soviet Policy in the Persian Gulf, 1968–1975." Unpublished Ph.D. Dissertation, University of Virginia, 1976.

3092. O'Neill, Bard E. *Petroleum and Security: The Limitations of Military Power in the Persian Gulf*. NSM Monograph 77-4. Washington, D.C.: Research Directorate, National Defense University, 1977. 22p.

4. Africa

a. GENERAL STUDIES

Books

3093. Legum, Colin et al. *Africa in the 1980s: A Continent in Crisis*. New York: McGraw–Hill, 1979. 232p.

3094. Stevens, Christopher. *The Soviet Union and Black Africa*. New York: Holmes and Meier, 1976. 236p.

3095. Stockholm International Peace Research Institute. *Southern Africa, the Escalation of a Conflict: A Politico–Military Study*. New York: Praeger, 1976. 235p.

3096. Weinstein, Warren, ed. *Chinese and Soviet Aid to Africa*. New York: Praeger, 1975. 316p.

Articles

3097. Albright, David E. "Soviet Policy." *Problems of Communism*, XXVII (January 1978), 20–39.

3098. Baker, Ross K. "Soviet Military Assistance to Tropical Africa." *Military Review*, XLVIII (July 1968), 76–81.

3099. Burns, Robert T. "Soviet-Cuban Enterprises in Africa." *U.S. Naval Institute Proceedings*, CV (July 1979), 28–33.

3100. Gann, Lewis H. "The Military Outlook: Southern Africa." *Military Review*, LII (July 1972), 59–72.

3101. Klimov, Andrei. "Africa Rejects 'Absolute Neutrality.'" *Soviet Military Review*, no. 1. (January 1972), 57–58.

3102. Legum, Colin. "The Soviet Union, China, and the West in Southern Africa." *Foreign Affairs*, LIV (July 1976), 745–762.

3103. Thompson, W. Scott. "The Soviet–Cuban Experience in Africa, 1974–1978." In: Richard E. Bissell and Chester A. Crocker, eds. *South Africa Into the 1980s*. Boulder, Colo.: Westview, 1979. Chpt. 7.

3104. Whetten, Lawrence. "The Soviet-Cuban Presence in the Horn of Africa." *Journal of the Royal United Service Institution for Defence Studies*, CXXIII (September 1978), 39–45.

Documents, Papers, and Reports

3105. Bell, J. Bowyer. *The Horn of Africa: Strategic Magnet in the Seventies*. Strategy papers, no. 21. New York: Published for the National Strategy Information Center by Crane, Russak, 1973. 55p.

3106. Copson, Raymond W. *Africa: The Soviet-Cuban Role*. CRS Issue Brief, no. 78077. Washington, D.C.: Congressional Research Service, Library of Congress, 1978.

3107. Rees, David. *Soviet Strategic Penetration of Africa*. Conflict Studies, no. 77. London: Institute for the Study of Conflict, 1976. 24p.

b. Specific Nations

(1) Angola

Books

3108. Harsch, Ernest and Tony Thomas. *Angola: The Hidden History of Washington's War*. New York: Pathfinder Press, 1976. 157p.

3109. Legum, Colin and Tony Hodges. *After Angola: The War Over Southern Africa*. New York: Africana, 1976. 85p.

Articles

3110. Bissell, Richard E. "Southern Africa: Testing Detente." In: Grayson Kirk and Nils H. Wellman, eds. *The Soviet Threat: Myths and Realities*. New York: Praeger, 1978. pp. 88–98.

3111. Chapman, Michael. "Civil War in Angola." In: Royal United Service Institution for Defence Studies. *R.U.S.I. and Brassey's Annual, 1976–77.* Boulder, Colo.: Westview, 1976. pp. 36–47.

3112. Ebinger, Charles K. "External Intervention in Internal War: The Politics and Diplomacy of the Angolan Civil War." *Orbis,* XX (Fall 1976), 669–679.

3113. Ignatyev, Oleg. "Angola Retrospect." *New Times* (Moscow), no. 34 (August 1976), 27–30.

3114. Larrabee, Steven. "Moscow, Angola, and the Dialectics of Detente." *World Today,* XXXII (May 1976), 173–182.

3115. Papp, Daniel S. "Angola: National Liberation." *Parameters,* VIII (March 1978), 26–39.

3116. Petersen, Charles W. "The Military Balance in Southern Africa." In: C. P. Potholm and Richard Dale, eds. *Southern Africa in Perspective.* New York: Free Press, 1972. pp. 298–317.

3117. Reed, David. "Angola's Made-in-Moscow War." *Reader's Digest,* CVIII (June 1976), 83–88.

3118. Vanneman, Peter and Martin James. "The Soviet Intervention in Angola: Intentions and Implications." *Strategic Review,* IV (Summer 1976), 92–103.

Documents, Papers, and Reports

3119. Crocker, Chester A. *Report on Angola.* CSIS Report. Washington, D.C.: Center for Strategic and International Studies, Georgetown University, 1976.

3120. United States. Congress. Senate. Committee on Foreign Relations. Subcommittee on African Affairs. *Angola: Hearings.* 94th Cong., 2nd sess. Washington, D.C.: U.S. Government Printing Office, 1976. 212p.

(2) Congo/Zaire

Books

3121. Abi-Saab, Genges. *United Nations Operations in the Congo, 1960–1964.* London and New York: Oxford University Press, 1978. 200p.

3122. Dayal, Rajeshwar. *Mission for Hammarskjold: The Congo Crisis.* Princeton, N.J.: Princeton University Press, 1976. 335p.

3123. Gordon, King. *The United Nations in the Congo: A Quest for Peace.* New York: Carnegie Endowment for International Peace, 1962. 184p.

3124. House, Arthur H. *U.N. in the Congo: The Political and Civilian Efforts.* Washington, D.C.: University Press of America, 1978. 435p.

3125. Lefever, Ernest W. and Wynfred Joshua. *United Nations Peace-Keeping in the Congo, 1960–1964: An Analysis of Political, Executive, and Military Control.* 4 vols. Washington, D.C.: Brookings Institution, 1966.

3126. Weissman, Stephen K. *American Foreign Policy in the Congo, 1960–1964.* Ithaca, N.Y.: Cornell University Press, 1974. 325p.

Documents, Papers, and Reports

3126a. United States. Congress. House. Committee on Foreign Affairs. *Immediate and Future Problems in the Congo: Hearings.* 88th Cong., 1st sess. Washington, D.C.: U.S. Government Printing Office, 1963. 22p.

3127. _____. Department of State. Bureau of Intelligence and Research. *Chronology of Significant Events in the Congo, January 1959– December 21, 1961.* Research Memorandum, no. RAF-16. Washington, D.C., 1961. 32p.

(3) Ethiopia

Articles

3128. Day, Bonner. "The Soviet Airlift to Ethiopia." *Air Force Magazine,* LXI (September 1978), 33.

3129. Papp, Daniel S. "The Soviet Union and Cuba in Ethiopia." *Current History,* LXXVI (March 1979), 110–114.

3130. Payton, Gary D. "The Soviet–Ethiopian Liaison: Airlift and Beyond." *Air University Review,* XXXI (November–December 1979), 66–73.

3131. "The Soviets Exercise Their Airlift Capability." *Air Force Magazine,* LXI (March 1978), 27.

Documents, Papers, and Reports

3132. Spencer, John H. *Ethiopia, the Horn of Africa, and U.S. Policy.* Cambridge, Mass.: Institute for Foreign Policy Analysis, 1977. 70p.

(4) Libya

3133.   Pajak, Roger F. "Soviet Arms Aid to Libya." *Military Review*, LVI (July 1976), 82–87.

(5) Somalia

Book

3134.   Farer, Tom J. *War Clouds on the Horn of Africa*. 2nd rev. ed. Washington, D.C.: Carnegie Endowment for International Peace, 1979. 183p.

Articles

3135.   Bell, J. Bowyer. "Strategic Implications of the Soviet Presence in Somalia." *Orbis*, XIX (Summer 1975), 402–411.

3136.   Chaplin, Dennis. "Somalia and the Development of Soviet Activity in the Indian Ocean." *Military Review*, LV (July 1975), 3–9.

3137.   Payton, Gary D. "Soviet Military Presence Abroad: The Lessons of Somalia." *Military Review*, LIX (January 1979), 67–71.

3138.   "Somalia: The Russians are on Africa's Horn." *Time*, CVI (July 21, 1975), 29–30.

3139.   "Soviet Airlift Saves Somali Nomads: Translated from *Pravda*, October 21, 1975." *Current Digest of the Soviet Press*, XXVII (November 12, 1975), 22–23.

3140.   Vanneman, Peter and Martin James. "The Soviet Thrust Into the Horn of Africa." *Strategic Review*, VI (Spring 1978), 33–40.

Documents, Papers, and Reports

3141.   Crozier, Brian. *The Soviet Presence in Somalia*. Conflict Studies, no. 54. London: Institute for the Study of Conflict, 1975. 29p.

3142.   United States. Congress. Senate. Committee on Armed Services. *Soviet Military Capability in Berbera, Somalia: Report*. 94th Cong, 1st sess. Washington, D.C.: U.S. Government Printing Office, 1975. 29p.

5. Asia

a. CHINA

Books

3143.   Bueschel, Richard M. *Communist Chinese Air Power*. New York: Praeger, 1968. 238p.

3144.   Middleton, Drew. *The Duel of the Giants: China and Russia in Asia.* New York: Scribner's, 1978. 231p.

3145.   Salisbury, Harrison. *War Between Russia and China.* New York: W. W. Norton, 1969. 224p.

Articles

3146.   Aarestad, James H. "The Sino–Soviet Border Dispute." *Forum,* no. 31 (Fall 1971), 92–100.

3147.   Petersen, Philip A. "Possible Courses of a Military Conflict Between the U.S.S.R. and P.R.C." *Military Review,* LVII (March 1977), 28–37.

3148.   Thach, Joseph E., Jr. "Modernization and Conflict: Soviet Military Assistance to the P.R.C., 1950–1960." *Military Review,* LVIII (January 1978), 72–92.

Documents, Papers, and Reports

3149.   Hinton, Harold C. *The Sino–Soviet Confrontation: Implications for the Future.* Strategy papers, no. 29. New York: Published for the National Strategy Information Center, by Crane, Russak, 1976. 29p.

b. NORTH KOREA AND THE KOREAN WAR

Books

3150.   Davis, Larry. *MIG Alley.* Warren, Mich.: Squadron/Signal Publications, 1976. 80p.

3151.   Futrell, Robert F. *The United States Air Force in Korea, 1950–1953.* New York: Duell, 1961. 774p.

3152.   Gardner, Lloyd C., comp. *The Korean War.* New York: Quadrangle Books, 1972. 242p.

3153.   George, Alexander L. *The Chinese Communist Army in Action: The Korean War and Its Aftermath.* New York: Columbia University Press, 1967. 255p.

3154.   Jackson, Robert. *Air War Over Korea.* London: Ian Allan, 1973. 175p.

3155.   McGovern, James. *To the Yalu: From the Chinese Invasion of Korea to MacArthur's Dismissal.* New York: Morrow, 1972. 225p.

3156.   Paige, Glenn D. *The Korean Decision, June 24–30, 1950.* New York: Free Press, 1968. 394p.

3157. Rees, David. *Korea: The Limited War.* New York: St. Martin's Press, 1964. 511p.

3158. Spanier, John W. *The Truman-MacArthur Controversy and the Korean War.* Cambridge, Mass.: Belknap Press, 1959. 311p.

3159. Stewart, James T., ed. *Air Power: The Decisive Force in Korea.* Princeton, N.J.: Van Nostrand, 1957. 310p.

3160. Whiting, Allen S. *China Crosses the Yalu: The Decision to Enter the Korean War.* 2nd ed. Stanford, Calif.: Stanford University Press, 1968. 219p.

Articles

3161. "Air War in Korea." *Air University Quarterly Review,* IV (Fall 1950, Spring–Summer 1951), 19–30, 47–72, 83–96; V (Winter 1951–Spring 1952), 86–92, 87–97; VI (Spring–Fall 1953), 83–89, 78–92, 114–127.

3162. Albright, Joseph G. "Two Years of MIG Activity." *Air University Quarterly Review,* VI (Spring 1953), 83–89.

3163. Black, C. L. "F-80 vs. MIG: History's First Jet Battle." *Flying,* XLVIII (March 1951), 13–15.

3164. "Communist Air Power in Korea." *Flight,* LXI (June 6, 1952), 678–679.

3165. Coughlin, William J. "Air Lessons of Korea." *Aviation Week,* LVIII (May 25, 1953), 23–24.

3166. Greenough, Robert B. "Communist Lessons From the Korean Air War." *Air University Quarterly Review,* V (Winter 1952), 22–29.

3167. Jessup, Alpheus W. "Red Pilots Sharpen Their Skill in Korea." *Aviation Week,* LV (December 17, 1951), 11–13.

3168. Knight, Charles. "New Air War: [F-86] Sabres vs. MIGs." *Collier's,* CXXVII (April 21, 1951), 26–27.

3169. Seung-Kwon, Synn. "Reflections on the Korean War: Soviet–North Korean Relations." *East Asian Review,* I (Autumn 1974), 267–285.

3170. Soltys, Andrew T. "Enemy Antiaircraft Defenses in North Korea." *Air University Quarterly Review,* VII (Spring 1954), 75–82.

3171. Thresher, R. D. "Yak in the Sun." *Flying,* LV (July 1954), 18–19.

3172. Thyng, Harrison R. "Air-to-Air Combat in Korea." *Air University Quarterly Review,* VI (Summer 1953), 40–45.

3173. "U.S. vs. Russian Planes." *U.S. News and World Report,* XXXII (March 14, 1952), 24–25.

3174. Vandenburg, Hoyt S. "We're Really Fighting Russia Now." *U.S. News and World Report,* XXXI (December 14, 1951), 19–21.

3175. Weyland, Otto P. "We Fight Russia's Warplanes: Report, With Supplementary Editorial Analysis." *Flying,* XLVII (September 1950), 15–17.

Documents, Papers, and Reports

3176. Brooks, Robert O. *Russian Airpower in the Korean War.* Maxwell AFB, Ala.: Air Command and Staff College, Air University, 1964.

3177. United States. Congress. Senate. Committee on Armed Services. *The Military Situation in the Far East and the Relief of General Douglas MacArthur.* 5 vols. 82nd Cong., 1st sess. Washington, D.C.: U.S. Government Printing Office, 1951.

c. Afghanistan

3178. "Afghanistan Takeover: Why the Russians Acted." *U.S. News and World Report,* LXXXVIII (January 14, 1980), 22–26.

3179. "Afghanistan: The Soviets Dig in Deeper." *Time,* CXV (January 21, 1980), 36–38.

3180. Ali, S. "Accepting the Limits of Aid." *Far Eastern Economic Review,* CV (August 31, 1979), 27–28.

3181. DeBorchgrave, André. "The 'New' Afghanistan." *Newsweek,* XCV (January 21, 1980), 34–35.

3182. "How the Soviet Army Crushed Afghanistan." *Time,* CXV (January 14, 1980), 20–23.

3183. Martin, Robert P. "Russia's No-Win War in Afghanistan." *U.S. News and World Report,* LXXXVII (October 15, 1979), 89–90.

3184. Nielsen, John. "Russia's Afghan Coup." *Newsweek,* XCV (January 7, 1980), 18–22.

3185. _____. "Soviet Afghanistan." *Newsweek,* XCV (January 14, 1980), 28–30.

d. The Indo-Pakistani Conflicts

Books

3186.   Arora, J. S. B. *War With Pakistan, 1971.* New Delhi, India: Army Publishers, 1972. 208p.

3187.   Ayoob, Mohammed. *The Liberation War.* New Delhi, India: Chand, 1972. 292p.

3188.   Banerjee, Jyotirmey. *India in Soviet Global Strategy: A Conceptual Study.* Columbia, Mo.: South Asia Books, 1977. 201p.

3189.   Choudhary, Sukhbir. *The Indo–Pakistani War and the Big Powers.* New Delhi, India: Trimurte Publications, 1972. 195p.

3190.   Drieberg, Trevor. *Towards Closer Indo-Soviet Co-Operation.* New Delhi, India: Vikas, 1974. 182p.

3191.   Jackson, Robert. *South Asian Crisis: India, Pakistan, and Bangladesh—a Political and Historical Analysis of the 1971 War.* New York: Praeger, 1975. 240p.

3192.   Jain, Rajendra K. *Soviet-South Asian Relations, 1947–1978.* 2 vols. New York: Humanities Press, 1979.

3193.   Kapur, Harish. *The Soviet Union and the Emerging Nations: A Case Study of Soviet Policy Towards India.* London: Joseph, 1972. 124p.

3194.   Kaushik, Devendra. *Soviet Relations With India and Pakistan.* New York: Harper & Row, 1971. 119p.

3195.   Mellor, John W., ed. *India: A Rising Middle Power.* Boulder, Colo.: Westview, 1979. 374p.

3196.   Palit, Dharitri K. *The Lightning Campaign: The Indo–Pakistan War, 1971.* Compton, England: Compton Press, 1972. 172p.

3197.   Pushpinder, Singh. *Aircraft of the Indian Air Force, 1933–1973.* New Delhi, India: English Book Store, 1974. 180p.

3198.   _____. *A Guide to Airpower in Asia and the Pacific.* New Delhi, India: Guide Publications, 1971. 200p.

3199.   Ray, Hemen. *Indo–Soviet Relations, 1955–1971.* Bombay, India: Jaico Publishing House, 1973. 302p.

3200.   Siddiqui, Kalim. *Conflict, Crisis, and War in Pakistan.* New York: Praeger, 1972. 217p.

3201. Singh, K. Rajendra. *The Politics of the Indian Ocean*. New Delhi, India: Thomson Press, 1974. 252p.

3202. Vali, Ferenc A. *Politics of the Indian Ocean Area: The Balance of Power*. New York: Macmillan, 1976. 272p.

3203. Ziring, Lawrence, ed. *The Sub-Continent in World Politics: India, Its Neighbors, and the Great Powers*. New York: Praeger, 1978. 240p.

Articles

3204. Arzan, Singh. "The Indian Air Force and Its Role in the Country's Defence." *Journal of the United Service Institution of India*, CDXXI (October–December 1970), 409–415.

3205. Ashlock, J. R. "India's Experience Reveals MIG Problems." *Aviation Week and Space Technology*, LXXIX (November 4, 1963), 33–34.

3206. Barclay, Cyril N. "The Indo-Pakistani War." *Army*, XXII (May 1972), 20–26.

3207. Barnds, William J. "The Soviet Union Chooses India." In: *India, Pakistan, and the Great Powers*. New York: Published for the Council on Foreign Relations by Praeger, 1972. Chpt. 5.

3208. Bowles, Chester. "America and Russia in India." *Foreign Affairs*, XLIX (July 1971), 639–651.

3209. Budhraj, Vijay. "Moscow and the Birth of Bangladesh." *Asian Survey*, XIII (May 1973), 482–495.

3210. Chau, P. R. "Indo-Soviet Military Co-Operation: A Review." *Asian Survey*, XIX (March 1979), 230–244.

3211. Chopra, Pushpindar W. "India and the MIG-21." *U.S. Air Force Fighter Weapons Review*, (Spring 1974), 18–26.

3212. Choudhury, G. W. "The Dismemberment of Pakistan, 1971." *Orbis*, XVIII (Spring 1974), 179–200.

3213. _____. "Moscow's Influence on the Indian Subcontinent." *World Today*, XXVIII (July 1972), 304–311.

3214. Costa, Benedict. "The 14-Day War, Blow-by-Blow." *Illustrated Weekly of India*, XCIII (January 16, 1972), 6–17.

3215. Dil, Shaheen. "The Extent and Nature of Soviet Involvement in the Bangladesh Crisis." *Asian Quarterly*, no. 3 (1973), 243–259.

3216. "E," pseud. "India vs. Pakistan: Formula for War." *Flight International*, C (December 16, 1971), 987–991.

3217. Guha, S. B. "Pakistan's Air Power." *Institute for Defence Studies and Analysis Journal*, II (October 1969), 124–149.

3218. Hanne, William G. "From Moscow: South by Southeast." *Military Review*, LVI (January 1976), 47–55.

3219. Hasan, Zubeida. "Soviet Arms Aid to Pakistan and India." *Pakistan Horizon*, XXI (Fall 1968), 344–355.

3220. Horn, Robert C. "Indian–Soviet Relations in 1969: A Watershed Year?" *Orbis*, XIX (Winter 1976), 1539–1543.

3221. "The India–Pakistan War: A Soviet View." *Current Digest of the Soviet Press*, XXIII (January 11, 1972), 8–10.

3222. "Indian Air Power Isolates Pakistani Forces in the East." *Aviation Week and Space Technology*, XCV (December 13, 1971), 15–16.

3223. Jackson, Robert. "The Great Powers and the Indian Sub-Continent." *International Affairs*, XLVIII (January 1973), 35–50.

3224. _____. "The Strategic Outlook for the Indian Sub-Continent." *Asian Affairs*, LIX (October 1972), 250–269.

3225. Jukes, Geoffrey. "The Soviet Union and the Indian Ocean." *Survival*, XIII (November 1971), 370–375.

3226. Kaul, Ravi. "The Indo–Pakistani War and the Changing Balance of Power in the Indian Ocean." In: Frank Uhlig, Jr., ed. *The Naval Review, 1973*. Annapolis, Md.: U.S. Naval Institute, 1973. pp. 172–195.

3227. Millar, Thomas B. "Soviet Policies South and East of Suez." *Foreign Affairs*, XLIX (October 1970), 70–80.

3228. Mustafa, Zubeida. "The U.S.S.R. and the Indo-Pakistan War, 1971." *Pakistan Horizon*, XXV (Spring 1972), 45–52.

3229. "Neutralist India Eyes Soviet MIGs." *Business Week*, (June 2, 1962), 91–92.

3230. "Pakistan Air Force Built Around the MIG-19." *Aviation Week and Space Technology*, LXXXIX (December 2, 1969), 42–46, 49–52.

3231. Qureshi, Khalida. "Arms Aid to India and Pakistan." *Pakistan Horizon*, XX (February 1967), 137–150.

3232. Rajasekhariah, A. M. "Soviet Arms Supply to Pakistan: Motives and Implications." *Modern Review*, CXXIII (October 1968), 706–710.

3233. Rikhye, Ravi. "Why India Won: The 14-Day War." *Armed Forces Journal,* CIX (April 1972), 38–41.

3234. Sen Gupta, Bhabani. "Moscow and Bangladesh." *Problems of Communism,* XXIV (March–April 1975), 56–68.

3235. Sharma, B. L. "Soviet Arms for Pakistan." *Journal of the United Service Institution of India,* XCVIII (July–September 1968), 223–238.

3236. Wheeler, Geoffrey. "The Indian Ocean Area: Soviet Arms and Interests." *Asian Affairs,* LIX (October 1972), 270–274.

Documents, Papers, and Reports

3237. Belke, Reece G. *Military Power in the Indian Ocean: A Comparative Analysis Between United States and Soviet Realization.* Research Report. Maxwell AFB, Ala.: Air Command and Staff College, Air University, 1969. 71p.

3238. Bhargava, G. S. *India's Security in the 1980s.* Adelphi papers, no. 124. London: International Institute for Strategic Studies, 1976. 27p.

3239. Graham, I. C. C. *The Indo-Soviet MIG Deal and Its International Repercussions.* RAND Paper P-2842. Santa Monica, Calif.: RAND Corporation, 1964. 18p.

3240. Millar, Thomas B. *Soviet Policies in the Indian Ocean Area.* Canberra Papers on Strategy and Defense, no. 7. Canberra: Australian National University Press, 1970. 22p.

3241. Tahtinen, Dale R. and John Lenczowski. *Arms in the Indian Ocean: Interests and Challenges.* Studies in Defense Policy. Washington, D.C.: American Enterprise Institute for Public Policy Research, 1977. 84p.

3242. United States. Congress. House. Committee on Foreign Affairs. Subcommittee on National Security and Scientific Developments. *The Indian Ocean—Political and Strategic Future: Hearings.* 92nd Cong., 1st sess. Washington, D.C.: U.S. Government Printing Office, 1971. 242p.

3243. Vogler, Charles C. *Soviet Expansion in South Asia.* Maxwell AFB, Ala.: Air War College, Air University, 1972. 68p.

Soviet Aerospace Arms and Assistance, 1945–1980

e. INDOCHINA

Research Note

THE AIR WAR fought by Americans in Indochina and the resulting air defense system built by the Soviets for the North Vietnamese are the subjects of extensive literature. The citations listed here are only a sample of what is available. For further information readers might wish to consult the author's *Air War Southeast Asia, 1961–1973: An Annotated Bibliography and 16mm Film Guide* (Metuchen, N.J. and London: The Scarecrow Press, 1979. 298p.).

Books

3244. Brown, Weldon A. *The Last Chopper: The Denouement of the American Role in Vietnam, 1964–1975.* Port Washington, N.Y.: Kennikat Press, 1976. 359p.

3245. Cooper, Chester L. *The Lost Crusade: America in Vietnam.* New York: Dodd, Mead, 1970. 559p.

3246. Drendel, Lou. *. . . And Kill MIGs.* Warren, Mich.: Squadron/Signal Publications, 1974. 63p.

3247. Emerson, Gloria. *Winners and Losers: Battles, Retreats, Gains, Losses, and Ruins from a Long War.* New York: Harcourt, 1978. 448p.

3248. Fitzgerald, Frances. *Fire in the Lake.* Boston: Little, Brown, 1972. 491p.

3249. Halberstam, David. *The Best and the Brightest.* New York: Random House, 1972. 688p.

3250. Hoopes, Townsend. *The Limits of Intervention.* Rev. ed. New York: McKay, 1973. 264p.

3251. Kirk, Donald. *The Wider War: The Struggle for Cambodia, Thailand, and Laos.* New York: Praeger, 1971. 305p.

3252. Lewy, Guenther. *America in Vietnam.* London and New York: Oxford University Press, 1979. 540p.

3253. Milheev, Iuri. *On the Side of a Just Cause: Soviet Assistance to the Heroic Vietnamese People.* Moscow: Progress Publishers [1970?] 127p.

3254. O'Ballance, Edgar. *The Wars in Vietnam, 1954–1973.* New York: Hippocrene Books, 1975. 204p.

3255. *The Pentagon Papers: The Defense Department History of United States Decision-Making on Vietnam.* The Senator [Mike] Gravel Edition. 5 vols. Boston: Beacon Press, 1971.

3256. Sharp, U. S. Grant. *Strategy for Defeat: Vietnam in Retrospect.* San Rafael, Calif.: Presidio Press, 1978. 324p.

3257. Sheehan, Neil et al. *The Pentagon Papers, the Secret History of the Vietnam War: The Complete and Unabridged Series as Published by the New York Times.* New York: Quadrangle Books, 1971. 677p.

3258. Van Dyke, Jon M. *North Vietnam's Strategy for Survival.* Mountain View, Calif.: Pacific Press, 1972. 336p.

3259. Warner, Denis A. *Certain Victory: How Hanoi Won the War.* Kansas City, Mo.: Sheed, Andrews and McMeel, 1978. 295p.

3260. Westmoreland, William C. *A Soldier Reports.* Garden City, N.Y.: Doubleday, 1976. 446p.

Articles

3261. Bearden, Thomas E. "What Really Happened in the Air Defense of North Vietnam?" *Air Defense Management,* (April–June 1976), 8–15.

3262. Burbage, Paul et al. "The Battle for the Skies Over North Vietnam, 1964–1972." In: A. J. C. Lavalle, ed. *USAF Southeast Asia Monograph Series,* vol. 1. Washington, D.C.: U.S. Government Printing Office, 1976. pp. 97–193.

3263. Butz, J. S. "Our Pilots Call Hanoi 'Dodge City.' " *Air Force and Space Digest,* XLIX (December 1966), 28–33.

3264. Dowd, John. "The Truest Sport: Jousting with SAM and Charlie." *Esquire,* LXXXIV (October 1975), 156–159.

3265. Nihart, Brooke. "The MIG Killers." *Armed Forces Journal,* CIX (July 1972), 32–35.

3266. "North Vietnam [Soviet] Airlift." *Military Review,* XLVI (October 1966), 102.

3267. O'Ballance, Edgar. "The Air Defense of North Vietnam." *Marine Corps Gazette,* L (November 1966), 78–79.

3268. Simler, George B. "North Vietnam's Air Defense System." *Air Force and Space Digest,* L (May 1967), 81–82.

3269. "Telephone Poles: The Bombing of Soviet SAM Missile Sites." *Newsweek,* LXVI (August 9, 1965), 22.

3270. Teplinsky, Boris. "Air War in Vietnam." *New Times* (Moscow), no. 51 (December 22, 1965), 11–14.

3271. _____. "The Air War Over Indochina." *International Affairs* (Moscow), no. 2 (February 1967), 40–47.

3272. United States. Central Intelligence Agency. "Communist Military and Economic Aid to North Vietnam, 1970–1974." *Congressional Record,* CXXI (March 7, 1975), 5767–5768.

3273. Van Staaveren, Jacob. "The Air War Against North Vietnam." In: Carl Berger, ed. *The United States Air Force in Southeast Asia, 1961–1973.* Washington, D.C.: Published for the Office of Air Force History by the U.S. Government Printing Office, 1977. pp. 69–100.

Documents, Papers, and Reports

3274. Eastland, James N. et al., eds. *Aces and Aerial Victories: The United States Air Force in Southeast Asia, 1965–1973.* Washington, D.C.: Published for the Office of Air Force History by the U.S. Government Printing Office, 1976. 188p.

3275. United States. Central Intelligence Agency. Office of Basic and Geographic Intelligence. *Indochina Atlas.* Washington, D.C., 1970. 17p.

3276. _____. Congress. Senate. Committee on Armed Services. Preparedness Investigating Subcommittee. *Air War Against North Vietnam: Hearings.* 90th Cong., 1st sess. 5 vols. Washington, D.C.: U.S. Government Printing Office, 1967.

3277. _____. _____. _____. _____. _____. _____: *Summary Report.* 90th Cong., 1st sess. Washington, D.C.: U.S. Government Printing Office, 1967. 10p.

3278. _____. _____. _____. _____. _____. *U.S. Air Force Tactical Air Operations in South–Asia, 1967: Hearings.* 90th Cong., 1st sess. Washington, D.C.: U.S. Government Printing Office, 1967. 12p.

3279. _____. Department of Defense. *United States–Vietnam Relations, 1945–1967.* 12 vols. Washington, D.C.: U.S. Government Printing Office, 1971.

6. The Pacific Area

a. INDONESIA

Books

3280. Hughes, John. *Indonesian Upheaval.* New York: McKay, 1967. 304p.

3281. Mahajani, Usla. *Soviet and American Aid to Indonesia, 1949–1968.* Athens: Ohio University Press, 1972.

3282. Stevenson, William. *Birds Nest in Their Beards.* Boston: Houghton, Mifflin, 1964. 280p.

3283. Sukarno. *Sukarno: An Autobiography.* Indianapolis, Ind.: Bobbs-Merrill, 1965. 324p.

Documents, Papers, and Reports

3284. Horn, Robert C., 3rd. "Soviet–Indonesian Relations, 1956–1966: A Case Study of Soviet Foreign Policy." Unpublished Ph.D. Dissertation, Fletcher School of Law and Diplomacy, Tufts University, 1969.

b. JAPAN AND THE KURILES

3285. "Echoes of Cuba: The Soviet Military Buildup on Shikotan and Two Other Isles in the Southern Kuriles." *Time,* CXIV (October 15, 1979), 64.

3286. "Soviets Accelerate Buildup in the Kuriles." *Aviation Week and Space Technology,* CXI (October 22, 1979), 24.

Appendix I: Late Entries, to May 1980

THE FOLLOWING CITATIONS were uncovered too late for inclusion in the main body of the bibliography. All entries are, however, keyed into the author index.

3287. "Against the Red Pilots." In: *Born in Battle,* no. 2: *The Air War in the Mid-East.* Hod Hashorn, Israel: Eshel-Dramit, Ltd., 1978. p. 48.
Russian–Israeli combat over the Suez Canal in 1970.

3288. "Air Defense Units—Training and Related Activities: Translated from *Krasnaya Zvezda.*" *Translations on USSR Military Affairs,* no. 1491 (January 23, 1980), 1–18.

3289. _____. *Translations on USSR Military Affairs,* no. 1497 (February 15, 1980), 1–8.

3290. _____. *Translations on USSR Military Affairs,* no. 1485 (March 20, 1980), 67–95.

3291. Andreyev, V. "Commander's Role in Flight Training Discussed: Translated from *Aviatsiya I Kosmonavtika,* September 1979." *Translations on USSR Military Affairs,* no. 1479 (December 10, 1979), 125–131.

3292. Anishchenko, L. "Maintenance Procedures in an Air Regiment Described: Translated from *Aviatsiya I Kosmonavtika,* October 1979." *Translations on USSR Military Affairs,* no. 1491 (January 23, 1980), 68–72.

3293. Aoki, Hideo. "F-111 vs. Su-19, Spearheads of Respective Camps: Translated from *Koku Journal,* February 1979." *Translations on USSR Military Affairs,* no. 1451 (July 16, 1979), 41–50.

3294. Astashenkov, P. "Designer Myasishchev's Future High-Speed Aircraft Described: Translated from *Aviatsiya I Kosmonavtika,* July 1979." *Translations on USSR Military Affairs,* no. 1471 (October 30, 1979), 40–45.

3295. Avdeyev, A. "Problems of Planning Flight Training Discussed: Translated from *Aviatsiya I Kosmonavtika,* July 1979." *Translations on USSR Military Affairs,* no. 1477 (November 29, 1979), 6–10.

3296. "Aviation Maintenance Activities Described: Translated from *Aviatsiya I Kosmonavtika,* August 1979." *Translations on USSR Military Affairs,* no. 1473 (November 6, 1979), 22–34.

3297. "Aviation Units—Training and Related Activities: Translated from *Krasnaya Zvezda.*" *Translations on USSR Military Affairs,* no. 1485 (January 2, 1980), 6–25.

3298. _____. *Translations on USSR Military Affairs,* no. 1490 (January 22, 1980), 1–20.

3299. _____. *Translations on USSR Military Affairs,* no. 1495 (February 12, 1980), 30–42.

3300. Belyayev, V. "Element Leader and Wingman Training Described: Translated from *Aviatsiya I Kosmonavtika,* August 1979." *Translations on USSR Military Affairs,* no. 1475 (November 14, 1979), 44–47.

3301. _____. "Helicopter Gunship Squadron Training: Translated from *Krasnaya Zvezda,* June 3, 1979." *Translations on USSR Military Affairs,* no. 1462 (September 7, 1979), 61–62.

3302. Bryukhovskiy, G. "Employment of Aviation in the Manchurian Operation Described: Translated from *Voyenno–Istoricheskiy Zhurnal,* August 1979." *Translations on USSR Military Affairs,* no. 1472 (October 31, 1979), 20–31.

3303. Chaplygin, G. "Helicopter Flight Training Described: Translated from *Aviatsiya I Kosmonavtika,* July 1979." *Translations on USSR Military Affairs,* no. 1471 (October 30, 1979), 28–32.

3304. Chizhezvskiy, V. "Bomber Squadron Training Described: Translated from *Krasnayz Zvezda,* June 5, 1979." *Translations on USSR Military Affairs,* no. 1462 (September 7, 1979), 62–64.

3305. Dunayev, P. "Biographical Information on Marshal Vladimir A. Sudets: Translated from *Voyenno–Istoricheskiy Zhurnal,* October 1979." *Translations on USSR Military Affairs,* no. 1487 (January 7, 1980), 84–86.

Appendix I: Late Entries, to May 1980   267

3306. Federyakov, G. "Importance of Interceptor Pilot Initiative Stressed: Translated from *Aviatsiya I Kosmonavtika*, June 1979." *Translations on USSR Military Affairs*, no. 1481 (December 13, 1979), 9–15.

3307. Fitkulin, O. "Training Activities in an Air Defense Missile Regiment: Translated from *Kommunist Vooruzhennykh Sil*, April 1979." *Translations on USSR Military Affairs*, no. 1464 (September 13, 1979), 1–9.

3308. Fox, Charles L. and Dino A. Lorenzini. "How Much is Not Enough: The Non-Nuclear Air Battle in NATO's Central Region." *Naval War College Review*, XXXIII (March-April 1980), 58–78.

3309. Frantsev, O. "Wartime Employment of Close Support Aviation Discussed: Translated from *Voyenno-Istoricheskiy Zhurnal*, July 1979." *Translations on USSR Military Affairs*, no. 1476 (November 28, 1979), 29–40.

3310. Gavrilov, S. "Testing for Aircraft Design Deficiency Described: Translated from *Aviatsiya I Kosmonavtika*, May 1979." *Translations on USSR Military Affairs*, no. 1471 (October 30, 1979), 8–12.

3311. Gorchakov, P. "Strategic Missile Force's Twentieth Anniversary Status Report: Translated from *Kommunist Vooruzhennykh Sil*, December 1979." *Translations on USSR Military Affairs*, no. 1502 (March 7, 1980), 45–55.

3312. Haselkorn, Avigdor. "The 'External Function' of Soviet Armed Forces." *Naval War College Review*, XXXIII (January–February 1980), 35–45.

3313. Izgarshev, V. "Helicopter Combat Capabilities Discussed: Translated from *Pravda*, September 20, 1979." *Translations on USSR Military Affairs*, no. 1480 (December 10, 1979), 50–53.

3314. Khomchich, M. "Capabilities of Bomber Maintenance Unit Described: Translated from *Aviatsiya I Kosmonavtika*, June 1979." *Translations on USSR Military Affairs*, no. 1481 (December 13, 1979), 29–34.

3315. King, Peter. "Two Eyes for a Tooth: The State of Soviet Strategic Doctrine." *Survey*, XXIV (Winter 1979), 45–56.

3316. Koldunov, Aleksandr. "Air Defense Troops Commander-in-Chief on Tasks and Capabilities: Translated from *Agitator*, March 1979." *Translations on USSR Military Affairs*, no. 1467 (October 5, 1979), 1–5.

3317. Konechnyy, Ye. "Air Base Guard Service Described: Translated from *Krasnaya Zvezda*, April 5, 1979." *Translations on USSR Military Affairs*, no. 1453 (August 10, 1979), 15–19.

3318. Korobov, A. "Control of Fighter-Interceptors Described: Translated from *Krasnaya Zvezda*, May 24, 1979." *Translations on USSR Military Affairs*, no. 1462 (September 7, 1979), 56–59.

3319. Kotikov, A. K. "Helicopter Development in the Soviet Union Described: Translated from *TRUD*, December 1, 1979." *Translations on USSR Military Affairs*, no. 1489 (January 16, 1980), 42–45.

3320. Loginov, A. "Mobile Air Defense Missile Crew Training Described: Translated from *Znamenosets*, April 1979." *Translations on USSR Military Affairs*, no. 1475 (November 19, 1979), 1–5.

3321. Martin, Robert P. "Russia's Arctic Superfort at Murmansk." *U.S. News and World Report*, LXXXVIII (March 3, 1980), 37–38.

3322. Mikhaylenko, I. "Wartime Operations—Moscow Air Defense Organization: Translated from *Voyenno-Istoricheskiy Zhurnal*, December 1979." *Translations on USSR Military Affairs*, no. 1588 (March 27, 1980), 64–72.

3323. "Missile Units—Training and Related Activities: Translated from *Krasnaya Zvezda*." *Translations on USSR Military Affairs*, no. 1484 (December 27, 1979), 32–52.

3324. _____. *Translations on USSR Military Affairs*, no. 1489 (January 16, 1980), 1–10.

3325. Moroz, Ivan M. "Psychological and Moral Training of Airmen Discussed: Translated from *Sovetskiy Voin*, August 1979." *Translations on USSR Military Affairs*, no. 1473 (November 6, 1979), 5–14.

3326. "'Neman' Troop Training Exercise Activities." *Translations on USSR Military Affairs*, no. 1481 (December 13, 1979), 38–88.

3327. Nikolayev, P. "Regiment Commander Describes Training: Translated from *Krasnaya Zvezda*, May 17, 1979." *Translations on USSR Military Affairs*, no. 1462 (September 7, 1979), 50–53.

3328. Pajak, Roger F. "Soviet Arms Aid in the Middle East Since the October War." In: U.S. Congress. Joint Economic Committee. *The Political Economy of the Middle East, 1973–1978: A Compendium of Papers*. 96th Cong., 2nd sess. Washington, D.C.: U.S. Government Printing Office, 1980. pp. 445–485.

3329. Pervov, A. "Wartime Maneuvering of Reserve Aviation Units Described: Translated from *Voyenno–Istoricheskiy Zhurnal*, September 1979." *Translations on USSR Military Affairs*, no. 1483 (December 20, 1979), 70–78.

Appendix I: Late Entries, to May 1980 269

3330. Popov, O. "Maintenance Procedures Described: Translated from *Krasnaya Zvezda*, May 18, 1979." *Translations on USSR Military Affairs*, no. 1462 (September 7, 1979), 55–56.

3331. Rudnyy, N. "Medical Role in Flight Training Described: Translated from *Krasnaya Zvezda*, April 13, 1979." *Translations on USSR Military Affairs*, no. 1455 (August 10, 1979), 62–66.

3332. Safronov, P. "Wartime Photoreconnaissance Operations Described: Translated from *Voyenno-Istoricheskiy Zhurnal*, May 1979." *Translations on USSR Military Affairs*, no. 1452 (July 20, 1979), 30–35.

3333. Samoylenko, Ya. "Wartime Operations—Control of Airborne Landings: Translated from *Voyenno-Istoricheskiy Zhurnal*, December 1979." *Translations on USSR Military Affairs*, no. 1588. (March 27, 1980), 20–29.

3334. Shigin, M. "In an Air Defense Missile Battalion: Translated from *Krasnaya Zvezda*, May 19, 1979." *Translations on USSR Military Affairs*, no. 1463 (September 12, 1979), 77–80.

3335. Shurygin, Vladislav. "Orenburg Aviation School Activities Described: Translated from *Sovetskiy Voin*, July 1979." *Translations on USSR Military Affairs*, no. 1473 (November 6, 1979), 14–21.

3336. Sinikov, A. "Need for Knowledge of Flight Theory and Practice Stressed: Translated from *Aviatsiya I Kosmonavtika*, July 1979." *Translations on USSR Military Affairs*, no. 1471 (October 30, 1979), 26–28.

3337. Skubilin, V. "Aviation Technical Training Aspects Discussed: Translated from *Aviatsiya I Kosmonavtika*, October 1979." *Translations on USSR Military Affairs*, no. 1490 (January 22, 1980), 29–35.

3338. Sorokin, A. "Award of Sniper Rating [to Fighter Pilots] Discussed: Translated from *Krasnaya Zvezda*, June 16, 1979." *Translations on USSR Military Affairs*, no. 1462 (September 7, 1979), 66–70.

3339. Sozinov, V. "Improving the Deployment of Air Defense Troops Discussed: Translated from *Voyenno–Istoricheskiy Zhurnal*, October 1979." *Translations on USSR Military Affairs*, no. 1487 (January 7, 1980), 19–30.

3340. Stadnikov, A. "Fuel Economy Measures in an Aviation Unit Described: Translated from *Krasnaya Zvezda*, May 5, 1979." *Translations on USSR Military Affairs*, no. 1458 (August 23, 1979), 1–4.

3341. Tolubko, Vladimir F. "Tolubko on Tasks of Strategic Rocket Forces: Translated from *Sovetskiy Voin*, November 1979." *Translations on USSR Military Affairs*, no. 1489 (January 16, 1980), 49–52.

3342. "Training of Strategic Missilemen Described: Translated from *Sovetskiy Voin*, June 1979." *Translations on USSR Military Affairs*, no. 1463 (September 12, 1979), 54–60.

3343. Tyukhtin, N. "Aviation Maintenance Personnel Training Described: Translated from *Aviatsiya I Kosmonavtika*, September 1979." *Translations on USSR Military Affairs*, no. 1477 (November 29, 1979), 19–23.

3344. United States. Air Force. *Net Assessment of USAF-SAF Fighter Pilot Training (U)*. Washington, D.C.: HQ, Department of the Air Force, 1978. 164p.

3345. Uppert, Guenter. "Capabilities of Soviet Air Defense Troops: Translated from *Soldat und Technik*, June 1979." *Translations on USSR Military Affairs*, no. 1454 (August 3, 1979), 32–36.

3346. Ushakov, S. "Organizational Development of Long-Range Aviation Described: Translated from *Aviatsiya I Kosmonavtika*, August 1979." *Translations on USSR Military Affairs*, no. 1475 (November 19, 1979), 33–37.

3347. Veksler, L. "Helicopter Assault Landing in Mountains Described: Translated from *Aviatsiya I Kosmonavtika*, August 1979." *Translations on USSR Military Affairs*, no. 1475 (November 14, 1979), 38–40.

3348. Vereykin, A. "Pilot Reconnaissance Training Described: Translated from *Aviatsiya I Kosmonavika*, August 1979." *Translations on USSR Military Affairs*, no. 1475 (November 14, 1979), 40–43.

3349. Vysotskiy, V. "Aviation Maintenance Methods and Results Described: Translated from *Aviatsiya I Kosmonavtika*, July 1979." *Translations on USSR Military Affairs*, no. 1471 (October 30, 1979), 52–57.

3350. Yermov, V. "In an Air Defense Missile Regiment: Translated from *Krasnaya Zvezda*, May 12, 1979." *Translations on USSR Military Affairs*, no. 1463 (September 12, 1979), 74–77.

Appendix II: List of Journals Consulted

*Academy of Political Science
   Proceedings
A.E.I. Round Table
Aero Album
Aero Digest
Aeronautical Engineering Review
Aeronautics
Aeroplane
Aerospace Daily
Aerospace Engineering
Aerospace Historian
Air Classics
Aircraft
Aircraft Engineering
Air Defense Magazine
Air Defense Management
Air Force
Air Force and Space Digest
Air Force Magazine
Air Force Policy Letter for
   Commanders
Air International
Airman
Air Pictorial
Air Pilot
Air Power
Air Power Historian
Air Progress
Air Trails
Air Training
Air University Quarterly Review
Air University Review*

*America
American Aviation
American Aviation Historical Society
   Journal
American Legion Magazine
American Mercury
American-Scandinavian Review
An Cosantoir
Annals of the American Academy of
   Political and Social Science
Antiaircraft Journal
Armed Forces and Society
Armed Forces Journal
Armed Forces Journal International
Armed Forces Management
Armor
Army
Army Information Digest
Army, Navy, Air Force Journal
Army Quarterly
Asian Affairs
Asian Quarterly
Asian Survey
Astronautics and Aeronautics
Atlantic
Atlantic Community Quarterly
Automotive and Aviation Industries
Aviation
Aviation Age
Aviation News
Aviation Week and Space Technology
Boeing Magazine*

Bulletin of the Atomic Scientists
Bulletin of the Institute for the Study of the History and Culture of the USSR
Business Week
Canadian-American Slavic Studies
Canadian Army Journal
Canadian Aviation
Canadian Journal of Political Science
Collier's
Commander's Digest
Comparative Politics
Congressional Digest
Contact
Cooperation and Conflict
Countermeasures
Current Digest of the Soviet Press
Current History
Data
Defense and Foreign Affairs Digest
Defense '80
Defense Monitor
Department of State Bulletin
East Asian Review
Eastern Europe
Electronic Warfare
E.M.O Digest
Far Eastern Economic Review
Field Artillery Journal
Flight
Flight Management
Flying
Flying Review International
Foreign Affairs
Foreign Policy
Fortune
Forum
Harper's
Hawk
Historian
History, Numbers and War
Illustrated London News
Impact of Science on Society
India Quarterly
Infantry
Intelligence Digest
Interavia
Interceptor
International Affairs (London)
International Affairs (Moscow)
International Defense Review
International Journal
International Security
International Security Review
International Studies Quarterly
Interplay of European-American Affairs
Israel Horizons
Joint Services Recognition Journal
Journal of Conflict Resolution
Journal of Contemporary History
Journal of Modern History
Journal of Palestine Studies
Journal of Peace Research
Journal of Politics
Journal of Social and Political Studies
Journal of the Royal Aeronautical Society
Journal of the Royal United Service Institute
Journal of the Royal United Service Institution for Defence Studies
Journal of the United Service Institution of India
Life
Look
McGill Law Journal
Macleans
Marine Corps Gazette
Mechanical Engineering
Midwest Journal of Political Science
Midwest Quarterly
Military Affairs
Military Engineer
Military Review
Missiles and Rockets
Modern Review
Moment

Appendix II: List of Journals Consulted

National Air Review
National Defense
National Guardsman
National Review
Nation's Business
NATO's Fifteen Nations
Naval Aviation News
Naval War College Review
Navy
New Middle East
New Outlook
New Republic
Newsweek
New Times (Moscow)
New York Times Biographical Service
New York Times Magazine
19th Century
Orbis
Ordnance
Pakistan Horizon
Parameters
Pegasus
Political Quarterly
Political Science Quarterly
Popular Mechanics
Popular Science
Problems of Communism
Queen's Quarterly
RAF Flying Review
RCAF Staff College Journal
Reader's Digest
Reporter
Ripon Forum
Round Table
Royal Air Forces Quarterly
Russian Review
Saturday Evening Post
Scholastic
Science Digest
Science Studies
Scientific American
Sealift
Sea Power
Signal
Skyways
Slavic Review
Social Justice Review
Soviet Literature
Soviet Military Review
Soviet Review
Soviet Studies
Space/Aeronautics
Spaceflight
Stanford Journal of International Studies
Strategic Review
Strategy and Tactics
Survey
Survival
Swiss Review of World Affairs
TAC Attack
TacAir Warfare Center Quarterly Report
TAF Review
Technology Weekly
Time
Translations on USSR Military Affairs (U.S. Department of Commerce, Joint Publications Research Service)
True
U.S. Air Force Fighter Weapons Newsletter
U.S. Army Aviation Digest
U.S. Naval Institute Proceedings
U.S. News and World Report
Vital Speeches
Washington Post Magazine
Western Flying
Wings
World Marxist Review
World Politics
World Today
Worldview
World War II Magazine

Appendix III: Selected Soviet Aerospace Biographies

IN EXAMINING THE sections on personnel it became apparent that a need existed for a compendium of Soviet aerospace biographies. Data is presented below on fifty-three individuals of varying importance, either as aerospace commanders, pilots, or designers, during our period. Due to unevenness of source material, some biographies are more complete than others.

Abbreviations

A: award
ADD: Long-Ranger (bomber) Aviation, World War II
as: aerospace service
bttn: battalion
CC: Central Committee
Cent: Central
Chmn: Chairman
Cmte: Committee
CO: Commanding Officer
Col: Colonel
Col.Gen: Colonel General
convoc: convocation
CoS: Chief of Staff
CP: Communist Party
CPSU: Communist Party of the Soviet Union
DA: Long Range (bomber) Aviation Command
DC: Deputy Commander
del: delegate
dep: deputy
dept: department
distr: district

div: division
ed: education
FDC: First Deputy Commander
flt: flight
GU-VVS: Soviet Army Air Force
HQ: Headquarters
Mjr: Major
Mjr. Gen: Major General
O: Order of
po: Party offices/political officer
PVO-Strany: National Air Defense Force
r: rank (final or most recent)
regt: regiment
ret: retirement or retired
so: staff officer
sqn: squadron
SRF: Strategic Rocket Forces
Supr. Sov: Supreme Soviet
VTA: Military Air Transport Command
VVS: Soviet Air Force

Filipp A. Agaltsov

b: 1900
ed: Graduate, Military–Political Academy, 192–
as: Joined Red Army 1919 and fought in Civil War, 1919–1921; soldier/officer, CO, various units, 1921–1937; CO, regt, Spanish Civil War, 1938–1939; CO, air regt, div, corps, participant in Battle of Kursk (1943), 1941–1945; CO, air corps and DC, VVS, 1946–1962; CO, DA, 1962–1969; Inspector–Advisor, Inspectors General Group, USSR Ministry of Defense, 1969–
r: Marshal of Aviation
A: O Lenin; other decorations and medals
po: Member, CPSU, 1919; DC, GU-VVS for Political Affairs, 1937–1938

Yevgeniy N. Andreev

b: 1926
ed: Graduate, Airborne Forces School, 1955
as: Joined Soviet Army, 1943; parachute tester, made over 1,500 drops, including one of 25,458 meters from the stratostat "Volga" (1962), 1944–1966; no information after 1967
r: Col, Soviet Army
A: Hero of the Soviet Union

Sergey N. Anokhin

b: Moscow, 1910
ed: Graduate, Moscow Gliding School, 193–.
as: Joined GU-VVS, 1930; parachute and glider instructor, 1936–1945; pioneer jet aircraft test pilot, 1945–1962; no information after 1962
r: Col of Aviation
A: Hero of the Soviet Union; Hon. Test Pilot; Hon. Master of Parachute and Gliding Sports; O Lenin; other decorations and medals

Oleg K. Antonov

b: Troitsry, Moscow Region, February 7, 1906
ed: Graduate, Gliding School, 1926; Aviation Facility, Leningrad Polytechnical Institute, 1930

as: Dep Chief Designer, then Chief Designer, Tushino Glider Construction Plant, 1930–1936; Chmn, Commission for the Inspection of Design Offices, Plants, and Gliding Schools, 1936–1941; civil aircraft and glider designer for Special Purpose Aviation, 1941–1945; Head, Experimental Design Dept, USSR Ministry of Aviation Industries, 1946–1961; Designer General, USSR Ministry of Aircraft Industries, 1962–.
A: Stalin Prize; Lenin Prize; Hero of Socialist Labor; O the Red Banner of Labor; O Lenin (2); Hammer and Sickle Gold Medal; other honors
po: Member, CPSU, 1945; dep, USSR Supr. Sov of 1958 convoc

Aleksandr A. Arkhangelsky

b: 1892
ed: Graduate, Moscow Higher Technical School, 1918
as: Central Institute of Aerodynamics and Hydrodynamics, 1918–1933; toured aviation plants in U.S., 1933; headed the engineering group which designed and built the SB bomber, 1934; Acting Chief Designer, Experimental Aircraft Construction Plant, Central Institute of Aerodynamics and Hydrodynamics, 1935–1941; Chief Designer, Kazan Bomber Plant, 1942–1947; participated in jet bomber and jet passenger plane development, 1947–1955; Dep Designer General, Experimental Design Bureau, USSR Ministry of Aviation Industries, 1955–; no information after 1960
A: Hon. Science and Technical Worker of RSFSR; O Lenin (3); Stalin Prize (2); Hero of Socialist Labor; O the Red Banner of Labor

Pavel F. Batitskiy

b: Kharkov, 1910
ed: Graduate, Calavry School, 1929; Frunze Military Academy, 1938; Academy of the General Staff, 1948
as: Joined Soviet Army, 1924; CoS, 26th Infantry Div, then CO, 128th Infantry Corps, serving on Northwest, Voronezh, 1st and 2nd Ukrainian, and Belorussian Fronts, 1941–1945; CoS of an air defense region, 1948–1950; Chief of Main Staff and DC, VVS, 1950–1953; FDC, Moscow Military Distr, 1953–1954; CO, Moscow Air Defense Distr, 1954–1965; FDC of General Staff, USSR Armed Forces, 1965–1966; CO, PVO-Strany and Dep USSR Minister of Defense, 1966–1978; ret 1978
fr: Marshal of the Soviet Union
A: Hero of the Soviet Union; O Lenin (4); O Kutuzov (2); O Suvorov, 2nd Cl.; O the Red Banner (5); other decorations

po: Member, CPSU, 1938; dep, RSFSR Supr. Sov of 1959 convoc; dep, USSR Supr. Sov of 1962–1978 convoc; del at 1956, 1959, and 1961 CPSU Congresses; member of Moscow City CPSU Cmte, 1958 and 1960; cand. member, CC, CPSU, 1961–1966; member, CC, CPSU, 1966–1978.

Sergei A. Bobylev

b: Lenino, Kalinin Oblast, 1922
ed: Unknown
as: Soviet Army po, 1941–1945; po, then DC of Pol. Admin. at Main Party HQ, then chief of a political dept in a military academy, then Chief, Political Dept in the Pol. Admin., Kiev Military Distr, then FDC, Pol. Admin. of the Leningrad Military Distr and of the Soviet Army in East Germany, 1945–1971; member of the Military Council and Chief of Pol. Admin., Leningrad Military Distr, 1971–1975; DC of Pol. Admin. (for PVO-Strany), HQ of Soviet Army and Navy, 1975–
r: Col. Gen, Soviet Army
po: Member, CPSU, 1941; dep to Supr. Sov RSFSR, 1975–

Anatolii I. Brandys

b: Nizhnedneprovsk, August 1923
ed: Graduate, War Flying School, 1943; Air Force Academy, 1950; Academy of the General Staff, 1959
as: Joined Soviet Army, 1941; frontline soldier, then pilot, various fronts, 1941–1945; so and later professor at various military academies, 1945–1977
r: Col, VVS
A: Hero of the Soviet Union (2): O Lenin; O the Red Banner (4); other decorations
po: Member, CPSU, 1944

Yuri A. Gagarin

b: Gzhatsk Rayon, 1934
ed: Graduate, trade school, 1951; Saratov Aeroclub, 1955; Orenburg Military Aviation School, 1957
as: Joined VVS, 1957; fighter pilot, various sqn, 1958–1959; cosmonaut training, 1959–1961; first manned orbital flt in Vostok I, 1961; goodwill

ambassador to various countries, 1961–1964; killed in crash of MIG-15 trainer, 1968
r: Flt Mjr; Space Pilot, Class I
A: Hero of the Soviet Union; Tsilokovsky Gold Medal; Gold Medal of the International Aviation Federation; Gruenwald Cross, Cl.I; Hero of Socialist Labor; Hon. Master of Sport of the USSR; other decorations
po: Member, CPSU, 1960; dep, USSR Supr. Sov of 1962 convoc; member, CC, All-Union Komsomol, 1962

Dimitriy B. Glinka

b: Dnepropetrovsk Oblast, 1917
ed: Graduate, Air Force Academy, 1945
as: Joined Soviet Army, 1937; fighter pilot on Crimean, Southern, North-Caucasian, 4th, 2nd, and 1st Ukrainian Fronts, flying 350 combat sorties and shooting down 56 aircraft, 1941–1945; attended World Conference of Democratic Youth, 1945; ret 1946
r: Col, VVS
A: Hero of the Soviet Union (2); other decorations
po: Member, CPSU, 1942; dep USSR Supr. Sov of 1946 convoc

Aleksandr Y. Golovanov

b: 1903
ed: Civil Air Fleet Pilot's School, 1930
as: Joined Red Army and fought in Civil War, 1918–1921; platoon and company CO and chief in a CHEKA courier section, 1921–1927; pilot on special assignments, 1931–1934; pilot for senior CPSU and govt. officials, 1934–1935; CO, special aircraft detachment, Northeast Siberia concentration camp admin., 1935–1936; pilot for eminent CPSU and govt. officials, 1937; FDC, then Head, Mobilization Dept, Main Board, Civil Air Fleet, 1938–1941; joined GU-VVS, 1940; CO, Long Range Aviation, later reorganized as 18th Air Army, taking part in Belorussian, Koenigsburg, and Hungarian operations, 1942–1945; CO, DA, 1946–1953; removed from office, 1953; no later information
r: Chief Marshal of Aviation
A: Thirteen medals and decorations
po: Member, CPSU, 192–

Petr. A. Gorchakov

b: 1917
ed: Graduate, Military–Political Leningrad Academy, 1954
as: Joined Soviet Army, 1938; secretary of a party bureau of a regt, war commisar, CO of a regt for political affairs, head of pol. dept of a rifle div on the Briansk, Central, and 4th Ukrainian Fronts, 1941–1945; head, pol. dept, of various associations; FDC of pol. admin. of a mil. distr; member, Military Council and Head of Pol. Admin., Baltic Provinces Military Distr, 1945–1970; DC of Pol. Admin. (for SRF), HQ of Soviet Army and Navy, 1970–
r: Col. Gen, Red Army
A: Hero of the Soviet Union; other decorations
po: Member, CPSU, 1939; member, CC, Latvian CP, 1966–1971; dep to USSR Supr. Sov of 1970 convoc; cand. member, CC, CPSU, 1971–

Mikhail M. Gromov

b: 1899
ed: Red Army Aviation School, 1918
as: Instructor, Moscow Air Force School, 1918–1921; test and experimental flyer, made several record-breaking flts, including 1937 Moscow–North Pole–San Jacinto route, 1921–1941; CO, long-range air corps on Kalinin Front, 1942–1943; CO, 1st Air Army, 1943–1945; test pilot, 1945–ret; no information after 1967
r: Col. Gen of Aviation
A: Hero of the Soviet Union; O Lenin (4); other medals and decorations
po: Member, CPSU, 1941

Mikhail I. Gurevich

b: 1893
ed: Graduate, Aircraft Construction Facility, Kharkov Technical Institute, 1925
as: Aircraft designer, 1933–1937; Dep Chief Designer, Moscow Aircraft Plant No. 1, then dep to A. I. Mikoyan, Director and Chief Designer, Experimental Design Bureau, USSR Ministry of Aviation Industries, 1937–1976; with Mikoyan designed all early MIG fighters; died November 1976
A: O Lenin; Stalin Prize (4); other decorations

Aleksandr S. Iakovlev

b: 1906
ed: Graduate, N. E. Zhukovskiy Air Force Academy, 1931
as: Worker in shops of the Zhukovskiy Academy, 1924–1927; engineer in an aircraft plant, factory head and head of a main admin. unit, USSR Ministry of Aircraft Industries, 1931–1957; Chief Designer of USSR Ministry of Aircraft Industries, 1957–; no information after 1976
r: Col. Gen Engineering Technical Services
A: Stalin Prize (6); O Lenin (8); O the Red Banner; other decorations
po: Member, CPSU, 1938; dep to USSR Supr. Sov of 1946 convoc

Sergey V. Ilyushin

b: Vil. of Dilyalevo, March 1894
ed: Graduate, flying school, 1917; Zhukovskiy Air Force Academy, 1926
as: Private hangar worker, mechanic, Russian and Red Armies, 1914–1919; pilot, GU-VVS, 1919–1925; Director, Aircraft Construction Section, Science and Technical Cmte, Main Air Force Board, and Asst. Chief, Air Force Test Institute, 1926–1936; Chief, Experimental Aircraft Construction Board, USSR Pop. Cmte of Aviation Industries, 1936–1947, and designed the famous IL-2 aircraft; Prof., Zhukovskiy Air Force Engineering Academy, 1948–1956; Designer General, State Cmte on Aviation Engineering, USSR Council of Ministers and Member, USSR Academy of Sciences, 1957–1977; died February 1977
r: Col. Gen of Engineering Technical Services
A: Hero of Socialist Labor (2); Stalin Prize (7); O Lenin (7); Lenin Prize; other decorations and medals
po: Member, CPSU, 1918

Nikolay P. Kamanin

b: Vladimir Oblast, 1909
ed: Graduate, Zhukovskiy Air Force Academy, 1938
as: Joined Soviet Army, 1927; CO, air detachment, 1933; CO, air unit which helped save the crew of the icebreaker *Chelyuskin*, 1934; so, various air units, 1934–1941; CO, air corps of 2nd Air Army, 1941–1945; FDC, DOSAAF, 1953–1958; Director, Space Pilot Training, 1959–ret; no information after 1965
r: Lt. Gen of Aviation
A: Hero of the Soviet Union; O Lenin; other decorations
po: Member, CPSU, 193–

Vladimir K. Kokkinaki

b: Novorossiysk, June 1904
ed: Graduate, Borisoglebsk Flying School, 1929
as: Joined Soviet Army, 1925; soldier, 1925–1927; transferred to GU-VVS, 1927; fighter pilot, instructor, flt CO, test pilot for some 100 aircraft of new design, (made non-stop [1938] Moscow–Khabarovsk–Vladivostok) 1931–1965; test pilot and chief inspector, USSR Ministry of Aviation Industries, 1941–1945; Head, Testing Service, USSR Ministry of Aviation Industries, 1945–1965; instructor for test pilots and Chmn, USSR Federation of Air Sports, 1965–
r: Mjr. Gen of Aviation
A: Hero of the Soviet Union (2); O Lenin (5); O the Red Banner (3); O the Red Star (4); other decorations and medals
po: Member, CPSU, 1938; dep USSR Supr. Sov of 1937 and 1946 convoc

Aleksandr I. Koldunov

b: September 1923
ed: Graduate, Kachinskaia Air Force School, 1941; Military Air Academy, 1952; Academy of the General Staff, 1960
as: Joined Soviet Army, 1941; fighter pilot, later, CO of a flying unit and sqn on Southwestern and 3rd Ukrainian Fronts, and shot down 46 enemy aircraft, 1941–1945; CO, various fighter aviation units, 1946–1952; CO of an air regt, 1952–1960; FDC, Baku Air Defense Distr (PVO), 1960–1969; attached to USSR Ministry of Defense, 1969; CO, Moscow Air Defense Distr (PVO), 1970–1975; FDC, PVO-Strany, 1975–1978; CO, PVO-Strany and Dep USSR Minister of Defense, 1978–
r: Marshal of Aviation
A: Hero of the Soviet Union (2); other decorations and medals
po: Member, CPSU, 1944; can. member, CC, CPSU, 1971–1978; member, CC, CPSU, 1978–

Ivan N. Kozhedub

b: Obrazheevska, Sumy Oblast, June 1920
ed: Graduate, Chushchevsk Military Flying School, 1941; Command Facility, Zhukovskiy Air Force Academy, 1949; Voroshilov Gen. Staff Higher Military Academy, 1956
as: Flt instructor, Chushchevsk Military Flying School, 1941–1942;

fighter pilot, air sqn and regt CO on Kursk, Dnieper, Korsun-Shevchenko, Jassy-Kishinev, Berlin operations and on 2nd Baltic Front, flew 330 sorties, took part in 120 air battles, and shot down 62 enemy aircraft, became the top allied ace of the war, 1941–1945; fighter pilot and so, various VVS Guards air units, 1945–1955; VVS Inspector of Flt Training, 1956–1973; Chmn Aero Sports Federation, 1972–1978; Military Inspector–Advisor of Inspectors General Group, USSR Ministry of Defense, 1978–
r: Col. Gen of Aviation
A: Hero of the Soviet Union (3); O the Red Banner (7); O Lenin; O the Red Star (2); other medals and decorations
po: Member, CPSU, 1943; dep USSR Supr. Sov 1946 convoc

Stepan A. Krasovsky

b: Glukhi, Mogilev District, August 1897
ed: Graduate, Zhukovskiy Air Force Engineering Academy, 1936
as: Po and so in various Red Army air detachments, 1918–1921; CO, Ivanov–Voznesensky Air Detachment, Moscow Military Distr, 1927–1934; CO, dive-bomber brig. and later CO, 147th High-Speed Air Brig., Leningrad Military Distr, 1934–1938; briefly removed from CO during purges, but restored as CO, Murmansk Air Brig. and Murmansk air region, 1938; CO, air forces of the 14th Army in the Russo–Finnish War, 1939–1940; FDC, Air Forces, North Caucasian Military Distr, 1940–1941; CO, Air Forces, 56th Army, 1941–1942; CO, 2nd Air Army, then CO, Air Forces, Southwestern Front, 1942–1943; CO, 2nd Air Army, 1943–1945; CO, air forces of various military distr, incl. Kiev and Belorussia, 1945–1956; Head, Gagarin Air Force Academy, 1956–1968; attached to USSR Ministry of Defense, 1968–1976; no information after 1976
r: Marshal of Aviation
A: Hero of the Soviet Union; O Lenin (6); O the Red Banner (3); O Suvorov 1st and 2nd Cl.; O the Red Star; other decorations and medals
po: Member, CPSU, 1918; dep Ukr. Supr. Sov of 1947 convoc; voting del, 1956 and 1961 CPSU Congresses; member, Central Auditing Commission, CPSU, 1961

Nikolay I. Krylov

b: 1903
ed: Secondary
as: Soldier, Russian Civil War, 1919–1921; so in the Far East, 1921–1938;

CO, infantry div, 1939–1941; CoS, Odessa Fortified Area and 1st Black Sea Army, 1941–1942; CoS, 62nd Army, 1942–1943; CO, 21st Army on the Western Front, 1943; CO, 5th Army on the Belorussian Front, 1944; so, Far Eastern Front, 1945; CO, Special Army Group on Sakhalin and Kurile Islands and FDC, Far Eastern Military Distr, 1945–1955; CO, Urals Military Distr, 1955–1957; CO, Leningrad Military Distr, 1957–1960, headed a military del (1958) to Sweden; CO, Moscow Military Distr, 1960–1963; CO, SRF and USSR Dep Minister of Defense, 1963–1972; died January 1972
r: Marshal of the Soviet Union
A: Hero of the Soviet Union (2); O Lenin (4); O the Red Banner (4); other decorations and medals
po: Member, CPSU, 1927; dep USSR Supr. Sov of 1950, 1954, 1958, 1962–1972 convoc; voting del at 1956, 1959, and 1961 CPSU Congresses; member, CC, CPSU, 1961–1972

Pavel S. Kutakhov

b: August 16, 1914
ed: Graduate, Military School for Pilots, 1938; Higher Officers' Tactical Flying Course, 1949; Academy of the General Staff, 1957
as: Joined Soviet Army, 1935; Flt CO, Russo–Finnish War, 1939–1940; fighter sqn and regt CO on the Karelian Front, flew 367 sorties, took part in 63 air battles, shot down 14 aircraft alone, and 24 with assists, 1941–1945; various so positions in military distr, 1946–1964; air force CO, Odessa Military Distr, 1965–1966; so, USSR Ministry of Defense, 1967–1968; FDC, VVS, 1968–1969; CO, VVS and Dep USSR Ministry of Defense, 1969–
r: Chief Marshal of Aviation
A: Hero of the Soviet Union; Gold Star Medal; O Lenin; other decorations
po: Member, CPSU, 1942; dep USSR Supr. Sov of 1969 convoc; member, CC, CPSU, 1971–

Aleksandr I. Makarevsky

b: Mushkovichi, Smolensk Oblast, April 1904
ed: Graduate, Bauman Technical College, 1929
as: Member, eng. staff, Central Aerodynamical Institute, 1927–1950; Director, Central Aerodynamical Institute, 1950–1960; instructor, Moscow Physical–Technical Institute, 1969–

A: Hero of Socialist Labor; O Lenin (3); other decorations
po: Member, CPSU, 1943

Aleksey P. Maresev

b: Volgograd Oblast, 1916
ed: Graduate, School for Military Pilots, 1940; Higher Party School, 1952
as: Flt CO in air regt, Volkhov Front, 1941–1942; in mil. hospital for amputation of both legs, 1942–1943; sqn CO in Guards air regt and credited with 15 air combat victories, 1943–1945; member, Soviet del to 1st and 2nd World Congresses of Peace Partisans, 1949–1950; member, Soviet del to Congress of the Internat'l Fed. of the Resistance Movement, 1954; member, Soviet Cmte for the Defense of Peace, 1954–1955; Exec. Secr. and Presidium member, Soviet War Veterans Cmte, 1956–; no information after 1960
r: Mjr, VVS (ret)
A: Hero of the Soviet Union; O Lenin; other decorations and medals
po: Member, CPSU, 1944

Artom I. Mikoyan

b: Vil. of Sanain, 1905
ed: Graduate, Zhukovskiy Air Force Engineering Academy, 1936
as: Designer and head of a design section and bureau, 1937–1958, designed MIG fighters with M. I. Gurevich (q.v.); visited Germany to study Nazi aircraft construction methods, 1945; Designer-in-Chief, State Cmte for Aircraft Engineering, USSR Council of Ministers, 1958–1970; died December 1970
r: Mjr. Gen Engineering Technical Services
A: O Lenin (4); Hero of Socialist Labor (2); Stalin Prize (3); other decorations
po: Member, CPSU, 1925

Aleksandr A. Mikulin

b: February 1895
ed: Unknown
as: Aircraft designer, 1923–1925; Chief Designer (aircraft engines), Institute of Automobile Engines, 1925–1942; general aircraft engine

designer, 1943– with emphasis on jet propulsion after 1946; no information after 1965
r: Mjr. Gen Engineering–Technical Troops
A: Stalin Prize (4); O Lenin (3); other decorations and medals
po: Member, CPSU, 1954

Mikhail L. Mil

b: 1906
ed: Graduate, Aircraft Construction Facility, Moscow Higher Technical School, 1930
as: Junior engineer, engineer, senior engineer, Experimental Aerodynamics Division, Central Aerohydrodynamics Institute, 1930–1939; designer, Experimental Design Bureau, Moscow Aviation Institute, 1940–1947; Chief Designer and Director, Experimental Design Bureau for Helicopter Construction, State Cmte for Aviation Engineering, USSR Council of Ministers, 1947–1970; died January 1970
A: Lenin Prize; other decorations
po: Member, CPSU, 1930

Kirill S. Moskalenko

b: Vil. of Grishino, April 1902
ed: Graduate, Dzerzhinsky Artillery Academy
as: Cadet, troop and battery CO, 1920–1936; CO, artillery regt, 1937–1940; brig., corps, then army CO, 1941; CO, 1st Guards Army, Stalingrad Front, 1942; CO, 40th Army, Voronezh Front, 1942–1943; CO, 38th Army, 1st and 4th Ukrainian Fronts, 1944–1945; so, Moscow Military Distr, 1945–1953; CO, Moscow Military Distr and Moscow Garrison, 1953–1960; CO, SRF and Dep USSR Minister of Defense, 1960–1962; Chief Main Inspectorate, USSR Ministry of Defense, 1962; Dep USSR Minister of Defense, 1966–
r: Marshal of the Soviet Union
A: Hero of the Soviet Union; O Lenin (5); O the Red Banner (5); other decorations and medals
po: Member, CPSU, 1926; dep USSR Supr. Sov of 1946, 1950, 1954, 1958, and 1962 convoc; member, CC, CPSU, 1956–1962

Georgiy K. Mosolov

b: 1927
ed: Graduate, Air Force School, 1948; Moscow Air Force Institute, 1959
as: Flying instructor, 1958–1961; test pilot, set height and speed records in E-66 aircraft (1962), 1951–1962; briefly in hospital for crash injuries, 1962; 1961–1963–ret; no information after 1967
r: Col, VVS
A: Hero of the Soviet Union; O Lenin (2); other decorations
po: Member, CPSU, 195–

Vasiliy V. Okunev

b: 1921
ed: Graduate, Dzerzhinski Artillery School, 1950; Academy of the General Staff, 1961
as: Joined Soviet Army, 1936; soldier and officer, CO of an antiaircraft tank sqn and CO of an antiaircraft div, 1936–1944; CO of an artillery regt, CoS, FDC, and CO of various antiaircraft units, div, and distr, 1944–1966; CO, Moscow Antiaircraft Defense Distr (PVO), 1966–1970; CO, Soviet SAM Expeditionary Corps in Egypt, 1970–1972; attached to USSR Ministry of Defense, 1972–1974; FDC USSR Antiaircraft Defense Troops (PVO), 1974–1976; ret, 1976
r: Col. Gen, Soviet Army
A: O the Red Banner; other decorations and medals
po: Member, CPSU, 1941; cand. member, CC, CPSU, 1971–1976; Dep USSR Supr. Sov of 1970–1976 convoc; del CPSU Congresses, 1966–1971; member, Cent. Auditing Commission, CPSU, 1966–1971

Georgiy N. Pakilev

b: Unknown
ed: Unknown
as: CO, VTA of VVS, 1969–; author of book *Soviet Military Transport Aviation*, 1974; piloted VTA An-22 in record-breaking flt, 1975; no other information available
r: Col. Gen of Aviation

Aleksandr I. Pokryshkin

b: Novosibirsk, 1913
ed: Graduate, Perm. Aviation Engineering School, 1933; Advanced Training School for Aviation Personnel, 1934; Kacha Aviation Flying School, 1939; Frunze Military Academy, 1940; Academy of the General Staff, 1957
as: Joined Soviet Army, 1932; flt aviation mechanic, Krasnodoe, 1934–1936; fighter sqn, regt, div CO in Caucasus and on 1st and 2nd and 4th Ukrainian Fronts, engaged in 156 air battles and shot down 59 enemy aircraft, 1941–1945; so and CO in PVO-Strany, 1945–1971; Chmn, DOSAAF, 1972–
r: Marshal of Aviation
A: Hero of the Soviet Union (3); O Lenin (3); O the Red Banner (4); other decorations and medals
po: Member, CPSU, 1942; dep USSR Supr. Sov of 1946 convoc; cand. member, CC, CPSU, 1976–; member, Commission for Foreign Affairs, Soviet of Nationalities, USSR Supr. Sov of 1958; del at 1959 and 1961 CPSU Congresses; member, USSR Supr. Sov del to France, 1964; member, CC, Ukrainian CP, 1960–1971

Aleksei N. Prokhorov

b: Rozhdestvenskoe, Voronezh Oblast, January 1923
ed: Graduate, Balashov Military Flying School, 1942; Air Force Academy, 1950
as: Joined Soviet Army, 1941; flew 238 combat missions for GU-VVS, 1941–1945; so, VVS, 1945–1966; teacher, 1967–
r: Col, VVS (ret)
A: O the Red Banner (3); O Lenin; O the Red Star (2); other medals
po: Member, CPSU, 1943

Vasiliy V. Reshetnikov

b: Unknown
ed: Unknown
as: Bomber pilot, GU-VVS, 1941–1945; so, DA, 1945–1963; CO, div of 2nd Long Range Air Army, 1963–1968; CO, DA of VVS, 1969–
r: Col. Gen of Aviation
A: Hero of the Soviet Union; Hon. Military Pilot of the USSR; other medals
po: Member, CPSU, 194–

Aleksei K. Riazanov

b: Kochetovka, Tambov Oblast, February 1920
ed: Graduate, V. P. Chkalov Aviation School, 1939; Frunze Military Academy, 1950; Academy of the General Staff, 1958
as: Joined Soviet Army, 1938; pilot, flt CO, FDC 4th Fighter Air Regt, 1941–1945, flew 509 sorties downing 31 German aircraft alone and 16 with assists; so, VVS, 1945–1962; FDC, PVO-Strany, 1962–1976; ret, 1976
r: Col. Gen of Aviation
A: O Lenin (3); O the Red Banner (4); O the Red Star (2); other decorations and medals
po: Member, CPSU, 1942

Sergey I. Rudenko

b: Korop, Chernigov Oblast, October 1904
ed: Graduate, First Military Aviation School, 1927; Zhukovskiy Air Force Academy, 1932; Special Course, Zhukovskiy Air Force Academy, 1936
as: Joined Soviet Army, 1923; fighter pilot, 1927–1930; CO, sqn, brig., airborne div, 1936–1941; CO, air force of the 61st Army, 1941; FDC, air forces of the Kalinin, Volkhov, and Southwestern Fronts, 1942; CO, 16th Air Army at the Stalingrad, Don, Cent Belorussian and 1st Belorussian Fronts, 1942–1945; CO, 1st Air Army in East Germany, 1945–1949; CoS, VVS, 1949–1950; CO, DA and DC, VVS, 1950–1953; CoS and later FDC, VVS, 1953–1969; Head, Gagarin Air Force Academy, 1968–1973; Military Inspector–Advisor of Inspectors General Group, USSR Ministry of Defense, 1973–1978; no information after 1978
r: Marshal of Aviation
A: Hero of the Soviet Union; O Lenin (5); O the Red Banner (4); Suvorov Order, 1st and 2nd Cl.; other decorations and medals
po: Member, CPSU, 1928; dep, USSR Supr. Sov of 1946 and 1962 convoc; dep, RSFSR Supr. Sov of 1955 and 1959 convoc; del, 1961–1966 CPSU Congresses; cand. member, CC, CPSU, 1961–1966

Andrey G. Rytov

b: Unknown
ed: Unknown
as: Bttn CO, Spanish Civil War, 1937–1938; attached to 2nd Air Army,

1941–1945; po, various mil. distr 1945–1955; head, pol. board, VVS, 1955–1959; Dep Head, Main Pol. Board of the Soviet Army and Navy, 1959–1967; died 1967
r: Col. Gen of Aviation
A: O Lenin; other decorations
po: Member, CPSU, 194–; dep, USSR Supr. Sov of 1962 convoc; del at 1961 CPSU Congress; cand. member, CC, CPSU, 1961–1967

Afanasiy F. Shcheglov

b: 1912
ed: Graduate, Frunze Military Academy and Academy of the General Staff
as: Joined Soviet Army, 1929; CO, regt, div, army corps, 1941–1945; so and field CO, various mil. distr, 1945–1959; CO, Baku Air Defense Distr (PVO), 1960–1965; FDC, PVO-Strany, 1966–1976; ret 1976
r: Gen, Soviet Army
A: Hero of the Soviet Union; O Lenin; other decorations and medals
po: Member, CPSU, 1939; dep, Ukr. Supr. Sov of 1955 and 1959 convoc; dep, USSR Supr. Sov of 1962 convoc; del, at 1956, 1959, 1966–1976 CPSU Congresses; cand. member, CC Azar CP, 1960–1964; member, CC, Azar CP, 1964–1965

Grigoriy F. Sivkov

b: 1921
ed: Graduate, Zhukovskiy Air Force Academy, 1940; Air Force Engineering Academy, 1952
as: Joined Soviet Army, 1939; pilot, flt and sqn CO, completed 243 missions, 1941–1945; eng. so, various mil. distr, 1945–1951; teaching associate, Zhukovskiy Air Force Engineering Academy, 1952–; no information after 1967
r: Col, Engineering Technical Troops
A: Hero of the Soviet Union (2); O Lenin; other decorations and medals
po: Member, CPSU, 1943

Nikolay S. Skripko

b: Bolderaia, near Riga, November 1902
ed: Graduate, Military Pilot's School, 1927; GU-VVS Higher Tactical

Flying School, 1938; Advanced Course, Voroshilov Higher Military Academy, 1950
as: Joined Soviet Army and fought in Civil War, 1919–1921; instructor and CO, air units, regt, div, and 3rd Aviation Corps, 1927–1941; CO, air force of the 5th Army and FDC of air force on the Southwestern Front and ADD, 1941–1945; FDC, DA, 1946–1949; CO, VTA and Air Landing Forces, later, Head, Military Transportation Aviation Dept, VVS Main Board, 1950–1955; CO, VTA, 1955–1969; Military Inspector–Advisor, Inspectors General Group, USSR Ministry of Defense, 1969–; no information after 1975
r: Marshal of Aviation
A: O Lenin (2); O the Red Banner (5); O Suvorov, 1st and 2nd Cl.; other decorations and medals
po: Member, CPSU, 1927; dep, USSR Supr. Sov of 1962 convoc; del at 1961–1966 CPSU Congresses; member, Central Auditing Commission, CPSU, 1961–1966

Ivan S. Stepanenko

b: 1920
ed: Graduate, Military Flying School, 1941; Frunze Military Academy, 1949; Academy of the General Staff, 195–
as: Joined Soviet Army, 1940; flt and sqn CO, Southern, Bryansk, North Caucasian, 2nd Baltic, and Leningrad Fronts, took part in 112 air battles and shot down 32 enemy aircraft, 1941–1945; so, VVS, 1945–ret; no information after 1967
r: Maj. Gen of Aviation
A: Hero of the Soviet Union (2); O Lenin; other decorations and medals
po: Member, CPSU, 1942

Vladimir A. Sudets

b: Nizhnedneprovsk, October 1904
ed: Graduate, GU-VVS Military Technical School, 1927; Military Flying School, 1929; Academy of the General Staff, 1950
as: Joined Soviet Army, 1925; pilot, flt and sqn CO, 1929–1938; so, main admin., GU-VVS, 1938–1939; CoS, air div, Russo-Finnish War, 1939–1940; CO, air regt, 1941; CO, air div, 1941–1942; CO, fighter air corps, 1942–1943; CO, 17th Air Army, 1943–1945; Chief of Main Staff and DC, VVS, 1946–1949; CO, Higher Air Force Officers' Course, then CO, air army, 1951–1955; FDC, VVS, 1955–1958; CA, DA, 1955–1962;

292   *Appendix III: Selected Soviet Aerospace Biographies*

CO, PVO-Strany and USSR Dep Minister of Defense, 1962–1966; Military Inspector–Advisor of Inspectors General Group, USSR Ministry of Defense, 1966–
r: Marshal of Aviation
A: Hero of the Soviet Union; O the Red Banner (5); O Lenin (4); O Suvorov; 1st and 2nd Cl.; other orders, decorations, and medals
po: Member, CPSU, 1924; member, CC, Belorussian CP, 1954–1956; del at 1956 CPSU Congress; dep, RSFSR Supr. Sov of 1959 convoc, dep at USSR Supr. Sov of 1962–1966 convoc; cand. member, CC, CPSU, 1961–1966

Pavel O. Sukhoi

b: 1895
ed: Graduate, Moscow Higher Technical School, 1925
as: Draftsman, designer, section head, and Deputy Chief Designer, Dept of Experimental Aircraft Construction, Moscow Center, Aerodynamics Institute, 1924–1933; Head, Section for Designing Experimental Record Long-Range Aircraft, Experimental Design Bureau No. 46, 1932–1955; Director, Joint Design Bureau, State Cmte for Aviation Engineering, USSR Council of Ministers, 1955–1975; died September 1975
A: O Lenin (2); Stalin Prize (2); Hero of Socialist Labor
po: Member, CPSU, 193–; dep, USSR Supr. Sov of 1958 and 1962 convoc

Pavel A. Taran

b: 1916
ed: Graduate, Military Flying School, 1938; Academy of the General Staff, 1957.
as: Joined Soviet Army, 1937; pilot, Russo–Finnish War, 1939–1940; flt and sqn CO, Ukrainian and Baltic areas, 1941–1945; so, VVS, 1945– ret; no information after 1960
r: Maj. Gen of Aviation
A: Hero of the Soviet Union (2); O Lenin; other decorations and medals
po: Member, CPSU, 1942

Appendix III: Selected Biographies

Vladimir F. Tolubko

b: Krasnograd, November 25, 1914
ed: Graduate, Academy of Tank and Armored Troops, 1941; Academy of the General Staff, 1951; Higher Course, Academy of the General Staff, 1968
as: Joined Soviet Army, 1932; soldier, officer cadet, tank, platoon, company CO, 1932-1938; tank sqn CO, CoS of a tank div, CO of a tank brig., and CoS of a tank corps on the Leningrad, Kalinin, and 3rd Ukrainian Fronts, 1941-1945; CoS of a div, CoS and FDC of a corps, aide to the Supr. CO, Soviet Forces in Germany, then CO of an army, 1946-1960; FDC, SRF, 1960-1968; CO, Siberian Military Distr, 1968; CO, Far Eastern Military Distr, 1969-1972; CO, SRF and Dep USSR Minister of Defense, 1972-
r: General of the Army
A: O Lenin (2); O the Red Banner (4); O the Red Star(2); other decorations, orders, and medals
po: Member, CPSU, 1939; dep, USSR Supr. Sov of 1970 convoc; cand. member, CC, CPSU, 1971-1976; member, CC, CPSU, 1976-

Aleksei A. Tupolev

b: Moscow, May 1925, son of A. N. Tupolev (q.v.)
ed: Graduate, Moscow Aviation Institute, 1949
as: Member of design bureau headed by A. N. Tupolev, 1950-1963; professor, 1964-
A: Stalin Prize; O Lenin (3); other orders and decorations
po: Member, CPSU, 1959

Andrey N. Tupolev

b: Vil. of Pustomazovo, January 15, 1888
ed: Graduate, Moscow Higher Technical School, 1918
as: Dep Director and founder of the Central Aerohydrodynamics Institute of Moscow, 1918-1935; Director, Design Bureau, Central Aerohydrodynamics Institute, 1922-1938; visited Britain as a guest of the Royal Air Force, 1934; visited Germany and U.S. to study aircraft construction, 1936; accused of "divulging aviation secrets" to Germany, arrested, and jailed, 1937-1939; while in prison, designed dive bomber, 1938-1939; released and returned to his design bureau, 1939; visited Britain twice in 1956; responsible for over 100 aircraft designs, includ-

ing the TU-4 based on interned U.S. B-29s and Russia's first jet airliner, the TU-104; died December 1972
r: Lt. Gen of Engineering Technical Troops
A: O Lenin (8); O Suvorov, 2nd Cl.; O the Red Banner (2); O the Red Star; Stalin Prize (3); Lenin prize; other decorations
po: Not a CPSU member; dep, USSR Supr. Sov of 1954, 1958, and 1962 convoc; visited U.S. with Premier Khrushchev, 1959

Konstantin A. Vershinin

b: Borkino, 1900
ed: GU-VVS Academy, 1932
as: Joined Red Army and fought in Civil War, 1919–1921; company and battn CO, 1926–1929; so, GU-VVS, 1933–1940; CO, special fighter training unit, 1940–1941; CO, fighter air div, 1941–1942; CO, air force on North Caucasian Front, then CO, 4th Air Army, 1943–1945; CO, VVS, 1946–1949; CO, air force, Baku Military Distr, 1949–1957; Head, Zhukovskiy Air Force Academy, 1957; CO, VVS and USSR Dep Minister of Defense, 1957–1969; ret 1969; died December 1973
r: Chief Marshal of Aviation
A: Hero of the Soviet Union; O Lenin; other orders, decorations, and medals
po: Member, CPSU, 1919; dep, USSR Supr. Sov of 1946, 1954, 1958, and 1962 convoc; member, CC, Azar CP, 1956–1957; voting del, at 1956, 1959, and 1961 CPSU congresses; cand. member, CC, CPSU, 1952–1956; member, CC, CPSU, 1961–1969

Aleksandr S. Yakovlev

b: Moscow, April 1906
ed: Graduate, Zhukovskiy Air Force Engineering Academy, 1931
as: Soviet Army motor mechanic at Frunze Military Airport, 1923–1925; designer, Dept of Experimental Aircraft Construction, Main Air Force Board, 1931–1934; Chief Designer, Experimental Design Bureau, 1934–1956; USSR Dep Pop. Commisar and USSR Dep Minister of Aviation Industries, 1940–1956; Chief Designer, USSR Ministry of Aircraft Industries, 1956–; designer of trainers, helicopters, fighters (YAK series), and other jet aircraft
r: Col. Gen of Engineering Technical Troops
A: O Lenin (7); Stalin Prize (6); Hero of Socialist Labor (2); Hammer and Sickle Gold Medal (2); other decorations and medals
po: Member, CPSU, 1938; dep, USSR Supr. Sov of 1946 convoc

Appendix III: Selected Biographies

Nikolay D. Yakovlev

b: 1898
ed: Unknown
as: Head, Chemical Laboratories, Main Artillery Admin., Soviet Army, 1920s–1935; Chief of Artillery, Kiev Special Military Distr, 1935–1941; Head, Main Engineering and Technical Artillery Admin., 1941–1945; Head, special board for the development of rockets and atomic weapons, Main Artillery Admin., USSR Ministry of Defense, 1945–1957; FDC, PVO-Strany, 1958–ret; no information after 1965
r: Marshal of Artillery
A: O Lenin (4); other decorations and medals
po: Member, CPSU, 1923; dep, USSR Supr. Sov of 1951, 1955, and 1959 convoc

Aleksandr N. Yefimov

b: Kantemirovka, February 1923
ed: Graduate, Military Flying School, 1942; Zhukovskiy Air Force Academy, 1951; Academy of the General Staff, 1957
as: Joined Soviet Army, 1941; pilot and later, flt and air attack sqn CO, Western and 2nd Belorussian Fronts, completed 222 combat missions, 1941–1945; so and CO, various air units, VVS, 1945–1966; CO, air forces, Carpathian Military Distr, 1967–1969; DC, VVS, 1969–1970; FDC, VVS, 1969–
r: Marshal of Aviation
A: Hero of the Soviet Union (2); O Lenin (2); O the Red Banner (3); other decorations and medals
po: Member, CPSU, 1943; dep, USSR Supr. Sov of 1946, and 1969 convoc; dep Latvian Supr. Sov of 1966 convoc; del at 1966 and 1969 CPSU congresses; author of articles in journal *Aviatsiya I Kosmonavtika*

Semen F. Zhavoronkov

b: 1889
ed: Graduate, Military-Political Academy, 1926; Myasnikov Pilots School, 1933; Voroshilov Naval Academy, 1949
as: Director, USSR Naval Aviation, 1941–1949; Chief, Main Board, Civil Air Fleet, 1949–1957; FDC, Main Board, Civil Air Fleet, 1957–1959; no information after 1960
r: Marshal of Aviation
A: O Lenin (2); O the Red Banner (4); other decorations and medals
po: Member, CPSU, 1917

Appendix IV: Charts

Chart I
The Soviet High Command

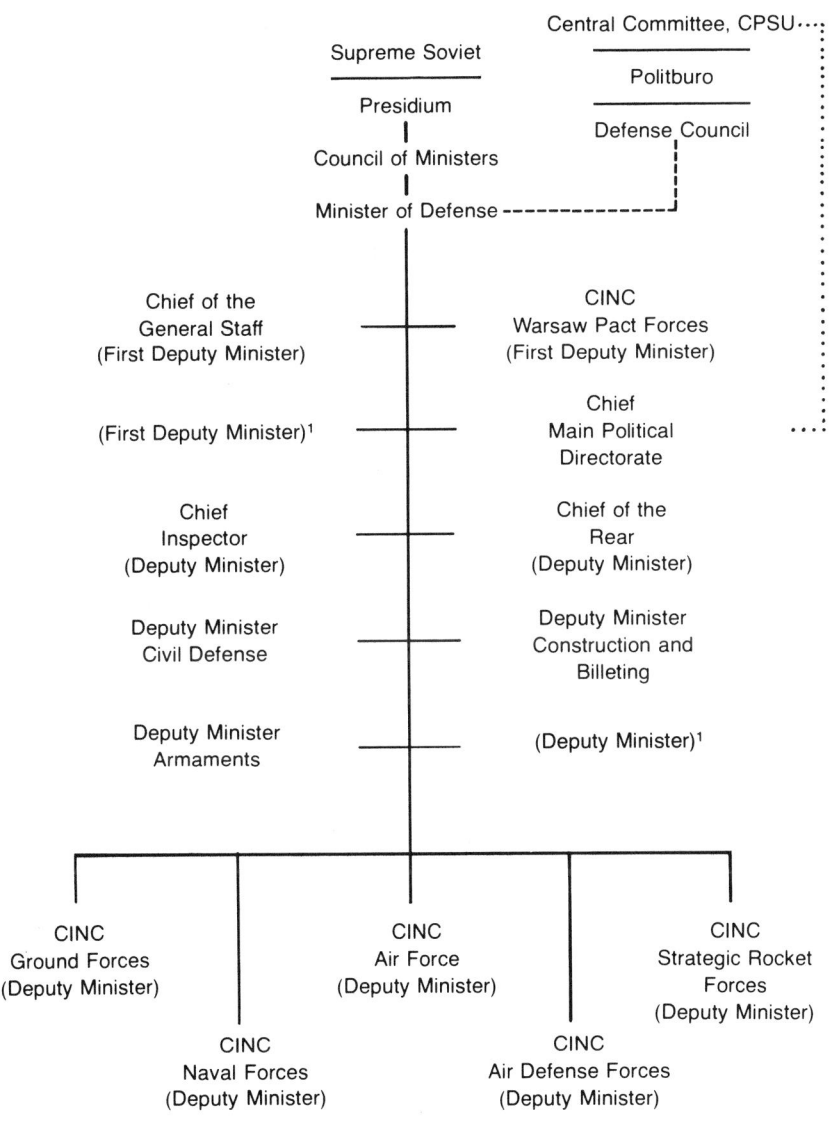

Chart II
Operational Commands

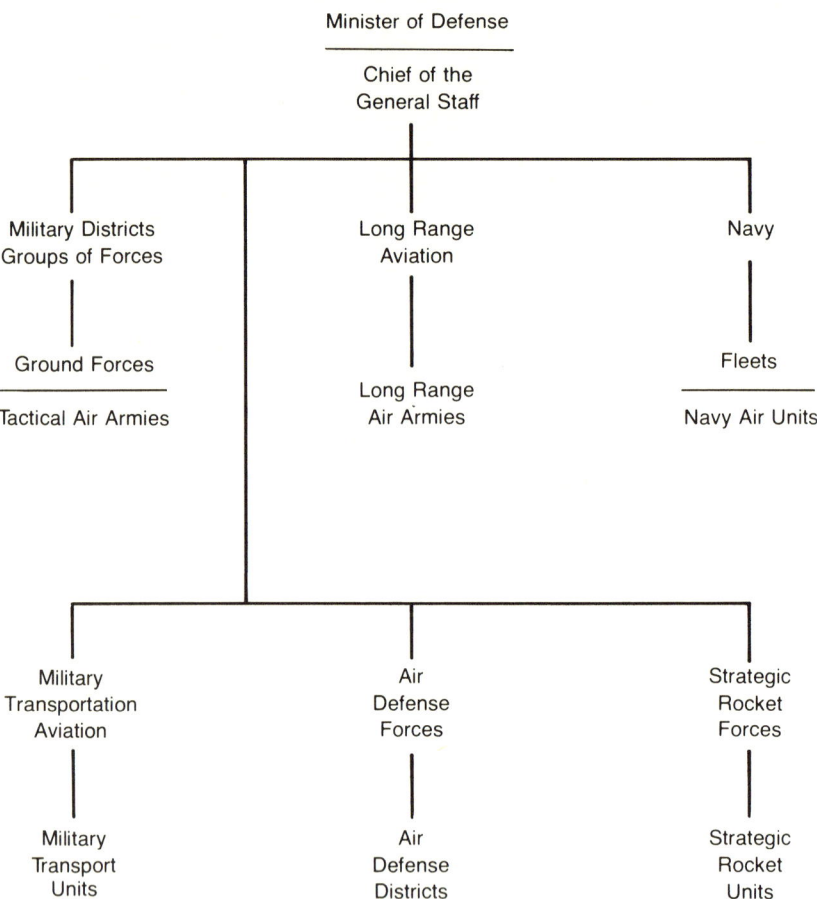

NOTE: The degree of operational authority the general staff has over the navy, long range aviation, national air defense and strategic rocket troops is unknown.

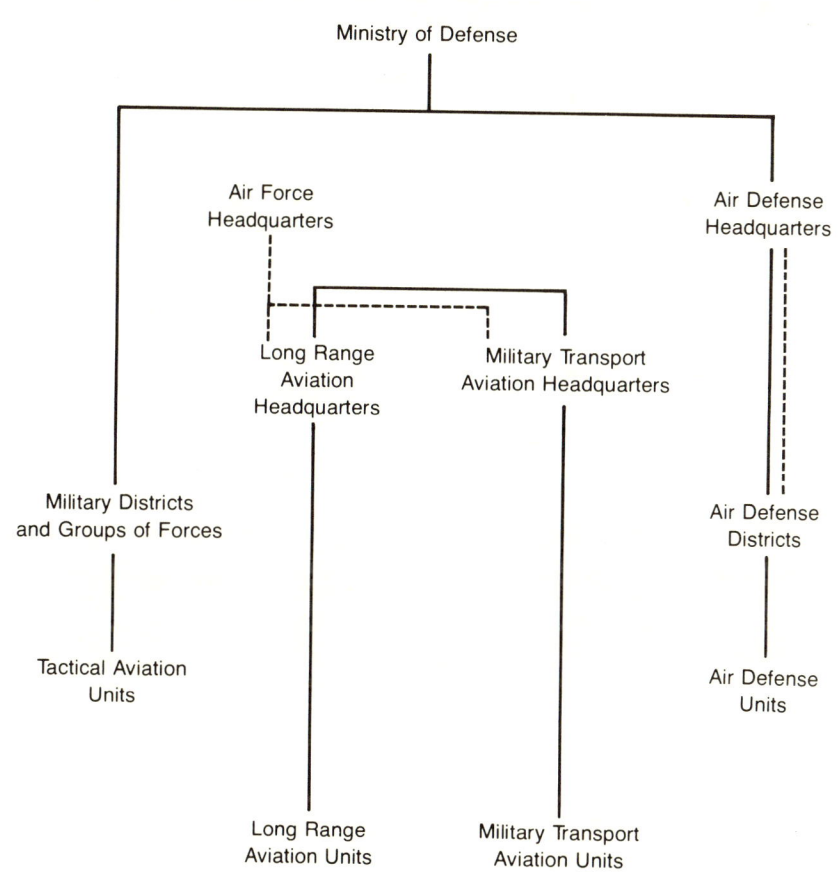

**Chart III
Relationship of Soviet Air Force
to the Ministry of Defense**

Chart IV
Air Force High Command

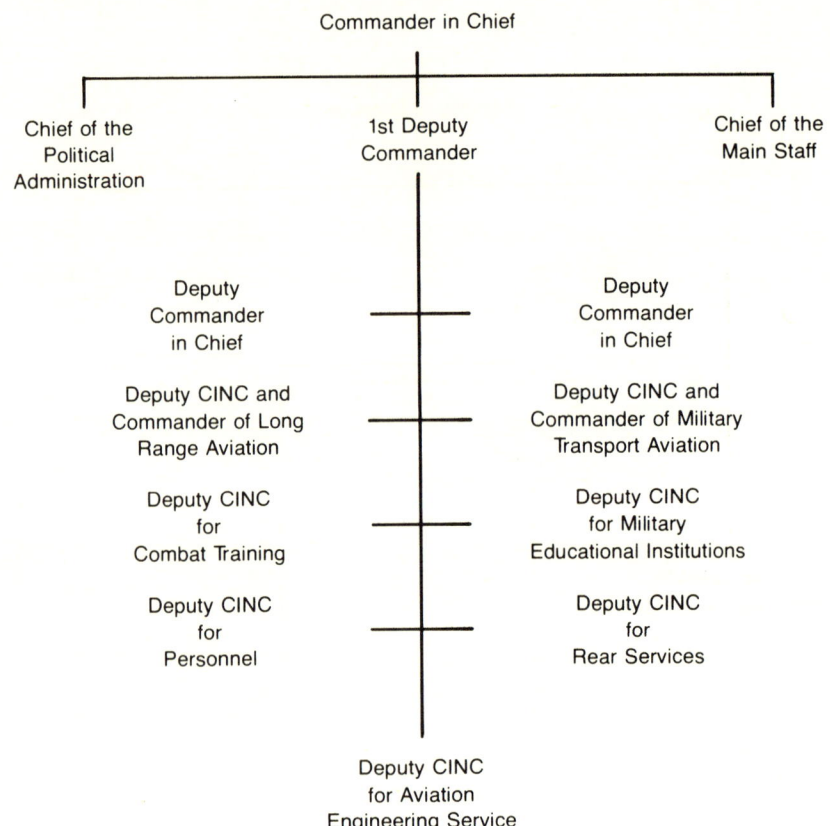

Chart V
PVO–Strany High Command

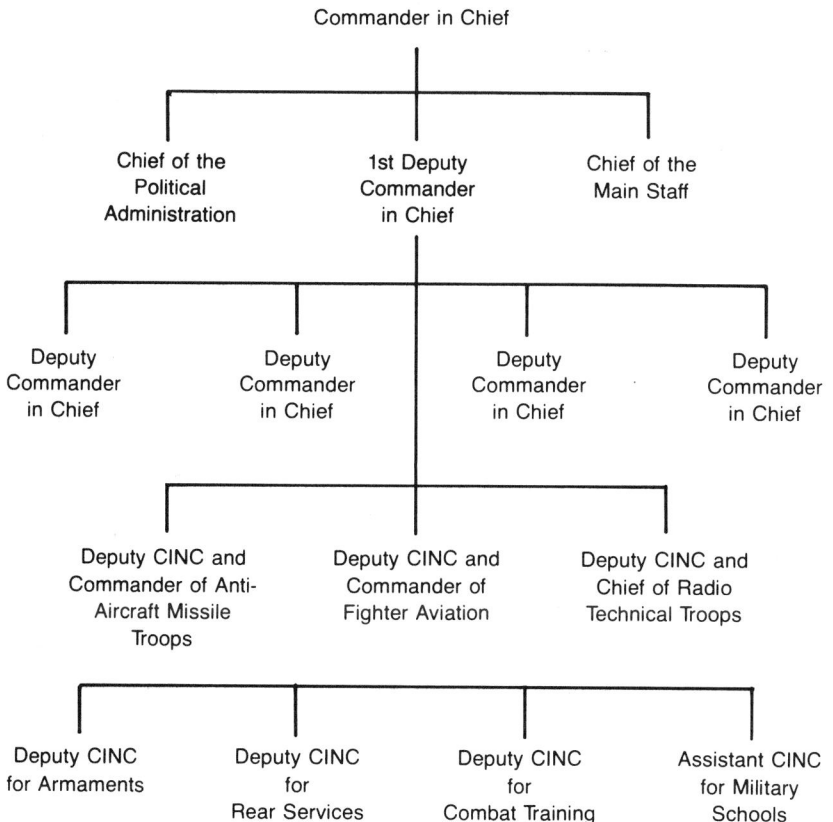

Chart VI
Territorial Organization of PVO

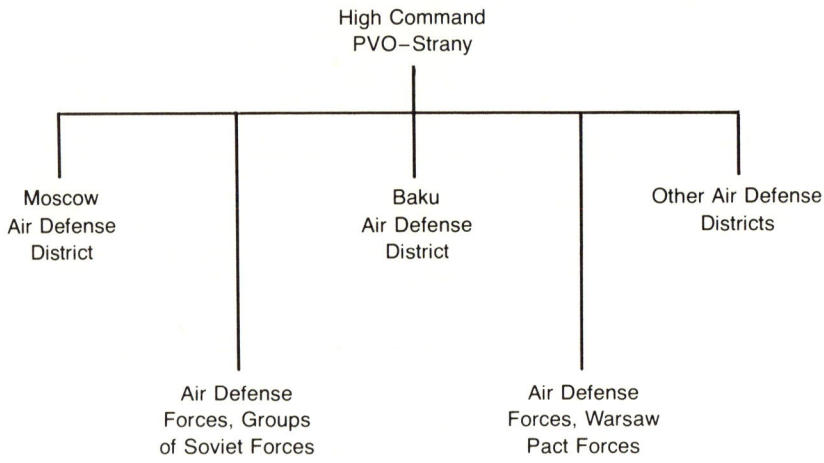

Chart VII
Organization of Headquarters Strategic Rocket Forces

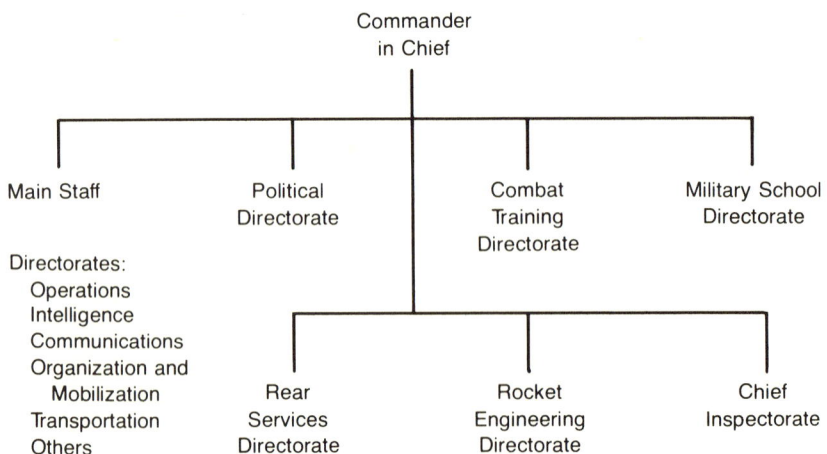

Author Index

Aarestad, James H., 3146
Abel, Ellie, 2828
Abir, Mordechai, 3078
Abi-Saab, Genges, 3121
Abshire, David M., 854
Ackley, Richard T., 1496
Adams, D., 2532
Adams, Henry H., 238–241
Adomeit, Hannes, 2879
Adrianov, A., 1651
Adwill, James, 2137
Aerospace Industries Association of America, 139
Agal'tsov, Filipp A., 1288, 1652
Ahnstrom, D. Newell, 2138
Alberts, Donald J., 3033
Albright, David E., 3097
Albright, Joseph G., 3162
Albritton, Britt L., 1051
Alex, Ralph, 2151
Alexander, Arthur J., 1004, 1052–1053, 1103
Alexander, Jean, 606, 626
Alexeyev, N., 1060
Ali, S., 3180
Allen, Luther, Jr., 1532
Allen, William E. D., 277–278
Allison, Graham T., 2829
Allon, Yigel, 2880
Allward, Maurice, 2016, 2087, 2233
Alsop, Joseph, 1460, 2881, 2953
Amelchenko, V., 1397, 1786
American Association for the Advancement of Slavic Studies, 66
American Enterprise Institute for Policy Research, 2533
American Historical Association, 4–7
American Security Council, 2609
Amoia, Alba, 174
Anders, Wladyslaw, 279
Anderson, Jack, 1461
Anderton, David A., 1061, 1167, 1850, 1946, 1965, 2058, 2072
Andrews, John, A.C., 105

Andreyev, V., 3291
Anischenko, L., 3292
Antonov, Oleg, K., 1136–1137
Anttonen, Ossi, 220
Anureyev, I., 1026
Anzulovic, J. V., 237
Aoki, Hideo, 3293
Araldsen, O. P., 2761–2762
Archer, Robert D., 1947, 2059
Arkill, Basil, 2195
Arlazorov, Mikhail, 627, 1138
Armitage, M. J., 2694
Armstrong, John A., 280
Arnold-Foster, Mark, 243
Arnold, Joseph C., 1289
Arora, J. S. B., 3186
Artemiev, Vyacheslav P., 800–801
Arzan, Singh, 3204
Asanov, D., 1456
Ashlock, J. R., 3205
Ashmore, Edward B., 2248
Aspaturian, Vernon V., 2535
Aspin, Les, 2433, 2536–2537
Asprey, Robert, B., 723
Astashenkov, P., 1062, 3294
Attar, Chand, 8
Atkeson, Edward, B., 955, 1533
Avdeyev, A., 3295
Awanohara, S., 2017
Ayling, Keith, 682
Ayoob, Mohammed, 3187
Azar, Edward, E., 2883

Baar, James, 1790, 2238
Babenko, I., 1606
Bachelor, John, 647
Backoften, Joseph E., 1351
Badeau, J. S., 3007
Bader, William B., 2635
Bailer, Severyn, 770
Bailey-Cowell, G. M., 855
Baker, David, 1020
Baker, Ross K., 3098

Balabolin, M., 1791
Baldwin, Hanson W., 244–245, 547, 1966, 2326
Banerjee, Jyotirmey, 3188
Banks, Arthur S., 99
Barber, Ransom E., 856, 1535
Barclay, Cyril N., 3206
Barclay, Glen St. J., 226
Barker, Arthur J., 3002, 3022, 3034
Barmin, V., 1653
Barnaby, Frank, 2327, 2680
Barnds, William J., 3207
Barnett, Frank R., 1536, 2434
Barnett, Roger W., 1537
Barrett, Raymond, 857, 2538
Barron, John, 802, 1640, 1642
Barry, Carol B., 790
Barry, Donald D., 790
Barshevsky, Vasilii, 2152
Bartenev, S., 985
Bartlett, Dewey F., 2723
Bartz, Karl, 317
Basiuk, Victor, 1021
Batchelor, John, 1850
Bates, E. Asa, 1815
Batov, P. I., 502
Baumbach, Werner, 318, 349
Bavousett, Glenn B., 607
Baylis, John, 834
Bayliss, Gwyn M., 9
Bazanov, Petr V., 1654, 1766–1767
Bearden, Thomas E., 1430–1431, 3261
Beasley, Robert D., 2884
Beck, Leonard N., 1290
Becker, Abraham S., 986, 1004, 2930–2932, 3079, 3089
Beecher, William, 1816
Beitzel, Robert, 541
Bekker, Cajus D., pseud., see Berenbrok, Hans D.
Belke, Reece G., 3237
Bell, J. Bowyer, 2851, 3105, 3135
Bell, Robert G., 2509
Bellamy, Ian, 2539
Belov, M., 1352–1355
Belyayev, V., 3300–3301
Bender, Roger J., 319
Bennett, Ralph K., 2018, 2540
Beregovoy, M. T., 1398
Berenbrok, Hans D., 320
Berlovskiy, N., 1769
Berman, Robert P., 1159
Berner, Wolfgang, 146
Bernstein, Barton, J. 2836–2837
Berry, F. Clifton, Jr., 2636
Bertram, Christopher, 2328
Bethell, Nicholas W. B., 423, 508

Betit, Eugene D., 529, 2695
Bhargava, G. S., 3238
Bialer, Seweryn, 580, 1609
Bidwell, Shelford, 835, 2681
Bigler, Willima B., 2nd, 2185
Biörklund, E., 1538
Bird, H., 1063
Biryuzov, S., 1655
Bissell, Richard E., 3110
Black, C. L., 3163
Blake, Peter J., 1356
Blau, George E., 424
Blechman, Barry M., 2355, 2435
Blesse, Frederick C., 1291
Blixt, Melvin D., 2885
Bloemertz, Günther, 321
Blond, Georges, 597
Bloomberg, Marty, 11
Bobylev, Sergey A., 1399, 1432
Bochkov, B. V., 1400
Boman, Truman R., 1292, 1497, 2251
Bond, P. S., 188
Booda, L., 2696
Booth, Ken, 992, 2622, 2637, 2697
Borawski, John, 2698
Borgart, Peter, 1433, 2120, 2129, 2699
Borovykh, A., 1656
Borsuk, A., 1657
Botlorff, Robert M., 79
Bottome, Edgar M., 2329, 2522
Bourdon, M. W., 629
Bowles, Chester, 3208
Bowman, Buddy, 1293
Bowman, Marvin S., 568
Bowman, Norman J., 100, 2234
Bowyer, Chaz, 565
Bradbrooke, Joan, 2139
Braddock, J. V., 2808
Bradshaw, Russell, 569
Bradsher, Henry S., 2098
Bramlett, David A., 1357
Brandon, Deane R., 548
Braybrook, Roy M., 1967, 1988, 1992, 1998–1999, 2009, 2032, 2043, 2047, 2051, 2073, 2082, 2088, 2095, 2113, 2134
Brehat, Victor, 1385
Breitkopf, Hans, 2252
Brennan, Donald G., 2461
Brewster, Owen, 1169
Breyer, Siegfried, 2763
Brindel, Charles L., 2462
Britt, Randolph, 1434
Brock, William E., 2541
Brodie, Bernard, 1521
Broekmeijer, M. W. J. M., 1435
Brog, David, 1294

Author Index

Brooks, Robert O., 3176
Brown and Shaw Research Corporation, 2667
Brown, Dallas C., Jr., 2700
Brown, David, 246
Brown, George S., 1498, 2356, 2542
Brown, Harold, 724, 2357, 2543–2544
Brown, Joseph M., 101
Brown, Michael J., 2228
Brown, Neville, 1817, 2545, 2701, 2742, 2886
Brown, Thomas A., 2546
Brown, Weldon A., 3244
Brownlow, Cecil, 987, 1108–1109, 1216, 1948, 2020, 2222, 2253–2255, 2358–2359, 2811
Brundtland, Arne O., 2764
Brunicardi, D. N. P., 1217
Bryukhovskiy, G., 3302
Buchan, Alastair F., 2523, 2743
Buckley, James L., 2463, 2610
Budhraj, Vijay, 3209
Bud'ko, A., 1738
Buel, Larry V., 190
Bueschel, Richard M., 3143
Bullock, John, 3023
Burbage, Paul, 3262
Burke, Gerald K., 1539, 2360
Burke, John C., 80
Burney, John C., 803
Burns, Richard D., 14
Burns, Robert T., 3099
Burrell, Raymond E., 2744
Burroughs, E.G., 581
Burt, Richard, 15, 2702
Buteux, Pierre, 2703
Butz, J. S., 1027, 1218, 1358, 1818, 2256, 2361, 3263
Bykov, V.L., 2704
Bystry, N., 1436

Cabrita-Matias, A., 2765
Cade, David J., 858
Cady, Steven E., 2362
Caidin, Martin, 478
Cain, Charles W., 1110, 1133, 1851, 2046, 2089, 2136
Caldwell, Cy, 1295
Caldwell, Erskine, 425
Caldwell, Lawrence T., 2510, 2705
Calvocoressi, Peter, 247
Cameron, Neil, 2547
Canby, Steven L., 2745
Candlin, A. H. S., 859
Cane, J. W., 1028
Carlton, David, 2330

Carmichael, Thomas N., 248
Carrell, Paul, pseud., see Schmidt, Paul K.
Carter, Kit, 249
Cate, James L., 253
Cecil, Robert, 426
Center for Strategic Studies, 2439, 3090
Chabanier, A., 2766
Chaney, Otto P., Jr., 1065
Chant, Christopher, 102, 322, 479
Chaplin, Dennis, 3136
Chaplygin, G., 3303
Chapman, Michael, 3111
Chapman, W. C., 1219
Chase, Alan C., 2933
Chau, P. R., 3210
Chaudhuri, N. J., 2638
Chedleyev, N., 373
Cheredichenko, M. I., 934
Cherednichenko, V., 1658
Cherikow, Nikolai, 2117
Chizhezvskiy, V., 3304
Chodes, John J., 2331
Chopovskiy, V., 1610
Chopra, Pushpindar W., 3211
Choudhary, Sukhibir, 3189
Choudhury, G. W., 3212–3213
Christyakov, I., 482
Chuikov, Vasilii I., 449, 520
Chupov, V., 1792
Churba, Joseph, 2934
Churchill, Winston S., 250
Citizens' Panel on Defense, 2363
Clark, Alan, 281
Clark, Donald L., 860, 1220
Clarke, Bruce C., 2548
Clause, D.M., 1296
Clemens, Walter C., Jr., 2436, 2464, 2639
Clemow, John, 2220
Cliffe, Trevor, 2746
Cline, Ray S., 2332–2333
Close, Robert, 2796
Coates, William P., 358
Cobb, Tyrus W., 1402, 2549–2550
Coffey, Joseph I., 2465, 2682
Cohen, Samuel T., 1170, 2707, 2798
Colby, Carrol B., 1852
Coleman, Herbert J., 1111, 2799, 2887
Collier, Basil, 251–252
Collins, Edward M., 956
Collins, John M., 2524–2525, 2551
Colton, Timothy J., 791
Committee on the Present Danger, 2437
Condon, Richard, 221
Confino, Michael, 2852
Congressional Information Service, 57
Congressional Quarterly, Inc., 92–93
Conquest, Robert, 792

Constable, Trevor J., 353, 594
Constant, James, 2364
Cook, Charles M., 549
Cook, Fred J., 1457
Cooke, David C., 608
Cooling, B. Franklin, 3rd, 16
Cooper, Bryan, 647
Cooper, Chester L., 3245
Copley, Gregory, 725
Copson, Raymond W., 3106
Cordes, Harry N., 2365
Cordesman, Anthony H., 2525, 2888
Cordier, Sherwood S., 2797
Cornwell, E. L., 1853
Costa, Benedict, 3214
Cottrell, Alvin J., 2889–2890, 2905, 2955
Coughlin, William, 1112, 3165
Council on Foreign Relations, 19
Cox, Frederick J., 2956
Cox, John, 2235
Crabb, Merle L., 2209
Craig, William, 450
Crane, Robert D., 854, 1540, 2838
Craven, Wesley F., 253
Crawford, Natalie W., 1451
Critchley, Julian, 427
Crocker, Chester A., 3119
Croizat, Victor J., 3080
Crosby, Ralph D., Jr., 2839
Cross, Roy, 609, 1171–1172, 1232, 1859, 1897, 2054, 2708
Crowe, Barry, 185
Crozier, Brian, 147, 1173, 3141
Crump, Roger L., 3036
Currie, Malcolm R., 1499, 2258
Cynk, Jerzy B., 509

Danchenko, A. M., 1649
Daniel, Donald C., 2526, 2611
Daniel, James, 2830
Daschke, Carl E., 1359, 2186
Davies, Merton E., 1819
Davis, C. E., 2236
Davis, Jacquelyn K., 2467, 2747, 2516
Davis, Larry, 3150
Davis, R. J., 1890
Davison, Michael S., 2800
Dawisha, Karen, 2891, 2949
Day, Bonner, 2061, 3128
Dayal, Rajeshwar, 3122
Dayan, David, 3003
Dean, Donald W., 103
Deane, Michael J., 793, 804, 829, 1029
DeBorchgrave, André, 2957, 3181
De Huszar, George B., 836
Deitchman, Seymour J., 713, 1297

DeMaiziere, Ulrich, 2801
Denisenko, P., 1659
Denisov, Nikolai, 375, 526
DePorte, Anton W., 2683
DeSeversky, Alexander P., 2334
Desoutter, Denis M., 1854
Despres, John H., 538
Detzer, David, 2831
Deutscher, Isaac, 1298
DeVore, Charles, 1030
DeVore, Ronald M., 20, 2892
DeWeerd, Harvey A., 1820
Dewey, Arthur E., 2767
Dewitt, N., 1031
D'Hoop, Jean Marie, 34
Dial, Jay F., 666
Dick, J. C., 2366
Dickson, Paul, 1785
Digby, James F., 2313
Dil, Shaheen, 3215
Dimant-Kass, Ilana, 2893
Dinerstein, Herbert S., 1522, 1541, 1589, 2612
Dismukes, Bradford, 2651
Divine, Robert A., 2832
Dixon, Robert J., 3039
Dobbs, Theodore, 2768
Dobrov, G., 1740
Dokuchayev, I., 1612, 1741
Donnelly, Christopher, 805, 1848, 2737
Donovan, John, 2854
Dornan, James E., Jr., 1500
Dornberger, Walter R., 1542
Doty, Paul, 2468
Douglas, Albert, 1221
Douglass, Joseph D., Jr., 861, 1523–1524, 1543, 1590, 2684
Dowd, John, 3264
Drane, Leslie, 1325
Dreisziger, N. F., 435
Drendel, Lou, 3246
Drieberg, Trevor, 3190
Drozdov, V., 1613
Drum, Karl, 359
Dubrov, V., 1299–1300
Dudley, Harrison G., 2769
Dudnik, A., 1770
Duffy, John J., Jr., 2438
Dulacki, Leo J., 862
Dunayev, P., 3305
Duncan, Charles W., Jr., 1661
DuPre, Flint O., 550
DuPuy, R. Ernest, 104, 254
Dupuy, Trevor N., 104–105, 1544, 2855
Duval, G. R., 615
Dyer, Philip W., 2709
Dzirkals, Lilita, 539

Author Index 309

Eaher, Ira C., 2021–2022, 3040
Eastland, James N., 3274
Eates, John I. H., 2583
Ebinger, Charles K., 3112
Edmonds, Martin, 1222
Eide, Asbjorn, 2623, 2629
Eisenhower, Dwight D., 1481
Ekman, Michael E., 530
El-Badri, Hassan, 3024
Ellis, Paul, 2210
Ely, Louis B., 714, 1333
Emerson, Gloria, 3247
Emme, Eugene M., 837
Encyclopedia Americana, 255
Engle, Eloise, 222
Enser, A. G. S., 21
Erickson, C. T., 1207
Erickson, John, 360, 376, 428, 483, 771–772, 863–868, 943, 1160–1161, 1174–1177, 1334, 1360, 1545, 1614, 2552–2553, 2710–2714, 2748–2749, 2770
Ermath, Fritz W., 806, 1546
Esposito, Vincent J., 270
Estep, Raymond, 22
Evron, Yair, 2960

Faber, Harold, 323
Fadeyev, Aleksandr A., 464
Farer, Tom J., 3134
Fast, Harriet F., 1615
Fay, John, 2140
Federyakov, G., 3306
Fedorov, A., 1742
Fedorov, P., 1663
Fedulov, M. V., 1453
Feist, Uwe, 324
Feuchtwanger, E. J., 1161–1162
Fil'chenko, L., 1665
Fischer, Robert L., 2809
Fitkulin, O., 3307
Fitzgerald, Charles G., 503
Fitzgerald, Frances, 3248
Fitzsimons, Bernard, 256
Ford, Corey, 551
Foreign Policy Association, 2511
Forsythe, David P., 2894
Foster, John S., Jr., 988, 1177a, 2554
Foster, R. B., 2750
Fox, Charles L., 3308
Foye, James, 186
Francillon, René J., 324
Frank, Lewis A., 1547, 2469, 2512, 2624
Frantsev, O., 3309
Freedman, Laurence, 2555
Freedman, Robert O., 2856–2857, 2895–2897, 2962

Freidel, Frank, 24
Fricker, John E., 1208, 1949, 2114, 2153, 2173
Friedman, William S., 1372, 1386, 1616, 1970
Frisbee, John L., 1403
Froelich, David V., 1950, 2011, 2025, 2036, 2052
Frolov, B., 494
Fromm, Joseph, 2368–2370
Fuller, Curtis, 377
Fullerton, John, 1223, 1335, 1361, 1387
Fulrong, R. D. M., 2771
Funk, Arthur L., 25
Futrell, Robert F., 3151

Gabelic, Andro, 2898
Gablehouse, Charles, 2141
Galay, Nikolai, 773–774, 870–872, 989, 1115–1116, 1548
Gale Research Co., 187
Galen, Justin, 2556
Gallagher, Matthew P., 282, 838, 873
Galland, Adolf, 325–326, 350
Gallik, Daniel, 990
Galvin, John R., 1350
Gann, Harry, 687
Gann, Lewis H., 3100
Garber, Max, 188
Garder, Michel, 715
Gardner, Floyd C., 3152
Garanin, Viktor, 1666
Gareau, Frederick H., 1549
Garman, W. Y., 189
Garn, Jake, 2371
Garrett, S. A., 2557
Garthoff, Raymond L., 378, 531–532, 727–729, 775, 807–808, 839–840, 874–880, 1224–1226, 1301–1303, 1502, 1550–1552, 2260, 2470–2472, 2558, 2640
Garwin, Thomas, 2559–2560
Gascogne, Alvary, 881
Gastello, V., 1794
Gasteyger, Curt W., 882, 2821
Gatland, Kenneth W., 1821, 2237, 2261–2265
Gault, Owen, 688, 695
Gavrilov, S., 3310
Geiger, George J., 1336, 1893, 1993, 2155, 2266–2267, 2319–2320
Geisenheyner, Stefan, 2772, 2812, 2899
Geneste, Marc, 2802
Gentili, Roberto, 309
George, Alexander L., 3153
George, Theodore, 2156–2157

Germany. Auswartiges Amt., 429
Germany. Wehrmacht, Oberkommando, 283
Getler, Michael, 2268
Geyer, Georgie A., 2858
Gebhrardt, Alexander O., 776, 1617
Gilbert, James, 1855
Gilbert, Stephen P., 2628, 2641–2642, 2668
Gilson, Charles M., 1894
Ginsburgs, George, 2643
Gladych, Michael, 1151, 1373, 1953
Glassman, Jon D., 2859, 2935
Glushko, Valentin, 1067
Gnusar'kov, V., 1667
Goerlitz, Walter, 451
Golan, Galia, 2860, 2900, 2996
Goldhamer, Herbert, 957, 2440
Gompert, David C., 1525
Goodlin, Chalmers H., 1940, 1954, 1972
Goodpaster, Andrew J., 2715
Goodspeed, D. J., 310
Gorchakov, P., 809, 1503, 3311
Gordon, Andrew, 883
Gordon, King, 3123
Gorokhov, K., 1337
Gouré, Leon, 884, 958, 1526
Graham, Daniel O., 991, 2335
Graham, I. C. C., 3239
Gray, Colin S., 885–886, 1338–1339, 1438, 1504, 1518, 1553, 1591, 2372–2374, 2473–2476, 2561–2563
Grayson, Benson L., 533
Great Britain. Air Ministry, 327
———. British Museum, 26
———. Public Records Office, 27
Grechko, Andrei A., 284, 469, 716
Green, Herschal, 570
Green, Murray, 887, 959
Green, William, 107, 151, 351, 648–651, 675–676, 678, 683–684, 691, 710–711, 1068–1073, 1163, 1171, 1208, 1228–1232, 1340–1341, 1374–1375, 1467, 1668, 1856–1864, 1895–1897, 1955, 1961, 1973–1974, 2045, 2063–2065, 2074, 2375, 2708
Greenberg, Milton, 196
Greenhut, Jeffrey, 3041
Greenough, Robert B., 3166
Greenwood, John T., 379, 1065
Greenwood, Ted, 1822, 1849
Gregory, W. G., 2127
Grey, Ian, 591
Griffith, Herbert F., 564
Griffiths, D. R., 2564
Grigor'yev, Mikhail G., 1505–1506, 1618
Griswold, Laurence, 2773, 3081
Griswold, W. S., 1898

Gromov, Mikhail M., 380
Grossman, Vasilii S., 501
Groves, Will W., Jr., 755
Grushevoy, K., 468
Guderian, Heinz, 285, 311
Gudymenko, Yu, 1669
Guha, S. B., 3217
Guillaume, Augustin, 361
Gukasov, G., 1771
Gunston, William T., 108–110, 355, 652, 1117, 1452, 1899–1902, 1934, 2269
Gurevich, Mikhail I., 1139
Gurney, Gene, 111, 257
Gusev, V., 1795

Hackett, John W., 2685
Haddaway, George E., 1233
Hadik, Laszlo, 201
Hagan, Kenneth, 2840
Hagerty, James J., Jr., 540
Hahn, Walter F., 1554
Haig, Alexander M., 2376
Halberstam, David, 3249
Halley, James J., 1332
Halperin, Morton, 888–889
Hamlett, Bruce, 2477
Hammond, Thomas T., 28
Handel, Michael I., 3042
Hanne, William G., 3218
Hanrieder, Wolfram F., 190
Hansen, Lynn M., 1342, 2158
Hansen, Philip, 992
Hardt, John P., 993
Harkavy, Robert E., 2625, 2630
Harrigan, Anthony, 3082
Harsch, Ernest, 3108
Harvey, David, 2270
Hasan, Zubeida, 3219
Haselkorn, Avigdor, 1429, 2644–2645, 3312
Hawkins, D. G., 1619
Hawks, Ellison, 653–654, 685
Haworth, David, 2774
Hayes, Grace P., 105, 216
Haykal, Muhammad H., 2861
Hayward, P. H. C., 191
Healy, Denis, 2775
Head, Robert G., 1074, 1670–1671
Heaps, Leo, 1810
Heflin, W. A., 192
Heikal, Mohamed, 2950
Heilbrunn, Otto, 841
Heiman, Leo, 2271, 2813
Heinl, Robert D., Jr., 730
Heinlein, Joseph J., Jr., 810
Hellman, Harold, 2142
Henk, Daniel W., 1405

Henn, Peter, pseud., see Schentl, Alfons
Hensel, Howard M., 3091
Henzel, H. W., 460
Herold, Robert C., 1032
Herter, Christian A., 1468, 1481
Herzog, Chaim, 3025, 3043
Hess, William N., 583
Hessman, James D., 2377, 2565–2567
Hewish, Mark, 1209, 2210
Hewish, Michael, 110
Hicks, Edmund, 571
Hiestand, Harry H., 1439
Higgins, Trumbull, 286
Higham, Robin, 29, 258
Hilton, Richard, 731
Hines, Kerry L., 2212
Hinterhoff, Eugene, 890, 2378, 2567–2568, 2646, 2814
Hinton, Harold C., 3149
Hoag, Malcolm W., 2613
Hoagland, John H., 2669
Hobbs, Richard, 1527
Hochman, Sandra, 1811
Hodges, Tony, 3109
Hoeber, Amoretta, 1524, 2569–2570
Hoeber, Francis P., 152
Hoeffding, O., 419
Hoehn, William E., Jr., 1004
Hoffman, Hubertus, 2324
Hoffman, Susan, 14
Hoffmann, Stanley, 2571
Holbrand, Carsten, 2336
Holder, L. D., 484
Holford, D. J., 2012
Holler, Frederick L., 30
Hollist, W. L., 1033
Holloway, Bruce K., 2572
Holloway, David, 811, 891–892, 1034–1035, 1054
Holmes, R. L., 1343
Holst, Johan J., 2337, 2441, 2776
Holzmann, Franklyn D., 983
Honan, W. H., 2815
Hood, Joseph W., Jr., 2442
Hooftman, Hugo, 1865
Hoopes, Townsend, 3250
Horelick, Arnold L., 893–894, 1592, 2846, 2932, 2991
Horn, Robert C., 3220, 3284
Hottinger, Arnold, 2964
Hotz, Robert, 381, 1075, 1118, 1153, 1234, 1469, 1903–1904, 3008
Hough, Jerry F., 794
House, Arthur H., 3124
Houston, N. S., 696
Howard, John, 362
Howard, Michael, 842
Howard, William E., 1790, 2238

Hoyle, Martha B., 260
Hrubiak, H., 1105
Hubble, John G., 2830
Hughes, John, 3280
Hughes, Peter, 2478
Huisken, Ronald, 2327
Hunt, Herman L., 2792
Hunter, Robert E., 2936
Hurewitz, J. C., 3083
Hurley, James A., 383
Hyland, William G., 968

Ignatyev, Oleg, 3113
Ilke, Fred C., 2573
Infield, Glenn B., 567, 572
Institut zur Enforschung der U.S.S.R., Munich, 765–768
Institute for Strategic Studies, 960
Institute of World Affairs, 154
Intelligence International, Ltd., 155
International Institute for Strategic Studies, 157, 732, 994, 2272, 2574–2576, 2716, 2965
Intriligator, Michael D., 1593
Irving, David, 328
Israel. Agranant Commission of Inquiry, 3069
―――. Ministry of Foreign Affairs, 2992
Ivanov, B., 1304, 1311, 1672
Ivanov, G., 1772
Ivanov, S., 534
Ivanov, V., 1744
Izgarshev, V., 1388, 1673–1674, 3313

Jabber, Fuad, 2901
Jablonski, Edward, 261
Jackets, L. A., 566
Jackson, Gary L., 1345
Jackson, Robert, 363, 584, 599, 2143, 2862, 3154, 3191, 3223–3224
Jackson, William D., 2479
Jacobs, Walter D., 1555–1556
Jacobsen, Carl G., 895, 2577, 2626–2627, 2647
Jacobsen, Hans A., 287
Jahn, Egbert, 1036
Jain, Rajendra K., 3192
James, Martin, 3118, 3140
Jarecki, Franciszek, 1620, 1977
Jasani, Bhupendra, 1823
Jennings, Richard M., 2443
Jenson, John W., 1557
Jessup, Alpheus W., 1978, 3167
Johnson, A. Ross, 2717, 2751, 2810
Johnson, Gerald E., 573
Johnson, Means, Jr., 2816–2817

Johnston, Robert E., 574
Joint Committee on Slavic Studies, 70
Jokel, G., 2718
Jokinen, Pertti, 230
Jonas, Anne M., 896
Jonbert, Philip, 1377
Jones, Chester G., 1452
Jones, Christopher D., 812, 2648
Jones, David R., 112, 161, 1406
Jones, Isaac R., 961
Jones, Robert H., 542
Jordan, George A., 543, 552
Jörgensen, K., 1558
Joshua, Wynford, 2628, 2668, 2902–2903, 3125
Jukes, Geoffrey, 440, 452, 480, 897, 3225
Julian, Thomas A., 579

Kadyshev, V., 1675
Kahan, Jerome H., 2841
Kalashinik, M., 813
Kaldor, Mary, 2629
Kalinayev, S., 1676
Kallistov, D. P., 288
Kang, Young H., 1594
Kapeliuk, Amnon, 2966
Kaplan, Fred, 2274
Kappel, Lon C., 2080
Kapur, Harish, 3193
Karikh, A., 384, 1305, 1440
Kass, Ilana, 2863
Kassel, Simon, 1055
Kassing, David B., 152
Kaul, Ravi, 3226
Kaushik, Devendra, 3194
Kaysen, Carl, 2578
Keegan, George J., Jr., 2381
Keegan, John, 113–114, 215, 430
Keep, John, 2649
Kelleher, Catherine, 795
Kemp, Geoffrey, 2338, 2904, 2937
Kemp, Jack F., 2433, 2579
Kennedy, Robert F., 2833
Kennedy, W. V., 1179
Kerr, Walter B., 364, 453
Kershaw, J. A., 1005
Kesselring, Albert, 289
Key, William G., 1236
Kharlamov, S., 1677
Khomchich, M., 3314
Khrushchev, Nikita S., 843–844, 1482, 1596
Killen, John, 329
Kilmarx, Robert A., 365, 420, 2818, 2905
Kimche, Jon, 2906
Kime, Steve F., 814
Kincade, W. H., 898

King, Horace F., 1944, 2055
King, Peter, 3315
Kintner, William R., 1528, 2444, 2456
Kirk, Donald, 3251
Kirk, Grayson, 2339
Kirkpatrick, Lyman B., Jr., 431
Kirsanov, P., 1678
Klaas, Philip J., 1812, 1824–1825
Klare, Michael T., 2513
Klenberg, Jan, 2793
Klepacki, Waclaw, 705
Klieman, Aaron S., 2864
Klimov, Andrei, 3101
Klochikhin, L., 1679
Kluge, Alexander, 454
Knebel, Fletcher, 1906
Knight, Charles, 3168
Knoke, Heinz, 330
Knorr, Klaus E., 2842
Kochnovskii, N. A., 385
Kock, F. H. C., 2719
Kohler, Foy D., 1559, 3026
Kolcum, Edward H., 1826, 2967–2970
Koldunov, Aleksandr I., 1407, 3316
Kolkowicz, Roman, 796, 815, 830–831, 899, 1056, 1595, 2481, 2580
Koltunov, G. A., 485
Komarov, N., 386
Kondioglo, A., 1796
Konechnyy, Ye., 3317
Konev, I., 495, 513
Konkov, N., 1680
Konnov, A., 1745
Konoplyov, Vasilii, 1037
Konyukhov, A., 1681
Korb, Laurence J., 2445
Korbonski, Andrzej, 2752
Korobov, A., 3318
Kotch, W. J., 3010
Kotikov, A. K., 3319
Kotov, Mikhail, 470
Kournahoff, Sergei N., 366
Kozhevnikov, M., 387–388
Kozicharow, E., 733
Kozlov, L., 231
Kozlov, S. N., 1607
Krasnov, A., 1306, 1441
Krasovskiy, S. A., 1180
Kravchenko, G. S., 562
Kreipe, Werner, 356
Krivinyi, Nikolaus, 115, 1210
Kruzhin, Petr, 777
Krylov, Konstantin K., 995, 1038
Krylov, Nikolai, 734, 1507–1508, 1621, 2276–2277
Kuban, Boris, 816, 1408, 1622–1623
Kuby, Erich, 521
Kucherov, Bertha, 33

Kulikov, N., 1682
Kurian, George T., 116
Kurochkin, P. A., 817
Kurov, N., 471
Kutakhov, Pavel S., 389, 1237–1244
Kuts, S., 1683
Kuznetsov, V., 1684
Kuzovov, V., 818

Labrie, Roger P., 117
Laird, Lael, 390
Laird, Melvin R., 1509, 2382
Lambermont, Paul M., 2144
Lambert, Mark, 2001
Lambeth, Benjamin S., 962, 1597, 2383–2384, 2446, 2482
Langford, David, 1022
Lantzer, Lawrence, 2847
Lanz, J. E., 193
Laqueur, Walter Z., 2865–2866
Larrabee, Steven, 3114
Larson, David L., 2834
Larson, Thomas B., 2340
Lashchenko, P., 496
Laske, Robert M., 901
Latour, Charles, 1827
Latter, B., 3046
Lavreichuk, V., 1746
Law, Bernard A., 611–612
Leach, Barry R., 432
Lebedev, V., 1145
Lebedew, L., 1747
LeCheminant, Pierre, 902
Lederrcy, E., 472
Lee, Asher, 331, 600, 1164, 1181–1183, 1211–1212, 1245–1249, 1307, 1409, 2278–2279
Lee, Benjamin S., 1979
Lee, William T., 735, 903, 984, 996–998, 1560
Leebaert, Derek, 2686
Lefever, Ernest W., 3125
Legault, Albert, 2527
Leggett, Robert E., 999
Legum, Colin, 163–164, 3093, 3102, 3109
Legvold, Robert, 736, 2650
Lellouche, Pierre, 904
Lelyushenko, D., 514
LeMay, Curtis E., 2341
Lemnitzer, Lyman, 2385
Lenczowski, George, 2867, 2907
Lenczowski, John, 3241
Lens, Sidney, 2342
Leonard, George B., Jr., 1624
Leonidov, N., 1326
Leontin, L., 905
Levesque, Jacques, 2822

Levine, Isaac D., 2386
Levinthal, David, 290
Lewis, Jesse W., Jr., 2614
Lewy, Guenther, 3252
Lewytzkyj, Boris, 769
Liberatare, E. K., 2163–2164
Liddell-Hart, Basil H., 262, 436, 445, 2528
Lindberg, Folke, 2777
Lindsay, G. R., 2527
Liska, George, 2529
Liss, Witold, 673, 677, 679, 693
Locksley, Norman, 2819
Lodge, J. E., 689
Loginov, A., 3320
Logvinenko, B., 2107
Lomov, N. A., 1023, 1039
London, Kurt, 737
London. Instytut Historyczny imienia Generala Sikorskiego, 510
Long, Anne K., 2841
Long, J. F. L., 738, 906, 1510, 1561, 2066
Loosbrook, John F., 1184, 1625
Lord, Carnes, 1828
Lorenzini, Dino A., 3308
Losev, G., 2108
Lowe, George E., 2343
Lowenthal, Mark M., 2509
Lowther, William, 2387, 2582
Lucas, Stevan R., 1519
Lucier, C. E., 2388
Luck, Edward C., 2483
Lukas, John, 263
Lukas, Richard C., 515, 544, 554–557, 563, 575
Lumsden, Malvern, 2199
Lundin, Charles L., 224
Luukkanen, Eino A., 223
Luttwak, Edward, 194, 1598
Lyons, Graham, 291

McBride, James H., 2389, 2583
McCagg, William O., 292
MacCaskill, Douglass C., 535
McConnell, James M., 832, 2651
McConnell, Robert B., 2670
MacDonald, Hugh, 1384
McDonnell, John, 907, 992, 1078–1079
McDowell, Ernest R., 697
McFarland, Marvin W., 516
McGovern, James, 3155
McGuire, Frank G., 2280
McGuire, James D., 2281
MccGwire, Michael, 1562, 2653
McKenzie-Smith, Robert H., 3048
Mackintosh, Malcolm, 717, 739, 908–912, 963, 1410, 1563–1564, 2584, 2652, 2753
Macksey, Kenneth, 246

McLane, Charles B., 2868
McLaurin, Ronald D., 2869
McMichael, Scott R., 2803
McPeak, William S., Jr., 2754
McQueen, Arthur D., 1411
McWhinnie, A. J., 2390
Mahajani, Usla, 3281
Mahoney, Shane E., 740, 913, 1032
Makarov, V., 1685
Maks, Leon, 511
Malaparte, Curzio, 465
Malinovskiy, Nikolay F., 819
Malinovsky, Rodion Y., 914–915, 1511, 1686
Mallon, Lloyd, 1250
Mallory, Walter H., 118
Malone, Daniel K., 1442
Malyanchikov, S. V., 1565
Malzeyev, Alexander, 2188–2189
Mamayev, V., 1797
Maney, Rhoi M., 2213
Mangold, Peter, 2870, 2997
Manning, Stephen O., 3rd, 558, 741
Mansfield, E. G. N., 2778
Maratoff, Paul, 277
Marriott, John, 165, 1829, 2202, 2214, 2282, 2344
Marsh, Roger, 2203
Marshall, Samuel L. A., 3012
Martell, Paul, 216, 312
Martin, Glen W., 1566
Martin, Laurence W., 2530, 2585
Martin, Robert P., 916, 3183, 3321
Marzari, Frank, 2391
Mason, Francis K., 219
Mason, Herbert M., Jr., 655
Mason, R. A., 1162
Mastro, Joseph P., 1308
Mataxis, Theodore C., 2283
Matloff, Maurice, 545
Matsulenko, V., 917
Matwiczak, Kenneth M., 2165
Maule, Henry, 264
May, M. M., 2392
Mechan, John F., 2687
Meehan, James L., 3rd, 1773
Meir, Golda, 3049
Melekhin, Aleksey D., 1512
Meller, R., 1908
Mellor, John W., 3195
Menaud, S. W. B., 1251, 1414
Menaul, Stewart, 2720
Menken, Jules, 984a
Meos, Edgar, 589, 601
Mergien, A., 3070
Merritt, Allen S., 2438
Metcalf, Arthur G., 2484–2485
Mets, David R., 391

Meyer, John C., 1327
Mezerik, Avraham G., 1483
Michel, Henri, 34, 265
Middleton, Drew, 2345, 3050, 3144
Mikhaylenko, I., 446, 3322
Mikhaylov, V. A., 2314
Miko, Francis T., 2514
Mikoyan, Artom I., 1080
Mil'chenko, N., 1415
Milheev, Iurii, 3253
Millar, Thomas B., 2654, 3227, 3240
Miller, B., 2655
Miller, D. M. O., 2804
Miller, Edward E., 667
Miller, Jay N., 1956
Miller, Mark E., 1029
Miller, Martin J., Jr., 1567
Miller, Ronald, 1024
Millett, Alan, 16
Milstein, Jeffrey S., 2939
Milstein, Michael A., 2486
Minasyan, M. M., 293
Minnehan, Thomas J., 1368
Miryukov, L., 392
Mishuk, M., 1309
Mitchell, Douglas D., 2515
Mizrahi, Joseph V., 332
Modrzhinskaya, Ye. D., 845
Molchan, G., 1416
Mollow, Andrew, 266
Mondey, David, 121, 1814
Monks, Alfred, 919, 964, 1252, 1378, 1570
Monroe, Elizabeth, 3071
Moore, John, 1912, 2871
Moore, Otis C., 1830
Moore, Robert P., 1382
Moorer, Thomas H., 2587, 2721
Morgan, Henry G., Jr., 2779
Moroz, Ivan M., 820, 1688, 3323
Morrison, Philip, 1832
Morton, I., 1913
Morton, Louis, 36
Morzik, Friedrich, 333
Moskalenko, Kirill S., 497, 1513
Moulton, Harland B., 2346
Moulton, James L., 2780
Mrazkova, Damela, 294
Muckerman, Joseph E., 2nd, 1571
Mueller, Robert, 249
Mughisuddin, Mohammed, 3075
Mulley, Frederick W., 920
Munro, Colin, 1866
Munson, Kenneth G., 613–614, 656, 686, 1166, 1867–1868, 1885, 1945, 2130, 2056, 2145, 2194
Murphy, Charles J. V., 2393–2394
Murphy, Margaret, 1689
Murphy, Paul J., 1689

Author Index

Murray, Bruce C., 1819
Murray, Michael P., Jr., 1690
Mustafa, Zubeida, 3228
Myers, Joe B., 1362
Myles, Bruce, 2193
Myrdal, Alva, 2347

Nanes, Allan S., 2395
Nash, Henry T., 2615
Nathan, James A., 1471
Nekhoroshkov, L., 1344
Nekrasov, F., 634
Nemecek, N., 635
Nemecek, Vaclav, 2075
Nerlich, Uwe, 2337
Nes, David G., 2909
Nesbitt, Robert L., 2794
Neupokoev, F., 2221
Nevskii, N. A., 1572
New, George, 1691
Newhouse, John, 2457
Newman, Stephanie G., 2630
New York Public Library, 37
Nielsen, Andreas, 334
Nielsen, John, 3184–3185
Nihart, Brooke, 3265
Nikitin, V., 1798
Nikolayev, P., 3325
Nitze, Paul, 1573, 2588–2589
Norby, M. O., 122
Norman, L. B., 1492
Norman, Lloyd, 2396
North, D. M., 2026
Novikov, A., 1692
Novikov, M., 504, 1134
Nowarra, Heinz J., 615
Noyes, James H., 3076
Nunn, Sam, 2487, 2723

O'Ballance, Edgar, 718, 742, 2397, 3005, 3028, 3254, 3267
Obukhov, V., 1751
O'Doherty, John K., 1253
Odom, William E., 1693
Ognibene, Peter J., 2488
Oleynik, A., 1694
Oliver, Luis G., 2977
Olmstead, Merle, 2200
Olmstead, William S., 1737
Olton, Roy, 197
Onacewicz, Wlodzimier, 922
O'Neill, Bard E., 3051, 3092
O'Neil, William D., 2100
Ordway, Frederick I., 2239
Orlov, V., 1799
Orlov, Yu., 1417

Orvik, Nils, 2782–2783
Osborn, Robert C., 2351
Ott, Lester, 712
Ownes, Rasher, 668

Paananen, Lauri, 222
Pachter, Henry M., 2835
Page, Stephen, 3077
Paige, Glenn D., 3156
Pajak, Roger F., 2671, 2940, 2979, 2999, 3133, 3330
Palit, Dharitri K., 3029, 3196
Paneth, Donald, 123
Panofsky, Wolfgang K. H., 2591
Panov, B., 447
Panyalev, Georg, 2006, 2013–2014, 2027, 2041, 2101
Papp, Daniel S., 923, 3115, 3129
Pappageorge, John G., 924
Papworth, Peter M., 2724
Paquier, Colonel, 352
Parkinson, Roger, 124
Parrish, Michael, 39, 394, 487, 778
Parrish, Thomas, 125
Parry, Albert, 2240, 2289
Parson, Nels A., Jr., 1529
Parsons, Iain, 126
Partridge, Eric, 195
Passingham, Malcolm, 705, 1389
Patrick, Stephen B., 2725
Pauker, Guy J., 2447
Pavlov, Dmitri, 466
Payne, Samuel B., Jr., 2489
Payton, Gary D., 3130, 3137
Pcrhal, E. M., 2070
Peck, J. L. H, 2071
Peckman, Joseph A., 2348
Pederson, John C., 2843
Peresypkin, I. T., 421
Perimutter, Amos, 3052
Perlmutter, William, 1869
Perry, Geoffrey E., 1833–1837
Pervov, A., 3326
Petersen, Charles W., 3116
Petersen, Phillip A., 925, 1165, 1514, 1915, 3147
Petrov, A., 1752
Petrov, Vladimir, 433
Petrovich, G. V., 1083
Pfaltzgraff, Robert L., Jr., 2444, 2456, 2490, 2516, 2747
Phillips, Reynolds, 2081
Phillips, Richard L., 1369
Phillips, Thomas R., Jr., 1255, 1418
Philpott, Bryan, 335
Pickert, Wolfgang, 461
Pierce, Max R., 2941

Pimlot, John, 267
Pioro, Tadeusz, 926
Pipes, Richard, 1574, 2688
Pirie, Anthony, 2144
Pirogov, Petr, 1641
Plano, Jack C., 196–197
Plocher, Hermann, 336–338
Plotnikov, G., 536
Podgornyy, Ivan D., 1419
Pokryshkin, Aleksandr I., 592
Polezhayev, V., 1753
Polk, James H., 2805
Pollinger, Gerald, 1860–1861
Polmar, Norman, 1870, 2241, 2399
Polyakov, A., 1420
Ponamarev, A. N., 1443, 1800
Popkov, V., 1444
Popov, O., 3327
Porter, Richard W., 1084, 1813
Possony, Stefan T., 1310
Potter, W. C., 2491
Potts, Ramsay D., Jr., 395
Powell, Craig, 2400
Powell, Hickman, 690
Powers, Francis G., 1458, 1472–1474
Pratt, Clayton A., 2806
Preisser, Chester J., Jr., 2993
Prendergast, William, 2517
Preston, Anthony, 295
Pretty, Ronald T., 1445, 2242
Price, Alfred, 339–341
Price, David L., 3084
Price, Wesley, 1257
Price, William, 2401
Prikhodchenko, G., 1801
Prinz zu Loewenstein, H., 822
Prokofyev, N., 527
Proskuryakov, V., 2204
Pryadko, P., 1754
Pryadko, Y., 1775
Pshenyanik, G., 396
Public Affairs Information Service, 86
Punnett, D. I., 1163
Pushpinder, Singh, 3197–3198
Puzanov, A., 1695

Quandt, William B., 3053, 3072
Quester, George H., 2824
Quick, John, 198
Qureshi, Khalida, 3231

Ra'anan, Uri, 2631, 2656, 2910–2912
Rabin, Sheldon T., 999
Rajasekhariah, A. M., 3232
Rake, Alan, 167
Ralph, John E., 1041

Ramazani, R. K., 2657
Rand Corp., 64
Randle, Kevin D., 1475
Ranger, Robin, 2726
Ransom, Harry H., 1476
Rasmussen, Robert D., 2807
Ratley, Lonnie O., 3rd, 488
Rattinger, Hans, 2727
Ray, G. D., 397
Ray, Hemen, 3199
Raymond, Walter J., 199
Rebrov, M., 1141, 1148, 1957
Record, Jeffrey, 3054
Reed, David, 3117
Reed, Thomas C., 2492
Rees, David, 3107, 3157
Rehm, Allan S., 965
Reid, Alan, 128
Reinhordt, G. C., 1575
Reitz, James T., 1391
Remes, Vladimir, 294
Remington, Robin A., 40
Rentschler, Frederick B., 2402
Reppert, John C., 2493
Reshetar, John S., Jr., 797
Reshetnikov, Vasilii V., 399
Retalliata, J. T., 1984
Rey, Gabriel, 2913
Reznichenko, Vasilii, 1576
Rhinelander, John B., 2459
Riccardelli, Richard F., 1345
Rice, Michael S., 669
Richelson, J. T., 1577
Rieckhoff, Herbert J., 400
Rikhye, Ravi, 3233
Ringold, Herbert, 560
Ritchie, Donald J., 1087, 2290
Rizika, J. Wilford, 1088
Robertson, Bruce, 1871–1872
Robinson, Clarence A., Jr., 1042, 1776, 1958, 2068, 2291, 2403–2404, 2494–2495
Rodwell, Robert R., 3055
Rogers, Leighton W., 561
Rohwer, Jurgen, 287
Ro'i, Yaacov, 2872–2873
Rokossovosky, K., 489
Romaneski, Albert L., 2784
Ropelewski, R. R., 3056
Rose, John P., 1447
Rosecrance, Richard N., 2531
Rosen, Stephen J., 2914–2915
Ross, Dennis, 1578
Ross, Thomas B., 1459, 1480
Rosser, Richard F., 2405
Rougeron, Camille, 401
Royal Institute of International Affairs, 169
Rubenstein, Murray, 2028

Author Index 317

Rubinstein, Alvin Z., 2632, 2916, 2951
Rubner, Michael, 41
Rudel, Hans-Ulrich, 342
Rudenko, Sergii I., 505
Rudnyy, N., 3331
Rudolph, James D., 3000
Ruffner, Frederick G., Jr., 200
Rummel, Rudolph J., 846, 927, 2406
Rush, Myron, 1592
Rust, Kenneth C., 576
Ryabov, V., 719
Ryan, Cornelius, 522
Ryzhov, V., 1697

Sadat, Anwar, 2952
Safronov, P., 1698–1699, 3332
Sagan, S. D., 3057
Salisbury, Harrison E., 296, 467, 3145
Salminen, S., 232
Salo, Mauno A., 233
Samoylenko, Ya., 3333
Sargent, Eric, 616
Sarvanto, James, 234
Sas, Anthony, 437
Savitskii, E., 402
Savitskiy, Yevgeny R., 1422–1423
Savkin, V. Ye., 847
Savosin, S., 1311
Sawers, David, 1024
Sayle, Murray, 2029
Schaefer, Henry W., 1000
Schaerf, Carlo, 2330
Schatunowskii, George, 1700
Schemmer, Benjamin F., 2407, 2593
Scherer, John L., 170
Schertl, Alfons, 343
Schiff, Zeev, 3030
Schleicher, Rolf, 1701
Schlesinger, James R., 2408
Schlieper, Fritz, 1632
Schmidt, Paul K., 297–298
Schneider, Mark B., 1188, 1579, 2497–2498
Schneider, William, Jr., 152, 744, 776, 1346, 1392, 1580, 1617, 2728
Schroter, Heinz, 455
Schultz-Naumann, Joachin, 473
Schurmann, Franz, 2350
Schuster, Edward J., 1043
Schwabedissen, Walter, 367
Schwarz, Urs, 201
Scianna, Philip P., 1599
Scott, Fraser, 1189
Scott, Harriett F., 720, 779–780, 823, 966–967, 1528, 1702–1703
Scott, William F., 42, 720, 928, 1190–1191, 1393, 1424, 2658

Scoville, Herbert, 2217, 2351, 2499
Scowcroft, Brent, 2409
Scribner, Jeffrey L., 784, 2410, 2659
Seamans, Robert, 1347, 2594
Seaton, Albert, 299, 441, 593
Sella, Amnon, 438, 2917–2918
Selle, Herbert, 462
Sellers, Robert C., 129
Selyodkin, V., 1633
Sen Gupta, Bhabani, 3234
Sergeyev, O., 1704
Seth, Ronald S., 442, 456
Seung-Kwon, Synn, 3169
Seymov, P., 1705
Shackleton, N. A., 929
Shafter, Richard A., 2296
Shaknazarov, G., 2595
Shamir, Shimon, 2852
Sharma, B. L., 3235
Sharp, F. R., 2785
Sharp, U. S. Grant, 3256
Shaw, John, 457
Sheehan, Neil, 3257
Sherman, Robert, 2297, 2411
Shigin, M., 3334
Shlaim, Avi, 3058
Shchitov, G., 1706
Sheldon, Charles S., 2nd, 1839–1840
Sherman, Robert, 2297, 2241
Shesterin, F., 1448
Shevchenko, N. A., 1765
Shirer, William L., 268
Shoemaker, Robert, 3015
Shores, Christopher F., 225, 235, 246, 313, 344, 585
Shrader, Cecil L., 930
Shtemenko, Sergei M., 300, 368, 403–405, 517
Shtoda, A., 1090
Shulman, Marshall D., 2500, 2660
Shulsky, Abram N., 2672
Shurygin, Vladislav, 3335
Shutov, Z., 490, 498, 506
Siddiqui, Kalim, 3200
Sidelnikov, I., 1425
Sidorenko, A. A., 848, 1363
Sidorov, P., 931
Sienkiewicz, Stanley, 2501, 2596
Silant'yev, A. P., 1267
Simakov, Ye., 406
Simler, George B., 3268
Simon, Reeva S., 43
Simpson, Benjamin M., 3rd, 1581
Simpson, John, 1091
Sims, Edward H., 586, 1287
Singh, K. Rajendra, 2984, 3059, 3201
Sinikov, A., 3336
Sin'kevich, V., 1394

Sinyutin, V., 1756
Sjaastad, Anders C., 2786
Skirdo, M. P., 1582
Skorikov, G., 1268
Skrylnik, A., 824
Skubilin, V., 3337
Slocombe, Walter B., 2518
Slominski, Martin J., 2502
Smart, Ian, 2316
Smirnov, Aleksandr V., 1707
Smith, David A., 1635
Smith, Myron J., Jr., 44
Smith, Peter C., 345
Smith, R. G., 825
Smith, W. Y., 745
Smolansky, Oles M., 2874, 2918–2919, 3085
Snell, Edwin M., 545
Snider, Lewis W., 2875
Snow, Edgar, 694
Snow, R. N., 1328
Snyder, Jack L., 1600
Snyder, Louis L., 269
Sobel, Lester A., 2823, 3031
Sokol, Anthony E., 932
Sokolovskii, Vasillii D., 849, 933–934
Solovyov, Boris, 481
Soltys, Andrew T., 3170
Sonnenfeldt, Helmut, 968
Sorahan, Joseph R., 1841
Sorokin, A., 1708–1709, 2205, 3338
Sozinov, V., 3339
Spaatz, Carl, 1274
Spahr, William J., 785, 935
Spaight, James M., 408
Spanier, John W., 3158
Speed, Roger D., 1530
Spencer, John H., 3132
Spielmann, Karl F., Jr., 838, 1094, 1531
Spier, Hans, 2755
Spurr, Robert, 1843
Sqarlato, Nico, 1873
Starr, Michael, 936
Staar, Richard F., 172, 1197, 2663
Stadnikov, A., 3340
Stadnyuk, Ivan, 1784
Stamps, T. Dodson, 270
Standish, J. F., 3086
Stares, John, 2413
Stebbins, Richard P., 174
Steeg, George F., 1845
Steiger, George, 1313
Steinbrunner, John, 2559–2560
Stepanov, V., 1803
Stern, Ellen, 2633
Sterne, Joseph R. L., 2787
Stevens, Christopher, 3094
Stevens, Edmund, 577

Stevens, J. H., 641
Stevenson, Adlai E., 3rd, 2598
Stevenson, William, 3282
Stewart, James T., 3159
Stockholm International Peace Research Institute (SIPRI) 130, 175, 2634, 2689, 3095
Stockwell, Richard E., 1095–1096, 1213, 1636
Stoessinger, John G., 850
Stoiko, Michael, 1495
Stolley, R. B., 2921
Stone, Jeremy J., 2503
Stratton, Andrew, 2414
Strauz-Hupé, Robert, 937–938
Strawson, John, 302, 523
Stroud, John, 369, 2118
Stukel, Donald J., 2519
Suchenwirth, Richard, 346–347
Sukarno, 3283
Sulimov, Y., 751
Sullivan, David S., 2504
Sullivan, R. R., 2601
Sullivan, William K., 2788
Sulyanov, A., 1712
Sutton, Anthony C., 1025
Sutton, George P., 2303–2304
Sutton, John L., 2673
Swanborough, F. Gordon, 651, 1275–1276, 1863, 1874–1875, 1882–1884, 1933–1934, 2146
Sweetman, Bill, 110, 1894, 2042, 2103
Szkoda, W. E., 518

Tahtinen, Dale R., 2942–2943, 3241
Talbert, Ansel E., 2731
Talbot, Strobe, 2458
Talbot-Booth, Eric, 617–618
Tanin, Ye., 2218
Tapman, Thomas F., 1637
Taylor, A. Marjorie, 202
Taylor, Alan J. P., 271
Taylor, John W. R., 131–133, 176, 619, 1097–1098, 1166, 1198–1200, 1277–1278, 1646, 1814, 1846, 1876–1887, 1935–1936, 1996, 2007, 2037, 2044, 2053, 2084, 2091, 2096, 2115, 2119, 2147, 2149–2150, 2177, 2181, 2194, 2233, 2243–2245, 2305
Taylor, Michael J. H., 133, 2130, 2148–2150, 2244–2245
Taylor, Peter P. W., 2198, 2732
Teplinsky, Boris, 3270–3271
Thach, Joseph E., 493, 3148
Thee, Marek, 2623
Thomas, John R., 1449, 1585
Thomas, Robert C., 200

Thomas, Tony, 3108
Thompson, W. Scott, 2448–2449, 2674, 3103
Thomson, I. W., 752
Thomson, Jeffrey R., 2352
Thresher, R. D., 3171
Thyng, Harrison R., 2827, 3172
Timmons, Richard F., 3061
Tinazero, A. A., 2317, 2616
Titz, Zdenek, 512, 519
Tkachenko, N., 1757
Tokaev, G. A., 409
Toliver, Raymond F., 353, 594
Tolstoy, S., 1364, 1780, 1805
Tolubko, Vladimir F., 314, 1586, 3341
Toyne-Sewell, T. P., 3062
Trainor, James, 2844
Trapans, A., 1809
Trilling, Leon, 1099, 1650
Trofimov, R., 2110
Trudeau, Garry, 290
Trusov, V., 1728
Tsipis, Kosta, 2306, 2318
Tsyganov, Nikolay G., 1639
Tsymbal, Nikolay A., 826
Tuchman, Barbara W., 3018
Tully, Andrew, 524
Turbiville, Graham H., Jr., 499, 1365–1366, 1781, 2735
Turchenko, V. V., 1453
Turley, G. H., 3063
Turner, Roscoe, 2416
Turner, Thomas, 2035
Turney, Alfred W., 443
Tuzov, N., 1315–1316
Twining, Nathan F., 1280
Tyukhtin, N., 3343

Uebe, Klaus, 370
Ulsamer, Edgar, 1045–1048, 1100, 1202, 1516, 1847, 1937, 2307, 2417–2424
Ulstein, Egil, 2795
Underhill, Garrett, 1395
Union of Soviet Socialist Republics, Ministry of Defense, 203, 371
———. PVO-Strany, 1454
———. Soviet Information Bureau, 1488
United Nations. Dag Hammerskjold Library, 95
United States. Air Force, 757, 1329, 3344
———. ———. Academy, Library, 46a
———. ———. Air University, 969
———. ———. Library, 65, 90
———. ———. Air Forces in Europe, 357
———. ———. Arms Control & Disarmament Agency, 204, 1006
———. ———. Army, 47–48, 205, 758–761, 1455, 2756
———. ———. Air Forces. Navy Division, 703
———. ———. Air Forces. Training Division, 703
———. ———. Military Academy. Library, 49
———. ———. ———. Department of Military Arts and Engineering, 303
———. ———. ———. Military History Institute, 50
———. Blue Ribbon Defense Panel, 2617
———. Central Intelligence Agency. National Foreign Assessment Center, 1007–1013, 1057, 2675, 2848, 3272
———. ———. Office of Basic and Geographic Intelligence, 3275
———. ———. Office of Political Research, 786–789, 2827, 2944
———. Congress. House. Committee on Armed Services, 177–178, 1601, 2450
———. ———. ———. Committee on Foreign Affairs, 2618–2619, 2945–2946, 3126a, 3242
———. ———. ———. Joint Economic Committee, 1014–1019
———. ———. ———. Committee on International Relations, 2676–2677
———. ———. Senate. Committee on Armed Services, 179–180, 1330–1331, 1602, 2620, 2757, 2849, 3142, 3177, 3276–3278
———. ———. ———. Committee on Foreign Relations, 1489, 1603–1604, 2451–2452, 2520, 3120
———. ———. ———. Committee on Government Operations, 970
———. ———. ———. Select Committee on Intelligence, 2453
———. Department of Defense, 181, 206, 2454, 3279
———. ———. Defense Intelligence Agency, 762, 1285, 1428, 1520, 3073
———. Department of State, 2505, 3127
———. Government Accounting Office, 2678
———. Joint Chiefs of Staff, 207
———. Library of Congress, 51–52
———. National Defense University, 2621
———. National Technical Information Service, 96
———. Superintendent of Documents, 97
———. War Department, 134–135, 208, 646
Uppert, Guenter, 3345
Urbach, Walter, Jr., 2192
Uryuzhnikov, V., 1317–1319, 1729
Ushakov, S., 3346

Vail-Motter, T. H., 546
Vakhramyev, A., 2604
Vali, Ferenc A., 3202
Van Cleave, William R., 2246
Van Creveid, Martin, 3074
Van den Berk, L. J. M., 939
Vandenburg, Hoyt S., 3174
Vandyk, Anthony, 1101, 1939, 1986, 1997, 2426
Van Dyke, Jon M., 3258
Van Ishoven, Armand, 354
Vanneman, Peter, 3118, 3140
Van Staaveren, Jacob, 3273
Van Veen, E., 1349
Vasilevsky, A., 448, 507
Vasil'yev, B. A., 827, 1383
Vazhin, F., 1320
Veksler, L., 3347
Veraksa, Ye., 410–415
Vereykin, A., 3348
Vernon, Graham D., 940, 2758
Vershinin, Konstantin A., 474, 1281–1282, 1321–1322, 2219
Vetrovoy, P., 1782
Vickery, William W., 2820
Vigor, Peter H., 753–754, 851, 941–943, 1783, 1848, 2427, 2737
Viksne, J., 3065
Viktorov, G. M., 755
Vishenkov, Vladimir M., 1763
Voaden, Denys J., 626, 1102, 1851
Vogler, Charles C., 3243
Volkov, L., 1155
Von Manstein, Erich, 304, 475–476, 491
Vorona, Jack, 1049
Vorontsov, G., 500
Vidrin, I. F., 1649
Vysotskiy, V., 1806, 3349

Wagner, Abraham R., 2876
Wagner, Ray, 704
Wakebridge, Charles, 3066
Wakeford, Ronald C., 2239
Walen, W. W., 1730
Walker, Walter, 2789–2790
Walker, Wayne T., 603, 658
Wallace, M. D., 2428
Walsh, Robert L., 578
Waltermire, Jacob B., Jr., 2994
Ward, Richard, 225, 348
Wargo, Peter M., 1367
Warner, Denis A., 3259
Warner, Edward L., 798, 833, 1050
Warnke, Paul C., 2610
Waters, H. R., 2845
Weal, Elke C., 621
Weber, Hans H., 11

Weeks, Albert L., 2429
Weinstein, Warren, 3096
Weissman, Stephen K., 3126
Weizman, Ezer, 2877
Wells, Norman E., 1450
Werth, Alexander, 305, 444, 458
Wessell, Nils, 2339, 2605
Wesson, Robert G., 828
Westmoreland, William C., 3260
Wetmore, Warren C., 2008, 2207, 3019–3020
Wettern, Desmond, 2791
Weyland, Otto P., 3175
Whaley, Barton, 434, 439
Wheatcroft, Andrew, 215
Wheeler, Earl G., 2606
Wheeler, Geoffrey, 3236
Whetten, Lawrence L., 852, 2353, 2739, 2923–2926, 2947, 2987–2988, 3067, 3104
Whitaker, Joseph, 182
White, D. Fedotoff, 372
White, William L., 1490
Whiting, Allen S., 3160
Whiting, Kenneth R., 236, 416, 422, 763, 944–945, 1283, 1323–1324, 1587
Wieczynski, Joseph L., 136
Willenson, K., 1648, 2826
Williams, E. S., 1638
Williams, Louis, 2878, 3032
Williams, Mary H., 273
Williams, Philip, 3068
Willoughby, Charles A., 1479
Willrich, Mason, 2459
Wilson, Gill R., 1940
Wilson, Peter A., 2311
Wilson, William T., 946
Winchester, James H., 1284
Windrow, Martin C., 219, 348, 622
Winston, D. C., 2030, 2128, 2430–2431, 2928
Wint, Guy, 247
Winter, William J., 623
Wise, David, 1459, 1480
Wise, Terence, 137
Wohstetter, Albert, 2432, 2607
Wohstetter, Roberta, 2850
Wolfe, Thomas W., 756, 782, 853, 947–952, 971–982, 1205, 1206, 1588, 1605, 2506–2507, 2521, 2679, 2690, 2740, 2759–2760, 2948
Wolk, Herman S., 953
Wong, Sybil, 1811
Wood, Derek, 1864, 1941
Wood, Tony, 355
Wragg, David W., 209, 1214
Wright, Denis, 3087
Wright, Gordon, 274

Author Index

Yakolev, Aleksandr S., 1106, 1156–1158
Yakubovsky, I., 477
Yancey, George P., 2455
Yefimov, Aleksandr, 1731
Yermov, V., 3550
Yeuell, Donovan P., 954
Yodfat, Aryeh Y., 2929, 2990, 3078, 3088
York, Herbert F., 2508, 2741
Yost, Charles W., 2664, 3021
Young, Frederick W., 2608
Young, Peter, 275–276, 3006
Yudin, I., 1426
Yurkin, A., 1732

Zabavskaya, L., 590
Zacharoff, Lucien, 418
Zaehringer, Alfred J., 1059, 1517, 2312
Zagoria, Donald, 2665
Zakharov, A., 1764
Zakharov, M., 316
Zhal'nerauskas, R., 1733
Zharko, V., 1734, 1942
Zemskov, V. I., 764
Zheltov, V., 1807
Zhigarev, V., 1943
Zhukov, A., 1735
Zhukov, B., 1808
Zhukov, Georgii K., 306, 492, 528
Zhuplatov, N., 2111
Zhuravlev, V., 1736
Ziegler, Janet, 54
Ziemke, Earl F., 307, 525
Zieser, Benno, 459
Zimin, G., 1427
Ziring, Lawrence, 3203
Zorza, Victor, 2666
Zubkov, I., 308
Zvenzlovsky, A., 463